OUT OF THE STORM

The Life and Legacy of Martin Luther

Also by Derek Wilson

Rothschild: A story of Wealth and Power
Sweet Robin: Robert Dudley Earl of Leicester
Hans Holbein: Portrait of an Unknown Man
The King and the Gentleman: Charles Stuart and
Oliver Cromwell 1599–1649
In the Lion's Court: Power, Ambition and Sudden
Death in the Reign of Henry VIII
All the King's Women: Love, Sex and Politics in the
Life of Charles II
Charlemagne: The Great Adventure

OUT OF THE STORM
The Life and Legacy of Martin Luther

Derek Wilson

HUTCHINSON
London

Published by Hutchinson 2007

2 4 6 8 10 9 7 5 3 1

Copyright © Derek Wilson 2007

Derek Wilson has asserted his right under the Copyright, Designs
and Patents Act 1988 to be identified as the author of this work

First published in Great Britain in 2007 by
Hutchinson
Random House, 20 Vauxhall Bridge Road,
London SW1V 2SA

www.randomhouse.co.uk

Addresses for companies within The Random House Group Limited can be found at:
www.randomhouse.co.uk/offices

The Random House Group Limited Reg. No. 954009

A CIP catalogue record for this book is available from the British Library

ISBN 9780091800017

The Random House Group Limited makes every effort to ensure that the papers used in its
books are made from trees that have been legally sourced from well-managed and credibly
certified forests. Our paper procurement policy can be found at:
www.randomhouse.co.uk/paper.htm

Typeset by Palimpsest Book Production Limited,
Grangemouth, Stirlingshire

Printed and bound in Great Britain by
William Clowes Ltd, Beccles, Suffolk

Contents

List of Illustrations

Introduction

'To be great is to be misunderstood' and I suppose it follows from Emerson's dictum that the great must suffer the attentions of generations of biographers all claiming to understand them. Martin Luther was a seminal figure in the progress of western thought, as intensely controversial in his own day as his ideas have been controversial ever since. He was a massive mountain dominating the historical landscape so that it is impossible to ignore him and equally impossible to deny his significance. His own internal struggle to find meaning and purpose in life became so dramatically externalised as to make him a representative man for the ages. His intellectual depth was combined with a vigorous journalistic style so that he could bring profound truths within the mental compass of the common man. He was one of those rare individuals who single-handedly forced the march of time into a new direction. He helped to shape sixteenth-century Europe and, therefore, seventeenth-century America, eighteenth- and nineteenth-century colonial societies worldwide, and the political ideals upon which western-style democracy rests. As such, he has not escaped the efforts of writers over the last four and a half centuries. For much of that time he was the victim of Catholic enemies who set out to vilify him and also of Protestant friends intent on rejecting every slur on their hero's character. But Brother Martin was always too big to be monopolised by the Church and certainly too big to be made captive by one section of it. He has been claimed as a great German nationalist, as a proto-Marxist who freed ordinary people from ecclesiastical tyranny and even, in John Osborne's play, *Luther*, as a free-thinking, coarse-mouthed role model for anti-establishment youth.

My own objective in *Out of the Storm* is simple but certainly not modest. I want to provide the non-specialist reader with an account in English of the life of Martin Luther, warts and all, and an assessment of his impact on his own time and subsequent ages. The first part of that function has hitherto been admirably fulfilled for millions of people by Roland Bainton's *Here I Stand*. Writing in the immediate aftermath of the Second World War, this American scholar produced a sensitive and sympathetic religious biography of one of the greatest of all Germans, a man widely regarded in his own country as one of the fathers of German nationalism. Bainton's work originated in lectures delivered to theology students at Yale, Hartford, Bonebrake and Gettysburg seminaries but it worked for non-specialists because it broke out of the prison of dry, earnest, partisan controversy which still dominated intellectual debate and told the heroic story of a great individual.

So, why reinvent the wheel? I believe there are two compelling reasons for retelling the Luther story in popular format for a new century: the world has changed and Reformation scholarship has changed. The students for whom Bainton wrote – and the same doubtless holds good for many outside the lecture hall who read and enjoyed *Here I Stand* – were men and women of religious commitment. They were raised in a Christian environment and, therefore, understood something of the profundities of sin, faith, righteousness and justification with which Luther struggled. We live now in a secularised age and for most people these theological issues are incomprehensible and, probably, irrelevant. Western man today is switched off by 'religion'. But not by spirituality. Church attendance has declined dramatically throughout Europe and even in the USA it is not as common as it was in the 1950s. However, as has been frequently observed, spirituality tends to increase in almost inverse proportion to the decline of organised religion. People need some outlet for their sense of the sacred and will always seek answers to the fundamental questions of existence. Hence the proliferation since the 1960s of New Age movements, transcendental meditation, eastern mysticism and a bewildering variety of cults. Luther is significant in this situation because he was bent on a similar quest. His overpowering spiritual longings were not being met by conventional religion. Step by painful step he set out on his own pilgrimage towards an individual understanding of eternal truth. His story, therefore, is relevant in a new way to a new age.

Reformation historiography over the last half century has been a battlefield of new interpretations and revisionist theories. Once upon a time the conflict was a simple one; it was waged between those, on the one side, who believed that Luther's movement delivered Europe from a decadent, power-crazed, theologically bankrupt medieval church and those on the other who extolled the virtues of undivided Catholicism and could not forgive Luther for breaking it up. The same partisan viewpoints continued in evidence, though expressed with greater sophistication and backed by new research, in the writings of, among many others, A. G. Dickens (*The German Nation and Martin Luther*), Steven Ozment (*The Age of Reform*; *The Reformation in the Cities*; etc.) and Heiko Oberman (*Luther: Man Between God and the Devil*) and Catholic apologists such as Eamon Duffy (*The Stripping of the Altars*, etc.), Richard Marius (*Martin Luther: The Christian Between God and Death*) and Christopher Haigh (*English Reformations*). At the same time and much in the spirit of the ecumenical movement other authors were looking at the Reformation and Counter-Reformation from a different angle, stressing what they had in common, rather than what divided them. They saw continuity between medieval and sixteenth-century movements to purify the Church and revitalise its message; e.g. A. D. Wright, *The Counter-Reformation*. Another academic initiative, spearheaded by Keith Thomas's *Religion and the Decline of Magic*, proposed that all Reformation historiography was barking up the wrong tree; the real sixteenth-century conflict was not between rival Christianities but between Christianity and a multi-faceted, primitive folk religion. Any reliable new biography must, without becoming bogged down in detail or sterile argument, sift the grains of gold from the silt of academic controversy and use them to adorn the narrative.

To claim that Martin Luther is everlastingly relevant is not to disguise the difficulty faced by the reader in making the transition from the twenty-first century to the age of the reformer. As Oberman pointed out, 'We must be prepared to leave behind our own view of life and the world: to cross centuries of confessional and intellectual conflict in order to become his contemporary' (*sic*).[1] But, like all hazardous adventures, the rewards outweigh the difficulties. I hope that the reader, like me, will find himself caught up in the exciting adventures of this most human of all intellectual celebrities, a man who, to use modern jargon, not only talked the talk but walked the walk. He was that rare phenomenon, a man of total conviction who had the courage to follow his beliefs wherever they led. Thanks to the huge volume of his written works which have survived – books, pamphlets, sermons and letters – and which are augmented by the detailed observations of contemporaries, we can obtain a remarkably detailed picture of Luther. He emerges not as a remote figure, to be admired or despised from afar, but as someone we can readily understand – a rumbustious enthusiast given to occasional bouts of depression, a practical joker, an affectionate husband and father, a preacher of thundering oratory, a man who enjoyed life and was certainly no puritanical killjoy. Luther possessed the faults that mirrored his virtues – stubbornness to match courage; vulgarity to match humanity; impatience with others to match his own self-discipline; generosity which matched his own indifference to creature comforts; a warm heart for friends which matched his unflagging hostility towards his opponents. To get to know this man is a rewarding experience.

Having done that, we have to move from the particular to the general. We must face questions of interpretation: what difference did Luther make in his own time? what has been his impact on history? in what ways has he moulded western thinking? *Out of the Storm* is the second in a series of books in which I am trying to suggest some answers to the question 'What is Europe?'. In *Charlemagne: The Great Adventure* I laid out the parameters of the subject, showing how an empire which scarcely outlived the life of its founder had yet lodged an idea in the common consciousness. Throughout the High Middle Ages missionary, military, political and cultural endeavours brought into being 'Western Christendom', founded on the reality and the myth of Charlemagne's achievement. It was a society bound together by common worship, common religious beliefs, a common language spoken by all the leaders of its intellectual life, and by allegiance to the pope and (in part) the Holy Roman Emperor. But this unity was only apparent. The triple-crowned pope claimed universal overlordship as Christ's representative and the sustainer of a common Christian culture. Yet increasingly the princes of Europe regarded him as a territorial magnate, like themselves, but one who had tax-paying subjects in every realm and representatives who interfered in regional politics. It was their misfortune that they could not deal with the pope on a purely political level. As long as his agents, the clergy, had control of the means of grace and, therefore, man's eternal destiny, it was a brave ruler who would openly oppose him. Medieval history has many examples of such confrontations, of which the best known to British readers is that of Henry II and Becket. In 1515 Henry VIII might optimistically assert that, 'kings of England in time past have never had any superior but God only' but the fact was that the odds were heavily weighted in favour of Rome. From time to time influential religious thinkers had emerged who had urged the exclusion of the Church from earthly wealth and temporal dominion but protestors such as Wycliffe,

Hus, the radical Franciscans and the Fratricelli had all been branded as heretics and dealt with accordingly.

It was Martin Luther who succeeded where others had failed. He evolved a theology which absolved territorial rulers from Roman overlordship just as it delivered individual souls from the tyranny of the sacramental system. As a result Western Christendom ceased to be a recognisable entity. The Holy Roman Empire was henceforth a title without substance. Expressed in crude terms, Luther created a 'North–South divide'. The supreme irony is that all this happened at precisely the time when the Emperor Charles V had succeeded in building up the largest continental empire since Charlemagne's.

Such devastating upheaval was well beyond anything that Luther wanted, planned or hoped for. He would have been appalled at the disintegration of Europe, the proliferation of Christian sects and the bloodshed of the so-called 'wars of religion'. He would have disclaimed responsibility. In his – essentially medieval – mindset ultimate causation lay with God and the devil. Chaos resulted when Satan triumphed. What Luther claimed to have done was release into the world the countervailing word of God. The formula may not have been quite as simple as Luther proposed but his evaluation of his own lifework was, in essence, right. Potentially he placed a vernacular Bible in every household. It was that free access to the source book of the Christian faith that forever freed Protestants from the institutional church and encouraged free thought in every area of life. If we clearly grasp that, we are at least some way towards understanding Martin Luther.

I

The Hour and the Man
1483–1517

'I am an uncivilised fellow, who has lived his life in the backwoods'

On the Bondage of the Will, 1525

1

Sturm und Drang*

The Scene: A dusty highway near the free city of Erfurt in high summer. Peasants work in the ripening grain fields stretching to the forest fringe. The air is heavy with sullen afternoon heat and to the distant south the sky above the Thuringian mountains is black with an approaching storm.

A solitary figure comes into view striding purposefully towards the city. He is a thickset young man, recognisable from his cap and the satchel of books on his back as a student from Erfurt university. He is deep in thought and not until the first heavy drops of rain come thudding into the dry ruts at his feet does he realise that he is in danger of a soaking. He casts around for shelter and begins to run towards a clump of trees. All around him the landscape is suddenly alive with livid lightning flashes. The ground trembles with the crashing timpani of thunder. He stumbles forward, terrified and alone under the fury of the heavens which, as he well knows, is nothing less than the wrath of God. Then a light, brighter and more lurid than any of the others flashing among the swirling clouds, explodes around him. With an earth-splitting crack a thunderbolt strikes the ground a mere matter of metres away. The force of it throws him off his feet. Petrified, he lies in the mud able to do no more than gabble frightened prayers. 'Holy St Anne, holy St Anne, save me! Let me live! Please, let me live! Mercifully hear me and I will become a monk.'

That is a fanciful reconstruction of the dramatic event which happened to Martin Luther on 2 July 1505 but the actual circumstances must have

* 'Storm and Stress'

been just as momentous for he looked back on it as the major turning point in his life. He was true to his panicking vow. He dared not be otherwise; to play fast and loose with the awesome God of the storm would be to put at risk his eternal soul. Fifteen days later he presented himself at the Augustinian house in Erfurt as a novice monk. From that moment his life took a new direction. So did the life of Europe – and the world.

There is always more behind such Damascus Road experiences than the simple events themselves reveal. Young Martin's inner turmoil was greater than the electric ferocity of the tumbling clouds. Spiritual forces were already propelling him towards the cloister and he was doing his best to avoid them. Like St Paul, he had been 'kicking against the goads' until God was obliged to employ drastic means to bend the disobedient young man to his will. So, at least, it seemed to the logic Martin derived from his religious upbringing.

The troubled student had been born twenty-two years before, in November 1483, and baptised on St Martin's Day (11 November). His parents, Hans and Margaretta (known in the family as Hanna) Luther (or Lüder), belonged to that group of struggling but upwardly mobile 'working-class' people who are the backbone of any stable nation. It was their outlook on life and Martin's ambivalent attitude towards it that formed the bedrock of his later development. Gross Hans (so called to distinguish him from a younger brother, Klein Hans) came from moderately prosperous farming stock in the small Thuringian town of Möhra but, as a younger son, he had had to make his own way in the world. Being a canny and thrusting young man he did that rather well. First of all he married into the professional classes. His bride was a Lindemann. Her family was well established in the nearby, prosperous city of Eisenach, where for generations they had been doctors, lawyers, teachers and civic dignitaries. The couple moved far away from home and family to settle in Eisleben. Hans had resolved to find work in the recently opened copper mines, but was there more to this decision to strike out on their own? This was an age in which society was fairly static and to put a hundred kilometres of rough, hilly terrain between themselves and their own people must have been an upheaval. Can it be that the Lindemanns disapproved of their Hanna throwing herself away on one of those rough Luthers? Hans' family had a far from savoury reputation. One of his brothers made frequent court appearances charged with acts of violence. It is useless to speculate on the reasons why Martin's parents decided to make a fresh start but the fact that they did so is evidence of a determined and courageous spirit which they certainly passed on to their son. Gross Hans was not the sort of man to be deflected from a chosen course of action by the disapproval of his 'betters'. Nor was Martin.

The reformer's later recollection of his parents' life in the early years of their marriage was one of hardship. 'My father was a poor miner,' he said. 'My mother carried all her wood home on her back. It was in this way that they brought me up.'[1] Like many people who have risen from humble origins, Luther was ambivalent about his working-class background. He could be proud of the honest toil by which his parents had improved their lot while disdaining the vulgarity and herd instincts of ignorant 'peasants'. It was soon after the birth of Martin, their second son, that Hans and Hanna moved to nearby Mansfeld. Mining was backbreaking and dangerous but it was better paid than work on the land and less dependent on the changing seasons. Hans was able to save enough to buy into a mine-owning syndicate. Later, he enjoyed sufficient standing in the community to borrow capital for the development of his business. Steadily his affairs improved but so did Gross Hans' expenses and the size of his family. By 1505 Hanna had borne him four sons and four daughters. Life was always a struggle for the ambitious entrepreneur and Hans could never count himself a rich man. What he could do, however, was give his children a better start in life than he had had. It was a matter of pride for him to do so and he may well have felt himself to be under the watchful eye of his socially superior in-laws. Some sons could follow him in the business but others would not be pitched out, as he had been, to fend for themselves in a harsh world. Young Martin showed promise from an early age and his parents decided to invest sacrificially in his education.

Apart from this significant fact there seems to have been nothing remarkable about his upbringing. He always remembered his parents with affection, while acknowledging that they were strict. His father could be jovial good company, especially when he had a few beers inside him, and his mother was both pious and loving. But neither of them hesitated to wield the stick and Martin recollected that it had been Hanna who, on one occasion, thrashed him till the blood flowed.

As to his religious training, it undoubtedly followed the pattern of conventional piety and routine rituals that were the norm amongst the lower orders in northern Germany. Men and women of every degree were acutely aware of living at the interface of two worlds – the physical and the spiritual. To vary the metaphor, they occupied a no-man's-land fought over by angelic and demonic hosts. Here signs and wonders were part of everyday experience and miracles were eagerly looked for. Special places – churches, shrines, holy wells – were foci of heavenly power. Others – forest depths, mountaintops, river banks – might be the very thresholds of hell, where devils, elves and hobgoblins lurked. No one doubted the power of magic or the authority of particular individuals to exercise it.

> It was inevitable that the priests, set apart from the rest of the community by their celibacy and ritual consecration, should have derived an extra *cachet* from their position as mediators between man and God. It was also inevitable that around the Church, the clergy and their holy apparatus there clustered a horde of popular superstitions, which endowed religious objects with a magical power to which theologians themselves had never laid claim.[2]

Theologians might not claim it but few priests, monks or friars were inclined to disavow the supernatural gifts upon which their hold over simple folk depended. The social framework of every European state was hierarchically structured and the authority of the clergy depended ultimately on the spiritual sanctions they possessed. Priests alone could 'make Christ' on the altar. They alone could absolve sins. Their prayers were efficacious for the repose of departed loved ones. And one way to achieve heaven was to be buried in a monastic habit. Preaching underlined this salvation magic but was far from being the only medium employed to maintain the influence of ecclesiastical professionals over the laity. Medieval Christianity was essentially a visual religion of garish colours and dramatic shapes, a chaotic jumble of images in stone, paint, stained glass and, increasingly, cheap propaganda prints. Illiterate parishioners gazed on a bewildering array of dramatically illustrated scenes – biblical episodes, saintly miracles, moral tales, apocalyptic visions – with no means of relating them to each other or to their own lives.

The ubiquitous representation which made the greatest impact was the 'doom' traditionally set up over church entrances or on chancel arches. This showed Christ the judge separating humanity into sheep, chosen to enjoy the eternal blessedness of heaven, and goats being dragged by demons into the grisly maw of hell. It was by playing on the fear of the unknown that the priestly hierarchy kept their talons on the minds of the people. They taught that only within the ship of the Church and its sacramental

Sinners consigned to hell for failing to keep the divine law

system could the devout soul journey safely through the perilous seas of this world and come safe to haven.

But the clergy were not alone in holding sway over the imaginations of ordinary folk. Other supernatural forces were at work, or were believed to be at work. When one of her infant children died, Hanna Luther did not attribute the tragedy to the inscrutable will of God or seek within herself the reason for divine judgement. She accused one of her neighbours of *maleficium*, witchcraft. Young Martin was brought up on numerous stories of occult visitations. He accepted as self-evident that such evil-inspired people existed and that one should wear charms, recite incantations, sprinkle the hearth with holy water and employ such other resources as the Church provided to ward off their attacks. The Stygian unknown is the breeding ground of fantasy and just as outer space today provides unlimited scope for imagining worlds peopled by superior beings, some of whom have visited Earth in flying saucers, so, in the sixteenth century, the mysterious origins of illness, animal diseases, bad weather and undeserved misfortune were readily attributed to ill-disposed

The *Schutzmantelbild*. The Virgin Mary, representing the Church,
extends her protective cloak around the faithful

persons who possessed secret powers and might well be in league with the
devil. Statistics compiled in West Germany in 1986 suggested that a third
of the population still believed in the existence of witches. If that is the case
in our own sophisticated, materialistic and rational age it is not difficult to
understand how such beliefs could be universal in the sixteenth century.
Popular religion among the illiterate masses in Europe was, thus, a hotch-
potch of Christian dogma, Christian myth and pagan survivals. There were
numerous other forces active within the Church – revivalist preachers,
publishers of vernacular devotional treatises, humanist scholars and members
of lay communities following a regimen of personal holiness and public
service. We shall have to explore these later. For the moment we must content
ourselves with the common religious experience with which Luther grew up.
He tells us very little about the personal beliefs of his parents so we must
assume that they shared the observances common to their class. That would
have involved weekly attendance at mass but reception of communion probably no more than twice a year, devotion to the miners' patron saint, Anne
(supposed maternal grandmother of Jesus), keeping of the numerous holy
days and festivals prescribed by ecclesiastical authority, occasional confession

and possibly rare excursions to some not-too-distant shrine to gaze on saintly relics and offer prayers for particular needs. As was not (and is not) uncommon, it was the woman of the household who was more devout than her husband. A colleague of the reformer, who met Frau Luther in later years, recorded that she possessed all the 'virtues which are fitting in an honourable woman [and] shone especially in modesty, fear of God and prayer, and other upright women used to take her as an example of virtue'.

The precocious child was sent to school probably at the age of five. In the Mansfeld *Grundschule* the elements of reading, writing and Latin grammar were instilled in him by the crude but effective methods of rote learning and the application of the birch when he failed in his lessons. Only by such mechanistic and harsh methods could the teacher (who will have had at most one assistant) have kept control of his lively charges. Within one room he had to instruct three classes – beginners, intermediates and seniors. For all but the most gifted pedagogues the work came down to either dominating the pupils or being dominated by them. Not surprisingly, Luther spoke scornfully of primary education in later years. However, what he resented most was not the beatings (and he tells us that on one occasion he was thrashed fifteen times in a single day) so much as the poor Latin that he was taught. The language of the Church and scholarship had become corrupted over the millennium since the silver age of Tacitus, Juvenal and Pliny and it would be many years before the Renaissance rediscovery of pure classical style reached Saxony.

Martin's next educational move, at the age of thirteen, was of short duration but may well have had a profound influence on the impressionable adolescent. A friend of his was being sent to a famous school at Magdeburg, some seventy kilometres from Mansfeld, and it was decided that Martin should accompany him. The institution was run by the Brethren of the Common Life, a revivalist order which had swept like a breath of fresh air through the conventional monastic spirituality of northern Europe. Their movement, which had begun over a century earlier in the Netherlands, was summed up in the title they gave it – the *Devotio Moderna*, the 'New Devotional System'. Like traditional religious orders the followers of this way gathered together in single sex communities to follow a life of prayer, meditation and service. But that was where the similarity ended. The brothers and sisters of the Common Life followed a more open, more fluid rule than their cowled colleagues. Though many clergy belonged to the order, it was essentially a lay movement and there was even room within it for families. Preachers of the order held out to their hearers a pathway to holiness which did not, of necessity, take the monastic life as its point of departure. To men and women who were looking for something more than the passive role allotted to the laity in church life it offered a quality and intensity of religious experience hitherto only available within the cloister. Followers of the New Devotional System were urged, by ascetic practices, to turn away from the world and model their lives on that of Jesus, and the most popular devotional book produced by the order took as its title, *The Imitation of Christ.* The instant popularity of this manual by Thomas à Kempis indicates that there were thousands of ardent souls looking for something more than formal religion. First printed in Augsburg in 1486, it went through more than twenty imprints in Germany alone before the end of the century. Readers identified with the anguish of the writer, who felt his heavenly longings chained to his worldly nature:

> Here a man is defiled with many sins, ensnared with many passions, held fast by many fears, racked with many cares, distracted with many curiosities, entangled with many vanities, compassed about with many errors, worn away with many labours, burdened with temptations, enervated by pleasures, tormented with want. O, when shall these evils be at an end? . . . O merciful Jesu, when shall I stand to behold Thee? When shall I contemplate the glory of Thy kingdom? When wilt Thou be unto me all in all?[3]

The Brethren of the Common Life had always taken a keen interest in education, knowing how vital it was to turn young minds towards the heavenlies before the distractions of the world took tenacious hold. They founded schools and ran hostels for students and their school at Magdeburg was famed for its high standards. It was only natural that the Luthers should jump at the chance to have their son enrolled there. Yet, within a year they had changed their minds and removed him. We are left wondering about the reason for their abrupt decision. Can it be that they were worried by the holy regimen of the brothers and the effect it was having on Martin? As well as the regular worship the boys had to attend there were talks and discussion groups aimed at explaining the mysteries of the faith and making it attractive to young minds. Through such instruction many adolescents came to offer themselves as trainee monks. One such was a young Dutchman by the name of Desiderius Erasmus, who we shall meet again. Aggravatingly, Luther's later, selective reflections had nothing to say about his response to this programme of instruction. However, one event did occur at Magdeburg which made an indelible mark on his embryonic self-concept. Someone pointed out to him a particularly emaciated mendicant friar. There were many such to be seen in the streets of the city, men who had espoused poverty and begged their bread from passers-by, but there was something particularly haunting about this stumbling Franciscan, who

> carried a sack like a donkey, so heavy that he bent under it but his companion walked beside him without a burden . . . He had so fasted, watched and mortified his flesh that he looked like a death's head, mere skin and bones; indeed he soon after died, for he could not long bear such a severe life.

But it was the identity of the ascetic, pointed out with whispered awe to the young student, that was especially poignant. He was Prince Wilhelm of Anhalt-Zerbst, a scion of the local ruling house. Whoever looked on this example of broken humility, Luther concluded, 'must needs be ashamed of his own worldly position'.[4] What did the thirteen-year-old boy and his classmates make of this spectacle as they discussed it among themselves and how did it relate to the instruction they were receiving from their earnest tutors? Dramatic sights stick in the mind while the daily routines of early life become blurred in recollection but it is the latter that, cumulatively, have the greater formative effect. Surely, it was at Magdeburg that Luther's thoughts began to turn towards the cloister.

That would explain his speedy withdrawal, for the possibility of their son becoming a monk or friar did not feature at all in his parents' plans. They wanted Martin to enter the wealthy, respected, professional class and had already decided that he was to be a lawyer. With this in view they removed him from the influence of religious enthusiasts and sent him to Hanna's home town of Eisenach, where he studied at the school of St George's parish. We might have expected that the Lindemanns would take their young relative under their wing but, for whatever reason, this was not the case. Instead, he was boarded with well-to-do merchant friends of the family, the Schalbes. In the 1560s, by which time Luther had become the subject of hagiographical writings and reminiscences, a story was told about how the boy came by his lodgings. It was said that Frau Schalbe had encountered Martin in church and, impressed by his singing and devotion, had decided to take personal care of him in return for his becoming the friend and protector of her own, much younger, son. If true, this would confirm that the essential change, for which the word 'conversion' is not too strong, had already come over the adolescent. He was seeking a spiritual destiny and one that would increasingly come into conflict with the career choice that had been made for him.

Whatever his psychological state, two facts are clear: the son of Hans Luther was still being held at arms length by his mother's people and he was now drawn into the circle of the pious Schalbes. If the boy's parents had hoped to wean him away from the spiritual pressures applied by the Brethren their tactics failed. Martin had exchanged the frying pan of the *Devotio Moderna* for the fire of Franciscan asceticism. His Eisenach hosts were enthusiastic and generous patrons of the Observant Friars, so called because they rejected any modification of their founder's rules of absolute poverty, chastity and obedience. Like the Brothers and Sisters of the Common Life, they, too, were reformists but they directed their zeal to following and encouraging others to follow an extremely austere pattern of life. They had separated from the more moderate wing (the Conventuals) of the Franciscan order (a separation formalised in 1517) and, because of their obvious personal privations (the example of Prince Wilhelm is a case in point) and commitment to preaching, they made a considerable impact. Heinrich Schalbe had endowed the Observant house, which was situated close to the nearby hilltop fortress of the Wartburg, and, with his family and friends, hung on the words of the holy friars. In later years Luther regarded the Schalbes' devotion with contempt. They had, he suggested, become mere grovelling servants to men who prided themselves on their own humility. Young Martin, therefore, during his most impressionable years came under the influence of two kinds of intense spirituality, one concentrating on internal devotion, the other on external privations. What they had in common was the pursuit of personal holiness as a means of commending the individual to God and, thus, deserving salvation.

However, we must be careful not to read back the man into the boy. The adolescent Martin was a lively, relaxed young man who was happy in his new school and who was becoming an accomplished scholar. The years away from home had given him a new confidence and helped him to overcome the natural shyness he had felt as a child. In Eisenach, a city for which he developed and maintained a warm affection, there was much to see and do. He and his friends must have made forays into the forest and gone fishing in the Hörsel or the Nesse. More solemn activities would have been centred on the splendid Gothic church of St George or, sometimes, on Romanesque St Nicholas' church. Excitement was always caused when the Elector of Saxony arrived with his colourful and exotic entourage to stay in the massive Wartburg Castle which brooded over the town from its hilltop position. Luther had many friends and the school regime was a distinct improvement on that of Mansfeld. Johann Trebonius, the master, was a gifted scholar and a teacher who managed to impart to his charges an enthusiasm for learning. Under his tutelage Martin's facility with Latin improved greatly and it was in the St George's school that he laid the foundation for that robust and fluent style that would give his writings their persuasive force. Yet, with the coming of the new century, came also the recognition that there was little more to be learned in Eisenach. The time had come to consider the next stage of his education. Hans Luther, who had already sacrificed much in equipping his son to join the social elite, decided to send him to university. And not just any university: Erfurt, where Martin went in 1501, could boast one of the best and most ancient seals of learning in Germany. Moreover its law school was second to none.

Twice the size of Eisenach, Erfurt was a thriving commercial and administrative centre as well as a university city. From the summit of Domburg hill the many spires of the cathedral and the church of St Severus watched over the sixth most populous city in the German lands, a city where traders from Poland, Venice, the Baltic states, France and the Netherlands rubbed shoulders in its bustling markets. Mercantile activity centred on the shop-lined bridge over the Gera, the Krämerbrücke, and a stone's throw away were the dye works from whose steaming vats came the woad which was Erfurt's primary export. In such a cosmopolitan entrepôt a young student could find many attractions and distractions. As in any university town, there were occasional fracas caused by the 'young gentlemen' and in 1509, which went down in the city annals as 'mad year', serious riots broke out entailing much bloodshed and property damage. There is no evidence of Luther taking part in such lawless behaviour but he later recalled that he carefully studied the 'courses' offered in the city's inns and whorehouses. Students were no less boisterous, energetic, arrogant and demonstrative then than they are now and Martin, like his friends, needed frequent breaks from the head-splitting concentration on the *quadrivium*.

This was the time-honoured programme of higher education by which the student ascended through the disciplines of arithmetic, astronomy, geometry and music to the philosophy of Aristotle and thence, for those bent on a clerical career, to theology, the queen of the sciences. Martin proved himself to be a gifted scholar, that is to say he jumped through the prescribed academic hoops without difficulty. He took his bachelor's degree in 1502 and his master's in 1505. He proved himself particularly adept at disputations, those regular confrontations at which students were required to argue propositions and counter-propositions according to strict rules of dialectic. Not for nothing did his fellows nickname him 'the philosopher'. Yet the mastering of logic produced by the *quadrivium* made him question its very basis.

The framework of all theological and philosophical teaching was 'scholasticism', which had started out as an intricate system of reasoning designed to make the Christian faith intellectually respectable and had developed over five centuries into a kind of academic scaffolding which served to prop up the dogmas of the Church. The arguments of the schoolmen were based on Aristotle and the early Church Fathers or, in practice, on official commentaries on these ancient authorities. Luther was very far from being the first scholar to feel disquiet about what had become an arid, second-hand way of handling divine truth. Almost a hundred years before, Nicolas of Clémanges, a Parisian theologian, had compared scholastic teachers to physicians who, having learned their craft, were content to discuss it among themselves while all around them people were dying of plague. Renaissance scholars in Italy had begun that 'back to the sources' movement which would spread across Europe under the name of humanism or the New Learning but this revolutionary tide had scarcely begun to lap at the walls or Erfurt while Luther was studying there. In 1505 he had only reached the stage of having doubts about the Church's handling of those deep truths entrusted to it – doubts by no means strong enough to act on. And why should he challenge the system? As long as he stayed within it the future looked bright. He felt justifiable satisfaction when he qualified for his master's degree, coming second out of a class of seventeen, and it gave him immense pleasure to witness his parents' pride when they came to Erfurt to watch him go in torchlight procession to receive his new honour. 'Oh, what a majestic and glorious thing it was,' he later wrote. 'I hold there is no temporal, worldly joy equal to it.' All that remained was to complete his study of law and to embark on a lucrative career.

However, there were fears and anxieties welling up inside him and try as he might to keep the lid fast shut upon them they kept escaping. It was the teaching of the Church that kept applying the crowbar to that casket of accusations and self-doubt. Martin was now of an age to pay close attention to sermons. In a city the size and importance of Erfurt there was much more preaching than in a backwater such as Mansfeld or even in Eisenach.

The parish clergy were better educated and the preaching orders of friars were more active. Moreover, thanks to the 'modern marvel' of printing, the serious, educated Christian could buy books of sermons to meditate on at leisure. Martin appreciated pulpit oratory and his trained mind was now equipped to entertain the written arguments set forth by the fashionable preachers of the age. What he learned from these sources about the way of salvation was scarcely encouraging.

The base line was that man was a sinner and could only set out on the road to God in sincere repentance. But there was the rub, for how could the anxious seeker know how genuine his own repentance really was? Did he really desire to make reparation to a loving God whom he had offended or was he more concerned about his own eternal welfare? One preacher estimated that the number of people capable of true contrition was, perhaps, one in thirty thousand.[5] It was the Church which came to the aid of the despairing sinner with its standard sacramental means of grace – masses, baptism, penance, unction – and such occasional aids as sermons, pilgrimages, indulgences and (for the wealthy) the purchase of holy relics. When Augustine wrote, *salus extra ecclesiam non est* ('there is no salvation outside the Church') he had specifically in mind these ritual observances by which the priestly profession helped to steer the human soul through this veil of tears towards heaven. However, it was for the individual, not only to live in obedience to mother Church and to avail himself of the benefits she offered, but to live righteously, which involved self-denial, works of charity and avoiding the snares of the world, the flesh and the devil. All this was extremely difficult in a secular environment, so that the surest way to inherit eternal life was to enter the cloister. Yet, even monks and nuns were not immune to temptation, as ribald stories and printed lampoons delighted to point out. What all this amounted to was that while salvation depended on the attainment of personal holiness no one could be certain of it. In 1431, for example, Joan of Arc outraged the examiners at her heresy trial because she claimed to know that she would be received into paradise, whereas they took it as axiomatic that 'on this earthly journey no pilgrim knows if he is worthy of glory or of punishment, which the sovereign judge alone can tell'.[6]

In moments of honest self-examination Martin certainly could not see a pious soul deserving of eternal bliss. He was a young man with a lust for life. He entered with enthusiasm into everything he undertook. He loved books and read widely outside his subject, delighting in such Latin authors as Cicero, Virgil and Livy. His study of the Bible probably began at this time for he later recalled that he *discovered* a copy in the university library.

It is difficult to believe that he had never before made the acquaintance of holy writ; there were many copies around, both in Latin and German. But laymen were not encouraged to study it for themselves; its complexities were best left for experts to unravel. When Luther began to turn the pages for himself, therefore, the contents may well have come as a revelation. The assiduous student also applied himself to his devotional exercises. But then he entered with equal enthusiasm into student pranks and the camaraderie of the beerkeller and the brothel. He was a highly successful young man with many friends and the world before him but in the darkness of lonely nights a much-favoured preachers' text may well have echoed in his brain: 'How shall it profit a man if he gains the whole world but loses his soul?'. Could it be that he was not destined by God for the legal profession? He may already have developed that profound contempt for the law that he often expressed in later years. 'Every lawyer is either a good-for-nothing or know-nothing' he asserted and he once told his own young son, 'If you should become a lawyer, I'd hang you on the gallows.'[7] Perhaps, the attraction of the cloistered life presented to him by the Brothers at Magdeburg continued to haunt him. There may also have been a spirit of youthful rebellion strewing rocks on his career path. That path had been chosen for him by his father and it would only be natural for Martin to believe that he deserved some say in his own destiny. We search the reformer's extensive writings and the biographical snippets provided by his friends in vain for any expression of deep affection for old Hans at this time. Father and son became estranged over Martin's decision to become a monk and the rift would not be healed for many years but it is more than likely that mutual ill-feeling had a longer history. All these impulses were in conflict. The twenty-one-year-old who, at the beginning of 1505, embarked on his studies of law was a man not at ease in himself. A modern psychiatrist would have identified him as someone heading for a breakdown. Of course, much of this is speculation. It is impossible for us to *know* what problems troubled his waking mind and what were those simmering in his unconscious.

What we can identify is the sequence of acts which brought on the eventual crisis. All of them had to do with death or the threat of death. His first close call was an accident with the sword which he carried when travelling as a precaution against brigands. Somehow it slipped from his belt, cutting into the flesh of his leg so deeply that it severed an artery. Only in the nick of time did companions manage to get him to a doctor who applied a tourniquet and dressed the wound. That night in bed the cut opened again and he lost more blood. Fortunately, someone else was on hand to save his life. The transitory nature of human existence came home to him once more soon after he gained his master's degree when a very close friend died suddenly. After that Martin tried to settle to his studies but found the law an uncongenial subject. His inclination was increasingly towards the theology faculty perhaps with the possibility of an academic career in mind. But that would be sure to provoke an argument with his parents. His proud father had just presented him with an expensive copy of the *Corpus Juris*, the lawyer's Bible. It was the most recent example of Hans Luther's personal sacrifice and his ambition for his son. The chances of continued parental support if he switched to theology would be nil. Of course, if he were to take the cowl and pursue the monastic route to higher education finance would cease to be a problem. But Martin knew full well that nothing would be more calculated to outrage old Hans. His father's outspoken opinions about 'lazy, good-for-nothing monks' were well known. Like many Germans of peasant extraction he regarded the religious life as a cop-out from the 'real' world of honest toil. Monks and nuns were the stock-in-trade of ale-house bawdy humour, habitually portrayed as gluttonous, drunken and libidinous.

Then came the news that his father had done something that would pre-empt further discussion. He had begun negotiations for the marriage of his upwardly mobile son into a local family of standing. For Martin the moment of painful choice had come. Marriage would disbar him from proceeding to a theology degree. He knew that if he rejected both a legal profession and the proposed bride his parents would be mortified. They would regard it as an act of gross ingratitude. They would lose face among the friends and neighbours to whom they had always boasted of their son's progress. But that had to be weighed against the risk of making a wrong and irreversible career move. The confrontation could no longer be avoided. It seems more than likely that Martin discussed with his father the possibility of a change of direction on the visit to his home in June 1505. Whatever the outcome of such a discussion, it is clear that the unwilling law student had a great deal on his mind as he made his way back to Erfurt.

God sends storms so that he may smite sinners with terror, and thus at last they may be converted . . . Why are the church bells rung against the tempestuousness of the air? . . . so that men, hearing their peals, may be aroused to call upon God lest he drown us on account of our sins as he drowned the whole world when the flood came. So when men hear the pealing of the bells against the storms of the sky, whether by day or night, they must fear for themselves, and humbly call on God to deal mercifully with us.[8]

So preachers exhorted their congregations and it was not merely superstitious countrymen who believed in divine intervention in daily life. After all, why should the Creator not make himself known through all his works? If he declared his beauty in the wayside flower why should he not proclaim his wrath in the tempest? Luther may have encountered rationalism in his readings of Cicero who, in the De divinatione, asserted that every natural phenomenon has a natural cause, whether or not we can discern it, but he would certainly have dismissed such statements as pagan unbelief. So, when the sky blackened on that sultry July day and thunder rumbled overhead and jagged lightnings stabbed the earth within metres of his stumbling footsteps, Martin was terrified. This was nothing but the judgement of God on a disobedient sinner who was resisting the divine will. He fell to the ground babbling out a prayer to his father's patron saint, St Anne. If his life was spared, he promised, he would not be disobedient to the heavenly vision; he *would* become a monk. On 17 July 1505, after a solemn leave-taking of his friends, he presented himself at the cloister of the Observant Augustinian friars.

The world would never be the same again.

2

'New Earth and New Heaven' – New Hell?

What *was* the world on which Luther was destined to have such an impact? For him it was about to shrink to the narrow confines of the Augustinian cloister at Erfurt. Even before that, his experience of a wider world had been limited in the extreme and, in the years ahead, he would rarely venture beyond the borders of his native Saxony. Yet his books, his disciples and the ideas that inspired them would spread devastatingly, like tremors from a seismic epicentre, to trouble the whole of Latin Christendom. But that entity – 'Latin Christendom' – which men had grown accustomed to calling by the alternative name of 'Europe', was itself in a state of convulsive change long before Luther's revolutionary expositions of the Bible burst upon it.

When Pope Alexander VI proclaimed that 1500 would be a year of jubilee, unprecedented crowds flocked to Rome from far and near. They came to make the ultimate pilgrimage. They came to be released from the consequences of their sins, for those who prayed at the holy sites, carried out the prescribed penitential acts and made the appropriate offerings to papal funds were granted plenary indulgence. The pope and his stage managers made sure that the jubilee was an outstanding success. It was promoted months in advance throughout Europe and its launch was impressively choreographed. For three days in the preceding December the bells of the city rang incessantly to herald the papal procession which made its exuberant way to St Peter's. The people cheered as Alexander was borne along on his throne, waving his hand over them in benediction. Before the Porta Sancta, sealed up with bricks, he was set down and walked barefoot to the door. A few ceremonial taps dislodged some of the bricks and soon the way was opened for the devout to flock through into the ancient and crumbling basilica. Eager as they were to pray for themselves and their loved ones who had already preceded them into purgatory, the visitors could not have been too distracted by holy thoughts to notice senior clergy openly parading with their whores, the pope's own son, Cesare Borgia, spearing bulls on the very steps of St Peter's and his daughter, Lucrezia, festooned with jewels, riding round the city with her gorgeous retinue. In the overcrowded inns they would have heard tales of feuds and murders and the grisly details of the assassination of another of the pope's sons, whose body had but recently been dragged out of the Tiber. Not that people had to visit Rome to be aware of the contrast between what the Church taught and how some of its leaders behaved. Songs, pamphlets and lampoons constantly held the ecclesiastical hierarchy up to ridicule or denounced scandal in high places. Yet these were the men who held the keys of heaven and hell – and frequently jangled then ostentatiously before the faces of the laity. It was one of many bewildering aspects of a bewildering age.

The year 1500 had a mystic significance beyond that which devout and superstitious people always attributed to *fins de siècle* because it came at a time when Europeans were aware that cataclysmic events were challenging old conventions. It was only two years earlier that Albrecht Dürer had issued that image which we always associate with the *Zeitgeist* of a Europe in transition from the 'medieval' to the 'modern' era, *The Four Horsemen of the Apocalypse*. It was one of fifteen woodcuts the twenty-seven-year-old artist designed for a book called *Apocalypse*, the work which made his reputation. It did so because it chimed in so perfectly with the prevailing mood.

These studies for the Revelation of St John, depicting in lurid and frightening detail the prophecies associated with the end of the world, expressed the fears of many people. In one sense there was nothing new about morbid concentration on sin, judgement and the impending wrath of God. Pessimism about the doomed human condition and the evil state of the world was a medieval preoccupation. Back in the fourteenth century the French poet, Eustache Deschamps had gloomily surveyed his own age:

> Age of tears, cravings and turmoil,
> Time of indolence and damnation,
> Age in decline, heading for dissolution,
> Time replete with horrors and dissembling,
> Lying age, full of pride and envy,
> Time lacking in honour and wise judgement.[1]

Albrecht Dürer, *The Four Horsemen of the Apocalypse*, 1498

As long as the basis for all theological and philosophical contemplation was the sinfulness of man, the snares of the world and the necessity of freeing the soul from the talons of the flesh and as long as the institutional Church was the only escape route to heaven, then who could gainsay the verdict that everything was going, quite literally, to the dogs – the hounds of hell? Certainly not the leaders of the Church, the foremost shapers of public opinion.

So, beyond the apparent significance of the round date, what special reasons were there for approaching the year 1500 with fear and trembling? Were worries about impending doom deeper and more widespread than they had been as long as anyone could remember? Did significant numbers of Europeans really feel that they were living in the end time? As artists, poets, statesmen, scholars, philosophers and churchmen peered over the edge of the new century, were they more apprehensive than usual? The answer to these questions is 'yes'. There was a general dis-ease based on a consciousness that the grinding tectonic plates undergirding society were moving with increased violence to produce profound changes to the very fabric of Latin Christendom. Those changes were both geopolitical and cultural.

A new power had risen up which threatened to engulf the Christian world. Ever since the time of Charlemagne, Christian Europe had preserved its geographical integrity and even extended its frontiers. Scandinavian and Lithuanian pagans had been brought within the fold. The Crusades had ultimately failed in their objective of rescuing the Holy Land from the scourge of Islam but they had checked the Arab advance around the Mediterranean basin and they had all but destroyed the Byzantine Empire, whose Orthodox Christians were hated as heartily as the followers of Mohammed. In the Iberian peninsula the reconquest of Moorish territory had proceeded steadily until, in 1492, the last Muslim ruler was expelled. But in the East Christendom became the victim of its own success. When a new Islamic state, the Ottoman Empire, on fire with holy zeal, burst from its Anatolian homeland the vestigial Roman Empire of the East crumpled before it. By 1400, this daunting enemy had overrun most of the Balkans. During the reigns of Murad II (1421–51) and Mehemmed II (1451–81) the Turks plunged ever farther westward. Constantinople fell to them in 1452 and by the end of the century Ottoman rule had reached the Hungarian border. In the central and western Mediterranean the politico-religious conflict was far from over. Following the *Reconquista* of Spain expeditions sent out by

Ferdinand of Aragon and Isabella of Castille (died 1504) occupied vital strongholds along the African coast between 1497 and 1510 but, thereafter, a united Spanish Crown transferred its maritime interests to Italy and the New World. This, as Fernand Braudel observed, was 'one of the great missed opportunities of history . . . Spain . . . failed to carry out her geographical mission and for the first time in history, the Straits of Gibraltar became a political frontier'.[2] European maritime endeavour, upon which the lucrative eastern trade depended, continued to be at the mercy of Barbary corsairs. But more terrifying to the inhabitants of the northern Mediterranean littoral were the raids of Arab slave traders. These marauders ranged far and wide, eventually reaching Ireland and Iceland. Stretches of Italian and French coastline were deserted as the inhabitants fled from the repeated threat from the slaving gangs. The heyday of the corsairs was yet to come but by the early years of the sixteenth century thousands of captives had been taken from their homes to serve in the harems and galleys of the Infidel. Stories of Muslim atrocities (doubtless often exaggerated) spread much farther and it would be impossible to overrate the fear engendered in Europe by a resurgent Islam. There were frequent calls for fresh crusades but the days when a pope could unite rival rulers in a concerted effort against the enemies of the faith were past. 'Taking up the cross' was good diplomatic rhetoric but when it came to turning deeds into action kings and princes found they had more pressing engagements.

Just how distracted Europe's rulers were by personal and dynastic ambition mingled with protestations of piety was shown by the tumultuous affairs of Italy during the momentous final decade of the fifteenth century. 1492 was both an *annus mirabilis* and an *annus horribilis*. The year that saw the Moors cast out of Spain and witnessed Christopher Columbus's first discovery of the fringe of the Americas, was also notable for the death of Lorenzo de Medici, the ruler of Tuscany, and the election to the papal throne of the infamous Rodrigo Borgia. Lorenzo, widely admired as the 'Wise' and the 'Magnificent', had raised Florence to the status of cultural capital of Europe by his patronage of the greatest painters, sculptors and architects of the day. During the golden age of the city Botticelli, Verocchio, Leonardo and Michelangelo were merely the foremost of a cohort of talented artists working there. But before Lorenzo died at the age of forty-three a new voice was heard in Florence, and its high-pitched, raucous and fervent sentences were not proclaiming the ruler's praises.

Bethink well, O, you rich, for affliction shall smite you. This city shall no more be called Florence, but a den of thieves, of turpitude and bloodshed. Then shall you all be poverty-stricken, all wretched, and your name, O priests, shall be changed into a terror ... I say unto you: 'Know that unheard times are at hand'.[3]

Girolamo Savonarola was the prior of St Mark's Dominican friary in Florence and a preacher so popular for his fiery eloquence that his sermons had to be delivered in the cathedral, the only building large enough to hold all those who wished to hear him. Because the congregation was so crammed he had a dividing curtain rigged up to prevent men and women immodestly jostling one another. For an hour or more at a time the standing audience was held spellbound by the ringing denunciations that echoed round the duomo. Decades later Michelangelo said that he could still hear in his head the strident, high-pitched voice delivering terrifying prophecies with utter conviction as well as the wailing and weeping of the hearers. Savonarola's targets were government corruption and the godless *dolce vita* of the citizenry.

There was nothing unique about the prior's outraged condemnation of sin nor even of his calling for public 'bonfires of the vanities' at which repentant Florentines were to commit their worldly fripperies to the flames. What was different was his fearless involvement in Italian politics. Obeying, as he declared, visions and revelations received directly from God, Savonarola condemned the Medici, the Vatican and the hierarchy of the Church. He foretold dire visitations of divine wrath and his prophecies seemed to be fulfilled when Italy suffered two invasions. The first was the appearance of a disfiguring, mentally debilitating, sexually transmitted disease – syphilis. The second was an army led by the King of France.

Charles VIII was scarcely less of a visionary (or megalomaniac) than the little Dominican. He, too, was ugly but possessed of a manic energy which caught others up in his enthusiasms. He had been reared on romantic and heroic legends and saw himself as a reincarnation of Charlemagne. Like Savonarola, he also believed himself set apart by God for a grand mission: he would lead the last great crusade which should deal once and for all with the Muslim menace. The first part of his strategy, however, had more to do with dynastic pride than the accomplishment of divine purpose. He had a hereditary claim to the Kingdom of Naples, which comprised all of southern Italy and Sicily. In 1442 this territory had been seized by Alfonso V, the Magnanimous, of Aragon and Charles was determined to restore the

Savonarola preaching in the Duomo

honour of the French royal house by reclaiming its Italian possessions. He was also very aware that with the crown of Naples went the titular over-lordship of the Kingdom of Jerusalem. Having mortgaged himself to the hilt in order to assemble a large army, the twenty-four-year-old king set out on his southward march in August 1494, with the sacred oriflamme, sup-posedly the standard which had once belonged to Charlemagne, borne before him. Savonarola welcomed his appearance as proof of prophecy and the Florentines fell even more under the preacher's spell. They chased the Medicean party out of the city and proclaimed a republic. In so doing they created a political vacuum. In the confused months that followed factions vied with each other to produce (and dominate) a new constitution. The only voice everyone listened to with respect was that of the prior of St Mark's. 'This Friar made no harangues in the streets, had no seat in the Councils of the State, yet he was the soul of the whole people, and the chief author of every law of the new government.'[4]

What followed was the first mini-reformation of the Reformation. Savonarola turned into reality his dream of making Florence a holy commonwealth. Moral renovation went alongside the introduction of democratic government. In one of his more famous sermons Savonarola

told the people that God intended to give them a new king. He paused
for effect while his congregation gazed up at the pulpit, waiting for him
to name their chosen ruler. Then, he declaimed, 'This new head is Jesus
Christ; he seeks to become your King!' Nor did his vision stop there.
'O, Florence, then wilt thou be rich with spiritual and temporal wealth;
thou wilt achieve the reformation of Rome, of Italy, and of all countries; the wings of thy greatness shall spread over the world.'[5] For a time
it seemed that heaven really would be created on earth. The cream of
Florentine society cast aside their jewels and embroidered clothes. Men
and women lived modestly, regular in their attendance at mass and given
to reading devotional books. Merchants stopped cheating their
customers. Bankers abandoned usury. The City of God even spread its
boundaries as travellers carried news of the exciting holiness experi-
ment and colporteurs did a brisk trade in the printed sermons of Florence's
man of destiny.

It could not last. Church leaders are always uncomfortable with holiness and for politicians 'power to the people' is never more than a slogan.
Those whom the new regime had deprived of power conspired against the
saviour of Florence. The behaviour of Charles VIII and the French helped
their cause. The army which had come to 'liberate' southern Italy behaved
like a locust horde, interested only in plunder. Neapolitan leaders soon
made common cause with Rome, Milan, Venice and Aragon to remove
the interloper. If Florence was to be enticed into what its promoters called
the Holy League Savonarola would have to be cut down to size. Alexander
VI ordered the 'troublesome priest' to Rome to explain himself and also
instructed him to cease preaching. Savonarola refused to comply with either
injunction. It was a decision he reached only after great anguish. Obedience
to ecclesiastical superiors was an ingrained habit but he had reached the
point all potential martyrs reach, the point where the inner voice of spiritual conviction becomes louder and more compelling than the threats
and blandishments of those who claim to speak for God. Now, the more
the pope alternately wheedled and thundered the less Savonarola respected
him. At one stage Alexander tried the bribe of a cardinal's hat but ended
by excommunicating the stubborn friar and threatening Florence with a
papal interdict. Only thus could the friar's enemies separate their quarry
from his large, popular following.

As the unholy alliance against him employed increasingly sordid tactics
Savonarola saw clearly that the real problem lay in the deep and widespread corruption of a Church in desperate need of reform:

O, prostitute Church, you have displayed your foulness to the whole world and you stink to Heaven. You have multiplied your fornications in Italy, in France, in Spain, and all other parts. Behold, I will put forth my hand, says the Lord, I will smite you, you infamous wretch; my sword shall fall on your children, on your house of shame, on your harlots, on your palaces, and my justice shall be made known . . . O priests and friars, you whose evil example has entombed this people in the sepulchre of ceremonial, I tell you this sepulchre shall be burst asunder, for Christ will revive his Church in his Spirit.

Affairs in Florence had not gone unnoticed elsewhere and messages of support arrived at St Mark's from many quarters. Thus emboldened, the fiery preacher now directed the gaze of his congregation farther afield and answered his critics with dire, if muted, warnings.

Write to France and Germany; write everywhere to this effect: That friar you know of bids you all seek the Lord and implore his coming. Haste at full speed, O you messengers! Think you that we alone are good? That there be no servants of God in other places? Jesus Christ has many servants, and great numbers of them, concealed in Germany, France and Spain, are now bewailing this evil. In all cities and strong places, in all manors and convents. There be some inspired with this fire of zeal. They send to whisper somewhat in my ear, and I reply: Remain concealed until you hear the summons, *Lazarus come forth!* I am here because the Lord appointed me to this place and I await his call, but then will I send forth a mighty cry that shall resound throughout Christendom and make the corpse of the Church to tremble even as the body of Lazarus at the voice of our Lord.[6]

The cataclysm would come just as Savonarola prophesied but the voice summoning the faithful to revolution would not be his. To oppose the intrigue, bribery and violence of his enemies the prior only had his oratory – and that was losing its novelty value. Charles VIII returned to France – and died months later of an apoplectic fit. The Florentines tired of enforced virtue. The divine blessings which Savonarola had promised the city failed to materialise. A mob stirred up by his political enemies stormed the convent and dragged him out to face a mockery of a trial before papal judges who arrived 'with their verdict already in their bosom'. On 23 May 1498, he was hanged and burned in the Piazza della Signoria and his ashes thrown into the Arno.

The rise and fall of Girolamo Savonarola was symptomatic, not of a new spirit that was abroad (the friar was almost pathologically orthodox and obedient to ecclesiastical authority until the last months of his life) but of the confusion and turmoil of the times. Spirituality and morality became intermingled with politics. Scoundrels grabbed power in the name of God. Christian leaders did deals with enemies of the faith (Alexander VI made a treaty with the Turks in 1498). Holy men became homicidal rivals (Florence's Franciscans turned out in force to gloat at the burning of Savonarola). The French invasion was the curtain-raiser to fifty years of warfare involving France, Spain and the Italian states. The tragedy for the leaders of Christendom was that they did not heed and, therefore, could not interpret the prophecies of the man they had hounded to death. It followed that they played their part in the fulfilment of those prophecies. Successive popes were preoccupied with the violent rivalries convulsing Italy. Even if the welfare of the universal Church had been their primary concern (and for some it certainly was not) they were too distracted by worldly affairs to be able to grasp the significance of the mounting challenges to traditional beliefs and practices. They comforted themselves with the knowledge that there had always been heretics and disobedient members of the flock and that disciplinary procedures were in place for dealing with them. In a word, they were complaisant.

In the year that Savonarola died the Church lost the services of another Dominican prior who shared the fiery zeal of the Florentine but expressed it in very different ways. His name was Tomás Torquemada, Grand Inquisitor in the kingdoms of Aragon and Castile. It was in this corner of the Christian world that the changing geopolitical alignments we have spoken of were most dynamic. Here a militant Christianity was on the march. After seven centuries of intermittent bloody conflict to rid the peninsula of alien faiths the leaders of Christian society were not disposed to deal leniently with their enemies. Muslim and Jewish residents were given a stark choice: leave, convert or die. Nor was conversion a soft option, involving nothing more than a token adherence to the religion of the conqueror. This was where the Inquisition came in. This organ of confessional thought police was first established in the thirteenth century. It always had two objectives: to preserve the unity of the faith by disciplining heretics and over-zealous enthusiasts; and to keep examination of doctrinal issues firmly in ecclesiastical hands by setting up Church courts to deal with suspected offenders. Where the Spanish Inquisition departed from the original model was in its appropriation by the state. Ferdinand and Isabella were sufficiently powerful to extract from Pope Sixtus IV in 1478 a papal breve authorising them to set up a joint commission. Effectively this meant that the Spanish Inquisition became a state tool for enforcing conformity and enriching the Crown from the confiscated property of convicted offenders. Later Protestant propagandists undoubtedly exaggerated the enormities of the Inquisition but the reality was terrible enough and it is not at all unjust that the name of Torquemada, who became Grand Inquisitor in 1483, has become a byword for sadistic persecution. The Inquisition displayed all the characteristics of a police state organ: religious and racial persecution (Orthodox Christians faced interrogation to discover whether they were of mixed blood), reliance on a network of informers, routine application of torture, public executions, sudden arrest and imprisonment without trial. Torquernada and his officials were an ecclesiastical KGB, independent of all local church and state authorities and answerable only to the Crown. No one was safe. The Archbishop of Toledo was imprisoned for over sixteen years and the eighty-year-old Archbishop of Granada fled to avoid capture. For the Inquisition did not only harry unbelievers and wild heretics. It was an unmuzzled hound which might be unleashed against anyone deemed by the Crown to be 'undesirable'. Individuals could be and were denounced for reasons of state or out of personal vindictiveness. During the period of its greatest power (c.1480–c.1580) thousands of the Inquisition's victims were sent to the stake or died as a result of imprisonment or torture.

What is ironical is that this insatiable beast which was turned on so many people who, like Savonarola, sought nothing but the reform of the Church was reared and trained for the purpose of reforming the Church. Spain on the cusp of the sixteenth century was in a ferment of expectation. The union of the crowns, the driving out of non-Christians, the onward momentum of the crusade against Islam, the annexation of Naples (Ferdinand regained control after Charles VIII's withdrawal in 1496), the expansion into newly discovered transatlantic lands – all these coupled with millenarian excitement served to build up a common perception of the new Spain as God's favoured nation destined to play a leading part in the world's endtime. Ferdinand of Aragon rose, as Machiavelli acknowledged, to be 'the foremost king in Christendom'. The pope certainly had to remain on good terms with such a man and flattered him by bestowing on him the title of 'The Catholic'. Rome did not dare question the

Jews being tortured, 1475

supremacy that Ferdinand exercised over the Spanish church. For his part, Ferdinand, forging a new nation from disparate elements, needed a church that would act as a unifying agency. It must be a church purged of all taint of heresy, compromise with Islam and Judaism, and the corruption which provoked criticism. This explains the rigid, unyielding religious policy that operated in his dominions. If free thought was not energetically rooted out it might grow into something which threatened the stability of the infant state. Thus, for example, when at the century's end Cordoba witnessed an outbreak of millenarianism – fed by the very successes of Ferdinand the Catholic – the Inquisition raged through the province with a merciless fury extreme even by its own standards. In a period of a few weeks almost 400 people were burned at the stake.

Meanwhile, Christopher Columbus, servant of that same Ferdinand and his queen, was claiming for himself an almost messianic role. He under-stood the 'other world' he had discovered in terms of biblical prophecy. It was the gateway, he proclaimed, not only to the ancient Eden of Genesis but to the new heaven and new earth of which the Revelation of St John spoke. Assuming the role of 'a prophet new inspired', the arthritic and prematurely aged explorer made several leaps of faith when he promised his patrons cascades of gold bullion, mass conversions of indigenous peoples to Christianity, the high favour of Almighty God and the success of Spanish arms in reconquering the Holy Land. In the same year (1502) that Columbus provided this roseate vision of Christian expansion, Vasco da Gama pointed the way to an earthly, mercantile paradise. His establishment of a Portuguese trading colony on the Indian coast at Cochin began a new era of direct contact between Europe and the Orient – the fabulous land flowing with silk and money, hitherto blocked by the 'iron curtain' of Muslim-controlled territory. Within a decade the world's shape had changed. Scholars, basing their studies on Ptolemy's *Geographike hyphegesis* (*c*. AD 170), had thought they understood the schema of creation and man's place within it. Now new maps were pouring off the presses which told them that things were not as they had believed them to be and every year seemed to produce a fresh discovery, exciting in itself and pregnant with bewildering implications for the future. These were certainly momentous times.

But what impact did stories of new found lands, conversion of Jews, battles against the Turks or burning of troublesome friars have on ordinary town and village dwellers throughout Europe and, specifically, in Luther's Germany? Historians peg out these events as significant markers of the transition from the 'medieval' to the 'modern' world but the real momentum of change was to be found in a stream that had long been running underground, steadily gathering its force until the time when it would gush forth in an unstoppable flood. It was a sense of insecurity, anxiety, resentment. European society was a simmering, unstable *frustrated* society aware of numerous grievances that it was unable to articulate adequately.

The deepest and most widespread unease sprang from frustrated national sentiment. In 1492, Conrad Celtis, poet laureate of the Holy Roman Empire, delivered a ringing speech at the opening of the new university of Ingolstadt:

> Resume, O men of Germany, that spirit of older times wherewith you so often confounded and terrified the Romans. Behold the frontiers of Germany: gather together her torn and shattered lands! Let us feel shame, yes, shame I say, to have let our nation assume the yoke of slavery and pay tribute to foreign barbarian kings.[7]

The German peoples shared a powerful mythology which reached back through the centuries to draw its vigour from the mingled legendary and factual deeds of Frederick Barbarossa, who resisted papal pretensions, Otto I, the 'hammer' of the Magyars, Charlemagne, revered as a saint in Germany, and so on back to one of the heroes of the Trojan War, claimed as the founder of the nation. Scholars made much play with the recently redis-covered writings of the Roman historian Tacitus, which told of the serious reverses imposed by local tribes on the invaders from across the Alps. Other patriotic propagandists were not slow to claim that it was Germany's destiny to rule Europe; had not Charlemagne, on Christmas Day, 800, wrested from the Byzantine emperor the crown of the Roman West?

Unfortunately for the possessors of this proud heritage, ambition and reality were poles apart. Indeed, it is questionable in what sense we can meaningfully use the word 'Germany' at all. The considerable area of central Europe which enjoyed a common language and a common cultural inher-itance was fragmented into a large number of political units. There were lands ruled by hereditary princes and dukes, territories which owed alle-giance to bishops and archbishops and self-governing, imperial 'free' cities. They all had their own currencies, trade regulations, customs and church-state relationships. They all came within the boundaries of the Holy Roman Empire and were 'unified' by fealty to the emperor and co-operation in the imperial parliament or Reichstag but the composition of this body indi-cates just how fractured 'Germany' was. It consisted, in round terms, of 120 senior clerics, 30 princes, the representatives of 65 cities and towns and six 'electors' (3 clerical and 3 lay). Members of this latter group, as their title suggests, had the right to elect the emperor. Far from providing a frame-work for centralised government this body was little more than a talking shop where representatives argued for the rights of their own constituen-cies. However, as the new century dawned the empire did have a focus of pride and cohesion if not of meaningful unity in the person of the man who donned the imperial crown in 1493. Maximilian I was acclaimed by several opinion formers as a fulfilment of prophecy, the second Charlemagne who would extend his rule over the Christian world and lead the last great crusade against Islam. It was a role he was determined to play and he made an impressive start. He was twice successful in wars against the French and added considerably to his Austrian inheritance by conquest and marriage. But Maximilian was very far from being a bluff, empty-headed soldier. He was a tireless administrator and mastered most of the languages spoken within the empire. He was a generous, not to say ostentatious, patron of artists and scholars (Albrecht Dürer, Albrecht Altdorfer and Lucas Cranach the Elder were among those who enjoyed his support and encouragement). His PR machine projected an image of Maximilian as the most cultured ruler of the age and the epitome of Christian chivalry. Within Germany the emperor was one element in the apocalyptic vision which fired popular imagination and inspired men to hope in their national destiny.

One of the few policy areas on which there was a large measure of agreement within the Reichstag and between Maximilian and his people was antipathy towards Rome. The Alps were a barrier of prejudice. Italians conventionally regarded Germans as barbarians and Germans thought of Italians as effete and corrupt. Resentment of papal interference in everyday life ran through society from top to bottom. Ever since Leo III had crowned Charlemagne in 800 the leadership of the Christian West had been disputed by popes and emperors. In 1440 the Italian humanist Lorenzo Valla exposed the *Donation of Constantine* as a forgery, thus kicking away the main crutch upon which papal supremacy in the temporal world had rested. This breathtakingly audacious ninth-century document had, until this point, appeared to provide incontrovertible proof that the pope was the sovereign authority throughout Latin Christendom. It purported to be a grant made by the Emperor Constantine to Pope Sylvester I in gratitude for his miraculous deliverance from leprosy. It ordained that,

> The sacred see of blessed Peter shall be gloriously exalted even above our Empire and earthly throne . . . as over all churches of God in all the world . . . We convey to Sylvester, universal Pope, both our palace and likewise all provinces and palaces and districts of the city of Rome and Italy and of the regions of the west . . .

Despite the seemingly unchallengeable evidence of the *Donation*, emperors *had* stoutly contested papal pretensions generation after generation on the grounds that they had received their *imperium* directly from God and, therefore, ruled by divine right over the lives and estates of all their subjects, lay and ecclesiastical. The same arguments raged at all political levels, for, when it came to the rich lands of the Church and the bishops and abbots who administered them, every prince, duke and city corporation wanted to keep them under their own control.

Another undercurrent of medieval European life was social restlessness. Those at the bottom of the social scale nursed a resentment that only awaited the emergence of bold leaders to express itself in disorderly conduct and those at the top lived in apprehension of peasant revolt. Authority and discipline were the most effective bonds tying communities together and the men in power habitually reacted (or over-reacted) to any suggestion of unrest. In 1476 there had been a particularly serious outbreak of trouble in the region of Würzburg, less than a hundred and fifty kilometres from the region where Martin's parents were growing up. The bishop had to deal with Hans Beheim, a charismatic rabble-rouser, known as the 'Drummer of Niklashausen'.

This self-appointed prophet was an ill-educated fellow who preached a muddled message of religious and social challenge. As well as the stock-in-trade demand for repentance and moral reform, he attacked oppressive taxation and demanded an egalitarian reordering of society, so that, 'pope, emperor, princes, barons, knights, squires, citizens, farmers and the common man will be the same, equal, one not owning more than the other and all will work'.[8] There was nothing original in the Drummer's utopian schema. Every peasant uprising in Europe proposed a programme of social levelling. A century earlier Wat Tyler's followers in England had demanded to know,

Hans Beheim, the Drummer of Niklashausen. A woodcut from 1493 shows Beheim, prompted by a Dominican, preaching to a crowd of country people

> When Adam delved and Eve span
> Who was then a gentleman?

Contradictory ecclesiastical teaching and practice helped to feed lower-class aspirations for change. What simple people observed and regarded with cynicism was that the biggest landowner in Christendom, the Church, constantly proclaimed the virtue of poverty and contempt for worldly goods. Teachers of the Jesus way, which urged disciples to lay up treasures in heaven and not on earth, could scarcely do otherwise but when bejewelled bishops exhorted the faithful to be content with their lot and accept the stratification of society as a divine given it seemed to be yet another example of the Christian leadership commanding, 'Do as we say, not as we do.'

Beheim received short shrift from the Bishop of Würzburg. He was arrested, denounced as a heretic, on somewhat dubious theological grounds, and duly burned. What is significant is the simple preacher's widespread appeal. Twelve thousand of his followers marched on the bishop's castle, demanding their hero's release, and had to be dispersed by episcopal troops. But that was very far from being the end of the matter. The Drummer was now venerated as a holy martyr and pilgrims flocked from far and wide to pay homage at the church where he had preached. No amount of official denunciation could stop them and it was only by razing the building to the ground that the authorities were eventually able to put an end to the practice. Beheim was far from being unique. His story may have come down to us because it was a particularly dramatic one or it may simply be that the records concerning him have survived better than those of other malcontents. Others there certainly were and both ecclesiastical and secular rulers had to be diligent in keeping the lid on simmering discontent.

By 1500 the political influence of the papacy was everywhere in decline. It was not only in Aragon and Castile that Rome had to do deals with reigning monarchs, making compromises and offering concessions in order to maintain a presence in the life of the state. The fiction of Latin Christendom was being stretched to breaking point. Culturally and spiritually Europe was still an impressive pavilion made from the strong, poly-chromed canvas of common language (for the religious and intellectual elite), common liturgy, common ecclesiastical structures and common doctrines. Yet, within this faith community there were many competing political entities, overlapping administrations and rival judicatures which created frustrations on a daily basis for all concerned. In Germany local and regional authorities grabbed whatever opportunities presented themselves to encroach upon the power of the spirituality. Long before the Reformation, devout German princes were assuming the supervision of monasteries and churches which ecclesiastic leaders were failing to reform. They purged convents of corrupt practices and even closed places of worship down altogether. They removed negligent clergy and insinuated into pulpits pastors of whom they approved. Naturally, the ecclesiastical hierarchy struck back wherever possible. The more it was weakened by the seeping away of papal authority, the more fiercely it clung to those structures and practices that had grown up over the centuries. The work of princely court and municipal council chamber was constantly impeded by the competing interests of a hugely complex set of ecclesiastical networks. As well as the administrative pattern of archdiocese, diocese and parish, there were the various monastic orders which were independent, not only of temporal authorities, but also of the secular church hierarchy. Clergy were free from prosecution under state law because the Church had its own courts. Since in some German cities more than ten per cent of the inhabitants could claim this 'benefit of clergy' it is scarcely surprising that many people despaired of obtaining justice.

Yet it was the financial burdens churchmen placed on their neighbours that rankled most with the economically hard-pressed members of society. The curia helped itself to 'annates', the first year's income of every newly appointed diocesan bishop and beneficed priest. To compensate for the draining away of gold across the Alps local clergy exploited to the full the charges they were entitled to make for their services. They imposed tithes and levied fees for hearing confessions, performing requiem masses, baptisms, marriages, burials and other rites. These were all explained as down payments ensuring residence in that great condominium in the sky. The whole sacramental system worked because spiritual and moral pressures were brought to bear on the laity to pay up cheerfully just as they were also urged to be generous to the mendicants who thronged the streets, to donate money to holy shrines and to purchase indulgences. Since all human beings were mired in sin, they were destined for an uncomfortable afterlife. Purgatory could not be avoided. All the devout could do was shorten their sojourn there by 'buying' the means of grace offered on the Church's 'market stall'. This is not an unfair metaphor. A substantial part of papal and episcopal revenues came from offering, at a price, exemptions from the Church's own moral and spiritual rules or absolution for breaking them. For example there were concubinage fees payable by parish priests to their bishops for the privilege of ignoring their celibacy vows. In *The Brothers Karamazov* Dostoevsky relates an imaginary encounter between Christ and a sixteenth-century grand inquisitor. In what is a pungently telling analysis the Church official points out the great favour the Catholic regime has done by lifting the burdens of conscience and free will from men's souls:

> . . . men rejoiced that they were once more led like sheep and that the terrible gift which had brought them so much suffering had at last been lifted from their hearts. . . Did we not love mankind when we admitted so humbly its impotence and lovingly lightened its burden and allowed men's weak nature even to sin, so long as it was with our permission?[9]

The 'deal' men struck with the institutional Church left them free to be religious without the burden of being devout. Theirs was a communal system of observances measured by feasts and fasts, festivals and fairs, linked as much with the agricultural cycle as the liturgical year. In what was basically for most people a hard life the familiar observances shared with their neighbours provided a comforting framework. The mass of European humanity, however much they might grumble, were at home in the old dispensation because they had never known and could not conceive anything else. 'The church was situated at the heart of men's lives – their emotional lives, their professional lives, and their aesthetic lives, if one can use that imposing word – of everything that was beyond them and everything that bound them together, of their great passions and their minor concerns, of their hopes and their dreams.'[10] Yet there were those who bitterly resented the control priests exercised over their lives even if they did not yet dare to challenge it. In the words of Hilaire Belloc, they had to 'keep a-hold of Nurse for fear of finding something worse'. What was particularly galling for them was that 'Nurse' was neglecting her charges and certainly not setting the prim and proper example that might be expected of her.

So, another aspect of the general frustration was dissatisfaction with a Church in need of reform. There certainly were, as we have seen, religious 'professionals' whose personal austerities, humble demeanour or eloquent preaching evoked awe and admiration but such were the exceptions rather than the rule. There were also many Church leaders who knew that there were grave disorders crying out for redress. Kings and princes added their voices to the chorus demanding change. Maximilian I and Charles VIII were among the many secular and religious heads who called for the summoning of a general council of the Church whose agenda would extend over a wide range of abuses. Everywhere preachers were to be found baying against moral corruption. Savonarola was certainly not unique. 'Reform' was very far from being a new idea. It was as old as Christianity. The high standards expected of Christians and explicit in the Gospel message ensured that every age produced its watchdogs whose role was to urge believers, and especially the leaders of the flock, to live up to their faith. It was for this reason that successive waves of reform had swept over Christian monasticism for hundreds of years, setting up new orders and bifurcating existing ones into strict and liberal movements. Diligent bishops carried out visitations and made efforts to improve the educational and moral tone of their clergy.

However, there were two obstacles to institutional reform, obstacles that would prove insurmountable. The first can be summed up in the maxim, 'A mission becomes a movement; a movement becomes a machine; and a machine becomes a monument.' The overriding preoccupation of any human establishment is self-preservation. There comes a time when it is incapable of the root-and-branch transformation necessary to recover the pure idealism of its founders. It has a vested interest in the status quo. Thus, for example, reigning popes routinely opposed appeals for a general council because of the challenge such a body might present to the authority of Rome. The medieval church could not reform itself from the top. There was simply too much at stake – politically, economically and socially. When visionary members of the hierarchy *did* press for reform – and herein lies the second obstacle – they thought in terms of *restoration*, of getting back to some age which, if not golden, was demonstrably better than the current one. The reality was that the problem was too deep and too wide for such simplistic solutions. After fifteen hundred years of exercising spiritual power, developing the doctrines and disciplinary procedures to buttress that power and suppressing radicals, mystics and zealots who posed inconvenient questions, nothing less than a complete shake-up would do.

The ace in the Catholic pack was spiritual sanction. The Church hierarchy was safe from radical reform as long as people believed, or at least accepted, its teaching. Of course, most of its sons and daughters lacked the intellectual equipment to challenge it. But was ignorance the only dam holding the flood that was about to break? Were there thousands of unhappy individuals only waiting for a reason to reject traditional doctrines? This is the sixty-four thousand dollar question historians have always had to face up to in their attempts to understand and explain the Reformation. Some have pointed to the material evidence for widespread devotion at the turn of the sixteenth century – the last flowering of the Gothic with its new shrines, chantries, chapels and expensively decked altars – to demonstrate that the new beliefs about to parade themselves were only espoused by minorities and that where they triumphed they had to be imposed upon reluctant populations. Others have argued from the persistence and spread of heresy that we are wrong to read too much into such externals; that the Reformation *was* an ideological revolution waiting to happen. It is self-evident that major historical changes are always brought about by minorities but it is also true, as Aristotle observed, that social stability depends on shared values. When those in authority can no longer depend on commonly held assumptions, institutions and even power itself are up for grabs. Then, the leaders of the state either have to accommodate themselves to the new ideas or impose the old ones by force. This is what happened over and again in different parts of Europe during the Reformation and the wars of religion that followed. It will never be possible to quantify the extent to which *homo religiosus* was passionately orthodox in his beliefs in the years around 1500. The vast majority of people simply did not leave religious testaments. We must rely entirely on the assembly of anecdotal evidence if we want to gauge something of the mood of the times.

The pace of change was to be set by urban dwellers because ideas always spread faster where populations are concentrated, where commerce and education attract a steady throughput of visitors and where the proportion of literate people is higher. So what evidence is there that religious life was flourishing or flagging in the towns and cities of Europe? Let us consider events in Strasbourg, a city of some 20,000 souls, standing at the crossroads between France, Germany, Italy and the Netherlands and open to all the intellectual and religious influences of the age. Between 1480 and 1520 its citizens were responsible for an impressive programme of pious works. New chapels were added to the cathedral and a great bell was hung and dedicated to the Virgin Mary. To the nineteen houses of religion already in existence was added the Convent of St Mary Magdalene. Several of the thirteen churches and two hundred chapels were freshly adorned with paintings, sculptures, tapestries and coloured windows. The annual festival of the Virgin drew thousands to throng the streets and process to the cathedral following images of the saint. Lay confraternities of tradespeople and craftsmen maintained altars, practised charitable giving and staged miracle plays. A casual visitor would have assumed that traditional religion was alive and well in Strasbourg. But there were other, less obvious signs that have to be recorded and interpreted. Membership of the religious houses was declining. So was their income. Over these years Strasbourgers gave less and less to the upkeep of monasteries and nunneries. Hawkers of papal indulgences similarly had a hard time of it seeking out customers. Printers, by contrast, did a brisk trade in vernacular Bibles, devotional manuals and religious pamphlets. Though, on the face of it, this might seem more proof of conventional piety, the picture is less clear when we explore *what* people were reading. The runaway bestseller was *The Ship of Fools* by Sebastian Brant, clerk of the city from 1503 to 1521. This German poem (also translated into Latin) was a scathing satire denouncing all the vices the author observed in contemporary society. Though it was by no means aimed exclusively at the clergy, there is no doubt that its popularity came in large measure from its appeal to a sizeable anticlerical element in society. Nor was Brant alone. The local Franciscan, Thomas Murner, attacked worldly monks and parish priests. 'When I want to hear God's word,' he complained, in *Guild of Delinquents*, 'all I get is the reading out of documents excommunicating peasants for their debts.' Criticism of the clergy was a popular drum to beat and ensured good sales. The gulf between priests and people was widening. In the 1490s there were several peasant risings directed at incompetent, absentee and avaricious clergy. It is not surprising that pastors were suspicious of lay religious activities, such as the confraternities and the founding of preacherships. The 'professionals' were probably right in viewing such initiatives as bids for independence by people who believed they were not getting what they wanted from their spiritual leaders. Within a very few years Strasbourg became one of the earliest and most extreme centres of reform. Among the gangs of angry vigilantes who went from church to church and convent to convent, turning out the inmates, pulling down statues and ripping holy pictures, were some of the people who had paid for monks to pray for them and installed or commissioned the works of art that were now being defaced.[11]

We have identified some of the frustrations that would eventually unleash themselves in orgies of denunciation, destruction and rejection of Church teaching. The Reformation was a protest movement and that accounts for most of its negative aspects. But it was much more than that; it was fundamentally an evangelical revival, bigger by far than any other that has punctuated the life of the European church but in essence no different to those movements associated with such preachers, mystics and writers as Francis,

Thomas à Kempis, Jonathan Edwards, Wesley and Billy Graham. By 'evangelical revival' I mean the dramatic impact of a gospel which is personal, biblical, affective and Cross-centred. The circumstances have to be right for such explosions of religious energy which lead to the conversion of hundreds of thousands of people and at the beginning of the sixteenth century the psychological climate was very right.

One way to gauge it is in the demeanour of worshippers. A modern Catholic historian laments the growth of individualistic lay piety and its undermining of the sacramental liturgy. People who were dissatisfied with the mechanistic recitation of the Latin service took to reading books of hours and primers while the priest got on with *his* mass. In this way books that were intended to strengthen conventional devotion could have the opposite effect: 'The religion of the laity came to consist more and more in their personal relations with God. A private prayer which seemed more effectively to bring the individual into conscious contact with God was more esteemed than communal prayer.'[12] The Church's own propaganda was working against it. So successfully had it inculcated a sense of sin into people that the more ardent members of the flock were desperately seeking ways to make their peace with God. Those who found the institutional means of grace superficial and inadequate were ready to look elsewhere.

Another litmus test is to be found in the change of popular attitudes towards what the Church called heresy. Over the centuries the hierarchy had fine-tuned the machinery designed to neutralise troublemakers who declined to believe what they were told to believe. It tried to deal sensitively with individuals and groups who questioned accepted doctrines. When pastoral guidance and discipline failed, more stringent measures were applied and in the last resort condemned heretics were excommunicated and handed over to the secular arm. Because disaffection usually bubbled up from the lower levels of society, princes and nobles, who had an inbred dread of peasant disorder, could, under normal circumstances, be relied upon to despatch the offenders. Whatever their differences with Rome and its agents, they understood well that Church and State stood or fell together. Moreover, the laity as a whole co-operated in the process. A family given the black spot by the Church courts would be ostracised by neighbours horrified by their crime and eager to distance themselves from the taint of heterodoxy. However, by the late fifteenth century public response to heresy trials was changing. Lay enthusiasm for persecution waned, especially in the towns. Civic authorities were increasingly reluctant to do the clergy's dirty work for them. Unless the accused were actual troublemakers, councillors preferred to turn a blind eye or, if pressed, to impose short periods of exile. Officially they certainly did not tolerate heresy but, in effect, their attitude amounted to an acknowledgement that citizens who conducted themselves responsibly in public might believe as they pleased in private.

Zealous churchmen who were determined to ensure the purity of the faith found themselves up against serious problems when heresy climbed the social scale, became tangled up with nationalism or when its advocates were protected by local rulers. The Hussites provide a case in point. Jan Hus was a teacher at Prague University who was burned at the stake in 1415 for allegedly spreading the opinions of the English heretic, John Wycliffe. Hus's condemnation had taken more than a decade of turbulent political manoeuvring to achieve and his enemies were triumphant. But not for long. For many years Hus had been revered as a Bohemian nationalist hero, who stood for independence from German domination and the purging of the Church from corruption. Now his death provoked a furious backlash. Several members of the Czech nobility joined the rebellion which broke out. The end result was the emergence of not one but two indigenous churches. The mainstream communion was the Utraquists and their more radical rivals were known as the *Unitas Fratrum* (The Union of Bohemian Brethren). Both were independent of Rome.

Hussite influence was not confined to Bohemia. Sympathisers and members of the Czech churches were to be found in many parts of Germany and in some cities the heretical assemblies were able to acquire their own buildings for worship. The popular view concerning the deplorable Hus affair that stubbornly held sway for more than a century was that the unfortunate man had been illegally done to death. A woodcut engraving of the 1520s shows the martyr being burned while the pope and a bishop look on gleefully. At the same time an angel carries the dead man's soul to heaven, while two laymen acknowledge him as a saint. In Luther's early days in the monastery at Erfurt his novice master confided that he shared the opinion that Hus's trial and condemnation had been a travesty of justice. Nor were the Hussites the only heretical groups active in Germany. Waldensians, whose movement could be traced back to the twelfth century, still operated in, usually, secret conventicles and there were numerous other groups who drew their colours from the rainbow hues of heterodoxy. Varieties of Christian belief had always existed

The martyrdom of Jan Hus, from a book of 1524. The Church
persecutes; ordinary people recognise Hus's holiness; and an angel
receives his soul into heaven

and this explains why Church leaders went to such lengths to preserve the
unity of the faith. But now they were losing the battle.

One reason for the proliferation of diverse religious opinions was the
availability of new information technology. In terms of its cultural impact
the printing press was the most significant innovation in world history
before the internet. To provide the raw material for the new industry a
process for the manufacture of cheap paper was developed. Thus, within
a very few years, the patient, painstaking and labour-intensive industry of
the monastic scriptorium became a thing of the past and the whole business of publishing and bookselling had begun. The international mercantile community had not been slow to realise the possibilities of Johannes
Gutenberg's development, in the 1450s, of a process for 'mass producing'
texts by means of a press using movable type. By 1500 every major town
and city in Europe had at least one print works and there were already in
existence more books than the world had ever seen – some thirty thousand
titles, running to over six million copies. It was this that would make it
possible, in Steven Ozment's words, 'for a little mouse like Wittenberg to
roar like a lion across the length and breadth of Europe'.[13] More than half
the books in print were on religious subjects and ranged from standard

theological texts for the use of scholars to cheap, heavily illustrated devotional works designed to appeal to the semi-literate.

To church leaders the new technology seemed to be, quite literally, a
godsend. It was a powerful tool for the task of educating the laity and re-
inforcing Catholic doctrine. Unfortunately, the printing press could also
be utilised by writers with challenging new ideas to propound and imper-
tinent questions to ask. From the very beginning of the commercial
publishing industry producers understood well the value of sensationalism.
Students, free-thinking scholars, cultured aristocrats eager for the latest
craze, renegade friars, members of huddled back-room sects – all these
provided a good market for books and pamphlets which lampooned the
establishment, denounced ecclesiastical abuses or daringly propounded
unorthodox ideas. There were good profits to be made from such potentially subversive literature, even if sometimes it had to be sold clandes-
tinely for fear of the authorities.

It is hard to conceive of the exhilarating sense of intellectual excitement and freedom thousands of people felt at being able to handle and
even own books. Objects that had hitherto only existed in monastic, university and aristocratic libraries, and thus never been seen by the vulgar, now
became familiar to all through bookshops and market stalls. The desire to
read which, till now, had only possessed scholars, merchants and admin-
istrators seized others. In Basel there survives a signboard painted in 1516
by Hans Holbein the younger and his brother, Ambrosius, for a public
teacher. The legend reads,

> For whoever wants to read and write German in the shortest possible
> time, even those who cannot read a single letter, who want to be
> able to write down and be able to read their debts. Satisfaction guar-
> anteed. Will take on burghers, journeymen, women and maidens,
> whoever needs to learn. Reasonable prices for instruction.[14]

As that advertisement suggests, the new technology not only spread
literacy across the social spectrum, it also gave a considerable boost to
vernacular languages and that, in turn, impacted on nationalism and
the sense of regional identity. Nor, as we have seen, was it only the
printed word that made an impact. Wood blocks and copper plates were
used to illustrate texts and assist those who were less than fluent readers.
Every man or woman prepared to con their letters might now set forth

on a seemingly limitless voyage of discovery. Radical thinkers like Desiderius Erasmus wholeheartedly approved this, believing that the dissemination of knowledge could only be beneficial. His friend, Thomas More, was, by contrast, alarmed to discover artisans and labourers presuming to read and debate holy writ and the controversial literature arising from it. He warned that only disaster could follow

> When an hatter will go smatter
> In philosophy,
> Or a pedlar wax a meddler
> In theology.[15]

But it was scholars and those who aspired to be scholars who were most deeply intoxicated by ready access to a whole new world of discovery and speculation. Like the Athenians of old, they 'spent their time doing nothing but talking about and listening to the latest ideas'.[16] Most of them did not consider themselves to be religious innovators; they were Renaissance men, rediscovering ancient truth and freeing it from barren scholasticism. On the other hand they did not shun the contemptuous taunt of traditionalists who dubbed them disciples of 'New Learning'. They were, indeed, bringing a new, fresh, bold, brave approach to ancient texts and the theological principles derived from them.

This is where the importance of printing really lies in relation to the Reformation. The intellectual conditioning of medieval scholars had rested upon reverence for the standard texts of the fathers and doctors of the Church. These works were, in themselves, precious objects, copied laboriously by scribes, generation after generation. Preservation was all – of the books themselves but also of the wisdom they contained. Impecunious students could only read the time-hallowed volumes in libraries and retain the information they contained by careful note-taking or rote learning. Now they could buy books, read them at their leisure, compare them with the works of other writers and commentators. They could study the criticisms of leading contemporary experts, even those who lived and taught in educational centres hundreds of miles away. In other words, they could stand in judgement on traditional teaching, instead of accepting it as a given. Students, who are always, almost by definition, rebels, forced the pace of change in universities. Courses were modernised. Every educational institution which aspired to be up to date added Greek and Hebrew – the languages of the early Bible texts – to its syllabuses. More and more classical and early Christian texts were published. Printing gave access, according to one's point of view, to either an Aladdin's cave or a Pandora's box of learning. The discoverer could take from it what he chose. New individualism had ousted old authoritarianism.

Everything was in place for a critic who would proclaim in robust prose the criticisms thousands of Europeans felt but had not, till now, dared to voice.

3

Monkery

For a dozen years Martin Luther strove with might and main to be a good monk. He could do no other. His bridges were thoroughly burned behind him. The emotional investment he had made in following what he believed to be his vocation was total. He was estranged from his family. He had cut himself off from his former life and friends. He had died to worldly ambition. Now that the great step had been taken he must have felt the relief of a difficult decision taken. He had met the requirement for discipleship laid down by Christ: 'Anyone who loves his father and mother more than me is not worthy of me . . . Whoever finds his life will lose it, and whoever loses his life for my sake will find it.'[1] He had chosen the 'more perfect way' and could reasonably look for that inner peace that had for so long eluded him.

There is little reason to suppose that he did not find it – for a time at least. However, we do have a problem in understanding Luther's monastic career. His later writings on the religious life are utterly condemnatory and he came to consider his Augustinian years as worse than wasted. 'In the cloister I lost both the salvation of my soul and the health of my body,' he complained in a sermon in 1531.[2] But such statements were made after he had turned his back on monasticism. His memories were coloured by that rejection and his combative teaching undoubtedly involved exaggeration. We can, I think, identify two aspects of the young monk's life during what have been called the 'years of silence'. There is the external Luther and the internal Luther. They did not start off in tension but gradually they pulled further and further apart until a violent sundering became inevitable.

To all outward appearances, between 1505 and 1517 Luther presented the picture of a gifted young monk, achieving above average promotion within his order and serving it by studying, teaching, writing and sharing in the work of administration. He had friends in the cloister as well as wise spiritual advisers to whom he turned when soul crises threatened to overwhelm him. He was not required to abandon the academic career which had always attracted him. On the contrary, his Augustinian superiors recognised his keen intellect and encouraged him to develop it – for the sake of his own spiritual health as much as the instruction of his pupils.

Luther the student was acquainted with all the religious houses in Erfurt and doubtless had personal contacts in some of them. This will have coloured his decision to present himself at the cloister of the Observant Augustinians. It was no casual choice. He did not pick out this particular house with a pin. In all probability he had discussed the quality of life in the Augustinian monastery with some of its inmates during the days when he was agonising over his career choice. There were two factors which may have influenced him. The first was the rigour of the regime practised in the Erfurt house. The order of Augustinian Eremites had been founded two hundred and fifty years earlier as one of the many attempts to reform European monasticism and call it back to its ascetic roots. The brothers were pledged to strict poverty, were to sustain themselves by soliciting alms from the Christian faithful and to pledge themselves to a rigid commitment to the liturgical routine of daily worship and prayer. Unfortunately, over the years the order succumbed to the creeping temptations of wealth and ease. Generous donations to its funds enabled it to build impressive conventual buildings and invest in income-producing property. Obedience to the rule became lax and by the mid-fifteenth century this reforming order itself stood in need of reform. A zealous move to raise the spiritual temperature led to a split in the order and the emergence of an 'observant' wing. In this 'holiness crusade' it was the Erfurt monastery that assumed the lead in Thuringia-Saxony. Its members had a reputation for taking their vocation very seriously and their way of life appealed to an ardent young student desperate to make his peace with God. On the other hand, had Luther been motivated entirely by ascetic zeal he could have chosen a community committed to more extreme austerities. As well as the Observant Franciscan at Magdeburg who had impressed him as a teenager, he saw on the streets of Erfurt Carthusians whose crippled bodies proclaimed their contempt for the flesh and groups of flagellants, who lashed their backs in public. Such extremes (which were condemned by many leading authorities) had no appeal for him.

The other attraction of the Augustinian cloister was its close connection with the university. Senior members of the monastery lectured in the philosophy and theology schools and it was a principle of the order to encourage monks who displayed talent to stretch their minds in academic study. That Brother Martin came into this category was obvious to his superiors from the very beginning. He had been one of the more successful students of his year and impressed his mentors with his work for his master's degree. There seemed every likelihood that he would prove to be an intellectual adornment to the monastery and the order. The Augustinians were urgently in need of new blood. Their numbers were in decline. In 1488 there were sixty-seven monks in the Erfurt house. Twenty years later the total had fallen to fifty-two. If the trend was to be reversed the order would need to attract more young men of Luther's calibre – intelligent, enthusiastic and totally committed to the austere lifestyle of the monastery. In fact the man who had rejected a legal profession in favour of the contemplative life was quite a 'catch' and could be held up as an example to other members of the student body who might be induced to follow his lead. Indeed, at least one of Luther's friends did do exactly that.

However, the new monk's academic activities had to be put on hold for a while. First he had to be fully initiated into the monastic way of life. During his novitiate year Martin was watched carefully to make sure that he possessed the dedication and stamina necessary to make a good monk. It was a year of real testing during which he had to be punctual at all the daily offices, show unquestioning obedience to his superiors, perform the most menial tasks without complaint and submit himself to close spiritual supervision by his confessor. To all outward appearances, Luther settled quickly into his new environment. His 'home' was now an impressive complex of buildings on the northern side of the city. The community might have been decreasing in number but their site was constantly widening and construction work was seldom at a standstill. In Luther's day the impressive monastery library was still a-building. The presence of masons and carpenters must have disturbed the serenity of monastic life, but it was also a testimony to the permanence of that life. Everything around the novice monk spoke of the timelessness of his vocation. The ancient buildings, the hallowed routine, the well-thumbed psalters, the hand-written and illuminated books replete with the wisdom of his spiritual forefathers all contributed to the comforting sense that Luther was part of a holy tradition that would continue until the day of the Lord's return. The soaring church was the centre of the community's life. Not only did they congregate there for the seven daily offices; individual monks were constantly engaged saying masses in the seven side chapels for the repose of those who had paid for this service. At his appointed place in the choir the new monk, who loved music, enjoyed participating in the ethereal plainsong which rose exultantly to the vaulted roof. If ever his mind wandered as he recited the familiar psalms and responses he could gaze on the stories of Christ and the saints vibrant in the great stained glass windows (but he would then be obliged to show contrition for his errant thoughts at his next confession). Two large courtyards, one cloistered, provided space for exercise and private contemplation during the inmates' few unoccupied moments. The refectory, sleeping quarters, library, infirmary, guesthouse and prior's lodging made up the remaining buildings on the site and beyond them were the garden and the little cemetery. Luther's own, private space was a bleak, unadorned cell, some three by two-and-a-half metres. This complex was his entire world. Seldom, if ever, during his first year did he venture outside the monastery's encircling walls.

Subjugation of personality was the prime object of his probationary training. He had to walk – quite literally – in utter humility, head bowed, eyes directed at the ground. He could speak to no one without the permission of the novice-master. In the refectory he had to serve his superiors, setting out plates and bowls and filling beakers. If ever he felt that he had been rebuked unjustly for clumsiness or inattention he had to suffer such treatment in silence. In addition to devotional reading he had to study and commit to memory the detailed rules of the order which covered every aspect of private and communal life. All this Luther accepted eagerly. He wanted nothing else but to be a good monk. So committed was he that the novice-master, Johann Greffenstein, had to restrain his enthusiasm. Greffenstein was a wise counsellor and one of the few monks for whom Luther later professed any respect. He was used to young men with over-acute consciences and when the zealous Brother Martin bombarded him with the minutiae of his sins he prescribed suitable reading matter and counselled him to strive for a sense of proportion. Undoubtedly it was concern for his eternal wellbeing that motivated Luther's scrupulosity but there was another reason why he had to get successfully through his trial year. His bitterly disappointed father had angrily suggested that Martin's 'calling' was an illusion or a deception. Whether or not the young monk admitted it to himself, he had to prove that old Hans was wrong.

He need not have worried. His superiors recognised his talents and his sincerity. Luther, they realised, had the makings of a model monk. Before the end of his novitiate he had been marked out as someone to be fast-tracked. Fortuitously, his arrival at the Erfurt cloister coincided with important developments within the order. Johann von Staupitz, a prominent theologian and administrator, had recently been appointed vicar general of the German Augustinians and he was determined to complete the work of reform in the houses under his charge. He wanted to make them all into Observant communities and he kept a sharp look out for members of the order who might help him in his campaign. Whether or not he became acquainted with Luther at this early stage is not clear but he must have heard of the promising new monk for it was only a matter of months before he took an interest in Brother Martin and began to influence his career.

One morning in the late summer of 1506 Luther was escorted into the chapter house where the entire company was gathered. He knelt before the prior and made the solemn vows which were required for full admittance to the order. After prayers a traditional hymn was sung during which he was invested with the white tunic, scapular and cope and the black cowled cotta. He was now a monk. He received from the prior a lighted candle as a symbol that he had entered the kingdom of light. The company now processed into the church where Luther knelt before the high altar and prayed aloud for God's blessing on his life as a monk. Finally, the prior led the community in interceding for their new brother, that, after a life of faithful service, he would be received into eternal blessedness. Then Luther was escorted to the stall in the choir which would be his until the day he died. The ceremony moved him deeply. Was this not what Thomas Aquinas, the thirteenth-century Church doctor, had written of as the 'second baptism'? Now Martin was as innocent as a newly christened baby and virtually assured of his place in heaven. He experienced hours, perhaps days, of euphoria.

But he was given little time to reflect on his new status. The next stages in his career had already been marked out for him. Almost immediately he began preparation for admission to the priesthood and, not long afterwards, he entered the theology faculty of the university because his prior ordered him to train as an Augustinian lecturer. Over the next six months he was admitted to each of the minor orders and was finally priested on 3 April 1507. 2 May was set for his first celebration of mass. It was to be a traumatic experience. As the day approached he fell into a state of nervous apprehension and that for two reasons. One was the sheer enormity of the awesome responsibility he was about to assume. According to what he devoutly believed, he was going to perform a miracle. Under his hands flour and water and the fruit of the grape would be metamorphosed into skin, bone and red and white corpuscles, the very body and blood of Christ. In preparation for the consecration a priest had to purify himself. The introspective and scrupulous Luther could not convince himself that he was ready for the great moment and this unnerved him, as he later recalled:

> When at length I stood before the altar and was to consecrate, I was so terrified by the words *aeterno vivo vero Deo* ['to thee, the eternal, living and true God'] that I thought of running away from the altar and said to my prior, 'Reverend Father, I'm afraid I must leave the altar.' He shouted to me, 'Go ahead, faster, faster!'[3]

The other problem that added to the celebrant's nerves was the presence of someone in the congregation from whom he had parted on bad terms almost two years earlier – his father. It was traditional for proud parents and family members to attend a relative's first mass and Hans had come with a party of twenty visitors. He presented a generous gift to the monastery. But did that mean that he was, at last, reconciled to the life his son had chosen to lead? In the event, the relationship was only partially restored, as Martin recorded in a letter to his father in 1521, after he had abandoned the cowl.

> It is now almost sixteen years since I became a monk, taking the vow without your knowledge and against your will. In your paternal love you were fearful about my weakness ... and you had learned from numerous examples that this way of life turned out sadly for many ... This fear of yours, this care, this indignation against me was for a time implacable. Friends tried in vain to persuade you that if you wished to offer something to God, you ought to give your dearest and best ... but you were deaf. At last you desisted and bowed to the will of God, but your fears for me were never laid aside. For I remember very well that after we were reconciled and you were talking with me, I told you that I had been called by terrors from heaven and that I did not become a monk of my own free will and desire, still less to gain any gratification of the flesh, but that I was walled in by the terror and the agony of sudden death and forced by necessity to take the vow. Then you said, 'Let us hope it was not a delusion and a deception.' That word

penetrated to the depths of my soul and stayed there, as if God had spoken by your lips, though I hardened my heart against you and your word as much as I could. You said something else too. When in filial confidence I upbraided you for your wrath, you suddenly retorted with a reply so fitting and so much to the point that I have hardly ever in all my life heard any man say anything which struck me so forcibly and stayed with me so long. 'Have you not also heard,' you said, 'that parents are to be obeyed?' But I was so sure of my own righteousness that in you I heard only a man, and boldly ignored you; though in my heart I could not ignore your word.[4]

The chronology of this relationship is not clear from that passage. Memory has conflated events. However, from other comments made by Luther and those recorded by some of his disciples it seems that Hans' rebuke about his son's rebellion against parental authority was delivered during the festivities following Martin's first mass. Although father and son were back on speaking terms and Hans had reconciled himself to making the best of a bad job, the old man was still deeply hurt and his son was profoundly conscious of it.

As well as sending to his father the moving letter above, Luther included it as the preface to a treatise on monastic vows which was published, in Latin and German, in 1522. Thus he wore his heart on his sleeve by revealing to the world what had passed between himself and his parent. In the monograph the author condemned others in characteristically robust language for doing precisely what he had done:

... you take your vows to a brazen godlessness which will not accept you unless you first forswear obedience to parents ... It greatly disturbs me that such audacity and impudence, glaringly mad though it is, rages furiously against the clear commandments of God ...[5]

When called upon to advise a young man how he should behave towards his father who was not yet weaned from 'papistical error', Luther counselled:

He should take care in every possible way not to offend his father by his liberty but should become the spiritual father of him who is his physical father. If for this purpose he adjusts himself to his father, he will not sin by attending mass and other profane rites.[6]

But this was not all Luther had to say on the subject. In conversation with friends he sometimes referred to the harshness of his upbringing and even blamed parental oppression for his decision to enter the monastery. This, then, is the point in the story when we have to probe deeper into Luther's early intellectual and emotional development and we must do so because so much of what is to follow hangs upon it. In the immaturity of youth he had made certain decisions (or become the victim of certain involuntary impulses) whose validity he was not convinced of in his heart of hearts and which he later repudiated. Yet even while confessing his errors of judgement – and, indeed, the sinfulness of those errors – he indulged the human failing of seeking others to blame. This lay close to the heart of his miserable self-doubt and agonised introspection over the next few years. He brooded on his parents' determination to force him into law, a profession for which he developed an intense hatred. So he had rebelled and taken the one step that could put him finally and irrevocably beyond his father's 'interference'. It was an Oedipean act that had killed all his father's hopes and dreams. But whatever escape the monastery afforded him, it could not free him from guilt and that guilt was underlined on the occasion of his first mass by a reconciliation with Hans that was only partial. However much he was in denial, he could never shake off the doubt that his monastic vocation might not be of God. That was why his father's words penetrated to the very depths of his soul and remained firmly lodged there. He tried to suppress them by rigorous spiritual discipline and zealous commitment to the monastic ideal but his efforts only ensured that they would intrude more and more into his conscious thoughts as the life of the cloister failed to provide the peace and assurance he was so ardently seeking.

For the time being, however, he could lose himself in his new studies. Perhaps theology, as well as challenging his mind, would solace his soul. Now he could devote hours each day to the garnered wisdom of the great doctors of the Church and he embarked on his reading with his accustomed enthusiasm and industry. Acres of paper and lakes of ink have been expended by scholars seeking to identify the 'forerunners' of Martin Luther. So devastatingly powerful were the broadsides of ideas he loosed off against so many traditions of medieval thought that historians and theologians have been reluctant to allow him complete originality. It has been assumed that he must have got his ammunition from somewhere. The development of Christian doctrine over the centuries has been progressive so it seemed reasonable to allocate Luther his position in the

never-ending carnival procession.
Another problem was that the
reformer was a thoroughgoing bibli-
cist; what he claimed to offer his
hearers and readers was straightforward exposition of the word of God.
But, surely, so the argument ran,
preachers had been doing that
throughout all the Christian
centuries. Luther could not have
been the first teacher in more than
a millennium to stumble on hitherto unknown truths. It must, therefore, be possible to discover his
antecedents. Unfortunately the
arduous quest is doomed to be unre-
warding and the reason for that was
succinctly stated by Luther himself:

Luther sanctified

'Living, nay rather dying and being damned make a theologian, not understanding, reading or speculation.' His intellectual breakthroughs came from
his own spiritual struggle, not from his wearisome working of the academic
treadmill. It was out of his own deeply felt personal experience that he
was able to speak to ordinary people rather than engage in esoteric debate
with ivory-towered specialists. Insofar as the scholastic masters he studied
between 1507 and 1517 exercised an influence on him it was a negative
one.

Study them he certainly did. He applied his brilliantly incisive mind to
all the standard texts he was expected to master. The basis for theological
study was the *Books of Sentences* of Peter Lombard (*c.*1100–60), an
anthology, commentary and treatise on the writings of the Church Fathers
and early medieval doctors. Generations of students had learned the fundamentals of doctrine in this second-hand way, not (necessarily) because
they were lazy but because books were rare and expensive. Original texts
were hard to come by and the *Sentences* were regarded as impeccably
orthodox by the ecclesiastical authorities. This systematisation provided a
useful groundwork for further study but was, when regarded as an authority
in itself, stultifying. The great thirteenth- to fourteenth-century thinkers,
Thomas Aquinas (1264–1323), Duns Scotus (1266–1308) and William of
Ockham (1290–1349), attempted to update Christian orthodoxy and make

it intellectually respectable by disposing of certain objections. Their primary concern was to make theology and philosophy, reason and revelation compatible. Captivated alike by Aristotle, the greatest of the Greek thinkers, who had logically argued for the existence of an 'unmoved mover' (i.e. a creator) and Augustine, the father of western theology, who had urged his students, 'understand, so that you may believe my word; believe so that you may understand the word of God,' they wanted to demonstrate that the two were in fundamental agreement on the human condition. This labour led them into the thickets of obscure philosophical speculation, through which each author hacked his own path. Later scholars and universities followed one or other of the masters and this led to rival schools of thought within the scholastic world. Thus, to the turgidness of Peter Lombard these later authors had added intricacies of esoteric argument as impressive as Gothic fan tracery.

Luther, however, was not impressed. We can clearly deduce his mounting frustration from the marginal notes he scribbled in the books he pored over in the library or the cloister: 'those grubs, the philosophers', 'the dregs of philosophy', 'that rancid philosopher Aristotle'. Writing to a friend in 1509, he indicated his weariness with the obscurity and irrelevance of so much that he was obliged to read:

> The study takes it out of me, especially in philosophy which from the beginning I would gladly have exchanged for theology, I mean that theology which searches out the nut from the shell, the grain from the husk, the marrow from the bone.[7]

He resented the intrusion of pagan philosophy into the study of Christian doctrine and from an early stage wanted to get to grips with the foundation documents, Augustine and the Bible itself. In this he was in tune with the humanistic spirit which was blowing through Europe's universities. A growing variety of early texts was available and to scholars of independent mind nothing but the originals would do. A word Luther often applied to his own theology was 'practical'. What he was looking for was not 'a good knock-down argument' but a faith to live by and to die for. He did not find it in the documents which expounded and defended the official doctrines of the Church. The more he read, the more disillusioned he became with many (though by no means all) of the medieval masters of Christian thought. His ruthless logic (which, ironically, had been developed by the philosophical studies he despised) exposed the gap between theological speculation and the daily experience of men and women trying to live their lives in accord with the will of God.

For example, the most important question facing the Church and its teachers was, 'How does salvation "work?"' Given that God is perfect and that man is sinful, how can the gulf between them be bridged? If the Christian is to be made fit to share eternity with his creator his life has to undergo a profound change. He must become 'righteous'. But how? The Church's best brains might have been able to tackle the question if they had had the necessary freedom and equipment. They possessed neither. They lacked freedom because, as we have seen, there could be no dethroning of the Church's means of grace. Since the entire Catholic edifice rested upon the efficacy of confession, penance, absolution and other rites it was heresy to challenge them. And scholars lacked the equipment because the foundation document they had to work with – Jerome's Latin Bible, the Vulgate – was defective, as humanist scholars were beginning to discover. Thus, theologians were like mariners who knew the destination they wanted to reach but were stuck in a ship with a jammed rudder and with only a faulty chart to navigate by. Scholasticism degenerated into futile arguments on issues upon which no human mind could possibly offer illumination.

The central problem was how someone could perform 'good works' (works of righteousness), i.e. works pleasing to God and meriting salvation. It was axiomatic that he could not by his own efforts achieve the necessary moral status. One school of thought asserted that as long as the sinner was trying his best God would 'infuse' grace into him, thus transforming his meagre efforts into something acceptable to heaven. No, no, said a rival group of theologians, the infusion of grace must come *first* because man's motives are inescapably tainted, so that he cannot even begin the process without divine aid. To the modern agnostic such obscurantist debate appears so fatuous that it is hard to imagine intelligent men indulging in it. But to men of the sixteenth century for whom this life was merely a testing ground for the greater world to come these things mattered. They certainly mattered to Luther.

It took ten years for Martin Luther to become a reluctant rebel and during those ten years he experienced three kinds of pressure. One was intellectual dissent. Another consisted of the labours put upon him by his order. The third was his agonising spiritual struggle to find peace with God. It is impossible to tease out these strands of his life and discuss them separately; they were tightly interwoven during these years of internal crisis.

His superiors were eager to make the most of their latest talented recruit.

Luther's awe-inspiring intellect and spiritual ardour marked him out for great things. He could with all honesty recall, 'I was a good monk and kept my order so strictly that if ever a monk could get to heaven by monastic discipline, I should have entered in. All my companions in the monastery who knew me would bear me out in this.'[8] Staupitz and the Augustinian leadership directed his career and monitored his progress very closely. Too closely. There can be no doubt that they pushed him with a relentlessness that brought him near to breaking point. In 1508, before he had even completed his baccalaureate in biblical studies, Staupitz ordered him to spend a year in the recently founded university of Wittenberg to deliver a course of lectures on Aristotle's *Nichomachean Ethics*. Scarcely had he returned to Erfurt the following autumn and received his degree when, again at the command of the vicar general, he began to study for a doctorate in theology. Staupitz was personally grooming him to be one of the order's leading preachers and teachers, a public figure who would win much acclaim for the Augustinian movement. A year later Luther was despatched to Rome on business for the monastery. He was given no time to settle back into the Erfurt routine for he was once more summoned to Witttenberg to lecture on the Bible and, eventually, to take the chair of biblical studies in succession to Staupitz. He had still not yet reached his thirtieth birthday.

All this activity and movement was demanding enough in itself but academic duties did not excuse a monk from the daily routine of the monastery or his responsibilities as a member of the community. He had to say masses in the conventual church and in parishes round and about where the brothers were responsible for services. Probably he was expected to take his share of begging expeditions in the surrounding countryside. The burden was almost intolerable, especially for someone as conscientious as Luther.

> When I was a monk I was unwilling to omit any of the prayers, but when I was busy with public lecturing and writing I often accumulated my appointed prayers for a whole week, or even two or three weeks. Then I would take a Saturday off, or shut myself in for as long as three days without food or drink, until I had said the prescribed prayers. This made my head split and as a consequence I couldn't close my eyes for five nights, lay sick unto death, and went out of my senses. Even after I had quickly recovered and I tried again to read my head went round and round.[9]

Ironically, the burden of study laid upon Luther by his superiors was intended, in part at least, to distract him from the spiritual torment he was undergoing and which lay at the root of his malaise. The only way we can understand his later vitriolic attacks on monasticism and the theology which undergirded it is by realising that for twelve years he was a man in love – in love with the life of a monk, in love with the pursuit of holiness which was the whole purpose of the monk's high calling. His devotion was total and that meant that his eventual disillusionment was equally complete. For years he wrestled with the fear that the one to whom he had pledged himself did not return his affection. She did not repay his ardour. She refused to give him what he sought from her. He went through agonies of loathing, directed now against his false mistress and now against himself for doubting her. When the divorce came Luther left angry, bitter and irreconcilable.

What places Luther among the most influential figures in Church history is his combination of spiritual intensity and intellectual brilliance. Many were the coenobites who, like him, struggled to achieve personal holiness by climbing the steep pathway marked out by traditional teaching. Yet, not only did it not occur to them to challenge orthodox doctrine; the very idea would have seemed the gravest sin. The Church was the repository of truth. It could not err. Their lot was simply to do the best they could within the system and hope at the end to find salvation. On the other hand, there appeared from time to time those, again like him, whose devotion to truth impelled them along a different route. These were the master logicians and their quest would not allow them to accept what offended against reason. Such scholars were so far in advance of the Church's conventional thinking that they were frequently branded as heretics in their own day, only to be recognised by later generations as men who had brought new illumination to old problems. William of Ockham was a case in point. He was drummed out of Oxford for unconventional views about the *Sentences* of Peter Lombard and later excommunicated by the pope for his opinions on the much more touchy subject of the level of poverty demanded of Franciscan friars. Both streams of experience met in Luther. It was only after years of agonised striving and discovering that the penitential system could not meet his spiritual needs that he was bold enough to find fault with the system and the rotten substructure of scholasticism that supported it. Logic compelled him to the audacious conclusion that if the system did not work for him it could not work for anyone. That it was fatally flawed.

What he longed for was assurance, certainty. He needed to *know* that all

the sacrifices he had made had not been in vain. That he had gained acceptance by God. That he had become 'righteous'. This was something that
orthodox teaching simply could not give him. Neither Thomist not Scotist
theology could tell him that he had achieved true repentance; that he had
been infused with the grace that metamorphosed his feeble efforts into deeds
worthy of eternal life; that his motives were pure – love of God, rather than
selfish concern for his own soul. He was trapped, doomed to ride perpetually
a fiendish carousel, that travelled mile after circular mile and arrived nowhere.

> I tried to live according to the rule with all diligence, and I used to
> be contrite, to confess and number off my sins, and often repeated
> my confession, and sedulously performed my allotted penance. And
> yet my conscience could never give me certainty, but I always doubted
> and said, 'You did not perform that correctly. You were not contrite
> enough. You left that out of your confession.' The more I tried to
> remedy an uncertain, weak and afflicted conscience with the tradi-
> tions of men, the more each day found it more uncertain, weaker,
> more troubled.[10]

Brother Martin was very far from being the only cloistered man or woman
with a bruised conscience. Introspection was a main plank of the contemplative life and one which could easily become infested with the dry rot
of morbidity. Some monks and nuns either were or became mentally unbal-
anced. They had been driven to take their vows by fear or guilt or self-
loathing or religious delusions. Wise counsellors within the orders were
experienced in identifying such disturbed souls and distinguishing them
from others whose problems arose from genuine spiritual scrupulosity. Luther
belonged to the latter group. He was mentally strong. Even in the midst
of anguish he could stand outside himself and try to analyse his problems.
Eagerly he read the Bible and devotional works in his search for solace.
He wore out his confessors with his earnest recitals of sins and pleas for
absolution. He avoided ascetic extremes, for though he later wrote about
his personal privations, these seldom seem to have amounted to more than
three-day fasts – pretty small beer in terms of the punishments others
inflicted on their bodies.

In all Luther's spiritual and intellectual problems the man who helped
him most was Johann von Staupitz. The vicar general developed a strong
personal interest in the earnest young monk and one that blossomed into
a close friendship. On his deathbed the older man declared that he felt

Johann von Staupitz

for Brother Martin something 'passing the love of women' and such words were entirely lacking the sexual innuendo with which a modern mind might invest them. They were also spoken years after Staupitz and Luther had parted company theologically and the young monk had abandoned the career path his mentor had designated for him. Staupitz became something of a father figure for Luther, an older man to whom he was linked by personal affection and a religious sympathy that old Hans would never be able to understand. And Luther would complete the comparison by turning his back on the Augustinian order just as he had refused to take up the legal profession. The fact that this relationship survived Luther's rejection of the ambitions Staupitz cherished for him is an indication of the personal magnetism that Luther possessed. The image of the introverted young monk obsessed with spiritual navel-gazing is obviously only one side of the picture. Certainly Luther went through periods of black depression when he retreated into himself and spoke to no one. He never fully shrugged off this particular demon and to the end of his days would retire into a room by himself when problems weighed heavily upon him. But when he emerged from anguished introspection into the sunlight of human intercourse he was a different man entirely; there was a clear divide between yin and yang. He was an honest, open, heart-on-sleeve extrovert; an enthusiast who plunged wholeheartedly into whatever he undertook. He wore his intellectual gifts lightly and was always ready for a joke, often of an earthy nature. He was a popular preacher, a charismatic opinion former and an irreverent debunker of establishment stupidity and pomposity. Here he is writing to a friend on the subject of a current *cause célèbre*, an attack by a rival scholar on Johann Reuchlin, the foremost Hebraist of the day:

> Up to this point . . . I considered Ortwin, that little 'poet' in Cologne, to be an ass. But as you see he has [now] become a dog, even more, a ravenous wolf in sheep's clothing, if not even a crocodile . . . I assume that finally he himself 'caught on' to his asinity (if I may use Greek in Latin), since our Johann Reuchlin pushed his nose in it. But since Ortwin has considered stripping off [his donkey skin] and clothing himself with the majesty of a lion, he has now instead ended up as a wolf or crocodile.[11]

As for Luther, he never failed to acknowledge the debt he owed to Staupitz. In letters and conversation he frequently praised his old mentor: 'I cannot forget or be ungrateful, for it was through you that the light of the Gospel began first to shine out of the darkness of my heart'; 'If Dr Staupitz had not helped me out . . . I should have been swallowed up and left in hell.'[12] The vicar general aided his protégé in three ways. As a wise and experienced spiritual counsellor he dealt with the earnest young man's scruples. When Luther referred to his superior's introducing him to the Gospel what he meant was that Staupitz forced him to fix his inner gaze on the Cross and not on his own sins, whether real or imaginary. Luther might be angry with himself and even with God but God, the God of Calvary, was not angry with him. The monk should stop torturing himself, totting up a spiritual balance sheet, and accept that his account had been settled by Christ. 'It was not a sign of great piety to mistrust the mercy of God but of stupid, obstinate and wholly unnecessary unbelief. Clinging to God's "No" when one should celebrate God's "Yes" in the gospel was the worst kind of unbelief.'[13] Staupitz also referred Luther to various writings by the German mystics. While all these wise counsels brought Brother Martin temporary relief, they seemed to be like welcome showers which refreshed him for a time but which did not reach right down to his spiritual roots. He still could not bridge the gap between the judgemental God of the medieval Church and the loving God of the New Testament and his unwavering commitment to logic would not allow him to accept the paradox of these two aspects of divinity.

Therefore, in addition, Staupitz undertook to tutor his young friend in his theological studies. He encouraged a cautious scepticism with regard to the competing scholastic schools of thought. Specifically, he cast doubt on the oppressive spiritual discipline (the 'method of confession') advocated to bring a sinner to unfeigned penitence. Staupitz pointed out that to believe that penitence was the first step towards achieving love for God was to put the cart before the horse. Only when we love God can we feel real contrition for our sins. The impact of this on Luther was dramatic:

> This your word stuck in me like some sharp and mighty arrow . . . and I began from that time onward to look up what the Scriptures teach about penitence. And then, what a game began. The words came up to me on every side jostling one another and smiling in agreement, so that, where before, there was hardly any word in the whole of Scripture more bitter than 'poenitentia' . . . now nothing sounds sweeter or more gracious to me.[14]

It was Staupitz who directed Luther to go back beyond the medieval doctors to the foundation documents of the Church – the Bible and the writings of Augustine. One day, probably in 1509, the vicar general was sitting beneath a pear tree in the monastery grounds. He summoned Luther to come and stand before him. He had chosen his moment carefully because he had something to say that he knew his companion would not want to hear. He charged the young monk, on his obedience, to study for his doctorate at Wittenberg. Luther was appalled. He protested that he was already overburdened with work. Proceeding to the higher degree would not only involve years of reading and preparing disputations, it implied a heavy programme of lecturing stretching into the years ahead. The extra load, he complained, would probably kill him. In that case, Staupitz grimly joked, God would doubtless find him a very valuable adviser in heaven. There was no more discussion.

Luther now became much more closely acquainted with the works of Augustine, who had brought a mind trained in pagan philosophy to the study of the Christian Scriptures. Of all the things he learned from the fourth- to fifth-century intellectual giant two would securely ballast his own theological vessel. Augustine had insisted on the primary authority of the Bible over the bishops and teachers of the Church and he had locked horns with the British scholar, Pelagius, over the issue of free-will and grace. Pelagius, in order to counter the moral decadence of his day, had urged men, of their own volition, to amend their lives and seek God. Augustine's response was clear and vigorous: the whole of humanity was alienated from its creator and no individual could by an act of will overcome the consequences of the Fall. The initiative in salvation remained wholly with God, who redeemed his chosen by the exercise of sovereign grace. In this Augustine was following Paul and as the teaching became clear to Luther he also embraced it. Thus it was that three great intellectual planets came into alignment. The German monk had a great deal in common with the apostle and the Bishop of Hippo. All three men forged their theology in the white heat of spiritual struggle and doctrinal conflict and all three were strong, self-assertive men who had been humbled by their inability to earn or even contribute to their own eternal wellbeing.

The third way in which Staupitz sought to help his disciple was by advancing his career. Keeping Luther busy with fresh study and new responsibilities was one means of diverting him from his own inner tensions. But the vicar general had other motives, political motives, for pushing Luther up the ladder, within the Augustinian movement. He was a fervent and enterprising reformer, determined to drag his order into the sixteenth century. Like all 'new brooms' he encountered resistance from conservative elements and people with a vested interest in resisting change. One way of overcoming opposition was to develop his own 'party'. Staupitz understood perfectly that if he was to succeed in his campaign to make the Augustinians a mighty force for good within the German states he would need to place his own supporters in important positions. Luther's rapid rise between 1508 and 1512 has to be seen against the background of change and conflict within German monasticism. But what began as a not particularly remarkable initiative to deepen the spirituality of one of the religious orders would develop into a challenge to both Church and State throughout Europe. Neither Luther nor his patron could possibly have foreseen the momentous events that would flow from his introduction to the world of imperial politics.

Staupitz was based at the Augustinian house in the little town of Wittenberg, which lay in that part of Saxony ruled over by the Elector Frederick III, the 'Wise'. Frederick was a devout, cultured, independently minded prince who developed a reputation for standing firm against any encroachments of imperial power on the rights of territorial rulers. But he had other, deliberately fostered, claims to fame. One was the encyclopaedic collection of holy relics, housed in the castle at Wittenberg. It may seem extraordinary that this prince who certainly merited his nickname and was discerning enough to patronise the leading artists, writers and scholars of the day should have been so credulous as to have spent a fortune on religious knick-knacks of spurious provenance. In 1509, his collection numbered 5,005 items and was still growing. It included one of the barbs from the crown of thorns, a hair from Jesus' beard and a piece of gold that had been offered by the magi at the crib of the infant Saviour. But this exercise in sensationalist superstition was commercially shrewd. It made Wittenberg a tourist attraction and a pilgrimage centre and that was very good for electoral revenue. Whether or not Frederick believed in the genuineness of all the relics his agents acquired (and he travelled widely himself, pursuing desired objects with the zeal of the compulsive collector), they were an excellent investment. Men and women flocked from far and near to gawp at the impressive display when it was on show to the public. Every All Saints' Day (1 November) the queue of the devout and the curious stretched down the main street from the castle to the parish church and the *Rathaus*. It was the best day of the year for local innkeepers, shop-keepers, souvenir peddlers and for the electoral treasurer. Every pilgrim to Wittenberg on relic day qualified for an indulgence which would knock centuries off his sentence in purgatory and the proceeds were shared between the elector and the Church authorities.

Much of Frederick's profit went to support his other great love, the university he had founded in 1502. The elector was determined that 'his' university should rival that of Leipzig, in the other part of Saxony (known as 'Albertine' or 'Ducal' Saxony) ruled by his relative, Duke George. In order that the new foundation should have kudos and attract students away from rival educational centres, Frederick decreed that it should be avant-garde, a 'modern' institution, at the cutting edge of radical scholarship. It was the first 'secular' university in Germany in the sense that its charter was not granted by ecclesiastical authority. In deliberately embracing the humanism which appealed to the rising generation of students Wittenberg's faculty heads had identified a niche market and eagerly exploited it. Staupitz had been a major player in bringing the university into being and was the first holder of the chair of biblical studies and dean of the theology faculty. However, his other responsibilities meant that he could not devote as much time as he wished to lecturing and it may have

Archduke Frederick of Saxony, 'The Wise'

been quite early in his university career that he began looking for a successor. In Luther he believed he had found the ideal candidate and this explains why the young monk was fast-tracked.

Being known as the vicar general's favourite was something of a mixed blessing for Luther. Although his academic career advanced with incredible haste, he was caught up in the rivalries and jealousies of the cloister. In 1506 Staupitz had himself appointed prior of all the Saxon Augustinian houses as well as vicar general of the Observants. This was a major step in his campaign to bring all the monasteries under a tighter discipline and a more rigorous following of the rule. Inevitably, some priors were suspicious of Staupitz's empire-building. At Erfurt there was actually a fear that merging the two wings of the movement would result in a relaxing of standards rather than otherwise. It was less than two years later that Luther was removed, presumably by Staupitz, to Wittenberg to lecture on Aristotle. This may mark the beginning of a tug-o-war between the vicar general and Luther's own prior. Certainly Luther was granted his baccalaureate at Wittenberg sooner than would have been the case at Erfurt and certainly his mother house demanded his return after less than a year. Then, within months, he was pressed by Staupitz to embark on his doctorate course.

The conflict between the vicar general and the recalcitrant houses was now hotting up. Staupitz and his opponents took their case to Rome and Luther found himself in the thick of it. He was a member of the Erfurt delegation despatched first to Halle to seek the support of the Archbishop of Magdeburg and then to Rome itself. Whatever his own thoughts on the issues involved, Luther was under instructions to plead his own monastery's case against the 'encroachments' of the vicar general, something he must have found difficult.

The eternal city! How privileged and excited Brother Martin felt to be travelling to the very centre of the Church's life. He was a country-bred northerner who had never ventured more than a hundred kilometres from his family home. Now, within days of his twenty-seventh birthday, he was to cross the Alps to the place where the bones of the great apostles and martyrs of the faith lay buried. He would be able to pray at the shrines which others, including his more senior brethren, could only dream of visiting. There can be no doubt that Luther looked forward to the trip with eager anticipation. He was aware of the cultural divide created by the Alps and of the German disdain for the soft, effete Italians but this prejudice was overlaid by his devotion to the mother church. He wanted to be impressed and, by and large, he was. He certainly did not leave after a month fulminating against the 'scarlet woman' or 'papal Antichrist'. If he saw with his own eyes evidence of corruption, sexual immorality and immoderate love of luxury he certainly did not react with the horror one might have expected from a monk devoted to a life of holy simplicity. He was probably too busy to concern himself with critical reflection. As well as the business which had brought him and his travelling companion to Rome he had sights to see and pious deeds to perform. There was the sacred seven-churches pilgrimage which began at St Paul's-without-the-walls and ended at St Peter's basilica. This exhausting tour, to be completed in one day, carried with it substantial reward in terms of remission of time spent in purgatory. Wherever possible Luther said mass at holy sites but here he found himself caught up in the indecorous scramble of local and visiting priests to say their office at the same altars. Queues of clock-watching clergy jostled each other to gabble the mass before rushing on to the next shrine. Luther remembered vividly in later years how his own devotions were interrupted by other priests urging him to 'hurry up'. This lack of reverence was in stark contrast to the overwhelming sense of awe he had experienced at his first mass and which he sought to replicate at every repetition of the liturgy. It seemed to him that in Rome familiarity with rites the officiants knew by heart had bred contempt. Some clergy even paraded scepticism and unbelief. There were those who at the solemn moment of consecration instead of the prescribed 'hoc est corpus meum' muttered, 'bread you are and bread you will remain'. However securely such experiences lodged in his unconscious to burst out later and provide evidence of the decadence of the papal regime, in 1511 Luther had no thought of challenging the Catholic establishment. As for his monastery's appeal to the general of the order, that failed totally. The little delegation was sent back to Erfurt with the message that the community was to show all obedience to the vicar general.

The welcome Brother Martin received on his return was distinctly cool. The brothers were divided over their response to the general's order and some may have felt that Luther had not stood up staunchly enough to his 'friend', Staupitz. This was a bad time for the Erfurt brethren; the tranquillity of cloister life was being assailed from within and without. 1510 has gone down in the city annals as the 'Mad Year'. There were several riots provoked by economic and political difficulties. A 'town and gown' fracas led to one of the university buildings being burned down. An unpopular city councillor was dragged out by the mob and summarily executed. The monastery could not avoid involvement. In an attempt to cool passions the brothers took the dead man's infant son as a hostage to prevent his family exacting revenge. However much the Augustinians tried to stay above the conflict or, at least, to exercise a calming influence, their sympathies for one side or the other were inevitably engaged. Scenes of frenzied mob rule certainly left an indelible mark on Luther's mind. He ever afterwards felt fear and contempt for popular revolt. It was in the midst of this chaotic, confrontational, lawless ferment that the monks had to try to resolve their own political differences. The spirit of the times made it virtually impossible for them to do so by calm, charitable debate. Personalities clashed, factions formed, support for policies was eagerly canvassed. This was the situation Luther walked into on his return in the spring of 1511. He took his stand with the minority party which was in favour of Staupitz. We may assume that he expressed his opinion firmly in chapter meetings and this cannot fail to have attracted taunts of 'turncoat'. Brother Martin had been sent to Rome to plead the cause of his community; he had come back a disciple of their enemy. Matters came to a head in September. Staupitz issued an ultimatum and gave the rebel-

lious houses two months to comply. Erfurt refused to be coerced. For Luther
the situation must have been intolerable. It will, therefore, have come as
a relief when he was, for a second and, as it turned out, final time despatched
to Wittenberg.

Frustratingly, we know nothing of the precise circumstances which led
to this momentous move. Did Luther's prior 'expel' him? Did Staupitz
'rescue' him? Was the transfer part of an attempt to cool the situation, a
solution welcomed by all parties? All that we can infer is that, though
some of the Erfurt Augustinians were not sorry to see Brother Martin go,
the manner of his going caused great offence. A year later he wrote to the
leaders of his former cloister in terms which suggest that their attitude
towards him had still not softened. The occasion for his letter was the
degree ceremony at which he was to be awarded his doctorate.

> I beseech you for the sake of Christ's mercy to commend me to God
> in your common prayers . . . so that God's will, gracious and blessed,
> may be with me. Further I beg you to honour me with your presence,
> if it can be done with any ease, and to partake in this my solemn
> 'parade' . . . for the sake of decorum and the honour of our Order,
> and especially our district. I would not presume, my fathers, to bother
> you with the inconveniences and expenses involved in such a journey,
> had the Most Reverend Father Vicar [Staupitz] not ordered it. In
> addition it would seem shameful, disgraceful and even scandalous
> that I should ascend to such dignity without you in Erfurt knowing
> of it, or being invited to it.[15]

There was obviously a real possibility that Luther's erstwhile colleagues
might boycott his big day. Further offence had been given them which
might well have made them distance themselves from one of their own
number who seemed to be getting too big for his boots. Their dispute with
the vicar general had come to an end in May 1512 and the rebel houses
had won. Staupitz, not wanting to impose his will by crude diktat, had
backed down. Doubtless this eased tension but feelings stirred over several
years could not be calmed in as many weeks and the Erfurt seniors had
another cause to be indignant with Staupitz – and Luther. The twenty-
eight-year-old monk should, technically, have applied to Erfurt university
for his doctorate but he could not have done so in 1512. Elevation to such
a dignity usually had to wait until the candidate had at least ten years'
teaching to his credit. Wittenberg, however, was a young university in a

hurry. It needed well-qualified lecturers to fill all its faculty posts, hence Luther's astonishingly rapid promotion. It can scarcely have failed to provoke jealousy from older men who believed themselves more deserving of the honour. It may well have seemed to the prior and his supporters that the sudden elevation of Brother Martin was a Parthian shot from the vicar general: having been thwarted in his grand design by the Erfurt house, he had retaliated by filching their brightest academic for his own university. This suspicion can only have been reinforced when they discovered that Staupitz had persuaded Elector Frederick to pay the expenses involved in the graduation ceremony on one condition – that Luther remained in Wittenberg for life.

As for Luther, he had now left the ancient and sophisticated city of Erfurt with its dreaming spires to take up residence in a town at 'the edge of civilisation'. It was a much smaller pool but he was now a big fish within it.

4

'Through open gates into Paradise'

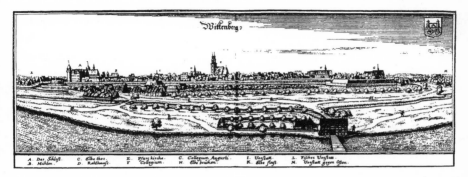

Wittenberg, at the right the monastery of the Augustinian Hermits

There was something schizophrenic about Wittenberg. When Luther arrived in the city he was to make famous, it had the immediate appearance of a mere backwater and a pretty muddy one at that. The contrast could hardly have been greater between the bustling metropolis of Erfurt with its dreaming spires and this town of some two thousand souls whose civic life was as sluggish as the River Elbe which meandered by it. Wittenberg had received its charter two centuries earlier and was technically a city but it boasted few buildings of any importance and most of its houses were mean constructions of timber and thatch. The former Slav lands to the North and East had been among the last to be thoroughly Christianised and Germanised and Wittenberg still had about it something of the atmosphere of a frontier town. Its people were fiercely nationalistic as only those can be who have long lived in close proximity to an alien culture. It may be for this very reason that they responded so warmly to Frederick III's ambitions for them. The elector's energetic patronage sprang from his determination to put the city on the map; to transform it into a cultural centre rivalling anything in the territory of his cousin George in Albertine Saxony. Saxony belonged to the Wettin family but had long been divided between the Albertine and Ernestine branches, between whom there was, inevitably, much rivalry. Frederick spent lavishly on the castle, the university, the Augustinian cloister and municipal buildings. He brought leading German artists to the city. Altarpieces by Dürer graced the church which served both the castle and the university. Lucas Cranach the Elder had arrived in 1505 as court painter to the elector and would spend the next forty-five years there presiding over an army of assistants in his large and busy workshop. Throughout the period that Luther lived in the city, Wittenberg was expanding. A printing industry developed to meet the needs of the university. The pilgrimage trade brought increased profit to local businesses. The university grew in size and stature. Some of the wealth thus generated was poured into more impressive town houses for the merchants and their growing families. And with all this went the development of civic identity and pride.

It is clear that Luther was glad to have escaped the bickering and personal animosities of the Erfurt cloister, for he felt keenly his rejection

Albrecht Dürer, *The Adoration of Magi*,1504. The Elector, Frederick the Wise, was an enthusiastic patron of Dürer and commissioned this alterpiece for the castle church at Wittenberg. Frederick was known as the Maecenas of the North

by his Augustinian brothers. Despite his entreaty, they had refused to attend his doctoral ceremony. Enemies in his mother house absolutely declined to accept his elevation. They could not even bring themselves to bow to the inevitable with a bad grace. They wrote letters of protest to the general of the order demanding Dr Luther's demotion. Over and again Luther was obliged to defend himself and this rankled with him. Two and a half years after his doctoral investiture he took the opportunity of a sermon during an Augustinian conference at Gotha to unburden himself in no uncertain terms. Ostensibly he was preaching against those who had opposed Staupitz's reform plans, but he also delivered a vituperative attack on those who indulged in gossip and backbiting. In this sermon we obtain the first glimpse of that combative style that he was to display during the years of his struggle against Rome. The argument is incisive, the language vividly vulgar. He compares the dissidents to pigs, 'whose shit stinks worse than that of any other animal'. Such invective may strike the modern reader as highly indecorous but it needs to be said that sixteenth-century protagonists were less squeamish; most of them did not hesitate to call a spade a 'bloody shovel'. However, denouncing one's enemies as agents of Satan was another matter and from this Luther did not shrink. His delivery was forceful, uncompromising and bolstered with scriptural proofs. One can imagine his pulpit positively shaking with the dynamic power of his righteous indignation. The 1515 Gotha sermon was certainly not an exercise in bridge-building.[1] Controversy was becoming second nature to Luther. When he believed he was in the right nothing would induce him to back down or compromise. He had alienated first his father and now his monastic brothers.

He was encouraged in this self-assertion by his enhanced status. Within the little world of Wittenberg Dr Luther's life was very different from the one he had experienced at Erfurt. Supported by Staupitz and, beyond him, by the elector, he enjoyed a growing celebrity. The small Augustinian community and the theology faculty both welcomed this talented young academic and he enjoyed popularity in the district as a preacher. In 1513 Staupitz thankfully yielded his professorial chair to his protégé and about the same time Luther became sub-prior of the Wittenberg monastery. In 1515 his authority within the order was increased when he was appointed district vicar of the Observant Augustinians in Saxony. This involved him in frequent tours of inspection to encourage and, where necessary, to discipline monks and priors. In September 1516 he ordered a change of regime at Neustadt:

. . . the root of your disorder is that you are not in concord with your head, the prior . . . Therefore, by authority of this office, I order you, Friar Michael Dressel, to resign from your office and [surrender] the seal. By the same authority I release you from the office of prior in the name of the Father, the Son and the Holy Ghost. Amen . . . It is not enough that a man be good and pious by himself. Peace and harmony with those around him are also necessary . . .[2]

As he wrote this letter Luther must have had in mind the sorry divisions in which he had been involved at Erfurt. The situation there had recently been resolved in a similar fashion when Luther's close friend, Johann Lang, was appointed to be prior at Erfurt. Lang had transferred from their mother house to Wittenberg with Luther and it would seem that his new posting was a move by Staupitz to bring the Erfurt Augustinians into line. It certainly made easier Luther's oversight of the monastery in his role as regional vicar. Of course, it was not just problems at Erfurt that he had to deal with. He was responsible for administrative details in the houses under his cure as well as their general spiritual wellbeing and the personal crises about which individuals wrote to him from time to time.

It is no wonder that he sometimes felt weighed down with the burdens of his multifarious activities in the order and the university. However, busyness was the price he willingly paid for his growing importance and we may detect a certain pride behind the letter he wrote to a friend describing his responsibilities in the university and the order:

I am a preacher at the monastery, I am a reader during mealtimes, I am asked daily to preach in the city church, I have to supervise the study [of novices and friars], I am a vicar (and that means I am eleven times prior), I am caretaker of the fishpond at Leitzkau, I represent the people of Herzberg at the court in Torgau, I lecture on Paul, and I am assembling a commentary on the Psalms . . . the greater part of my time is filled with the job of letter writing. I hardly have any uninterrupted time to say the Hourly Prayers and celebrate [mass]. Besides all this there are my own struggles with the flesh, the world and the devil. See what a lazy man I am![3]

That catalogue indicates how closely involved members of religious orders frequently were in the life of their local communities. They served as vicars in parishes roundabout. Their educational expertise was at the disposal of town and village councils (the townsmen of Herzberg were in dispute with the electoral court at Torgau, which was why they asked Luther to lend his eloquence to their cause). On top of all this Luther was involved in the regular tours of inspection to the monastic houses in his district. It is scarcely surprising, therefore, that he had little time for the daily offices. Yet, by 1516, the date of this letter, his detachment from the routine of monastic life seems to have been less troublesome to him. No longer is he setting aside Saturdays to catch up on his liturgical obligations. Something of the tension that had troubled him in his early cloister years seems to have evaporated. We must seek the reason for that not just in the transfer of his energies to his new and varied duties. Thanks to the in-depth Bible study that his lecture preparation imposed on him a seismic shift had taken place in his theological thinking. So we come to what has been called Luther's 'tower experience'.

Luther's description of his spiritual 'breakthrough' has become one of the classics of Christian literature along with the conversion experiences of St Paul, Augustine and John Wesley. At the very end of his life he recorded that enlightenment came to him in the library situated in the tower of the Wittenberg monastery as he prepared his biblical lectures and grappled with Paul's declaration in Romans 1.17: 'In the Gospel the righteousness of God is revealed, a righteousness by faith from first to last, as it is written, "the righteous will live by faith".' For anyone taking the standard, medieval understanding of 'righteousness' (*justitia*) this statement seemed to make no sense or, rather, to make the most abhorrent kind of sense. If 'righteousness' is that attribute of a just God whereby he deals with sinful men according to their desserts and if no man can be certain that he has merited acquittal in the divine tribunal then 'salvation' is a mockery. Luther recorded the misery this understanding of Paul's words forced on him:

> I was angry with God, saying, 'as though it really were not enough that miserable sinners should be eternally damned with original sin, and have all kinds of calamities laid upon them by the law of the ten commandments, God must go and add sorrow upon sorrow and even through the Gospel itself bring his justice and his wrath to bear!

If God was committed by his very nature to condemning all those who failed to achieve moral perfection then the central act of the Christian religion, which was re-enacted at every mass, the death of Christ on the cross, became pointless. Earnestly Luther scoured Scripture and the doctors of the Church for some sword which would sever this Gordian knot. Enlightenment came at last.

> I began to understand the justice [righteousness] of God as that by which the just lives by the gift of God, namely by faith, and this sentence 'The justice [righteousness] of God is revealed in the Gospel', to be that passive justice, with which the merciful God justifies us by faith, as it is written, 'The just lives by faith'.
>
> This straightway made me feel as though reborn, and as though I had entered through open gates into paradise itself.'[4]

Thus did Martin Luther come to unfurl the banner of 'justification by faith alone', beneath which he would march at the head of the Reformation and be followed by five centuries of Protestant believers. It was a monumental event in his own life and in the lives of Christians down the ages. It delivered Luther himself from that anguish of soul which had beset him since before he had entered the convent. It threw down a challenge to the official church. It struck the shackles from thousands of pious souls enslaved to superstition and empty ritual. For a myriad of reasons it caught the imagination of the age and sundered Europe into rival confessional camps. It is, therefore, easy to see why 'Luther's tower experience' has entered evangelical mythology as a moment of blinding revelation in which Luther rediscovered the heart of the Christian Gospel which had been lost for more than a millennium. But, like most myths, this rightly exalts the significance of the event while, at the same time, obscuring its actual details. History departs from legend at two points: the timing of the revelation and its uniqueness.

Luther's was not a Damascus Road conversion. In his memoir, written in 1545, the reformer dated his discovery to 1519. Yet, three years before that he was writing to an Augustinian colleague,

> . . . my dear Friar, learn Christ and him crucified. Learn to praise him and, despairing of yourself, say, 'Lord Jesus, you are my righteousness, just as I am your sin. You have taken upon yourself what is mine and have given to me what is yours. You have taken upon yourself what you are not and have given to me what I was not' . . . For why was it necessary for him to die if we can obtain a good conscience by our works and afflictions? Accordingly you will find peace only in him and only when you despair of yourself and your own works. Besides,

you will learn from him that just as he has received you, so he has made your sins his own and has made his righteousness yours.[5]

The words obviously express the writer's own profound experience and there could scarcely be a clearer statement of what, in theological jargon, is known as 'imputed righteousness', the transfer of Christ's righteousness to the repentant and believing sinner: 'God made him to be sin for us, who knew no sin, that we might be the righteousness of God in him' (II Corinthians 5.21). This is more than a legal fiction: God does not 'pretend' that we are guiltless; he actually makes us so by transferring Christ's perfection to us. Then, the accepted sinner is able to begin the process, by grace, of *becoming* righteous. Luther later explained it with a metaphor from sculpture: 'As the great artist sees the finished statue in the rough marble, so God sees already in the sinner, whom he justifies, the righteous man that he will make of him'.[6] Or, as he exhorted his Augustinian friend in 1516, 'keep your eyes fixed on what he has done for you and for all men in order that you may learn what you should do for others'.[7]

There was, then, no flash of insight which we can claim as the birth moment of the Reformation. Luther's realisation of the mystery at the heart of the Gospel grew within his questive mind as he prepared his lectures on various books of the Bible, the Christian foundation document of which he became, from about 1513, a devoted expositor. As he later explained, the concept of imputation opened up a new understanding of Scripture and of God:

I ran through the scriptures then, as memory served, and found the same analogy in other words, as the Work of God (opus) that which God works in us, Power of God (virtus Dei) with which he makes us strong, wisdom of God (sapientia Dei) with which he makes us wise, fortitude of God, salvation of God, glory of God . . .[8]

The impact of justification by faith was that it closed the gap between the sinner and the Saviour or, rather, it removed from that gap all the obstacles placed there by an institutionalised Church; those obstacles which masqueraded as actual aids to salvation, stones in a bridge spanning the great divide. It was as Luther began to realise that the Catholic hierarchy and the dogmas invented to support it were, in reality, keeping men and women away from God that he became so angry and so set upon a confrontational path from which there could be no turning back.

But had the medieval church really lost the Gospel and could Luther truly claim to have rediscovered it? Inevitably, when he took his lonely stand against the might of Rome one of the taunting criticisms thrown against him was, 'So you alone know the truth and all the saints and doctors of the Church are in error.' Catholic scholars like Thomas More claimed, in all honesty, that they could not understand Luther's theological objections to traditional doctrine. The Church had *always* recognised the need for faith. Many of the great doctors, from Augustine onwards, had emphasised it. Augustine had also interpreted *justitia Dei* passively, as the process whereby God makes believers just. The same teaching could even be found in the works of Peter Lombard.

And that really is the point. Luther's difficulty lay precisely in those words 'could also be found'. Yes, the doctrine of justification by faith was part of the vast corpus of orthodox Christian teaching but an unquiet soul like Luther's had to seek it amidst all the complexities of medieval theology. It was one tree in a forest, obscured from view by the luxuriant scholastic growth all around it. The Church should have been proclaiming loud and long the glorious truth that this holy God was also the God of love who, to be true to his nature, beckoned sinners to him and, through the Cross, both punished sin and absorbed that punishment within himself, thus providing free access to forgiveness and acceptance via repentance and faith. Instead, it proffered a multitude of intermediaries – priests, popes, saints – and a host of alternative aids to salvation – penance, sacramental absolution, the treasury of the saints (that heavenly credit balance deposited by the champions of the faith and available for lesser mortals to draw upon), pilgrimages, indulgences and all those 'works' by which alienated man might commend himself to God. The Catholic church had become a cluttered marketplace where a variety of theological, ethical and psychological merchandise was being energetically hawked to a bemused clientele. It should not surprise us that this was so, for the situation today is not markedly different. Among the bewildering variety of Christian denominations and networks some are wedded to sacramentalist ritual, some espouse fiery Pentecostalism, some see themselves as caretakers of old buildings and traditions, some proclaim an intellectualised liberal theology while others trumpet an unthinking fundamentalism and there are those which would have difficulty defining clearly what they *do* stand for. Were Luther to return he would find few churches marching proudly under the banner of the biblical evangel whose discovery had cost him so dear.

The Wittenberg doctor had had to fight tooth and nail to understand and experience that message. As a result he carried psychological, emotional and spiritual scars. Having captured the castle he would defend it with every fibre of his being and resist all who laid siege to it. Sometimes he would be overly protective, discerning enemies where there were none and cutting himself off from friends who were not one hundred and one per cent in agreement with his theology.

Volumes have been written on the subject of Luther's theological voyage to the safe haven of *sola fidei*. Fortunately, there is no need for us to chart again all the intricacies of his intellectual navigation; the times when he was borne along by favourable winds, the months spent becalmed by despair, the occasions when he had to steer in a new direction and the perilous moments when rocks and shoals appeared close at hand. Yet, nor can we ignore the traumatic spiritual journey of 1512–17. So much followed for himself and for the world from what he called his '*Anfechtung*'* that we need to be aware of its major elements. Our analysis will, of necessity, be an over-simplification.

Luther travelled via Staupitz, the German mystics, Augustine and the Psalms of the Old Testament to the Hellenistic-Semitic logic of St Paul. The young friar-academic had vast literary resources to draw upon in the monastic libraries at his disposal and he was obliged to read extensively in preparation for his own lectures and sermons. He was also aware of those new, humanistic patterns of thought with which the world of the European intelligentsia was abuzz. In all this ferment of old and new wisdoms a man could lose himself. What Luther needed was direction.

As we have seen, he was fortunate to find in Johann von Staupitz a sensitive and intelligent confessor. As an aid to devotion he recommended to the troubled young friar the works of the thirteenth- and fourteenth-century German mystics and, particularly, the sermons of Johann Tauler (c. 1300–61). These writings helped Luther – temporarily at least – in two ways. They diverted him from intellectual speculation. The mystical path is *experiential*. It takes as its starting point that God cannot be found by rational endeavour. The disciple is encouraged to achieve unity with God by literally 'losing' himself in the divine love. God is already present in the individual. Tauler called this a seed planted in the human soul and his master, the great Johann Eckhart (c. 1260–1328), used the image of a

---

* The word which Luther uses may be literally translated as 'temptation' but involves an emotional and spiritual intensity for which 'temptation' is an inadequate rendering.

'divine spark'. Secondly, and more fundamentally, Luther developed a theology of the Cross. He saw his earlier suffering not as proof of God's rejection but, on the contrary, as evidence of loving favour. As he wrote in the margin of his copy of Tauler's sermons, 'God does not act in us unless he first destroys us by the Cross and suffering.'

It is likely that Luther was able to make contact spiritually and emotionally with the mystics because of his own earlier experience of the lifestyle of the Brethren of the Common Life. Yet, try as he might to achieve religious ecstasy through contemplation and self-abnegating spiritual exercises, he found the blessed state of the mystic as elusive as the intellectual assurance of sins forgiven.

Luther's difficulty with mysticism was that he *was* a thinker, an academic. He had to have *answers* that satisfied his mind. The Gospel had to lie somewhere between the intricate sophistries of the scholastics and the emotionalism of the mystics. For God not to have made plain his eternal will for humanity would have been the most appalling cop-out imaginable. It was here that the intellectual rigidity of Augustine came to his aid. The first complete edition of the great doctor's works was published 1490–1506 and the more he read of Augustine the more Luther found in him a kindred spirit who had hammered out his theology on the anvil of spiritual strife and confrontation with heretics. Luther identified with Augustine's rejection of free-will. Augustine had opposed the Pelagians on this fundamental issue because to accept that man had the innate ability to please God would reduce Christianity to an exercise in ethics and render the Cross meaningless. Luther knew from his own desperate experience that he did not have it within him to will complete holiness. As he read Augustine's sermons and the *Exposition of the Psalms* he encountered what was for him a fresh understanding of the operation of divine grace.

Since man is wholly incapable of contributing to his own salvation the initiative must lie entirely with a sovereign God. Grace sets up an 'exchange' between Christ and the sinner: the Saviour takes on man's mortality (the penalty for sin) and barters for it his own perfection and immortality. This truth was nothing more nor less than that which St Paul had concisely stated: 'God . . . made him who knew no sin to become sin for us so that we might become the righteousness of God in him.'[9] Augustine did not shun the philosophical implications of this doctrine. Since, manifestly, all men and women did not embrace Christian salvation it must follow that a sovereign God exercised choice in these matters. The favoured ones were the 'elect', who were 'predestined' by God to receive the gracious exchange of spiritual status with Christ. The litmus test by which someone might know if he was among the elect was that he delighted in God and the Church's channels of grace. Medieval teachers had tended to fight shy of Augustine's hard-edged doctrine of predestination – the idea that a loving God has consigned some of his human creatures to heaven and, by logical extension, the remainder to hell, irrespective of their apparent virtues. Luther eventually distanced himself from the harsher implications of Augustinian thought but for the moment it hacked a path for him through the tangled thickets of theology to the ancient citadel of Holy Scripture.

In his role as Professor of Biblical Studies Luther had to get to grips more closely with the foundation document of the Christian faith. It was as he prepared his lectures on the Psalms (1513) and the Epistle to the Romans (1515) that the pattern of redemption became clear to him. Rather like archaeologists painstakingly and reverently removing the dirt of centuries from a Roman mosaic floor, Luther eagerly but carefully brushed aside the deposits of medieval interpretation until he could catch his breath at the beautiful, intricate yet dazzlingly clear design that lay revealed beneath.

It may occur to the modern reader to wonder why such a desperate seeker after divine truth had not simply opened the Bible in the early stages of his quest and saved himself years of angst. The answer is that the word of God lay behind a double-locked door fastened by ecclesiastical authority and traditional techniques of exegesis. Bishops and inquisitors over the centuries had learned that when portions of Scripture fell into the hands of unauthorised teachers the result was heresy and contempt for the institutionalised church. Therefore, the authorities guarded the sacred text from falling into the 'wrong hands'. They certainly could not be accused of ignoring it; rather they treated it with suffocating veneration. The liturgy was steeped in it. Monks spent long hours copying portions of it and adorning the text with sumptuous illustrations. Scholars sufficiently versed in Latin pored over it in abbeys and cathedral schools. Its more dramatic episodes were depicted in murals and stained glass and expatiated upon in sermons. But there was no coherent exposition of the written word. As one modern scholar has observed, 'Medieval liturgies are bewildering mosaics cut and shaped for a purpose out of the Scriptures; and if this process gives a prodigious enrichment to meaning, it obscures almost completely the flow and scope of the original.'[10] The biblical material presented to the people was like the gauze screen used in pantomime transformation scenes, sometimes concealing, sometimes displaying parts of the

set behind. Veneration for the holy text turned the book itself, as a physical object, into an icon. It was displayed, elaborately bound, on church
altars. It was carried in solemn processions. People expected their priests
to read out Bible passages over the sick and women in labour, or, if that
was beyond their powers, at least to touch them with the sacred tome.

Restricting access to the text did not present too much of a problem
to the authorities during the centuries when literacy was almost an exclusive preserve of the higher clergy and when all books were vastly expensive commodities. When princes and other wealthy patrons requested
gospels for their own private devotions the response was often ambivalent. Some clergy were content to issue beautifully decorated copies from
their scriptoria while others, like the eleventh-century scholar-monk Aelfric
advised them to stick to their own vocation and leave the Bible to experts.
After all, he pointed out, the Jews had had the Old Testament and look
what had happened to them! Of course, the Church's own scholars had
to be allowed access to the holy text and even to produce controversial
interpretations. Sometimes it happened that the dynamic of the divine
message broke through conventional glosses:

> I used to think that I had penetrated to the depths of Your Truth
> with the citizens of Your Heaven; until You, the Solid Truth, shone
> upon me in Your Scriptures, scattering the cloud of my error, and
> showing me how I was croaking in the marshes with the toads and
> frogs.[11]

So wrote one of the leading churchmen of the fourteenth century but he
had reached the position of archbishop before he experienced his breakthrough. A celebrated contemporary of Luther's, the Venetian Gasparo
Contarini, went through a similar spiritual crisis before stumbling on
divine grace in the New Testament. Contarini went on to become a cardinal
and would devote considerable effort to trying to reconcile Protestant and
Catholic partisans. Luther was, therefore, certainly not unique in falling
under the spell of the Bible but it took him months of agonising persistence.

The last obstacle he had to surmount was the method of exegesis
prescribed by centuries of tradition:

> When I was a monk I was a master in the use of allegories. I alle-
> gorised everything. Afterward through the Epistle to the Romans I

came to some knowledge of Christ. I recognised then that allegories are nothing, that it is not what Christ signifies but what Christ is that counts ... Jerome and Origen contributed to the practice of searching only for allegories. God forgive them.[12]

Since the Church was the guardian of Christian truth its teachers were obliged to find in Scripture and expound from Scripture those beliefs and attitudes which were officially approved. No one doubted that *every word* of the Vulgate supported traditional teaching. But the Bible is a difficult book (or, more accurately, collection of books). In parts the meaning is straightforward but in others it is obscure. There are elements that appear mutually contradictory and there were certainly some which, on straightforward reading, seemed to challenge prevailing doctrines and practices. For example, the Song of Songs, with its delightful exaltation of sexual love, was difficult to square with the official recognition of virginity as a blessed state superior to marriage. It was this coupling of biblical fundamentalism with 'political correctness' which made allegorical and figurative interpretations of the text vital. The exegete had to follow a strict pattern, probing every word for its 'hidden' meanings by means of symbolism and allusion. Martin began his lecturing career adhering strictly to this system. Thus, for example, when revealing the 'true' meaning of the Psalms, he told his students that by 'the sea' the writer meant the people of the world and by 'the mountains' he indicated the apostles. Above all, the Old Testament had to be shown as prefiguring the New and the lecturer who could produce subtle allusions to the work of Christ drew the admiration of his students and his peers.

But Luther could not keep up this obscurantist approach for long. He had respect for the plain meaning of the text and in order the better to get to grips with it he immersed himself in the study of Greek and Hebrew. In this he was aided by his close friend and confidant, Johann Lang. It was through Lang that Luther came into contact with that river of humanistic thought which was now rushing with growing velocity through the academic world of Europe and beginning to shift many of the embedded rocks of medieval assumptions. In 1516 Luther became one of the first scholars to acquire (for the monastery library) a copy of what would prove to be one of the literary cornerstones of the modern world. Erasmus's newly published *Novum Instrumentum* was a version of the New Testament in Greek following the best available documentary sources and provided with a Latin translation. Not only did it expose errors in the Vulgate (and, therefore, call in question medieval doctrines which could no longer claim to rest upon secure biblical foundations); it stood on its head the Church's attitude towards popular access to the holy writings. In his introduction Erasmus baldly stated

> I could wish that every woman might read the Gospel and the Epistles of St Paul. Would that these were translated into each and every language so that they might be read and understood not only by Scots and Irishmen, but also by Turks and Saracens . . . Would that the farmer might sing snatches of Scripture at his plough, that the weaver might hum phrases of Scripture to the tune of his shuttle, that the traveller might lighten with stories from Scripture the weariness of his journey.

This sentiment was not quite as original as generations of Reformation historians have liked to claim. Despite the disapproval of the authorities, there were, throughout Europe, many men and women of all social ranks who *were* reading the Bible or parts of it in their own tongue. The printing revolution had scarcely got underway in the late 1400s before vernacular Scriptures began to emerge from the presses. The Bible was the book above all others that people wanted to read and entrepreneurial printers were not slow to cash in on this demand. The first complete German Bible entered circulation as early as 1466 and other versions followed in various dialects. Erasmus was, therefore, not so much advocating a new policy as taking his stand clearly on one side of the argument.

With a more accessible Bible went new patterns of exegesis. It was almost twenty years since John Colet had drawn enthralled crowds to his lectures on *Romans* in Oxford. The humanist scholar did not reach the same conclusions as Luther about Paul's teaching on justification and grace but he captivated his audience with his fresh approach to Scripture. Colet consigned allegorical, tropological and anagogical readings to the lumber room of scholasticism. He excited some hearers and scandalised others by treating the New Testament as any other collection of classical writings. He studied Paul in his original context, emphasised the literal meaning of the apostle's words, then applied them to contemporary situations. This became the accepted method of the bold exegetics of the so-called New Learning. The Parisian humanist, Jacques Lefèvre d'Étaples, in his commentaries on the New Testament epistles had rejected human works from the divine scheme of salvation. This was in 1512, well before Luther's *sola fidei* discovery.

Luther the scholar could not fail to be influenced by the prevailing academic fashions but he never entered the ranks of the humanists. For a time he pursued a parallel course to the classically educated intelligentsia whose hero was Erasmus but he was always an individualist. He had trodden a hard road to reach his own enlightenment and he was not prepared to engage in polite debate about dearly bought truths. He found himself temperamentally at odds with university scholars who were captivated by elegance of style and often seemed to be as interested in the pagan authors of antiquity as they were in the lively oracles of God. There was a certain intellectual arrogance about this monk who lived his life on the margins of European civilisation, read widely in authors ancient and modern, garnered from them grains for his barn and then rejected them because they did not possess the whole truth as he came to understand it. In this way Luther turned his back on most earlier and contemporary writers – on Erasmus, on Tauler and on Nicholas of Lyra, the fourteenth-century Franciscan who wrote a monumental commentary on Scripture and was almost a lone voice calling for a literal understanding of the text. His uncompromising criticism emerges clearly in a letter he wrote to his friend George Spalatin (of whom more anon) in 1516:

> What disturbs me about Erasmus, that most learned man, my Spalatin, is the following: in explaining the Apostle [Paul], he understands the righteousness which originates in 'works' or in 'the Law' . . . as referring to those ceremonial and figurative observances [of the Old Testament] . . . Had Erasmus studied the books Augustine wrote against the Pelagians . . . and had he recognized that nothing in Augustine is of his own wisdom but is rather that of the most outstanding Fathers . . . then perhaps he would not only correctly understand the Apostle, but he would also hold Augustine in higher esteem than he has so far done.
>
> I definitely do not hesitate to disagree with Erasmus on this point, because in Bible exegesis I esteem Jerome in comparison to Augustine as little as Erasmus himself in all things prefers Jerome to Augustine. Devotion to my Order does not compel me to approve of the blessed Augustine; before I had stumbled upon his books I had no regard for him in the least. But I see that the blessed Jerome emphasizes and puts great weight on the historical meaning of Scripture. How amazing that he interprets Scripture better when he skims over the surface –

as for instance in his letters – than when he labours over it, as in his minor works.

The 'righteousness based on the Law' or 'upon deeds' is, therefore, in no way merely a matter of [religious] ceremonial but rather of the fulfilment of the entire Decalogue. Fulfilment without faith in Christ – even if it creates men who are wholly irreproachable in the sight of man – no more resembles righteousness than sorb apples resemble figs.

I ask you, therefore, to do the service of a friend and Christian and inform Erasmus of my thoughts. I hope and desire that he will be highly esteemed. But I am afraid that because of his fame many will take up the defence of the literal, that is, the dead, understanding [of Scripture], of which the commentary of Lyra, and almost all the commentaries written since St Augustine, are so full. Even [Jacques Lefèvre d'Étaples] a man otherwise spiritual and most sound – God knows – lacks spiritual understanding in interpreting divine Scripture; yet he definitely shows so much of it in the conduct of his own life and the encouragement of others.

You could call me rash for bringing such famous men under the whip of Aristarch [a second century BC Greek critic reputed to have an acid tongue] if you would not know that I do this out of concern for theology and the salvation of the brethren.[13]

In the fulness of time Luther allowed even his Augustinian marker buoy to drift away on the tide:

Ever since I came to an understanding of Paul, I have not been able to think well of any doctor [of the Church] . . . At first I devoured, not merely read, Augustine. But when the door was opened for me in Paul, so that I understood what justification by faith is, it was all over with Augustine.[14]

Like a man floundering in turbulent seas, Luther had grabbed at every piece of intellectual and spiritual flotsam that might support him. Each in turn had failed to provide sufficient buoyancy. But at last the works of Saul of Tarsus had come within his grasp and in the Church's first great theologian Luther found a soul mate. It is not surprising that this should be so for Paul's spiritual pilgrimage had been remarkably similar to Luther's own:

If anyone thinks he can trust in external ceremonies, I have even more reason to feel that way. I was circumcised when I was a week old. I am an Israelite by birth, of the tribe of Benjamin, a pure-blooded Hebrew. As far as a person can be righteous by obeying the commands of the Law, I was without fault. But all those things that I might count as profit I now reckon as loss for Christ's sake. Not only those things; I reckon everything as complete loss for the sake of what is so much more valuable, the knowledge of Christ Jesus my Lord. For his sake I have thrown everything away; I consider it all as mere refuse, so that I may gain Christ and be completely united with him. I no longer have a righteousness of my own, the kind that is gained by obeying the Law. I now have the righteousness that is given through faith in Christ, the righteousness that comes from God and is based on faith.[15]

Luther, too, had come to realise the utter futility of religious rituals and moral endeavour in the economy of salvation.

Everything he discovered went into his lectures and sermons and so forceful and persuasive a communicator was he that he began to make a name for himself in the intellectual world. Students began flocking to Wittenberg to sit at the feet of this exciting, radical new teacher. By 1517 a Wittenberg 'school' of theology was emerging. In May of that year Luther boasted to Johann Lang:

Our theology and St Augustine are progressing well, and with God's help rule at our University. Aristotle is gradually falling from his throne, and his final doom is only a matter of time. It is amazing how the lectures on [Peter Lombard's] Sentences are disdained. Indeed no one can expect to have any students if he does not want to teach this theology, that is, lecture on the Bible or on St Augustine or another teacher of ecclesiastical eminence.[16]

The fame or notoriety of little Wittenberg was highly gratifying to Luther's superiors. Staupitz had every reason at this stage to be proud of his protégé and pleased that his evaluation of the young monk's intellectual powers had been vindicated. Elector Frederick was delighted that the educational foundation which was his pride and joy had achieved such rapid celebrity. He had little understanding of the theological issues involved. What he did know was that Wittenberg University was being talked about, that students from far and near were enrolling in its courses, that the whole city was benefiting economically and that princely rivals proud of their own prestigious educational institutions could no longer dismiss Wittenberg as a cultural backwater. Luther might be a turbulent priest but whatever he was stirring up was good for the prestige of Electoral Saxony.

There is no record of Luther and Frederick ever having a serious conversation or prolonged meeting. But they had an intermediary who, because of his crucial influence, deserves to be hailed as one of the architects of the Reformation. George Spalatin was almost Martin Luther's exact contemporary. This Bavarian scholar was one of the first German thinkers to espouse humanism. While studying at Erfurt he joined the elite circle of Conrad Mudt, better known by his assumed classical name of Mutianus. These self-consciously avant-garde intellectuals venerated Erasmus and delighted to challenge establishment thinking with their new ideas. Spalatin was ordained priest in 1508 and the following year was summoned to Torgau to become tutor in the household of Prince George, the brother and heir of Frederick the Wise. The elector held him in high regard and Spalatin's promotion was rapid. As chaplain, secretary and councillor he became one of the most influential men in Saxony. Spalatin's regard for Luther blossomed into friendship and, to judge from extant letters, the royal servant looked to the university professor for guidance in spiritual issues. He also served as a link between Luther and the elector and between Luther and the humanist fraternity.

By 1517 Martin Luther was a celebrated teacher in his early thirties who was beginning to make a name for himself in the academic world. He enjoyed the adulation of his students, the support of his prince and the encouragement of friends like Spalatin and Lang, who urged him to publish his sermons and lectures. Did all this go to his head? Very possibly. It would be difficult for him not to have been tempted to intellectual arrogance and not surprising if he occasionally succumbed. He felt complete certainty about the enlightenment he had achieved by mental effort and anguished prayer and taught 'our theology' with total conviction. When he discerned an abuse in the Church which he, in company with other advanced thinkers, believed should be exposed and challenged, he took up the cause with his customary directness. The abuse in question was indulgences.

II
The Crisis
1517–1521

'God is impelling me, driving me on, rather than leading me. I cannot master myself; I want to be calm, yet I am driven into the midst of uproar.'

Letter of Luther to Staupitz, 20 February, 1519

5

'Out of love and zeal for truth'

When the coin in the coffer rings
A soul from purgatory springs

Johann Tetzel was a superlative salesman. He combined the showmanship and ingenuity of a P. T. Barnum with the eloquence of a Winston Churchill. This rotund, fiftyish Dominican friar was the front man for a money-raising campaign regarded by many in Germany as nothing less than an outrageous ecclesiastical scam. The jingle above was just one item from the stock-in-trade of a marketing genius who commanded an excellent understanding of the psychology of his audience. This ex-inquisitor began his campaign as hawker of cheap grace in January 1517 when he was appointed subcommissary for the sale of indulgences in the province of Magdeburg. In the following months he toured his district accompanied by a formidable entourage, designed to bring out crowds of the curious. As he approached a town he would be met by the local dignitaries and would then unpack from his cart all the paraphernalia necessary for an impressive entry. He and his robed acolytes would march in solemn procession preceded by a cross, a standard bearing the papal arms and a gold embroidered cushion upon which rested the symbol of his authority, Leo X's bull proclaiming the indulgence. On arrival at the market place, Tetzel would set up his pulpit, the tables of his clerks stacked with the bundles of impressive parchment certificates and the all-important coffers ready to receive the payments of the gullible. As soon as a sufficient crowd had gathered he would start to preach.

The Sale of Indulgences

His sermon was the sales pitch of a disreputable insurance rep peddling heavenly policies. He appealed to his listeners' self-interest. Histrionically he urged them to reflect on the peril in which their immortal souls were mired by their sins. How could they hope to escape the just penalty demanded by a holy God? They were doomed to suffer for decades, centuries, perhaps millennia the pains of purgatory. Indeed, they might never reach their ardently desired haven at all. Now the pope, who entirely desired their salvation, was coming to their rescue. 'All who are contrite and have confessed and made contribution will receive complete remission.' Tetzel's subtle propaganda did not end there; he also preyed on his hearers' guilt. 'Have mercy on your dead parents,' he exhorted. From beyond the grave fathers and mothers were imploring, 'Pity us, pity us. We are in dire torment from which you can redeem us for a pittance. We bore you, nourished you, brought you up, left you our fortunes. Will you let us lie here in flames?' A few coins, the preacher assured them, would secure eternal bliss for the donors and their loved ones.[1]

The Dominican's brash, tawdry commercialism was ultimately denounced by his employers but by then the damage was done. Tetzel had laid the powder trail and Luther had set his match to it. But how was it that overselling by a particularly unscrupulous agent became the catalyst for the entire Reformation? Indulgences had, after all, been around for centuries and had occasionally provoked disquiet among theologians. So, what was special about the 1517 indulgence and why did Luther's reaction to it lead to the sundering of Europe into rival camps? The answer is that Tetzel's activity was the *reductio ad absurdum* that exposed a practice bereft of theological justification and that, once exposed, it became obvious that what was at stake was not the practice itself but the authority which sanctioned it. Luther did not set out to attack that authority and was genuinely surprised by the storm that his initial reaction whistled up. It was only after opposing positions had been taken that the crisis deepened with a doom-laden inevitability. Two kinds of truth locked horns: the truth that Luther had discovered in the Bible and the truth asserted by the Roman establishment.

But we must not run ahead of ourselves. The corruption of the indulgence traffic touched Luther on a particularly raw nerve for it was one aspect of those penitential practices which his own inner turmoil had led him to reject. Tetzel was quite right in presenting his wares to all who were 'contrite, had confessed and made an offering'. Forgiveness, as all Christian teachers knew, was dependent on repentance and it was a priest's role to declare absolution to those who gave evidence of heartfelt penitence. Furthermore, there was no objection to those who had found peace with God making a donation which expressed both their gratitude and the depth of their determination to amend their ways. However, the formula, repentance + confession + penance + offering = absolution, was something that many ordinary people found difficult to grasp. For them indulgences were simply a matter of absolution and release from penance in return for payment and Tetzel was far from being the first to take advantage of this dangerously over-simplified common view. Luther's mounting unease with the situation arose from both his theological development and his pastoral experience. Traditional penitential doctrine left faith out of the equation. If, as he now believed, the elect were moved by God to that complete re-direction of life explicit in the word 'metanoia' (= 'repentance', something altogether deeper and more dynamic than 'penitence') and were justified through belief in the once-for-all sacrifice of the Cross, then forgiveness had nothing whatsoever to do with monetary payment. Nor was his objection a matter of theological nit-picking. He came face to face with the dire results of false teaching in his routine duties as parish priest. What was he to say to the man or woman he was preparing for death who confidently demanded absolution and produced a certificate declaring that a smooth passage through purgatory was assured by a payment for which this receipt bearing the papal seal had been received long ago? Such delusion was truly diabolical, for, as Luther declared when he went public with his objections to the indulgence traffic, 'Those who believe that they can be sure of their salvation because they have indulgence letters will be eternally damned, together with their teachers' (see below, p. 371).

As much as Luther had his eyes fixed on eternity, it is difficult to believe that he was not aware of the immediate and very worldly ramifications of the 1517 indulgence. The mission of Tetzel and his colleagues was inextricably twisted into the skein of papal and princely politics. A century later, the partisan Venetian historian, Paolo Sarpi, observed acidly of Pope Leo X that he would have been a model pope if his accomplishments in the artistic sphere had been matched by even the most rudimentary understanding of religion. It was not an entirely fair barb because the man installed in St Peter's chair in 1513 had spent a couple of years studying theology and canon law at the university of Paris. However, Leo's ambition was certainly to be remembered for glorifying the house of Medici and the city of Rome rather than glorifying God. Giovanni de Medici had grown up a pampered youth in the sumptuous court of his father, Lorenzo the Magnificent. As a younger son, he was designated for the Church. Various offices were obtained for him while he was still a child and he became a cardinal at the age of thirteen. The death of Lorenzo and the rise of Savonarola were disastrous for him. He and his relatives were driven into exile and it seemed that the great Florentine house was about to be eclipsed. During the troubled years which followed Giovanni suffered many humiliations, including capture and imprisonment by the French, and when a change in the volatile situation in North Italy gave him the opportunity to turn the tables on his enemies he grabbed it eagerly. He had become the head of the family after the death of his elder brother in 1503 and by intrigue and main force he regained control of Florence in 1512. The following year he managed to have himself proclaimed pope, thus becoming the head of the Church as well as the leader of a major Italian state. Although his nephew, Lorenzo (the dedicatee of Machiavelli's *The Prince*), technically ruled the republic, it was Leo who pulled the strings. This fat, flaccid, ulcerous primate set himself to raise the international status of the papacy in the face of the mounting threat of Spanish and French power. He tried by nepotism and patronage to extend Medici rule in Italy and to weld the papal states and neighbouring territories into a politically and militarily powerful unit and he set about making his own capital a Renaissance centre without rival. The son of Il Magnifico set a personal example in conspicuous consumption. The lavishness of his table and the sumptuousness of his crowded court were legendary. No contemporary prince could rival the generosity of his patronage of artists, scholars, musicians and buffone, the clowns in whom he took a special delight. Leo rivalled his father in extravagance but could not match the great Lorenzo for style and taste. The life of Leo and his household gave ample proof of the cultural equation, prodigality – flair = vulgarity. Rome did, however, benefit from its master's heedless generosity. He brought architects, sculptors and painters into the city and set them to work on new palaces, an improved road layout and the rebuilding of St Peter's and the Vatican apartments. His predecessor, Julius II, had gutted the twelve-hundred-year-old basilica of Constantine in defiance of a traditionalist and cost-conscious curia. What he planned to replace it was the biggest and most splendid church in the world. By the time of Julius' death the grandiose scheme had got little further than the drawing board of Bramante, the architect, and Leo inherited a vast, dusty building site. The new pope had no alternative but to continue the work and he hastened it forward with enthusiasm. Preoccupied with all these great designs, Leo paid scant heed to a little local difficulty which arose in Germany.

Even a prudent pope would have found it difficult to meet the cost of such ambitious plans. Household economies and trimming of personal expenditure would certainly have helped to balance the books but that was not Leo's style. Money slipped through his fingers like quicksilver and he was very soon in debt to all the major finance houses of Europe. However, he had one great advantage over his fellow Renaissance monarchs: he owned the milch-cow of the western church and had a myriad ways of extracting revenue from it. He ensured that conventional taxation was efficiently gathered. He sold cardinalates and other offices. He readily issued dispensations from sacred vows and other moral obligations to wealthy appellants. And he made full use of indulgences. In 1515, he issued the bull Sacrosanctis, declaring a plenary indulgence, ostensibly for the work on the new basilica. (In reality much of the cash collected went to funding his luxurious lifestyle.) It was, in fact, the renewal of an indulgence issued by Julius II in 1510 and against it he borrowed heavily from the Augsburg banking house of Fugger. Leo had no doubt that he was on a winner: how could the faithful fail to be impressed by the generous absolution on offer and who could doubt the importance of the holy cause for which the money was intended? From the other side of the Alps the perspective was different. People were weighed down by ecclesiastical imposts of one kind or another and cared not a fig for the beautifying of Rome. On the other hand, however, the terrors of hell and the pains of purgatory were very vivid in their imagination. Many would have happily welcomed a reason not to believe in the automatic grace of the penitential system but, failing that, what could they do but put their hands in their purses and pay what they could ill afford for the promise of eternal bliss?

Reception was also mixed among the princes of the Empire. Leo was certainly not without enthusiastic allies in the promotion of the new indulgence. Temporal and spiritual rulers were accustomed to profiting from such initiatives and received a rake-off for allowing the pope's sales team to operate in their territory. As we have seen, Frederick the Wise used indulgence revenue to fund his university and he was one of many. But the elector was among those who actually opposed the 1515 indulgence – for reasons of dynastic politics. He was keeping a wary eye on young Albrecht of Brandenburg, an ambitious member of the rival house of Hohenzollern. This prince was a bird of the same feather as Leo X – fat, sybaritic and power-hungry. By the age of twenty-four he was already Archbishop of Magdeburg and Administrator of the diocese of Halberstadt. Now he wanted to add the Archbishopric of Mainz to his portfolio. This required a papal dispensation which Leo was happy to provide – at a price. There were other heavy expenses connected with Albrecht's installation and he, too, had to resort to the Fuggers. How was he to recoup his outlay and pay the bankers their interest? The answer was obvious: he struck a deal with Leo. He would promote the indulgence in his lands in return for a share of the proceeds.

All this occurred during the time that Luther was refining his ideas about faith, repentance and forgiveness. He was becoming increasingly disturbed about the growing indulgence industry and cautious warnings against it featured in some of his sermons in 1516. As the academic star of Wittenberg University he was in a difficult position. If he was too forthright in his condemnation he would risk the anger of his patron who might reasonably claim that Luther was attacking him personally and undermining the financial basis of his own institution. Yet the biblical truth he was discovering left no room for indulgences, or certainly not for the more crass understanding of what indulgences could do. It was a distressing dilemma for him, even more so after he preached against indulgences on the feast of All Saints 1516, in a church packed with pilgrims come to see the elector's relic collection. As he had feared, this incurred Frederick's displeasure.

The next few months were a time of mental and spiritual torment. Luther tried to push the indulgence business to the back of his mind. His main academic activity in 1517 was marshalling a detailed attack on Aristotelianism. He wrote a commentary on the philosopher's *Physics* (now lost) and presided over a disputation on the subject in September. But there was no escaping the more pressing problem. Frederick had forbidden the selling of the *Sacrosanctis* indulgence in his territory but everyone was talking about Tetzel's antics. Luther was not alone in being scandalised by them and must have frequently discussed them and their implications with his students and colleagues. What made the issue more pressing was the fact that the salesman had published details of his itinerary and members of Luther's flock were rushing off to the nearest towns in Hohenzollern territory to buy their certificates. If these deluded people were putting their immortal souls in peril their pastor simply could not ignore the problem. As he explained to Staupitz a few months later, 'God is impelling me, driving me on, rather than leading me. I cannot master myself; I want to be calm [i.e. to avoid conflict], yet I am driven into the midst of uproar.'[2] His pastoral experience and devotional studies were raising within him an anger at the spiritual dictatorship exercised by some members of the clergy. As well as extracting money, they imposed punishments on men and women who failed to pay their tithes or to meet other obligations. This was an appalling abuse of their privileged position. What Luther did not realise at this stage was that such behaviour and its doctrinal justification went right to the top of the Church.

By the autumn he had decided on what he considered to be an appropriate, cautious and respectful intervention. This was the time that he came across a little sales manual issued under the archbishop's authority for the guidance of the indulgence traders. Here was no second- or third-hand report on Tetzel's tricks. It was a clear, black and white statement of the hard-sell, theologically and psychologically dubious methods Albrecht's agents were being instructed to employ. It was the final straw. Luther had to act. But how to do so without generating more heat than light? There is no doubt that Luther was very angry but he was also well aware that he had to navigate a path through a political minefield. He decided to try to keep any debate on an academic level, claiming the scholars' privilege of questioning official lexis and praxis. He also affected to believe that doctrinal errors were the result of distortion by agents and were not to be laid at the door of either the pope or the archbishop. He carefully prepared a twofold course of action, one private, one public. He prepared a little treatise on indulgences and sent it to Albrecht with a letter in which, in suitably humble language, he asked the archbishop to issue fresh instructions to Tetzel and Co. Simultaneously he advertised a debate on the whole subject of indulgences to be held in the theological faculty at Wittenberg. This latter was the famous 95 Theses.

> Luther, angered by Tetzel's impious and execrable debates and burning with the eagerness of piety, published *Propositions concerning indulgences.* . . and he publicly attached these to the church attached to Wittenberg Castle, on the day before the feast of All Saints, 1517.[3]

So wrote Philip Melancthon, Luther's long-term colleague and first biographer, and this simple statement has given rise to the dramatic legendary image of the black-robed monk striding truculently through the streets of Wittenberg and hammering to the castle church door the manifesto of the Protestant Reformation. Alas for popular myth! The event may not have happened and, if it did, it did not happen in such a self-consciously doom-laden atmosphere. Luther made no reference to this public act in any of his writings and Melancthon, the sole source of the story, did not arrive to take up a post at the university until the following year. What Luther *did* do was fully in line with academic convention. He distributed to various scholars a series of propositions on the theological implications of the sale of indulgences. Out of courtesy he sent a copy to his diocesan bishop and, at some point, he publicly advertised that leading experts had been invited to a disputation of his propositions. He invited interested parties either to attend or to send their comments by letter. There seems no reason to doubt that the church door provided the notice board for this declaration but the public announcement probably took place sometime in December, rather than on All Saints' Eve, and was quite a low-key event.

The *Disputation on the Power and Efficacy of Indulgences* (see Appendix) was not a wholesale attack on the medieval church. Its scope was strictly limited and it did not challenge doctrines (such as purgatory) which Luther would later reject. Nor did it explicitly question the pope's authority. Rather it claimed to enhance Leo's standing by exposing the scandalous practices carried out in his name and thus defusing criticism. The preface clearly set out Luther's intention:

> Out of love and zeal for truth and the desire to bring it to light, the following theses will be publicly discussed at Wittenberg under the chairmanship of the reverend father Martin Luther, Master of Arts and Sacred Theology . . .

Luther immediately made his appeal to Scripture and the remaining 93 theses may be seen as a commentary on the first two:

1. When our Lord and Master Jesus Christ said, 'Repent', he willed the entire life of believers to be one of repentance.
2. This word cannot be understood as referring to the sacrament of penance, that is confession and satisfaction, as administered by the clergy.

Luther affirmed several truths that stemmed from this: For the sincerely repentant and forgiven believer indulgences are unnecessary (36–37). The selling of indulgences may confuse people as to the necessity for heartfelt contrition (39–41, 49, 52). It is far better to devote energy and money to works of charity than to the purchasing of indulgences (43–45). The promises made by some indulgence hawkers are false (32–33, 35, 54, 71–78). Indulgences cannot remit penalties in purgatory (8–11, 17–22). He piously assumed that,

> If the pope knew the exactions of the indulgence preachers, he would rather that the basilica of St Peter were burned to ashes than built up with the skin, flesh and bones of his sheep. (50)

Luther attacked what he considered a misunderstanding of the 'treasury of merit', that heavenly bank balance into which Christ and the saints had supposedly paid and on which the pope could draw in granting remission to holders of indulgence certificates. 'The true treasure of the church is the most holy gospel of the glory and grace of God' (62). This was always available to all men, whether or not the pope issued indulgences, through preaching and the sacraments (58–61). He contrasted the 'treasures of the gospel' which were like nets with which 'one formerly fished for men of wealth' with the 'treasures of indulgences . . . with which one now fishes for the wealth of men' (65–66).

Having stripped away almost all the *raison d'être* of indulgences and exposed the abuses to which the system gave rise, what had Luther left? The answer is, very little. He allowed that the pope *could* remit penalties but only those that he had himself imposed or that had been imposed by canon law. Similarly, he could lift guilt from sinners but only 'in cases reserved to his judgement'. Beyond that his authority consisted in declaring God's forgiveness to the penitent and praying for souls in purgatory. In such matters he had no more influence than that of any other priest (5–6, 8, 25–26).

The gap between the earnest Wittenberg professor's vision of the Church and that of the luxuriating, worldly wise pope could scarcely have been greater and the 95 Theses certainly exposed the gulf. For all the cautious wording Luther employed and his determined diverting of guilt away from the earthly head of the Church, he must have realised that the responsibility for the corruption and theological error he so clearly identified could not be laid at the door of the pope's foot soldiers. Even if he did not fully grasp the implications of his academic exercise others were not slow to do so once the theses were in the public domain. It was in order to demonstrate that he was a devoted son of mother church that Luther concluded his disquisition with a section in which he listed the criticisms which *other* people were making of the indulgence trade. 'Why doesn't the pope use his own money to pay for St Peter's?' 'If the pope has the power to release souls from purgatory why doesn't he just do it – out of love, rather than for cash?' 'Is it not a scandal that a notorious evil-liver can pay for the deliverance of a soul from purgatory when the pope won't do it himself?', etc., etc. (81–90). Luther was, he declared, eager to save the leadership of the Church from 'slander or from the shrewd questions of the laity'. This was not just clever posturing. Luther knew that he spoke for many who were indignant, troubled or angry about the activities of Tetzel and his colleagues. It seemed to Luther that the way to lance the boil was to encourage debate among the Church's scholars so that abuses could be stopped, erroneous theology reformed, and the truth clearly set forth. His intentions were honest. But was he being naïve or canny in his forthright but respectful approach to the problem?

Attempting an answer to that question presents us with others: did Luther comprehend that the western church was facing an impending major crisis; that it was suffering a deep-seated disorder of which indulgence charlatanry was only an indicative skin blemish? Did he believe the Church was capable of reform? Did he believe himself to be called to challenge the religious establishment as the prophets of old had confronted the Jewish temple priesthood? If Archbishop Albrecht had replied, 'Thank you, Brother Martin. You're quite right. I will give instructions that these abuses are to be stopped,' would there have been no Reformation? As early as 1567 Pope Pius V revoked all indulgences which involved the payment of money, and the refinement of orthodox teaching made it clear that the relief of souls in purgatory could only be accomplished by prayer and not granted by the pope. On the narrow ground of indulgences, therefore, much might have been achieved by the open debate for which Luther called in November 1517. Three things seem to me to be quite clear. First, Luther was by nature combative. He had fallen out with his father and with his superiors at Erfurt. He was about to fall out with the Roman hierarchy. In years to come he would fall out with other evangelicals who could not see eye to eye with him on all points of doctrine. Secondly, the real issue, as his enemies were quick to point out, was one of authority. Luther rested his case on Scripture and reason, backed up by judicious quotation from the early fathers. Those who wanted to bring him to heel took their stand on the pope's unchallengeable right to define doctrine. Thirdly, the more publicity Luther's challenge received, the more sympathisers emerged to support him. It was not just his students who loyally – boisterously even – rallied to his cause; from all over Europe messages of support poured in to Wittenberg. The realisation that he spoke for far more people than he can have ever imagined strengthened his determination. It also ensured that the issue became increasingly sensitive for the religious establishment.

There was an extraordinary increasing momentum about the events of the next couple of years. To start with movement was slow, almost imperceptible. Luther seems to have been more interested in other theological matters, such as his ongoing attack on Aristotle. No scholars took up his invitation to a disputation. For some weeks it seemed that the 95 Theses were a non-event. They provided a subject for comment among the literati. But then, thanks to the printing press, unauthorised copies were soon circulating throughout Europe. By March 1518 Thomas More in England was reading them.

The seeds of Luther's new theology did not fall on unprepared ground. Amongst ordinary people the widespread grumbles about grasping and immoral clergy went hand-in-hand with a revived popular piety. Men and women seeking peace and comfort in an inward religion were scandalised about the clergy's obsession with externals to which they controlled the access. It was only a few years later that an Augsburg weaver wrote what many felt in his denunciation of priests who were out of touch with the spiritual needs of their people: 'O dear brother, see what their works are ... They say they have the holy spirit ... but the bible is as pleasing to them as a sow in a Jewish synagogue. For they prefer to preach indulgences, private confession, confirmation, last rites, holy salt, oil, spices ... eternal light, chalices, vestments.'[4]

Members of the ecclesiastical establishment were well aware of such feelings among peasants and artisans and lost very little sleep over them. The lower orders could be controlled and if discontent should develop into heresy they had ways of dealing with it. Heterodoxy was, habitually, a lower-class phenomenon. The majority of men and women investigated by the Holy Office were journeymen, semi-skilled workers, small traders and renegade priests, part-educated people who knew just enough theology to clothe their prejudices with reasoned argument. But something new was happening at the beginning of the sixteenth century and it took church leaders several years to realise its significance. Heresy was going up-market.

The book sophisticated European society was talking about after its first publication in Paris in 1511 was Erasmus' *Encomium Moriae, The Praise of Folly*. This audacious lampoon of contemporary mores proved to be far and away the most popular of the author's numerous works and went through more than forty editions in a quarter of a century, so, quite clearly, it struck a common chord. In it Erasmus pricked the bubble of religious life with the needle of satire. He pointed out the absurdities of scholastic theology, mocked the superstitious worship of saints, waxed indignant about the avarice and lust of monks, ridiculed the rivalry between religious orders, protested about prince-bishops who hired mercenary armies. But Erasmus' greatest scorn was reserved for the supreme rulers of the Church:

> ... the popes are generous enough with ... interdictions, excommunications, re-excommunications, anathematisations, pictured damnations, and the terrific lightning-bolt of the bull, which by its mere flicker sinks the souls of men below the floor of hell. And these most holy fathers in Christ, and vicars of Christ, launch it

against no one with more spirit than against those who, at the insti-
gation of the devil, try to impair or to subtract from the patrimony
of Peter. Although this saying of Peter's stands in the Gospel, 'We
have left all and followed Thee,' yet they give the name of his patrimony to lands, towns, tribute, imposts, and moneys . . . they fight
with fire and sword, not without shedding of Christian blood; and
then they believe they have defended the body of Christ in apostolic fashion, having scattered what they are pleased to designate
as 'her enemies'. As if the church had any enemies more pestilential than impious pontiffs who by their silence allow Christ to be
forgotten, who enchain Him by mercenary rules, adulterate His
teaching by forced interpretations, and crucify Him afresh by their
scandalous life![5]

Here was condemnation seemingly more direct and robust than anything
which had yet come from Luther's pen but the whole tone of the *Encomium
Moriae* was jocular. Erasmus was quite serious about the need to careen
the Christian ship, removing all the barnacles and weed which had accumulated over the centuries and cutting out worm-ridden timber. He pleaded
for a return to simple faith and devotion not dependent on externals. Yet
he had no intention of going to the stake for the cause of reform and he
hoped by satirising all aspects of society, secular as well as sacred, to get
his point across without causing too much offence.

As with all satire the establishment did not know how to take *The Praise
of Folly*. Some ecclesiastics, including Leo X, smiled knowingly, supposedly enjoying the joke and not wanting to strengthen its impact by seeming
to take it too seriously. Others were outraged and protested publicly about
the impudent smart alec who had presumed to pour scorn on holy things.
One prominent Dominican fixed a portrait of Erasmus to his wall so that
he could have the pleasure of spitting at it every time he went past. Quite
clearly, then, criticism was assailing the church hierarchy from several
directions and they were growing more sensitive to it. Certainly, the attack
mounted by a Wittenberg monk could not be passed over with a knowing
smile and an indulgent nod of the head.

It used to be said that 'Erasmus laid the egg that Luther hatched' and
it was not very long before the two names were being bracketed together
(much to Erasmus' anxiety and annoyance). In fact, Luther did not appreciate the Dutchman's lightheartedness. The issues both writers were dealing
with were, for him, far too serious to be dismissed simply as 'folly'. 'I am

reading our Erasmus,' he wrote to Spalatin in March 1517, 'but daily I dislike him more and more . . . he does not advance the cause of Christ and the grace of God sufficiently . . . Human things weigh more with him than the divine.'[6] However, such reservations were unknown to the outside world. To most interested parties Luther and Erasmus seemed to be singing from the same hymn sheet and their revolutionary refrains caused great excitement. When, within weeks, Luther's *Theses* were translated into German copies were eagerly snapped up and read throughout the land. Many people could not follow Luther's theological argument but they were at one with him in his contempt for the arrogant Dominicans.

Closer to home there were certainly some people who held their breath, nervous of an indignant reaction. The Elector Frederick commented 'the pope won't like this', Luther's bishop advised him to keep his head down and his Augustinian colleagues were anxious that there might be a furore that would bring the order into disrepute. The Archbishop of Magdeburg sent the theses to Rome, where an aloof Leo X simply handed the matter over to the head of Luther's order with the instruction to prevent the German monk spreading contentious theories.

There was one individual who could not adopt a laid-back stance. Johann Tetzel, understandably, considered that he had been made the subject of a scurrilous, libellous attack. He lost no time in hitting back and it was the bellows of his fury which raised the temperature of the conflict to white heat. Tetzel branded Luther a heretic and boasted that he would have him tied to a stake within weeks. The fiery Dominican had a series of counter-theses published which championed the conventional teaching on penance and indulgences. A batch of 800 copies reached Wittenberg in March. This provided Luther's students with an opportunity to demonstrate their support. If anything was to be burned it would not be their professor. A posse of them descended on the local bookseller, confiscated his stock of the new theses and made a public bonfire of them. It was over-reaction on both sides that turned a little local difficulty into a *cause célèbre*. Luther distanced himself from the antics of his young advocates and refused to emulate the knee-jerk reaction of his adversary. Part of the dominant image of the reformer that has come down to us is that of the pugilistic and verbally unrestrained controversialist. Certainly once the breach between Wittenberg and Rome had been opened up he became a no-holds-barred fighter who traded vulgarity and insults with his foes. But in these early months of the conflict he appears as a man determined to preserve the proprieties expected of a Christian priest and teacher. In the spring he was present in Heidelberg at a meeting of the Augustinian general chapter where he presented his strong views on scholastic theology. One young friar who listened to the debate was impressed not only with Luther's brilliant logic and persuasive communication skills but also his courtesy and his willingness to listen to other points of view.

At Heidelberg Luther was, of course, among friends. Members of his own order were protective of their troublesome celebrity even if many of them did not agree with him on all points. They certainly took his side in the growing confrontation with their old rivals, the Dominicans. For their part, Tetzel and his brethren grabbed with eagerness the stick with which they had been presented to beat the Augustinians. In the political life of the medieval church the black friars were the equivalent of the Soviet KGB, ruthless guardians of religious orthodoxy who used any and every means to extirpate heresy. They were answerable directly to the pope for the running of the Roman Inquisition and, by 1517, they had enjoyed three centuries of teaching and defending what they had themselves defined as truth. Widely feared and hated for their insidious methods in sniffing out critics of the religious establishment, the *domine canes*, 'hounds of God' (as they were commonly called in burlesque Latin) were extremely powerful in the curia and the inner circles of the Vatican. They had at least three reasons for being hypersensitive about Luther's challenge. Not only was he attacking their indulgence trade – he dismissed as arid and misguided their great hero, Thomas Aquinas, and (or so they claimed) he had encouraged people to question the authority of the pope. So fierce was Dominican opposition that Luther genuinely feared for his safety while travelling to and from Heidelberg. His enemies were intent on hauling him off to Rome to make an example of him which would act as a warning to the Augustinians not to harbour dangerous free-thinkers. As they set their well-oiled disciplinary machine in motion it could not have occurred to them that this time they would be facing a formidable adversary who had widespread public support and friends in high places. They were so accustomed to success in heresy proceedings that they could not stand back to evaluate the situation and its possible repercussions.

The chapter meeting was something of an oasis in the hostile atmosphere in which Luther increasingly found himself. He was received as something of an Augustinian hero. Some of his colleagues might not have been prepared to follow him down the path of radical theology but they were delighted to see their loathed Dominican rivals mauled by one of their own number. There is no indication that he was called upon to account to his superiors for his 95 Theses and when he laid down the burden of regional vicar he had the pleasure of seeing his old friend, Johann Lang, appointed in his place. For himself, Luther deliberately avoided plunging headlong into heated debate with Tetzel. He devoted several months of 1518 to a careful review and explanation of his opinions on indulgences. The Wittenberg theses had been merely debating points, rather than cogently presented arguments and their author was genuinely concerned that some of them might have been misunderstood or mischievously misrepresented. Not until August was he ready to set his *Explanations of the Disputations on the Power of Indulgences* before the public.

Tetzel, meanwhile, had not been idle. He had produced another set of theses, and this time he really had got to the heart of the matter. Determined to have Luther's scalp, he wasted little effort on arguments supportive of the efficacy of indulgences. Instead, he denounced his enemy as a heretic who had challenged the authority of the pope. Indulgences were beneficial to both the living and the dead *because the holy father said so.* Anyone, therefore, who denied the Church's teaching on indulgences was accusing the pope of error – a most damnable heresy. Tetzel bracketed Luther's name with those of Wycliffe and Hus. He even implicated Frederick the Wise in the dangerously erroneous teaching coming out of Wittenberg. Any prince who protected a suspected heretic, he said, was equally guilty. In thus shifting the ground of the argument Tetzel was doing more than hiding behind the papal skirts. He was identifying himself with the most extreme doctrines of the pope's authority and infallibility. In so doing he had, inadvertently, placed at the head of the Reformation agenda that issue which would inflame the passions of thousands of people from peddlers to princes: *potestas* – power and authority. Once the question, 'How does God rule in the kingdoms of the world?' was asked, it gave permission for a range of other disquieting questions to be posed: is the Church ruled by popes or general councils?; what is the relationship between the power of the bishop and the power of the magistrate?; are priests subject to the common law?; do priests have the power to 'make' God in the mass?; is the Bible the Church's sovereign authority and, if so, who may interpret it? These and other fundamental issues were clamouring to be heard. What Tetzel had done was open the door and let them in.

Luther saw clearly the thin ice onto which the conflict was leading him. He, too, knew that *potestas* was the real issue. That is why he was ultra-careful in his presentation of the *Explanations*. He dedicated the work to Leo X and protested his total devotion to the head of the Church:

> I let my book go out under the protection of your name, Holy Father, so that all well-meaning readers may know with what pure intentions I have sought to fathom the nature of ecclesiastical power and what reverence I hold toward the power of the keys. If I were as they describe me, the illustrious Elector Frederick of Saxony certainly would not suffer such a pestiferous boil in his university, for he is probably the greatest zealot for Catholic truth there is at the present time . . . Therefore, Most Holy Father, I cast myself at your feet with all that I am and possess. Raise me up or slay me, summon me hither or thither, approve me reprove me as you please! I will listen to your voice as the voice of Christ reigning and speaking in you. If I have deserved death, I shall not refuse to die.[7]

But this did not mean that he was crumpling in the face of opposition and was ready to abandon his convictions. He told his readers he was amazed that some theological points set forth for routine academic debate had become the subject of wide discussion. However, since this was the case, he had no alternative but to explain and defend what he had said and what he still believed. Only, now he went further. He opined that, if purgatory exists – and on this Luther for the first time cast doubt – the pope has no authority over the souls residing there. The only thing he can do is pray for them – an obligation he shares with all living Christians. In fact, he now stated unequivocally, papal power only extends over members of the Church Militant.

Luther's logic had carried him to the point of exposing theological error and confronting the corruption of those who lied to the people about religious and ethical matters in order to bolster their own power and to extort money. How could he be silent when these abuses were the subjects of ale-house gossip the length and breadth of Germany? The hierarchy could not go on sweeping this dirt under the carpet. Yet how could he hold fast to these accusations and, at the same time, avoid being singed by the martyrs' bonfire? The only way was to keep the debate theoretical and to make no personal attacks. Accordingly, Luther exonerated Leo X while pointing out that some of his predecessors had erred and others had led scandalous lives. When he turned his attention to the contemporary situation it was to lash the Roman hierarchy with his pen. It is 'a many-headed monster', an 'inferno of simony, licentiousness, pomp, murder and other abominations'. Christ's vicar is almost powerless to bring this vice-ridden executive back under control, 'for in what part of the Christian world do they ridicule the popes more than in that genuine Babylon, Rome?'[8] What the Church stood in urgent need of was – Reformation.

6

'Positively no chance of a revocation'

'If one would have let my writing go unhindered, everything would have been quiet long ago. The song would have been sung, and everyone would have become tired of it.'[1] So Luther claimed in a letter written to Frederick the Wise in January 1519. The writer indicated his willingness to consume a large portion of humble pie. He would admit that his criticisms had been expressed in intemperate language. He would urge his readers to remain loyal to the Roman church. He would indicate that he was now retiring from the fray. In fact, Luther insisted that he would do anything, 'if only I am no longer called upon to drag this matter out into the public [arena]'.[2] Unfortunately, the submissive effect was spoiled by the last, forthright sentence of the letter: 'But there is positively no chance of a revocation.'[3] The one and only thing the accused heretic would not do was recant his convictions. To have done so would have meant letting go the sheet anchor of his soul, acknowledging that his hard-won discovery of life-changing truth was a delusion, that what he profoundly believed to be divine revelation had been a satanic deceit. It was precisely this that his adversaries were determined that he should do. The use of any and every means to secure recantation was the only way the medieval church knew of dealing with heretics. Like any establishment under attack it reacted ferociously to challenge and its spokesmen were sanctioned to employ any tactics in its defence. They had the backing of a massive institution. They had the money and the influence necessary to stifle dissent. They held the power of life and death over ordinary people. Under no circumstances would they suffer the personnel or practices of the Church to suffer affront.

Thus, within a mere year of the posting of the 95 Theses, both sides had manoeuvred themselves into a position from which neither could retreat without conceding defeat.

Both parties were intransigent but Luther had some justification in claiming that it was the papal fundamentalists who had set the pace. Not only did they produce a succession of reactionary champions eager to go into the ring with this tyro from the backwoods; they also employed spiritual blackmail in the form of ban and excommunication as well as threats of physical violence against Luther and anyone who stood by him. The succession of events in the second half of 1518 reads like a thriller, in which the hero finds himself over and again caught in the machinations of a powerful enemy commanding a cohort of unscrupulous agents, from whom, one by one, he manages to escape.

Luther's most persistent and formidable opponent was Johann Maier von Eck, Chancellor of Ingolstadt University and probably the most accomplished controversialist the Church possessed. He was Luther's equal as scholar and preacher and, in fact, shared many of the reformer's concerns. Eck was a friend of humanist learning and a champion of free, academic debate. Luther was genuinely hurt, therefore, when this leading theologian for whom he had a considerable respect entered the lists against him. Here was no intellectually third-rate indulgence pedlar or devious-minded Dominican or Italian lackey of the curia. Eck was a fellow German who might have been expected to understand Luther's anxieties and to enter into unbiased debate.

Eck received a copy of the 95 Theses soon after they were published and, by March, he had riposted with a refutation of some of Luther's arguments in a treatise entitled *Obelisks*. Neither party wanted a public quarrel and relations might have remained at the level of polite disagreement had Eck's contribution not arrived in Wittenberg while Luther was away at the Heidelberg chapter meeting. In the professor's absence his colleague, Andreas Carlstadt, took up the cudgels on his behalf – and Luther must profoundly have wished that his friend had been able to restrain himself. The Most Reverend Lord Professor, Doctor Andreas Rudolf-Bodenstein von Karlstadt, Doctor of Theology, Doctor of Secular and Canon Law, Archdeacon and Deacon of All Saints Wittenberg was an eccentric, headstrong radical. Within a few years he went far beyond Luther's theological position, rejecting any distinction between priesthood and laity, dressing as a peasant and insisting that everyone call him 'Brother Andy'. As Professor of Thomistic Philosophy he was Luther's superior and by no means an intellectual lightweight. By 1517 he had fallen under Luther's spell but in his unbridled enthusiasm for Bible-based teaching he rushed in where his younger colleague would have hesitated to tread. He answered Eck's *Obelisks* with a theological broadside of no less than 380 theses which he later enlarged to 406, intending to demolish the Ingolstadt scholar utterly. He boldly asserted the supremacy of Scripture, denied that the pope had any authority to remit punishment for sin and posed several other propositions which could only alarm Eck and convince him that Wittenberg had become a hotbed of heresy. Eck was affronted at having been the recipient of an exuberant challenge from a second-rate intellect but he did not respond immediately, preferring to await Luther's reply. This came shortly in the form of an extended letter called *Asterisks*. The tone was conciliatory and it seemed that courteous relations would be restored but Eck considered himself duty bound to silence the strident voice which was calling ever more loudly from Elector Frederick's infant university. Saxony, it seemed to him, was producing its own Hus. In August 1518 he at last published a reply to Karlstadt and challenged him to a disputation. Negotiations for this went ahead during the autumn with Luther trying to keep the peace between the two rivals.

Meanwhile, the Dominicans were orchestrating their attack. Tetzel and his pack had their teeth firmly embedded in Luther's flesh and they were determined not to let go. Over the winter the Wittenberg professor had delved deeper into the nature of ecclesiastical power and, in May, he preached about the papal ban. If indulgences were the carrots of ecclesiastical discipline, ban and interdict were the sticks. They excluded 'contumacious offenders' from the Church and its benefits and were applied with increasing severity according to the resistance of the miscreants. Initially, the offender was banned from the sacraments and most of the life of the local community. He could not have his children baptised and if he died he could not be buried in consecrated ground. If he persisted unrepentant the clergy tightened the screw by extending the ban to his family and servants. Clergy most frequently used this weapon to force the lower orders to pay their tithes and other dues promptly but in their conflict with secular authorities churchmen seldom hesitated to use the interdict as a form of blackmail. This might extend from a convent extracting commercial privileges from a town council to a pope placing a whole nation under the greater interdict.

These penalties were only intended to apply in the temporal sphere and, even so, they were draconian enough. Malicious clergy had it in their

power to break up families, ruin businesses and even bring down kingdoms. What made the use of this form of coercion exponentially more
oppressive was the widespread belief – which the Church did little to dispel
– that penalties imposed on earth continued to apply in purgatory. It was
this aspect of the teaching that Luther challenged in his sermon. Since
only God, he insisted, had the power to save and damn, the souls in purgatory were totally beyond the jurisdiction of church leaders on earth, no
matter how exalted they might be. Moreover, anyone who suffered unjustly
from the evil machinations of the clergy had absolutely nothing to fear in
the next life.

> If . . . you die without the sacrament, if your corpse is thrust into
> unconsecrated ground, or even if it is dug out again and cast into
> the water, happy are you! Blessed is he who dies under such an unjust
> ban! For inasmuch as he has remained faithful to righteousness he
> shall gain the crown of life.[4]

Luther believed he was removing erroneous accretions from Catholic
doctrine. His enemies claimed he was undermining the Church's disciplinary system and ultimately the authority of the earthly head of the Church.
They were both right. Corrupt practice had made a nonsense of canon
law. When the clergy stubbornly maintained that practice they laid themselves open to criticism. Of all bodies the Dominicans were the most stubborn and, acting on the principle that ends justified means, they seized
on Luther's sermon, distorted it and sent a falsified report to Rome where
their colleagues triumphantly showed it to the curia as proof of the
Wittenberger's damnable heresy.

Tetzel, determined not to be left out of the hunt, published fresh diatribes.
In order to place himself on an equal footing with his adversary he had
his friends in Rome secure for him a doctorate in theology. In his reply,
which he tossed off in a few days, Luther called the writer's bluff. Tetzel
wanted to be treated as a scholar, did he? Very well, then he must expect
to have his lamentable methodology ruthlessly exposed.

> When he cites thousands of scholastic teachers, he puts too high a
> value on these worthless counters. If he had thought the matter over
> carefully, he would have found not many more than three, for the
> others are only yes-men and imitators.

As to Tetzel's handling of Scripture, Luther accused him of searching for proof texts and quoting them out of context like a sow snuffling around in a hay sack for grains of rye. Turning his fiery invective on Dominican theology, Luther complained,

> They say that he who buys an indulgence does better than he who gives alms to a poor man in extreme need. God help us, and they call themselves teachers of Christian people! In truth now, we no longer need to be alarmed when we hear how the Turks are dese-crating our churches and the cross of Christ. We have in our midst Turks a hundred times more wicked, who are utterly destroying our one and only sanctuary, the Word of God.

He was on popular ground when he castigated the Dominicans as 'bitten with the desire to burn' those they slanderously called heretics. By midsummer it was obvious that Luther's adversaries would stop at nothing to lay hands on him. That was why he now told them that he was ready to argue his understanding of the Gospel with Tetzel or anyone else, as long as they would come to Wittenberg.[5] He had no intention of meeting the Dominicans on their home ground. Certainly, he would not go to Rome which was where they wanted to put him on trial.

By July they had persuaded the pope to commence legal proceedings. As part of this process the Commissioner of the Sacred Palace, Sylvester Prierias (another Dominican), produced an indictment entitled, *Against the Presumptuous Theses of Martin Luther concerning the Power of the Pope.* It was couched in terms of outraged vindictiveness and its author did not hesitate to use the language of the gutter. Luther's reply, again dashed off and sent to the printer in a couple of days, rejected the charge of heresy on the grounds that no established Catholic dogma had been refuted. All Luther had done, he claimed, was assert his right to question the dubious ways some orthodox teaching was being interpreted and distorted by the Church's own agents. He was, by now, becoming well practised at fighting repeatedly over the same terrain. He marshalled his sources with devas-tating precision and became ever freer in his use of language. He repaid Prierias in his own vulgar coin, partly because he was genuinely incensed by the tactics of his enemies and partly with an eye to the wider public. Luther's greatest talent, now beginning to come to the fore, was as a commu-nicator. The enthralling lecturer and preacher was emerging as a brilliant author and journalist. His writing, whether in Latin or German, had a vigour and clarity which ensured that his works would be widely and eagerly read. Luther was determined that the world at large should follow his conflict with the authorities so that, even if they were able to silence him by fire or incarceration, the truth would not be stifled. Arguably the most important effect of his prodigious and compelling literary output was to spur other protagonists to enter into public debate. The 1520s would produce a positive snowstorm of pamphlets and books (see below, p. 214).

At the beginning of August Luther received an order from Leo X to present himself in Rome to face his accusers. This was the prologue to two months of high drama in which theological debate would become tangled with high politics and base personal conflict. The pope backed up his demand with an instruction, via the head of the Augustinian order, that Luther's superior in Saxony was to have the heretic arrested, manacled and thrown into prison, pending his transfer to Rome. Now that the crunch had come Luther turned to his patron for help. He asked Frederick to engineer the hearing of his case in Germany since only on home territory could he be sure of a fair trial and personal safety.

Now the fate of a north German academic was decided by relationships between the most important people in Europe. The Emperor Maximilian was in his sixtieth year and obsessed by thoughts of death. The numerous concerns and interests that had filled his long life were now reduced to two: he wanted to complete the impressive tomb on which Europe's finest craftsmen were working at Innsbruck and he wanted to ensure the succession of his elder grandson, Charles of Spain. To achieve the second of these grand designs, Maximilian had to woo the electors, especially the highly influential Frederick the Wise, and Frederick was not an enthusiastic supporter of the young Charles. Leo X was firmly opposed to the Spanish

Leo X

candidate. As ruler of Sardinia, Sicily and all of southern Italy Charles was an uncomfortably powerful neighbour of the Papal States. Leo lent his support, as the lesser of two evils, to Francis I of France, the recent conqueror of Milan. Thus, the pope also was obliged to court the Elector Frederick. In the political intrigues and manoeuvrings of the autumn of 1518 the issue of what to do with a German heretic played a minor but not insignificant part. Maximilian wrote to assure the pope of his support over the Luther business and hinted that Rome might be inclined to implicate Frederick in the errors of the man he was protecting. But Leo was in no position to adopt a heavy-handed attitude towards the prince. On the contrary, he held out inducements: the Golden Rose, the highest distinction the pope could convey and the possibility of more indulgences. He urged Frederick to show himself a good son of Holy Church by handing over the 'son of perdition'. But the elector kept his own counsel and everything would depend on what course of action he decided to take.

The next senior ecclesiastic to become involved in the Luther saga was the general of the Dominican order, Tomasso de Vio, known as Cajetan. This able man, recently raised to the cardinalate, is one of those individuals whose reputation has suffered because of his confrontation with Martin Luther. Had the course of history been different he might have been remembered as a leader of the Catholic reform movement. He was fifty and the leading Thomist scholar of the day who had taught metaphysics at Padua, investigated the continuing cult of Savonarola, and had been a major advocate of church reform. He denounced corruption at the centre of church life and instituted a programme of moral rigour within his order. Although he and Luther stood at opposite poles theologically (Cajetan was a convinced Aristotelian and a staunch upholder of papal authority), each had come to his present position via a genuine spiritual journey and the Dominican firmly believed that doctrinal purity guaranteed by papal fiat was the only secure basis for the faith, and therefore the salvation, of individual Christians. This severe but fair-minded and intelligent scholar was the man chosen by Leo for the most sensitive diplomatic job: that of papal legate in Germany.

What Cajetan discovered in the summer of 1518 came as a shock to this churchman who had spent all his life south of the Alps. Princes and nobles were resentful of the abuses of previous papal agents and suspicious of Leo's demand for financial aid, supposedly to fight the Turk. The cardinal advised his master that Germany's leaders needed handling with kid gloves and when Frederick requested the transfer of Luther's case from Rome to

Augsburg Cajetan advised the pope to agree. Thus it was that Luther's first examination for heresy took place in the thriving Bavarian commercial centre. The imperial free city of Augsburg, the third city of Germany with a population of some 30,000, was socially and intellectually a microcosm of central Europe. Cosmopolitan, prosperous and free-thinking, it was home to the banking families of Fugger and Welser and also to the artist families of Burgkmair and Holbein. Immigrants from neighbouring countries came to find employment in the print houses and weaving ateliers. They brought with them their own traditions and beliefs and, because Augsburg needed their industry and craftsmanship, the city fathers tended to turn a blind eye to their heterodox ideas. Thus, Bohemian Hussites were protected and calls from church leaders to outlaw other heretics often fell on deaf ears. If toleration of the unorthodox was one side of the coin, the other was loud criticism of the religious establishment. The bishop and the city council seldom saw eye to eye and there existed the usual clashes over privileges and tax exemptions between religious houses and the civic authorities.

Both Cajetan and Luther had cause to ponder that they were not among friends in Augsburg. The cardinal was under instructions not to bandy words with the errant son of the Church, but to demand recantation and, failing that, to despatch him in chains to Rome. However, Elector Frederick had urged him to hear Luther in a spirit of gentle fatherliness. He must have had grave doubts about his chances of accomplishing his mission. As for Luther, he set out with a sense of real foreboding. 'What a disappointment I shall be to my family,' he lamented as he contemplated the fire and the stake. Friends had obtained for the examinee an imperial safe conduct but Luther felt far from secure as he trudged the eight hundred kilometres of the long road south. He can have been far from encouraged by the many friends he met along the way who urged him to abort the arranged confrontation. He had already received a message from Staupitz, inviting him to join him in Salzburg, so that they could live and die together. But recalling how Jesus had set his face to go to Jerusalem, Luther smothered his anxiety and journeyed on. The stomach disorder to which he fell prey as he neared his destination was probably a result of nervous tension.

Luther arrived on 7 October and his sessions with Cajetan occupied the twelfth to the fourteenth of the month. In the recently terminated imperial diet at Augsburg the pope's emissary had achieved very little in the face of suspicion and stubbornness from the princes, so he was more determined than ever to obtain a favourable result in this case which touched his master so closely. The discussion began courteously enough. Luther appeared before the cardinal in the Fuggers' town palace and prostrated himself before the pope's representative. Cajetan graciously received the obeisance and assured the German friar of his fatherly concern for him. But everything about the setting of the interview and the body language of the main participants made it clear that this was not a meeting designed to establish the truth, nor even a tribunal. It was a court of audience. Cajetan sat surrounded by his Italian entourage of sniggering sycophants, perhaps on a raised dais, while Luther stood before him in the empty vastness of the hall. (After the first confrontation he was accompanied by a few friends including Staupitz.) As soon as the initial pleasantries were over the mood rapidly deteriorated. The two men were engaged in a dialogue of the deaf. Cajetan, indeed, made it clear that he had not come to engage in dialogue at all, thus frustrating Luther's desire to be shown precisely where he had fallen into error. What it all came down to was this: did Luther or did he not accept that the pope, by virtue of his guardianship of the treasury of the saints, had the power to remit punishments being suffered by souls in purgatory. Luther did not – because there was no support for such a claim in the plain word of Scripture.

Cajetan was the first to lose his cool. It was not just Luther's obstinacy which angered him. The monk was outfacing him by demonstrating his detailed knowledge of the Bible and the doctors of the Church. By this point Luther had had over a year to refine his understanding of the issues at stake. Every confrontation had sent him back to his sources and driven him to seek out new ones. He now had chapter and verse at his fingertips. Thus when the cardinal allowed himself, contrary to his instructions, to be drawn into discussion of theological matters he found himself dealing with a knowledgeable and fluent controversialist. Cajetan was not a patient man and as it became clearer that he was getting nowhere with the recalcitrant monk his temper became frayed. He tried everything he could think of to obtain a recantation. He ranted, he threatened, he held private talks with Luther's friends hoping to enlist their help, he even offered to overlook some of Luther's errors if he would only yield on the main substantive issue. All he received by way of reply was an assertion that the pope was subject to Scripture and a general council, an offer to submit his teaching to the judgement of the leading universities, and a request to appeal directly to the pope. (As Luther put it, the appeal would be from 'Leo ill-informed to Leo better-informed'.)

At the conclusion of the third interview Cajetan thundered, 'Get out! I don't want to see you again until you are ready to recant!' Luther's version of the 'end of the affair' was that he simply turned on his heel and left while the cardinal was still shouting. Both sides claimed victory or, rather, disclaimed defeat but the real significance of the Augsburg stalemate was that in defying the pope's representative Luther had unequivocally defied the pope. He had become the standard-bearer of revolt. It was an exposed and lonely position he now found himself in. During those tense October days Staupitz had released him from his obligations to the Augustinian order so that he could act in obedience to his conscience without compromising his Augustinian brethren. Luther later referred to this as his first excommunication. Poor Staupitz; he was pulled in two directions by his deep friendship for his protégé and his responsibilities to the order. He had a deep admiration for Luther's intellectual grasp and spiritual insights. He shared Luther's basic theological convictions. But he was worried by the younger man's increasing truculence and his impatience with matters of (what Staupitz considered) lesser importance. He stood by his colleague as long as he could at Augsburg and longer than many would have considered prudent. He talked with Luther long into the night, urging him to soften his attitude even if he could not change his mind. He pressed him, for his own safety, to go into hiding. He even tried to raise a collection to enable Luther to travel to some far haven. But, in the end, he was as powerless as Cajetan to bring about any real alteration in Luther's resolve. On 16 October, frustrated and, perhaps, even fearful for his own safety (Cajetan had threatened to include Luther's supporters in the inevitable papal ban which would be forthcoming), Staupitz slipped away from Augsburg without announcing his departure to anyone.

Oddly, what happened next was . . . nothing. The general expectation was that Cajetan would try to apprehend Luther and, under normal circumstances, he would have done just that. However, because of the delicate political situation between the pope and Elector Frederick, he hesitated to infringe the terms of Luther's safe conduct. Luther wrote to the cardinal respectfully explaining why he could not in conscience recant and indicating his intention to leave Augsburg. Cajetan did not dignify him with a reply. Four days of tense inactivity passed. Luther's supporters grew increasingly twitchy. They suspected, probably with good reason, that their angry and frustrated enemies were hatching a plot to seize or, perhaps, even to kill Luther. To circumvent this they grabbed the initiative. On the night of 20 October they smuggled their friend out of the city. Without any baggage, outer garment, weapon or even spurs, he slipped through a postern gate under cover of darkness, was plonked on a very indifferent horse (he was, in any case, a very indifferent rider) and set off northwards with a single guide. Luther later described the next few hours as the most uncomfortable journey of his life. When he reached Monheim, after a jolting ride of some eighty kilometres, he slithered, sore and stiff, from the saddle, his legs buckled and he promptly fell into a pile of straw.

The next day, at Nuremberg a historic meeting took place between two of the great figures of the age. Martin Luther came face to face with Albrecht Dürer. The artist had long been an admirer of the Wittenberg radical, though perhaps an even greater admirer of Staupitz. At Advent 1516 the Augustinian leader had preached a memorable sermon in Nuremberg, moving many with his exhortation to the congregation to embrace the love of God as demonstrated in the Cross. Modern readers may find it difficult to grasp just how moving and liberating this advocacy of personal, affective religion could be to hearers accustomed to exhortations to cling to the skirts of mother church as the only away of avoiding the eternal torments of hell. One result of Staupitz's preaching was the formation of the 'Sodalitas Staupiziana', the 'Staupitz Fellowship', a group of leading citizens whose desire for a deeper devotion prompted them to explore new religious ideas. Their guru drew attention to Martin Luther, his gifted apprentice, and, from November 1517, they had begun to follow his career with interest. One member of the Sodalitas, Christoph Scheurl, was already a committed disciple. As a lecturer at Wittenberg from 1507 to 1512 he had made the acquaintance of the young monk from Erfurt and it was Scheurl who became the eager agent for Luther's works in Nuremberg. It was almost certainly he who had organised, without permission, the circulation of the 95 Theses in southern Germany. Dürer also belonged to this band of free-thinkers and from this time he attached himself enthusiastically to the cause of the teacher from Wittenberg. The existence of such a coterie illustrates how tinder-ready was the intellectual stubble of Germany to receive the flaming brand of Luther's revolutionary thought. We can go a step further: Dürer provides a timeless link for us between the Reformation that was to come and the unquiet spirit of the German people that already existed. That pious anxiety reveals itself dramatically in such images as The Four Horsemen of the Apocalypse and the sketch of King Death.

'In order that no evil may befall Your Excellency on my account, I hereby declare that I am willing to leave your lands to go wherever the God of mercy will have me.'[6] So Luther wrote to Frederick the Wise days after his return home at the end of October. There were two reasons for this statement; two factors which would certainly cause embarrassment to his patron. One was the papal ban which Luther knew he must now expect. If its terms were extended to cover all who gave succour to the heretic then the results for the elector would be grave indeed. The other was Luther's fixed determination not to yield one iota to pressure from Rome. On the contrary, he had already begun work on a vigorous defence which he proposed to publish. The *Acta Augustana* would be a point-by-point account of all that had passed at Augsburg, so that the world would know how his willingness to have his opinions impartially considered by the Church's best scholars had been rebuffed by Cajetan. Luther was not prepared to allow his enemies to propagate their version of events unchallenged. There was no element of bluff in his offer to leave Saxony. The elector took Luther's words at face value and told him, via Spalatin, that it would be better for all concerned if he were to leave. Accordingly, Luther preached a farewell sermon to his congregation at Wittenberg and gathered his friends together for a final meal. Luther later recalled that it was while he was still at table that he received two letters from the elector. The first demanded to know why he had not already left. The second, which arrived hot on its heels, instructed him to delay his departure.

It has always been difficult to fathom Frederick's attitude to his brilliant, troublesome protégé. He was an intelligent ruler who enjoyed enormous respect among the princes of Germany. Not for nothing was he known as 'The Wise'. It was his custom to weigh up carefully all the pros and cons and to take counsel from his advisers before reaching a decision. Then, when he had made up his mind, he held firmly to his purpose and was not to be hustled out of it by interested parties. He was a dignified man who observed meticulously all the diplomatic and social protocols. Thus, he was careful never to get too close to Luther so that no one could accuse him of being under the reformer's influence. But aloofness did not imply that he would disown his servants if it became expedient to do so. For Frederick was also a man of honour who took seriously his obligation to those who relied on him for protection. There were several occasions on which he found the radical preacher and teacher absolutely infuriating. On the other hand, he was equally annoyed by the representatives of an Italian pope who were quite unscrupulous in seeking Luther's downfall.

Probably what finally weighted the balance of the elector's judgement in the 'Luther affair' was his passionate concern for and pride in his university. When he considered the contribution that Luther had made to the development and reputation of the new seat of learning in Wittenberg he realised that it would be unwise, unfair and ungrateful to jettison the professor – certainly as long as Luther could, with some justification, claim that he had not received a proper, impartial hearing.

It is scarcely an exaggeration to say that Luther *was* Wittenberg University. Frederick's foundation had got off to a very shaky start and few students of any calibre were attracted to it. Luther had put it on the map. As a radical teacher with exciting new ideas and a vigorous, engaging teaching style the young doctor of biblical studies was a celebrity and young men from all over Germany and beyond wanted to sit at his feet. At this very time the university authorities were making sweeping changes to the syllabuses. Aristotle was out, together with Aquinas's commentaries. Hebrew and Greek were given more prominence on the timetable and Wittenberg became only the second German university to establish a chair in Greek. It was awarded to a young graduate of Heidelberg and Tübingen by the name of Philip Melancthon. Steeped in humanist studies, the twenty-one-year-old scholar took up his new post full of zeal to rejuvenate classical and biblical studies by a return to original sources. By 1518 the student quarters of the small Saxon city were bursting at the seams. This certainly created problems for the citizens of Wittenberg but they were problems of growth. If Frederick had thrown Luther to the '*domini canes*' there would have been an eruption of protest from the younger element within his dominions and from many others besides who were beginning to identify the outspoken Augustinian as their David confronting the papal Goliath. The results of Luther's abrupt disappearance from the university could only have been disastrous for that institution. Whatever the reasons for his decision, Frederick eventually resolved not to disembarrass himself of his troublesome priest. He wrote firmly to Cajetan: since no one in his dominions had condemned Martin Luther as a heretic, except those who had a vested interest in so doing, his prince had no reason to take any action against him, unless the legate could provide him with proof of the friar's alleged false teaching.

It is probably true to say that, by the end of 1518, all the principals in this affair were anxious to wriggle out of the situation into which they had got themselves. Spalatin, Scheurl and other friends were passionately begging Luther to modify his language and retire gracefully from the fray.

For his part, Luther desired peace and, as we have seen, promised his patron that he would do anything to further it – except recant. In Rome the curia, now fully apprised by Cajetan of the unstable situation in Germany, decided to try diplomacy where power politics and theological confrontation had failed. They sent to the elector's court Karl von Militz, a young member of the Saxon minor nobility who was currently attached to the papal household. This latest emissary had no theology but that did not inhibit him from examining the professor of biblical studies. We do not know what Militz's terms of reference were but it is clear that he exceeded them unhesitatingly in his eagerness to succeed where others had failed. He was an ambitious young man seeking his fortune and having little but his wits and an engaging personality to rely on. He was gambling heavily on bringing off his mission in the winter of 1518–19. If he could pull the papacy out of the hole into which Dominican intransigence had pushed it his career would be made. Sadly, he was not equal to the task and, even if he had been, his endeavours would have come too late. The Reformation had begun and was developing an impetus of its own.

Militz's first move was to send a peremptory summons to Tetzel in Leipzig. He doubtless planned to issue a severe dressing-down to the indulgence pedlar as a means of earning Luther's goodwill. However, Tetzel refused to come. He said that he was afraid of being waylaid by Luther's supporters. He might well have had some justification for this fear but he must also have sensed the way the wind was blowing and realised that some of his erstwhile supporters now regarded him as a liability. He resolved to keep his head down. Luther, similarly summoned, made the long trek to the electoral residence at Altenburg, south of Leipzig, in the first days of January. He was allowed no time to recover from the journey for the latest papal envoy interviewed him straight away. Militz employed flattery, cajolery and carefully veiled threats and certainly made some impression on Luther. What agitated the friar most was the realisation of the impact his writings were having on the world at large. Militz reported that on his travels he had discovered that a majority of people were turning against Rome and that his masters in Italy were deeply worried about this alienation. Luther was genuinely alarmed also. For the first time he had an inkling of the bitter polarisation of German society created by the indulgence issue. Luther shared with all members of the 'settled' classes the fear of civil unrest and he was appalled at the thought that his activity might give rise to a widespread challenge to authority. This emerges clearly from a letter he drafted to Pope Leo as a result of his first session with Militz.

After protesting his undying obedience to the Holy See, the writer explains why the developing situation makes his recantation impossible:

> . . . through the antagonism and pressure of enemies, my writings are spread further than I ever had expected and are so deeply rooted in the hearts of so many people that I am not in the position to revoke them.

He promises to abandon the indulgences controversy as long as his enemies will do likewise. Moreover,

> I shall publish something for the common people to make them understand that they should truly honour the Roman church, and influence them to do so. [I shall tell them] not to blame the church for the rashness of [those indulgence preachers], nor to imitate my sharp words against the Roman church, which I have used – or rather misused – against those clowns, and with which I have gone too far. Perhaps by the grace of God the discord which has arisen may finally be quieted by such an effort.[7]

This letter was never sent. Militz, realising that the recantation issue was one on which his superiors would not back down and not wanting the rug to be pulled from under his own mediation, offered to intercede for Luther. The two men also agreed to have the heresy issue decided by the impartial mediation of the Archbishop of Trier. The meetings ended with a generous supper hosted by Militz during which the young diplomat larded his guest with flattery, tearfully protested his friendship and, on departure, kissed him warmly.

It all looked very promising but sugary diplomatic sauce could not smother the astringent taste of fundamental discord over religious truth. Militz might believe that he had found a formula to which both sides could subscribe while clinging to the conviction that they had yielded nothing of importance but Luther was, by now, distrustful of anything that came out of Rome. When he discovered what subsequently passed between Militz and Tetzel he actually felt sorry for his old adversary. The pope's emissary summoned the Dominican before him at Leipzig to face charges of embezzlement and sexual immorality. Tetzel was so utterly crushed that his health gave way. Luther saw this action for what it was, a stratagem to publicly humiliate the indulgence salesman without actually conceding anything on the theological issue of indulgences. Clearly, Rome was not interested in truth, merely in retaining power by any and every means.

This became all the clearer after 12 January. That was the day that Emperor Maximilian died. Leo X's need to seek an accommodation with Frederick was now even more urgent. He offered lurid blandishments to the elector if he would refuse his support to the Habsburg candidate, Charles of Spain. Not only was the Golden Rose now on offer; the pope invited Frederick to nominate a new cardinal and hinted that perhaps the eminent professor from Wittenberg might be a suitable recipient of this honour. The cynical Medici clearly believed that all men could be bought, including Frederick the Wise and Dr Martin Luther.

The papal entourage had every incentive to let sleeping dogs lie, at least until after the imperial election. For his part, Luther with difficulty restrained himself for several weeks. The one man who was intent on keeping the theological debate alive was Johann Eck. He had a reputation to maintain as an intellectual prize-fighter and his forte was the disputation. The disputation, in which two protagonists argued their case for hours or even days on end, at the end of which a judge proclaimed the winner, was a standard part of a scholar's training and people attended these contests to relish the exchange of witticisms and invective as well as telling argument. Conflict has always been the stuff of art and popular sub-art and the disputation takes its place in the wide range of public entertainment alongside *Hamlet* and TV soaps. In this medium Eck was a champion. His mental fists were at the disposal of any patron who had a case to be argued. Eck revelled in conflict, whether it was confronting heretics, arguing the properties of the physical universe or defending the right of the Fuggers to extract extortionate levels of interest from their customers. His weapons were wit, vulgarity, an encyclopaedic knowledge and formidable mental stamina (he once participated in a disputation that went on for nineteen days). As he watched Luther's rise to prominence he ached to lock horns with the radical monk. Like Militz, though with considerably more talent, he was eager to use Luther as a rung in the ladder of his own ambition. Eck's feud with Karlstadt rumbled on through the autumn of 1518 and a disputation was eventually arranged to be held in Leipzig the following spring. But Eck was not interested in a public contest with a minor celebrity. When he published the twelve theses he proposed to defend it was clear that Luther was his target. For his part, Luther was equally eager for the fray – he had all along been asking for an opportunity to test his propositions in an academic arena – but he was inhibited by his vow of silence and the elector made it clear that he would not give his blessing to his professor taking part in any new high-profile theological argument. Now, however, he could persuade himself that since the opposition had reopened the debate on indulgences he was released from his promise. He, therefore, prepared himself thoroughly for his forthcoming confrontation with his formidable opponent.

> . . . our Eck, that little glory-hungry beast, has published a small sheet of paper regarding his planned debate with Karlstadt at Leipzig after Easter. That foolish man obliquely attempts to satisfy his long-standing grudge against me; naming one person as contestant yet attacking someone else who has to handle the whole affair, he storms against me and my writings. I am fed up with that man's senseless deceit. As a result I, too, have published a refutation against him, as you will see from the enclosed printed material. This may, perhaps, be an occasion for Eck finally to treat this matter seriously, instead of as a game, as heretofore, and thus ill serve the Roman tyranny.[8]

So Luther grumbled to Spalatin on 7 February 1519. It is a far more important letter than at first sight might appear. The devil (quite literally) is in the detail. For the first time he confides confidentially to his friend that he now views the pope and the curia as 'the Roman tyranny'. Since Augsburg, Luther's thinking had advanced several squares on the chessboard. The publication he referred to was his own set of theses in opposition to Eck's. They covered old ground but there was one extremely significant addition:

> That the Roman church is superior to all others is proved only by the utterly worthless papal decrees of the last four hundred years. Against these stands the testimony of the authentic history of eleven hundred years, the text of Holy Scriptures, and the decree of the Council of Nicaea, the holiest of all councils.[9]

Luther's questioning of the authority of the papacy had reached a new stage and thanks to the abundance of written material he left we can recreate the natural progression of his thought. His realisation that salvation is by faith and not by human endeavour or routine performance of penance had convinced him that the Bible was the supreme authority in matters of faith – the Bible plainly understood without the subtle dialectic of scholasticism or the glosses of approved commentators. His understanding of Scripture cast doubt on the pope's power to remit penalties for sin. His attempt to draw attention to what he believed was an aberrant form of Catholic teaching brought the wrath of the ecclesiastical hierarchy down about his ears. The pope's own representatives had branded him a heretic and insisted that the visible head of the church on earth was superior to the written word of God. That could not be true, for if it was it would negate all Luther's profound spiritual experience to this point. *Ergo* the pope was *not* the final arbiter in matters of faith for the whole Church. Luther's fresh researches revealed that papal claims to primacy were based on misinterpretation of biblical proof texts and on the tenth-century Decretals of Pseudo-Isidore, a bundle of forgeries which claimed to demonstrate that all parts of the Church before the Council of Nicaea (325) had acknowledged the leadership of the Bishop of Rome. The fraudulent imposition of this corrupt Roman regime had prevented the emergence of a pure Germanic church. All this was revolutionary enough but one more thought, a logical progression from what had gone before, was now haunting Luther. He shared it tentatively with Spalatin on 13 March:

> I am studying the papal decretals for my debate. I speak this in your ear, I know not whether the pope is Antichrist or an apostle of Antichrist, so does he in his decretals corrupt and crucify Christ . . .[10]

There was no doubt about it, now. This *was* rank heresy.

7

'The time for silence is past'

Martin is of medium height, haggard and so emaciated with care and much study that one can almost count all the bones in his body. Nevertheless, he is still in the vigour of manhood. His voice rings clear and distinct . . . in his manner and social intercourse he is cultivated and affable, not at all gloomy and arrogant, always in a good humour, in company agreeable, cheerful and jocose. No matter how hard his opponent threatens him, he is always confident and joyous . . . Eck is a great, tall fellow, solidly and robustly built. The full genuinely German voice that resounds from his powerful chest sounds like that of a town crier or a tragic actor. But it is more harsh than distinct . . . His mouth and eyes, or rather his whole physiognomy, are such that one would sooner think him a butcher or a common soldier than a theologian. As far as his mind is concerned, he has a phenomenal memory. If he had an equally acute understanding, he would be the image of a perfect man. He lacks quickness of comprehension and acuteness of judgement, qualities without which all the other talents are vain . . . His gestures are almost theatrical, his actions overbearing; in short, the impression he gives is not at all that of a theologian. He is nothing more than an uncommonly bold, even shameless sophist.[1]

According to a member of Leipzig's humanist fraternity, these were the two personalities who squared up to each other in the debate of June–July 1519. The description is not wholly objective. Luther was the exciting, radical thinker everyone was eager to see, while Eck was a reactionary rhetorician whom no advanced thinker would regard as an original mind. Nevertheless, some interesting facts do emerge from the above passage. The image of Luther that has come down to us is that of a solidly built Saxon tending, certainly with increasing age, to fleshiness of features. The word picture of the haggard scholar acts as a corrective. It indicates just how much the repeated conflicts of 1518–19 were taking out of him. When he was not travelling or arguing with his adversaries he spent long hours writing detailed apologia of his own position, reading and making copious notes for the next stage of his ordeal. Nor should we suppose that he did not spend as many hours in agonised prayer. He was a man literally fighting for his life. He had taken on the might of Rome and some of his more unscrupulous foes would, he knew, use all the dirty tricks in their repertoire to bring him to the stake. They did so in the belief that they were pledged to defend the unity of the Church which was perpetually involved in wrenching out the weeds planted by the devil. Luther spoke often of his imminent martyrdom in words which sound melodramatic to our ear but were, in fact, well attuned to the reality of the situation as he saw it. He did not need Eck or anyone else to point out to him that, in his 'arrogance', he was setting his own theological understanding against the accumulated 'wisdom' of the Christian centuries. The conviction with which he spoke in debate or wrote in his tracts stemmed, not from empty-headed braggadocio, but from long and intense inner battles with doubt. How could he be right and the cohorts of Catholic scholars past and present be wrong? But, on the other hand, how could his understanding of the plain words of Scripture be at fault? His was the eternal dilemma of the honest dissident who sees clearly the perils of the path ahead but knows that he must tread it. Nor did he only foresee suffering for himself; in a letter of May 1519 he referred to the growing, sometimes violent, support he was receiving and prophesied the advent of 'massacres and war'.[2] Luther had as much interest in stability as all other men of good sense and his violently expressed abhorrence of violence in later years stemmed in part from his realisation that he had some responsibility for it.

He experienced that loneliness that comes to people who are surrounded by clamorous supporters with whom he could not fully identify because they did not really understand the issues at stake. He missed the wisdom of Staupitz who was still keeping his distance and he confided to his old mentor how alienated he felt from the world:

I beg you, pray for me, because I am quite confident that the Lord will constrain your heart to be disturbed on my behalf. I am a person who is both exposed to and enveloped by society [with its] drunkenness, sarcasm, carelessness, and other annoyances, not counting the problems which burden me on behalf of my office.[3]

The humanist writer who responded so favourably to Luther was typical of many who welcomed his radicalism in the early days of the Reformation. They were like the academics of ancient Athens (and, indeed, of all subsequent ages), of whom St Luke wrote that they 'liked to spend all their time telling and hearing the latest new thing'.[4] Intellectual novelty appealed to them and they recognised in Luther a scholar of truly formidable ability. Most of them would later desert the reformed cause when they realised that it demanded commitment to a new way of life and not just assent to a fashionable set of theological propositions. For the moment they supported him and scorned the 'sophist' Eck.

It was, however, Eck, the showy controversialist, adept at playing to the gallery and skilled in covering his lack of deep understanding under a smokescreen of well-remembered proof texts, who came to Leipzig with the support of the conservative majority. In reality, the members of the theological faculty were very unenthusiastic about the whole affair, which they regarded as both distasteful and likely to involve them in the political rivalry between their ruler, Duke George, and Elector Frederick. It was Duke George who overruled them, eager as he was to score points against his cousin and the upstart university of Wittenberg. The duke attended several of the sessions of the debate, gave Eck many signs of his favour and expected to enjoy the satisfaction of seeing the great heretic, Luther, mercilessly exposed once and for all under his jurisdiction.

Eck was, thus, already well ensconced among friends by 24 June, when the Wittenbergers entered the city, making a great show of their arrival. For this 'away fixture' Luther's younger supporters had decided to stage a striking demonstration of pride in their champion. Thus, the two wagons bearing the disputants and their immediate entourage were accompanied by a 'bodyguard' of two hundred halberd-waving, slogan-shouting students. The effect of their entrance was somewhat spoiled, however, when a wheel came off one of the wagons, and Karlstadt with all his books was pitched into the road.

The great debate for which intellectual Europe had waited so eagerly turned out to be a significant historical turning point but not in the way that any of its participants expected or intended. For them what they experienced was three weeks of ill-tempered and frustrating confrontation. Luther failed to gain that public hearing for his basic theological principles which he had been longing for. Eck failed to achieve the ringing, universal condemnation of the Wittenberg heresy for which he had been striving. Both men left Leipzig more than ever committed to their own convictions and determined to commend them to a Europe-wide audience. All this was immediately apparent to the two gladiators and their spectators. What would only become clear in the fullness of time was that the fiction of a united Christendom had been exposed and, once and for all, consigned to the dustbin of history. Leipzig was a thrusting hand on the tiller of international events. It set Europe and the world on a new course.

For the first few days the disputation was between Eck and Karlstadt, since it was Wittenberg's professor of theology who had issued the challenge. It was 4 July before the conflict everyone had come to see began. Majority opinion at this stage seems to have been that the Dominican was ahead on points. The great hall of Duke George's castle was packed with teachers and students eager to hear the Latin salvoes fired by the disputants but also by non-scholars who struggled with the ancient language and lacked the modern invention of simultaneous translation. At one point Luther broke off his discourse to explain in German the essential points of the debate. Each man had his own rostrum and mounted it in turn, though not without interruptions from the other side, supporting his arguments and accusations with remembered quotations (the competitors were not permitted to take books into the hall) from Scripture and the Fathers. The supporters cheered and jeered much as they would have done as spectators of a sporting contest. And between appearances rival gangs, like modern lager louts, assailed each other in the streets and, if Eck's complaints are to be believed, threatened the principals with violence. This confrontational entertainment was, to be sure, scarcely the most effective way of arriving at a greater understanding of divine truth but it was the convention and Luther and Eck both had to 'perform' in the ways expected of them. Beyond doubt, the Dominican was the more accomplished exponent of public rhetoric but his opponent was not without his own bag of tricks. When Eck ranted Luther sniffed ostentatiously at a posy of flowers. While Eck tried to stir his audience to righteous indignation, Luther tried to make them laugh. However, Luther was unable to prevent his enemy getting under his skin especially when he was accused of espousing the heresies of the condemned Bohemian, Jan Hus.

Debate ranged over several topics – purgatory, penance, indulgences – but the central issue and the one which engaged most time was that of authority. Eck had come to Leipzig to uphold the most extreme claims of the papacy and to denounce his adversary, along with all the wretched heretics of recent centuries who had sought to deprive the pope of his supremacy. Many scholars in the hall and in the wider world outside expected Luther to counter by claiming that final authority in matters of faith and practice lay with general councils of the Church and would have supported such a contention. Eck's masterstroke was that, very early in the debate, he goaded Luther into rejecting the infallibility not only of popes but also of councils. He denounced Luther as a follower of Wycliffe and Hus because those 'pestilential' heretics had also rejected Peter and his successors as leaders of the universal Church. The linking of the Wittenberger's name with that of Hus was a cunning tactic, not merely because Hus was a notorious schismatic, but because Bohemia and Saxony were bad neighbours. To the ancient rivalries between Czech and German speakers within Bohemia had been added the conflict between Catholics and Utraquists (members of the powerful Hussite church). Persecuted Catholics had fled across the frontier into the area around Dresden and Leipzig and there had even been border incursions. Eck was deliberately playing on popular prejudice. Luther hotly denied the taint of Hussitism. He was, in fact, little acquainted with the doctrines of the Bohemian heretic but he took advantage of a meal break to study his writings and the report of the Council of Constance which had condemned him. He discovered that Hus's judges had condemned, *en bloc*, thirty articles put forward by the accused without bothering to consider them individually. Luther's cursory examination led him to a momentous conclusion.

When he returned to the arena he was ready, as he thought, to blow away the fog his adversary had deliberately conjured up. He told the assembly, quite clearly, that he rejected the Hussite movement but that he also found fault with the proceedings at Constance in 1414–15. Some of Hus's beliefs he found 'most Christian and evangelical' and, as such, the Catholic Church was wrong to condemn them blindly. Luther clearly had in mind his own position and, possibly, that of other radical commentators like Reuchlin whose ideas were rejected on the basis of prejudice and without unbiased examination in the light of Scripture. And it was Scripture, Luther affirmed, which was *the* supreme authority for the Christian. He went on to be more specific. He asserted that popes can and have erred and that councils can and have erred. One of the mistakes Constance had made was in condemning

Hus's article which stated, 'It is not necessary for salvation to believe the Roman church to be superior to all others.' 'Now, I don't care whether it was Hus or Wycliffe who pointed this out', Luther said. The only thing that mattered was that it was true. For example, several of the great Greek Fathers of the Church had rejected the primacy of the Bishop of Rome. Were they to be dismissed as non-Christians? No. There was one universal Church and the pope was not its head. It followed that,

> It is not in the power of the Roman pontiff or of the Inquisition to construct new articles of faith. No believing Christian can be coerced beyond holy writ. By divine law we are forbidden to believe anything which is not established by divine Scripture or manifest revelation.[5]

This was the reasoned argument Luther delivered but it was not what some of the audience heard. It was enough for them that the speaker had expressed sympathy for the views of a justly condemned heretic. Duke George was heard to mutter a shocked oath and other spectators took their lead from him. It was at this point that Luther broke into German, determined that his hearers should not misunderstand his position.

> Councils have contradicted each other ... A simple layman armed with Scripture is to be believed above a pope or a council without it. As for the pope's decretal on indulgences, I say that neither the Church nor the pope can establish articles of faith. These must come from Scripture. For the sake of Scripture we should reject pope and councils.[6]

Thus did Luther set up the second twin pillar of the Reformation. Salvation was embraced *sola fidei* but also *sola scriptura*. This inevitably provoked the objection that neither Luther nor his followers were ever able adequately to counter: if a believer's understanding of the Bible is the only criterion of what is, for him, the truth, then farewell Christian unity and hail religious anarchy.

However, the claim that Luther violently rent the seamless robe of the Christian West by freeing the individual conscience is based on a fallacy. The traditional argument on which the massive edifice of medieval doctrine was built was that the Holy Spirit would lead his people into 'all truth'. Whether, in practice, this was guaranteed by papal diktat or conciliar debate was something that had been long argued about. By undermining both, Luther had brought down not the girding walls of Christendom, but, rather, the comforting conviction that such invisible walls existed. They did not.

> The more scholars understood the past, the more untenable became the contention that there had always been a consensus of the faithful about the most important doctrines and rituals. The Leipzig debate was in itself thumping proof that such a romantic notion could not be maintained except by those resolved to preserve it because they had a stake in it. That stake could be ambition, greed, status or reputation. It could also be the heart's desperate longing for certainty and meaning in this world and the next.[7]

The medieval Church had always been an association (sometimes a reluctant association) of regional and ideological entities upon which the Roman hierarchy had stamped itself. That hierarchy was a fallible human institution and the larger it grew, the more fallible it became. And the more fallible it became, the more it relied on sheer size and power to enforce its will. Luther did not undertake to dismantle the system under which his forebears had lived even though an increasing number of people were becoming disenchanted with it. What he did was to write the manual on how this might most effectively be achieved. He provided the spiritual and intellectual justification for actions which, without that justification, would have been nihilistic vandalism and anticlericalism.

But in the summer of 1519 this Reformation 'manual', comprising an astonishing number of works on a variety of theological topics, had not yet been completed, nor was Luther's intricate and comprehensive pattern of revolutionary ideals. He was still working his way towards that package of logical conclusions that would inevitably follow from his insistence on personal faith and the primacy of Scripture. The real importance of the Leipzig debate was that it prodded his enquiring yet reluctant mind more rapidly towards the as yet hazily observed destination.

The disputation itself ended both abruptly and inconclusively. On 15 July Duke George called a halt to the proceedings because he was expecting important guests and needed his castle back. The verdict was, as had been agreed, left to the universities of Erfurt and Paris and the rival camps would have to wait to see which of them received the endorsement of these august seats of learning. It goes without saying that the confrontation had generated more heat than light and that both Luther and Eck departed in anger, having conceded not the merest fragment of those convictions with which they had arrived. Both men believed their opponents had behaved shabbily and they had genuine cause for complaint about the robust displays of partisanship in which supporters engaged. Eck complained of drunken threats from the Wittenbergers. Luther claimed that Eck's people had been spreading scurrilous rumours, such as the story that he carried the devil about with him locked in a little silver box. Partisans were in no doubt that Luther was at war with or in league with the devil.

Luther and the devil – different perspectives. On the left, the devout monk receives a satanic challenge. On the right the reformer is depicted as in league with the devil.

Eck noisily trumpeted his 'triumph' over the heretics and was supported by his Leipzig friends. While the duke and the university received Luther and Karlstadt with conventional politeness, they feted his rival, with a sumptuous dinner and rich gifts and, after the Wittenberg party had left, Eck stayed on for eleven days enjoying the generous hospitality of his hosts. But when the posturing had ceased and the cheering had died down all that was left was a bad-tempered confrontation that had settled nothing. The dismal failure of Leipzig was underlined by the response of the adjudicating universities. The academic world was well accustomed to steering a tortuous path between the Scylla of papal obedience and the Charybdis of intellectual freedom and was not going to be man-oeuvred into doing the Inquisition's work for it. Not until the very end of the year did Erfurt deliver its formal response and it was not the one Duke George wanted to hear. The Saxon university declined to give a verdict. Its leaders found the whole affair embarrassing and distasteful. They did not, of course, say so but they managed to discover a technicality which, they claimed, rendered them unable to decide one way or the other. With Paris the duke faired even worse. The heads of the Sorbonne did nothing for almost two years. Finally, after much badgering from Leipzig, they appointed a committee which examined Luther's writings, adjudged some of them to be 'pernicious', but declined to give a verdict on the great debate. They informed Duke George that they would only undertake that disagreeable and time-consuming task for a swingeing fee. The duke was by now becoming disenchanted with theologians who could not agree among themselves. Some pestered secular authorities to pluck their chestnuts from the fire for them while others lampooned rulers as persecutors and puppets of Rome. When pressed to define clearly what was and what was not heresy – which was, presumably, part of their job – they shrank from the responsibility. George never ceased to be an opponent of Luther and not until after his death (1539) were Lutherans permitted freedom of worship in Albertine Saxony but Eck and his supporters could no longer count on the duke's unqualified patronage.

The Leipzig disputation was a *cause célèbre* and, as with many such, its importance lay, not in itself, but in its results. Like Dr Johnson, most people find delight in 'the conflict of opinions and sentiments' and the widely publicised arguments in Duke George's Pleissenburg reached a large, fascinated audience. It was not just scholars who weighed up the effects of verbal thrust and parry. By 1519 Europe was awash with amateur theologians who were reading their Bibles, writing popular pamphlets and discussing the issues of papal authority and clerical abuse in taverns and marketplaces from Brest to Budapest. People took sides in what was emerging as the most important issue of the day. It has become such a commonplace to refer to the Reformation as the 'revolt of the laity' that we are in danger of losing the sense of excitement that gripped so many ordinary folk in these tumultuous years. For the first time they were able to express openly their indignation, their anxiety and their doubts about the way the Church was run. Now it was the clergy who were on the defensive. They could no longer silence the honest questions and sincere misgivings of their flock with threats of ecclesiastical or divine sanctions and they lacked a coherent and exciting alternative with which to counter the evangelical message. For many, doubtless the majority, what was happening was bewildering but for others, especially the better educated, the new freedom was intoxicating.

So great was the sense of release that it would, in itself, create one of the Reformation's biggest problems. Over-zealous followers, as Luther discovered within a very few years, do not make the most reliable foot soldiers but, for the moment, he was vastly encouraged by the messages of support he received from all sorts and conditions of men. People flocked to out-of-the-way Wittenberg. The university was full to overflowing. Visitors, rather like pilgrims, made the journey to Luther's cell to seek his advice or discuss the progress of change in their own churches. The imperial postal system regularly delivered letters by the score. Writing to friends, Luther complained that he was in such great demand that he had little time for his own work. When we consider his phenomenal output during the months after the disputation (see below) we must conclude that either he was exaggerating or that his capacity for dealing with a wide range of issues and people at the same time was of an almost superhuman order.

The whirling snowstorm of pamphlets and treatises which swept across Europe in the next few months was not only generated by Luther and Eck. Apologists from both camps rushed to take part in the debate and the very intensity of the controversy attracted intellectual supporters to the Wittenberger's cause. The humanist camp identified him as a champion against that very obscurantism and stubborn adherence to discredited dogmas that they, too, loathed. The Leipzig disputants were not arguing in a vacuum over the issue of papal authority. It was one of the leading subjects of scholarly debate at this time. Lorenzo Valla's *Declamatio*, in which he had exposed the fraudulent *Donation of Constantine*, had been written as long ago as 1440 but had only recently appeared in printed form (Luther had not read it before his confrontation with Eck). The intellectual elite were scandalised by the traditionalists' dependence on assertion and unwillingness to submit their claims to objective scrutiny in the light of new knowledge. To them Eck seemed the very worst kind of arrogant, intolerant, closed-minded adversary and they readily took their stand behind Luther. Willibald Pirckheimer satirised the Dominican controversialist in a lampoon entitled *The Purified Eck*, in which he portrayed Eck as submitting to complex surgical treatment for the removal of his errors and vices. From Basel the gentle Oecolampadius entered the fray with a more reasoned refutation. The great Erasmus punned that the pope's champion had omitted the first letter from his name, for he was really a 'jeck', a fool.

On a practical level what mattered most to Saxony's great celebrity was the steadfast backing of the elector. Frederick had returned from the imperial diet at Frankfurt while the Leipzig debate was still in progress. His behaviour and demeanour at this gathering, which was a turning point in his life, tells us much about the stature of the man. He and the other six electors had come to cast their votes for a new emperor. Inevitably, they were under enormous pressure. They were the recipients of bribes, cajolery and impassioned special pleading. In all this Frederick was the principal target. The German princes looked to him as their natural leader. He had considerable influence on his colleagues. The pope had named him as his preferred candidate. Charles of the house of Habsburg and Francis, King of France, were the main contenders but in the event of the vote being split Frederick would almost certainly have emerged as the obvious compromise choice. The principal opposition to Frederick the Wise becoming emperor came from Frederick the Wise. He had no ambition to don the purple. As in all other matters he quietly kept his own counsel, resolved upon his course of action and, having done so, was not to be deflected from it. He actually emerged as leader after the first ballot but at that point he refused the honour and, in the second round, he gave his vote to Charles. Waverers on the electoral council followed his lead and the Habsburg was duly elected. Frederick showed the same consistency of purpose in his dealings with Luther. The papal curia placed increasing pressure on him to give his protégé up but, although he never wavered in his own orthodox faith and although Luther frequently tried his patience, Frederick stuck by his man.

Someone equally unflinching of purpose was Johann Eck. He was, by now, utterly obsessed with extirpating the Lutheran heresy and devoted all his time and energies to securing Brother Martin's excommunication. It is just conceivable that, even at this late stage, the 'Luther affair' might have dissipated like a passing storm had Eck been prepared to loosen his terrier-like grip. Friends urged Luther to make the kind of submission to Rome that would enable the curia to find a face-saving formula in order to end what was still regarded on the far side of the Alps as an annoying demonstration of German independence. For his part, Luther still stated his willingness to abandon his radical teachings – provided, of course, that they could be demonstrated to be against 'Scripture and reason'. There were also eirenic voices in the papal camp. Several orthodox leaders were embarrassed by their unattractive *condottiere*, Johann Eck. Karl Militz had not abandoned his fruitless campaign to end the conflict by diplomatic means and part of his strategy was now to make Eck a scapegoat who could be jettisoned in the interests of a negotiated peace. This tactic had been partially successful in the case of Tetzel. That unhappy man had actually died in Leipzig, depressed and abandoned by most of his erstwhile friends, soon after the disputation. His last contact with Luther was a note from his old adversary which he received on his deathbed, in which the reformer absolved him of blame for the escalating crisis. The indulgence hawker, Luther suggested, had been little more than a stalking horse for men with a more sinister agenda. There were, perhaps, few protagonists who, in such circumstances, would have been so generous and this reminds us that there was much more to Martin Luther than the pugilistic combatant with the untamed pen. Several contemporaries recorded his kindliness, good humour and affability and we know from the numerous causes that he championed that there was nothing feigned about his concern for those suffering at the hands of arrogant clergy or troubled in spirit by oppressive doctrines. For example, in December we find him appealing to the elector on behalf of the people of Kemberg, 'sucked dry' by 'sacrilegious taxes and ungodly plunderings', imposed for the support of the priesthood and religious fraternities.[8] Though the ill-tempered conflict which rumbled on through 1519 and 1520 took up an enormous amount of time and effort, it did not deflect the monk, priest and teacher from his pastoral responsibilities.

Eck knew full well that he had enemies within the orthodox intellectual establishment and it was partly out of a need to watch his own back that he stayed vigorously on the offensive. Through the Dominican grapevine he persuaded the theology faculties of Louvain and Cologne to condemn Luther's writings. He wrote his own report on the Leipzig disputation and made sure that it was well circulated. He followed up the face-to-face debate with derogatory pamphlets and encouraged friends in Leipzig and elsewhere to enter the fray with diatribes which Luther was obliged to spend time answering. He did so with his customary mix of earnestness, sarcasm and vulgar abuse. These exchanges were so much wasted ink and paper. Since the argument took the form, not of the trading of logical point and counterpoint, but of the confrontation of rival, supposedly divine, revelations, neither side could or would yield on the tiniest point. Final victory for Eck could only come as a result of brute force and that could only be authorised in Rome.

It was in the spring of 1520 that Eck arrived in the papal HQ and he immediately made an impact on the curial campaign. Up to this point response in Rome to the Saxon heretic had been diverse and desultory.

Leo X's primary concern had always been to extend papal (and, more specifically, Medicean) power in Italy. He had expended considerable effort in trying to prevent the election of Charles V but now that that was a *fait accompli* he concentrated his diplomacy on exercising as much influence as possible over the young emperor. Another challenge presented itself on the eastern frontier of Christendom where a twenty-six-year-old sultan had just inherited the Ottoman throne. His intentions were, for the moment, unknown but would not remain so for long. In 1521 he began that series of campaigns which would see Muslim forces march up to the gates of Vienna and establish bridgeheads in the western Mediterranean. History would come to know the new ruler in Constantinople as Suleiman the Magnificent. At home Leo was preoccupied with the building of St Peter's and the maintenance of a luxurious and culturally scintillating court. Thus, all in all, affairs among the 'barbarian' Germans did not figure largely in his consciousness. This, in effect, made it easier for Eck and the Dominicans to pursue their agenda.

Cajetan had been trying to impress on the ruling elite in Rome the inherent danger of the Lutheran revolution. Having travelled among the courts, towns and intellectual centres of Germany he knew how fertile was the seedbed upon which the new religious ideas were being scattered. But Cajetan was not greatly in favour with the Medicean elite and could be easily shouldered aside by more determined intriguers. Eck's reports delivered much the same message but they carried more weight because they were couched in terms of confident self-congratulation. Whereas Cajetan's mission had manifestly failed, Eck boasted of having trounced Luther in debate. The heretics, he claimed, were on the run and a vigorous follow-up on his triumph would put a stop to this pestilential movement once and for all. This was an attractive proposal to those who did not understand the situation in Germany and were eager for a quick and easy solution to the problem. Prior to Eck's arrival Cajetan and a group of Roman theologians had been studying the challenging ideas coming off the Wittenberg presses. They proposed a well-considered response that would distinguish between what was 'erroneous' and what was 'heretical'. They understood well the danger of making a martyr of Brother Martin or of further antagonising the international intelligentsia by issuing a blanket condemnation of his views. The Dominican lobby dismissed such caution as weakness and it was their insistence on an uncompromising demand for total recantation which carried the day.

Eck was given the chairmanship of a small committee charged with drafting a formal condemnation. By the beginning of May a papal bull was ready in draft and sent to Leo, who was hunting boar on his estate at Magliana. Doubtless it was the pope's favourite pastime that suggested the extravagant imagery with which the document opened:

> Arise, O Lord, and judge your cause. A wild boar has invaded your vineyard. Arise, O Peter, and consider the cause of the Holy Roman Church, the mother of all churches, consecrated by your blood. Arise, O Paul, who by your teaching and death have and do still illumine the Church. Arise, all you saints, and the whole universal Church, whose interpretation of Scripture has been assailed . . .

The bull itemised forty-one alleged heresies all of which, it declared, merited punishment. Having received Leo's approval, it was discussed by the sacred college of cardinals, who approved it *nem con*. They allowed Luther sixty days to submit and make a complete recantation. The chancellery engrossed the bull, dated it 17 July 1520, and had it printed in formidably impressive script to which the pope's lead seal (*bulla*) was affixed. Thus the most famous papal anathema of all time, *Exsurge domine*, fumbled its way into existence. It remained only to enforce it.

Easier said than done. When the bull was presented to Frederick, with renewed entreaty to hand over the miscreant monk, he ignored it. When Eck, as papal agent, embarked on his gleeful mission to have the bull proclaimed in the leading towns and cities of Germany he met, almost everywhere, sullen resistance. Church and university authorities were embarrassed and, in several cases, angry at being forced to join one or other of the rival camps when all they wanted was to stay out of the unseemly contest. The vicar general of the Bishop of Bamberg doubtless spoke for many when he expressed the hope that someone would drown 'that rascal Eck'. In several places where the bull was posted it was torn down or defaced. At Erfurt students threw copies into the river. The Archbishop of Mainz called a public meeting to denounce the heretic only to find the mood of the crowd so hostile that he had to flee in unseemly disarray. Even in Leipzig, where Eck might have expected a favourable reception, the university refused to publish the pope's denunciation. Not only that, he was forced to take shelter from student riots in the Dominican convent. He only had himself to blame. In a mood of spite he had added

Bulla contra errores
Martini Lutheri
et sequacium.

The papal bull, *Exsurge Domine*, issued against Luther in 1520

to the list of men being cited to face papal justice several of his own enemies, including such eminent humanist scholars as Pirckheimer. It thus seemed to the academic community at large that this typical Dominican was the sworn enemy of intellectual freedom and open debate. In his persecuting zeal he had squandered much of what little goodwill he still enjoyed among Europe's intelligentsia. At Wittenberg, the focal point of papal fury, the bull received its ultimate insult. Luther answered anathema with anathema. 'It is impossible for those to be saved who promote this bull or do not reject it', he wrote to Spalatin.[9] And he answered burning with burning. In some towns Leo's envoys had succeeded in organising bonfires of Luther's books. In December he responded by building a pyre of scholastic works and, as the flames rose higher, he flung *Exsurge domine* into them. The battle was literally heating up.

What really mattered during these months, what was truly pregnant with long-lasting consequences, was not the energetic campaigning of Eck, nor the cumbersome working of the curial machine, nor even the diplomatic stonewalling of Elector Frederick. It was the emergence of Martin Luther as the leading publicist of the age with a manifesto of breathtaking scope and audacity to set before the German people. The disputation had served as a catalyst to his honest, enquiring mind. As his taunting foe pushed him towards the abyss of heinous heresy Luther did not squirm away from the edge. He recognised with ever greater clarity that there was something fundamentally wicked about a monolithic Church which had driven many struggling souls to this very precipice. He went away from Leipzig to seek out the works of Hus and, having read them, confided to his confidants, 'We've been heretics all along without knowing it.' He found liberation in the realisation that down the centuries there had been Christians committed, as he was, to evangelical truth, and who, like him, had been forced to resist oppressive ecclesiastical institutions. To the taunt, 'Are you alone right and the Church wrong' he could now reply, 'I am not alone; many down the Christian centuries have thought as I think and many today are ready to stand at my side.' Thus emboldened, Luther explored the numerous implications of his brightening vision. In a truly staggering outpouring of books, pamphlets and printed sermons he addressed himself to a wide range of theological and devotional issues.

He resented having to defend himself against the ceaseless and repetitive attacks of his enemies. It was a distraction from his chief responsibility to teach and preach the true Gospel, and his irritation goes a long way towards explaining the impatient, coarse language in which some of his controversialist tracts were couched. It also partly explains why he threw himself into a positive frenzy of literary activity. Luther fully believed that his life expectancy was short. One way or another, his foes would achieve his destruction. If they could not have him sent to the stake they would resort to hired assassins. Rumours continued to abound – many of them fantastic. There existed, it was confidently asserted, a subtle doctor who had perfected a potion that would render him invisible. This he intended to use in order to get close to the arch-heretic and strike him down. So seriously were threats and suspicions taken that some of Luther's wealthier pupils and disciples put their castles at his disposal and urged him to take refuge. The reformer's standard response to such well-meaning offers was to assure his friends that he would cheerfully embrace martyrdom if called upon to do so. Indeed, it is scarcely possible to read some of his reflections on death without concluding that he had a morbid obsession with the subject. It was fear of death that had initially impelled him on his spiritual journey and it was the eradication of that fear that he had discovered to be one of the chief benefits of faith. The Christian should be able to exult with St Paul, 'O death where is thy sting; O grave where is thy victory?'[10] Yet Luther constantly struggled to retain his hold on the certainty of triumph and glory beyond the curtain of this world's stage. He could never totally free himself of this anxiety and if he returns over and again to the subject in his writings it is, as with every conscientious preacher, because he is preaching as much to himself as to others. The certain prospect of a martyr's death would have freed him from the last, grasping talons of doubt, for to share the final earthly sufferings of Christ would be, incontrovertibly, to share also his resurrection. In the meantime, Luther knew that he had to redeem every passing minute by broadcasting the seeds of Gospel truth as widely as possible.

Between 1519 and 1521 he published, sometimes in Latin and sometimes in German, treatises on: the art of dying, holy communion, baptism, the Lord's Prayer (and also a version of this for children), the Psalms, the Epistle to the Galatians, the Ten Commandments, penance, marriage, usury, the sufferings of Christ, confession and *Fourteen Consolers for the Troubled and Burdened* (a devotional tract written for the Elector Frederick when he was ill). These works fed the voracious presses of Wittenberg, Nuremberg, Augsburg, Strasbourg, Leipzig and Basel. Neither the print-masters nor the public could get enough of them and whatever Luther published ran inevitably to several editions. It was not just the controversy surrounding Luther that made his works so popular. If their appeal had simply been to the curious and the sensation-seeking they would have been no more than a nine-day's wonder. It was because the writer possessed passion and had developed a simple, direct and lively style that they spoke to so many people. As Robert Fife has pointed out, Luther had escaped from the dry-as-dust language of the academic theologian and embraced that of ordinary people:

Whether in Latin or German, whether addressed primarily to theologian or to simple believer, all these treatises ring with the same vivid, personal tone . . . but their message does not draw on historical or theological speculations. It echoes his experience as teacher and confessor in contact with men and women perplexed and terrified in a maze of popular usages and Church teachings and practices. To souls like these he speaks with an intimate understanding of their problems.[11]

A by-product of Luther's amazing energy and enterprise was that it kept his name before the public. Today 'celebrities' rely totally on their PR agents to sustain their fame. Media exposure is their oxygen; without it their reputation suffocates and they sink back into the dust of ordinary humanity. In the sixteenth century the printed word was the only way of keeping alive a Europe-wide reputation. Those who read Luther's works (or, in an increasing number of cases, had them read to them) were eager for more and printers responded to the demand. Thus the relentless buzzing of Eck and the swarm of Catholic protagonists had the effect of driving Luther on to develop his theology in ways that, without such agitation, he would not have done. Through the pages of the New Testament he made new, overwhelming, liberating discoveries. He felt like 'some watcher of the skies when a new planet swims into his ken'. He could not keep silent about these revelations. As his convictions matured, he noised them abroad with a skill which hidebound defenders of the status quo stood absolutely no chance of matching. For the supreme tragedy for the traditionalist cause was that it lacked a charismatic champion who could hold a candle to the reformer in intellectual brilliance and popular appeal. All Rome could produce was 'professional theologians concerned to write point-by-point refutations of Luther rather than to speak about religion to the common people or even to clothe the old Church in new and shining garments'.[12] Luther was the first publicist to exploit to the full the possibilities of the new communications technology and he had no serious rivals. The frustrated Church authorities hit back with negative weapons. Often it was ordinary people who felt the brunt of their attack. When they went to confession they were quizzed as to whether they had bought or read any of Luther's writings. If their answers were not satisfactory, absolution was withheld.

Of all the works that Luther wrote during this crucial period in his theological development two thrust their snow-capped peaks high above the rest of the range. The first was *To the Christian Nobility of the German Nation Concerning the Reform of the Christian Estate*, a breathtakingly bold theological essay with political implications which took the age-old discussion of the relationship between temporal and spiritual authority to altogether new heights. Medieval theory had asserted the existence of two distinct powers, temporal and spiritual, and given supremacy to the latter. Luther reversed this juxtaposition. For some time disciples who belonged to the ruling or administrative classes had been begging him for a statement of what bearing his new insights had on the theory and practice of power within states. What said Scripture on such issues as the right of the pope to levy taxes, the appointment of bishops, the status of clergy under civil law and the claims of Rome to worldly *imperium*? Such controversial questions, of course, touched the raw nerve of German nationalism and anti-Italian prejudice but they were also in line with current humanist debate. Machiavelli wrote his *Discorsi* and *Il Principe* in 1513, proposing draconian, ruthlessly pragmatic solutions to the confused state of Italian politics. In 1510, Edmund Dudley, a prisoner in the Tower of London, offered advice to the young Henry VIII in his *Tree of Commonwealth*, and drew attention to clerical abuses which it was the king's responsibility to eradicate. Eight years later, the French ex-minister, Claude de Seyssel, in *Le Grant Monarchie de France* upheld the right and responsibility of kings to control the lives of *all* their subjects, clerical and lay. And, in 1516, the most original of all contemporary treatises had appeared – Thomas More's *Utopia*, a wistful dissertation upon the impossibility of achieving a constitution which could perfectly balance the rights of rulers and ruled. Political theory was, thus, very firmly on the Renaissance agenda and would remain so for several decades. It was against this background that Luther offered his advice to the princes and nobles of 'the German nation', a title in itself designed to arouse patriotism among and underscore the distinct identity of those to whom the work was addressed.

'The time for silence is past,' the writer confidently begins, 'and the time to speak has come.' It may be that the appropriate moment to which he refers is the accession of a new emperor and certainly he laments in his opening paragraphs those of Charles' predecessors who have been 'shamefully oppressed and trodden underfoot by the popes'.[13] Later in the text he expands on this with a long historical exposition describing how successive popes bestowed the Holy Roman Empire on German leaders but retained ultimate authority in their own hands.

> We carry the title of empire, but it is the pope who has our wealth, honour, body, life, soul, and all that we possess. This is how they deceive the Germans and cheat us with tricks. What the popes have gladly sought was to be emperors, and when they could not achieve this, they at least succeeded in setting themselves over the emperors.[14]

Luther makes it very clear from the outset that the diabolical enemy which seeks to undermine all good order in the kingdoms of this world and which must now be repulsed in the name and power of a holy God is Rome. His theological argument takes as its starting point the priesthood of all believers. All Christians are called 'priests' in the Bible[15] and a man who has received episcopal consecration is not thereby transformed into a different kind of human being. What is clear from this is that Luther was not anticlerical. He never aligned himself with the widespread lay prejudice and anger directed at the clergy *per se*. What he was was antisacerdotal, i.e. opposed to any elevation of ordained Christians above their brethren by means of the supposed infusion of indelible character. Luther esteemed the clergy but regarded them essentially as functionaries, doing a job on behalf of the whole body of believers. There was, therefore, no difference in kind between a priest, a king or, for that matter, a cobbler. All were distinguished only by the work they did and the contribution they made to society.

> Since those who exercise secular authority have been baptised with the same baptism, and have the same faith and the same gospel as the rest of us, we must admit that they are priests and bishops . . . although, of course, it is not seemly that just anybody should exercise such office.[16]

The prince, says Luther, has his own function, clearly defined by Scripture. He is 'ordained of God to punish the wicked and protect the good'.[17] His authority must extend over all in his territory, priests and laymen alike. There cannot be one law for the clergy and another law for everyone else. At a stroke Luther had pulled down the high wall of legal privileges erected over the centuries by canon law. As he pointedly observed, 'If a priest is murdered the whole country is placed under interdict. Why not when a peasant is murdered?'[18]

Next he makes a frontal assault on the claim that only the Church – i.e. the priesthood – is the repository of divine truth, that the pope alone can correctly interpret Scripture. If that is the case, he argues, why bother with the Bible at all? 'Let us burn the Scripture and be satisfied with the unlearned gentlemen at Rome who possess the Holy Spirit!'[19] No, all are priests and, therefore, all have the right to read and interpret the Bible. Luther is quite unfazed by the logical conclusion of this argument – that it is a recipe for hermeneutical anarchy. It is fundamental to his whole stance on authority that it is not just scholars and theologians who are equipped to understand the word of God. That qualification would be little better than restricting access to Scripture to the pope and his minions. By reversing the relative positions of the papacy and holy writ and by insisting on the priesthood of all believers it necessarily followed that all and any Christians might judge the words and actions of the ecclesiastical hierarchy by the touchstone of Scripture. Luther himself had done this. He had tested the behaviour of the current papal regime and found it wanting. It was abundantly clear to him, as to most serious observers, that the Church stood in urgent need of reform, from the top down. It remained only to identify the offences that needed to be eradicated and decide who was to tackle them. This was where the German Christian nobility came in.

The greater part of the tract was given over to cataloguing the most glaring vices of the clergy. First to fall before Luther's flail was the osten-tatious luxury of the papal court and the cardinalate. When he came to describing how these princes of the Church funded their lifestyle he was on popular ground:

> Italy and Germany have many rich monasteries, foundations, benefices and livings. No better way has been discovered of bringing all these to Rome than by creating cardinals and giving them bishoprics, monas-teries and prelacies for their own use and so overthrowing the worship of God. You can see that Italy is now almost a wilderness: monas-teries in ruins, bishoprics despoiled, the prelacies and the revenues of all the churches drawn to Rome, cities decayed, land and people ruined because services are no longer held and the word of God is not preached. And why? Because the cardinals must have the income! No Turk could have devastated Italy and suppressed the worship of God so effectively. Now that Italy is sucked dry, the Romanists are coming into Germany . . . The 'drunken Germans' are not supposed to understand what the Romanists are up to until there is not a bishopric, a monastery, a living, a benefice, not a red cent left.[20]

The answer Luther proposed was to reduce the number of cardinals and to insist that the pope paid for them himself. He drew attention to what the German diet had already identified as a blatant abuse: the collection of papal taxes ostensibly to pay for the war against the Turk, which ended up swelling the papal coffers. These and other imposts should henceforth be rejected. For page after page the writer vented his spleen in detailed invective on the various ways in which the 'Roman Avarice' bled money from the nobles and their subjects. It is time, he says, for the leaders of Germany to take decisive action. They must call a halt to all these abuses.

And when a lackey comes along from Rome, he should be given a
strict order to keep out, to jump into the Rhine or the nearest river,
and give the Romish ban with all its seals and letters a nice cool dip.
If this happened they would sit up and take notice in Rome.[21]

In his clear distinction between spiritual and temporal authority Luther
rejected papal claims, frequently repeated since the coronation of
Charlemagne in 800, to suzerainty over the emperor. On the contrary, the
pope, no less than other clergy, was subject to civil law in all temporal
cases. Church courts only had competence to decide spiritual issues and,
even then, cases should be decided within the territory where the alleged
offences occurred and not cited to Rome. Papal legates should, henceforth,
be excluded from German territory. Luther was scathing about pilgrimages
which he wished to see abolished altogether and, similarly, the numerous
saints' days were to be done away with. This was another topic which
could be expected to play well with Luther's designated audience who were
frequently inconvenienced when servants or tenants absented themselves
for 'holy' observances. He was on home ground when he catalogued the
abuses of the monastic and mendicant orders and called for the help of
territorial magnates in regulating them.

When he came to the reorganisation of the secular clergy Luther was
much more revolutionary. He envisaged a congregational or, at least, a
local pattern of ministry:

> . . . it should be the custom for every town to choose from among
> the congregation a learned and pious citizen, entrust to him the office
> of the ministry, and support him at the expense of the congregation.[22]

Luther was in no doubt that control of church property lay in the hands
of landlords as did the right to appoint godly men as beneficed priests.
Such officials should not be required to be celibate. Luther's passionate
and lengthy disquisition on this subject has sometimes been taken as
evidence that he was tormented by sexual temptation but he was doing
no more than pointing out the scandal caused by the numerous, well-
publicised cases of clergy violating their vows to the vexation of their own
consciences and the ill-repute of the Church. Luther insisted that marriage
was an honourable estate from which clergy should not be excluded. Then,
before turning to the reformation he considered necessary in the temporal
life of the German states, he exhorted the nobles to make peace with the

Bohemians by acknowledging that their great hero, Hus, was unlawfully done to death and by submitting Utraquist beliefs to objective theological scrutiny.

Luther's criticisms of the civil life of Germany were brief and mild by contrast with his lengthy vituperation of the papacy. He was concerned at the moral state of the nation and he itemised the extravagance of noble courts – gluttony, prostitution and the lack of wholesome education for the young. It was time, he urged, for the ruling classes to take a firm hold on every aspect of government, admitting no interference from ecclesiastical bodies. They alone possessed the divine mandate and the power to carry out the work of reformation. Luther was the apostle of the nation state and may be said to have provided kings and princes with the justification they needed for assuming absolute power. But he was far from being alone. As the Roman church imploded and secular authorities took to themselves control of the external trappings of religious life (and the garnered wealth of abbeys and dioceses) most Renaissance thinkers supported (to a greater or lesser extent) this shift in the balance of power. It would be Calvin and the next generation of reformers who saw the dangers of unbridled state control and developed polities closer to the medieval model.

Luther dashed off this one-hundred-page vernacular exhortation to the German leadership in less than six weeks during May and June 1520. The next grenade lobbed into the Catholic citadel was in Latin and only half the length but it was equally destructive. In *Martin Luther's First Trumpet Blast Against the Babylonian Captivity of the Church*, published in October, the author sought to blow apart the traditional concept of sacerdotal priesthood. He chose to do so by enunciating a revolutionary sacramental theology. His argument took its inspiration from the exile of God's Old Testament people who were carried off into slave labour in Babylon in the sixth century BC. 'So fares today's Church,' Luther declares and the modern Nebuchadnezzar is the papacy. But there was more to the title than an arcane reference to the history of ancient Israel. 'Babylon' in the imagery of the book of Revelation and in all subsequent Christian polemic stood for the abode of Antichrist, the city of unspeakable whoredoms whose streets ran red with the blood of slaughtered saints. Rome through its priestly minions had enslaved God's people. They were held in thrall from cradle to grave by means of the seven so-called sacraments, those exclusive channels of grace by which alone struggling mortals could lay hold on heaven. It was these ministrations which both set the priesthood apart from the laity and gave them power over the laity. The writer set about removing the very *raison d'être* of that priesthood.

According to Luther's understanding of Scripture there were only three sacraments, not the traditional seven, and the three that remained were distorted by bad theology aimed at enhancing the prestige of the officiant and not at helping the recipient. He argued that only those rites and ceremonies were obligatory to Christians which were 'dominical', i.e. instituted by Christ for the purpose of deepening the relationship between the believer and God. Confirmation, ordination, marriage and extreme unction did not fall into this category. That left baptism, holy communion and penance (Luther later demoted penance from a sacrament to a valuable, though not obligatory, devotional exercise).

Having demonstrated how clergy abused the non-sacraments, Luther went for the Catholic jugular – the mass. The Lord's Supper had been ordained as a mystery in which Christ met *all* believers but the clergy had taken sole possession of it. They performed the mass whether there were lay people present or not. They denied the chalice to the laity. They claimed what was little better than a 'magical' power in 'making God' at the altar. They demanded that congregations believed the Aristotelian nonsense of transubstantiation. And, worst of all, they claimed to be re-enacting the sacrifice of Calvary at every celebration.

The orthodox doctrine of the mass had been defined three hundred years earlier at the fourth Lateran Council (1215). It having been long accepted by the medieval believer, set about as he was by all kinds of magic, that priests at the altar really did have the power to change bread and wine into flesh and blood by muttering the incantation *hoc est corpus meum*, some philosophical explanation had to be found to cover the obvious fact that no change was actually discernible in the elements. The answer seemed to be supplied by the Aristotelian distinction between the outward appearance of things (accidents) and their essence (substance). Thus, for example, we recognise a loaf of bread by its size, shape, texture, taste and smell but all these things do not constitute what is unique to bread – its 'breadness'. Theologians latched onto this concept and the Church's official teaching, as eventually honed by Thomas Aquinas, was that consecration did not simply set apart the elements for holy use but actually *changed* their substance without affecting their accidents. What still looked like bread was really flesh. To the rational mind this 'explanation' always presented problems but it was excruciatingly difficult to find an alternative which did not debase the sacrament. John Wycliffe, for example, had firmly rejected transubstantiation but until the end of his days he wrestled with the problem of how Christ was actually present in the Lord's Supper. For this was the fundamental 'given' from which the materialist and literalist medieval mindset could not escape. If Christ had said 'This is my body; this is my blood' then it was so.

Luther, too, was caught in this trap. The eternal Christ had, once, submitted to incarnation as a mortal human being, offering himself for the sins of the world. At the final judgement he would come in all his glorious majesty. In the meantime he came to his people through the word written and through the sacrament of the altar. This was a second incarnation, a daily renewed 'enfleshing'. Luther could not go the 'whole hog', as later reformers would, and interpret the communion service as an act of memorial featuring 'symbolic' bread and wine. He became just as angry with those who denied the real presence as he did with those who continued to cling to the absurdity of transubstantiation. Wherein, then, lay his unique protest about the mass and why was it so revolutionary?

He addressed himself to four fundamental aspects of contemporary sacramental theology. The first, as we have seen, was Aristotelian logic. This he regarded as having no place in Christian apologetic. The second was the centrality to his theology of saving faith. Just as a man or woman was made righteous by *faith*, so they received the gift of Christ in the sacrament by *faith*. It mattered not *how* the Saviour came in bread and wine. All the recipient had to do was believe that this was so and receive the miracle humbly, wonderingly and thankfully. Nor should the parishioner coming to the Lord's table think that he was performing a meritorious act which would win him divine favour. Luther had long since rejected 'works righteousness'. Now, if the holy transaction depended for its completion on the faith of the recipient, it had nothing whatsoever to do with the miracle-working power of the priest. Christ was not present in the mass by permission of the celebrant, but by his own gracious will. So, thirdly, Luther cut away the ground upon which sacerdotalism rested. The final abomination which Luther vehemently attacked was the idea of the mass as a repeated sacrifice. The priest had no power or authority to offer Christ to the Father on behalf of himself or other people, living or dead. To do so would suggest that the Saviour's death at Calvary was somehow inadequate.

Luther did not minimise the significance of the mass or seek to remove it from its central place in the life of the Church. Quite the contrary. The regular celebration was vital to his own life as a priest and when he presided at the altar he did all in his power to emphasise its dynamic power to underpin faith. He never forgot those two contrasting incidents from his early monastic years: the terror that overwhelmed him at his first mass as celebrant and the offhand, irreverent manner in which he had seen clergy in Rome gabble through the office. He wanted holy communion to be just that – holy and reverently observed and a means of vital communion between the believer and his Lord. He considered it appropriate that the laity should receive both bread and wine, though he did not make an issue of it (probably because he wanted to avoid being too closely associated with the Utraquists).

Devastating as all this was to the traditional life of the Church, Luther was no wild boar, rooting about in the vineyard and indiscriminately tearing up old beliefs and practices. He simply applied the solvents of *sola fidei* and *sola scriptura* to everything. What dissolved he cast aside but those conventional beliefs which passed the test were allowed to remain. That was why he was cautious about penance. From his monastic experience he knew the value of self-examination and confession. What he objected to was the use clergy made of the rite to assert and maintain their power over the laity and the encouragement the penitential system gave to such money-catching ploys as the sale of indulgences. In Luther's revised understanding of penance priests were not obligatory. Confession could as readily be made to a Christian brother or sister. The sacrament about which Luther had least to say was baptism. In the light of later disputes within the Protestant camp this may seem rather surprising. Since a man was only saved by faith it was logical, as Anabaptists later insisted, that baptism should follow conversion and infant baptism should be outlawed. Luther's argument was that baptism did not create or convey faith; it was only a sign of faith. The sincerity of a person's trust in God – whether baptised or unbaptised – was known only to God. The Church could not deny this sacrament to those who sought it. And, in an age of high infant mortality, it was both charitable and proper to bring children into the household of faith where they could, with sound, biblical instruction, be led to that commitment the sign of which they had already received.

When Erasmus read the *Babylonian Captivity* he was shocked and saddened. 'The breach is irreparable,' he sighed. Up to this point the doyen of the New Learning had applauded Luther's bold challenge to outmoded and obscurantist scholasticism, although the German's pugilistic manner had not been to his refined taste. But Erasmus saw clearly that Luther had now both burned his bridges and started a forest fire within Christendom. 'I knew there could only be one outcome,' he wrote to Spalatin, 'when I saw Luther taking on so many things at once, and with such ferocity. It was better to put up with what was wrong than try to mend it so clumsily.'[23] The ageing humanist was concerned for the wellbeing of Christendom but he was also worried about his own reputation. He felt himself caught in the middle in the battle raging in the intellectual world. Both eager radicals and outraged reactionaries called upon him to declare himself, something he was very unwilling to do. Erasmus genuinely believed that change could be brought about by gentlemanly debate and that Luther's bull-in-a-china-shop attitude was destroying all that the gradualist reformation was trying to achieve. He was, of course, wrong. The evangelical and institutional approaches to authority were diametrically opposed. The furious battle was joined not because Luther was by nature confrontational or because Rome enjoyed burning dissidents but because the papal cohorts refused to yield ground to the claims of Scripture and Luther would not take his stand on anything else. Erasmus was the man whose Greek New Testament had set scholars questioning fundamental doctrines. He was the man who had declared himself in favour of the farmer's boy reading the Bible at his plough. His tragedy was that he could not or would not follow matters through to their logical conclusions. The Dutch scholar was living and teaching in conservative Louvain when Luther's works were publicly burned there but we cannot imagine him leaving his study to go to the market square and stand on the edge of the cheering (and jeering) crowd. Within a year he had taken leave of Louvain in order to live in the more tolerant atmosphere of Basel. His retreat marks the end of the humanist phase of the Reformation. From this point the movement would be wrested from the hands of priests and academics and led by politicians, princes, demagogues, artisans and sword-brandishing militants.

The Church had been returned to the people because Luther had redefined it. He had exposed the medieval myth of a visible, organised body united in doctrine, liturgy and obedience to Christ's vicar on earth. Luther's Church was 'one holy, common, Christian Church, which is nothing else than the congregation or assembly of the saints, i.e. the good, believing men of earth, which is gathered, preserved, ruled by the Holy Spirit and is daily increased by means of the sacraments and the word of God'.[24] This assembly was invisible and did not depend for its existence on a clerical hierarchy or the mechanistic performance of penitential rites or pious acts. Membership was obtained by faith. The papacy had no universal control of this body. How could it have since it was the abode of Antichrist?

Luther did not tear asunder the seamless robe of Latin Christendom. He did not carve out Protestant 'free states' from what had been a Catholic 'empire'. It is vital that we grasp that fact. Medieval Europe was crazed with fault lines – ethnic, national and political, as well as liturgical, doctrinal and psychological. Church-state relations were not the same in Spain, Venice and Bohemia. Pockets of stubborn heresy existed in England and Switzerland. Nor were there simple lines to be drawn between what was orthodox and what was damnable error. Even the celebration of mass was confused by a wide variety of local 'uses'. The very concept of the Holy Roman Empire indicates an underlying schizophrenia, a polity at one moment secular and at another spiritual. Luther did not create the multitude of tensions to which Europe was prone. He simply gave them permission to exist. His new theology was a solvent eating into the weak conceptual glue which had held a heterogeneous group of peoples together for seven hundred years. 'Christendom' had been a fine idea. It had defined the greater part of Europe and distinguished it from neighbouring regions which were pagan or Muslim. It had powered the expansionism of the crusades and, more recently, overseas missionary endeavour. But 'Christendom' as a concept had outlived its usefulness. It could not answer the new questions men were asking. It could not contain the Renaissance dynamic. It could not hold in check vigorous emerging individualism. If Christianity was to survive in the changing world of the sixteenth century it had to be released from the cage of medieval constraint. It needed a fresh theological ground bass on which ordinary people could superimpose their own melodies. Martin Luther provided that harmonic foundation. It was the beginning of a new age.

> Wherever Luther's ideas penetrated . . . unity of culture, which continued only because of the commanding authority of the church, began to totter. Religion, philosophy, science and art now went their own several ways. Henceforth they developed independently according to their own inherent impulses . . . the synthesis which the Middle Ages achieved by submission to the *external* authority of the church is not compatible with the modern conception of culture.[25]

8

'Christ will give me the courage to despise these ministers of Satan'

As enduring as the legend of Luther nailing his theses to the door of the castle church is the powerful image of him defying the Holy Roman Emperor at the Diet of Worms with the words, 'Here I stand; God help me I can do no other.' Sadly, this vivid, heroic soundbite is no more reliable than the popular account of the posting of the manifesto against indulgences. But that in no way minimises the importance of the confrontation that took place at Worms in April 1521. It would be impossible to dissent from the verdict delivered a hundred years ago by the American scholar, Preserved Smith, that 'few moments in history have been at once so dramatic and so decisive'. It is one of the great ironies of history that just as Charles V was creating the biggest empire Europe had seen since the time of Charlemagne, Martin Luther was destroying its cultural unity from within. Whatever words the accused heretic actually spoke, the Diet of Worms was one of the major turning points of history.

Yet the appearance of the condemned heretic before the lay assembly of the Empire was very far from being a foregone conclusion. In fact, during the preceding six months the fixture was on, off and on again as the parties concerned tried to bring about their own conclusions to the troublesome Luther affair. The various contenders either did not want the trial to take place at all or wanted it to be held on their own terms.

The young emperor (he celebrated his twenty-first birthday on 24 February 1521) was a man of wide vision and even wider responsibilities. In the opera, *Don Carlo*, it is said (or, rather, sung) of Charles V, 'He aspired to rule the world, regardless of him who guides the stars in their

constant course in the sky. His pride was immense, his error profound.'
Charles would spend his thirty-five years as ruler of the western world's
largest empire in a constant struggle to assert and achieve goals that were
pious, imperial, dynastic and impossible. All his passions were summed up
in the declaration he made to the imperial diet:

> You know that I am born of the most Christian emperors of the noble
> German nation, of the Catholic kings of Spain, the archdukes of
> Austria, the dukes of Burgundy, who were all to the death true sons
> of the Roman church, defenders of the Catholic faith, of the sacred
> customs, decrees and usages of its worship, who have bequeathed all
> this to me as my heritage and according to whose example I have
> hitherto lived ... Therefore I am determined to set my kingdoms
> and dominions, my friends, my body, my blood, my life, my soul upon
> [the unity of the Church and the purity of the faith].[1]

That all sounded very well and there is no doubt that it was sincerely
meant but, equally, there is no doubt that in practice Charles stood no
chance of balancing all his ambitions. The political realities of holding
together his vast, disparate patrimony were not compatible with simple
idealism. Thus, for example, this emperor who saw protection of the Church
as his solemn duty would, within seven years, send his troops to sack Rome
and make the pope his prisoner (see below, pp. 246 ff.). More immediately, his forces were fighting rebellious subjects in Spain and he had unfinished business with Francis I. The French king was a mere six years older
than the emperor and Europe was to be the tiltyard where these two charismatic champions would strut their competing ambitions for a quarter of
a century. Francis had been Charles' rival for the imperial crown and was
striving to create an alliance strong enough to challenge Charles' position
in Europe. Only the previous summer he had spent lavishly on the Field
of Cloth of Gold, a diplomatic tour de force aimed at seducing Henry VIII
of England away from his friendly relationship with Spain. Meanwhile
Habsburg lands in the East were threatened by the warlike posturing of
Suleiman the Magnificent.

It was Charles' misfortune that the Luther affair, historically the most
important issue that would face him during his reign, confronted him
before he had attained real political and diplomatic maturity. His own
opinion of the troublesome monk was quite clear. When he was presented
with a copy of the *Address to the Christian Nobility* he tore it up in a rage.

But he was caught between the warring parties and he vacillated. During the preparations for the Worms diet he came face to face with the tensions within his empire. In most of his rag-bag of territories Charles ruled by right of inheritance but in Germany he held the crown by consent of the electors, chief among whom was Frederick of Saxony. He was anxious to win Frederick's support and negotiations were already in hand for a marriage alliance between their two families. The elector and his colleagues had varied feelings about Luther but they were all united in upholding imperial law and it dictated that no subject could be placed under the imperial ban without a hearing before a commission appointed by the emperor. It was to just such an impartial tribunal that Luther made his appeal in the autumn of 1520. The Church having refused him his day in court, he appealed to what he considered a higher authority. This was consistent with his complaint about the 'encroachment' by the papacy on the judicial preserves of the secular power which he had made in his *Address to the Christian Nobility* and he knew that several members of the imperial council were sympathetic towards it.

> From Rome, however, Charles received a clean contrary message:
> The authority of the Holy See should not be prejudiced by subjection to the judgement of the laity. One who has been condemned by the pope, the cardinals and prelates should be heard only in prison. The laity, including the emperor, are not in a position to review the case. The only competent judge is the pope. How can the Church be called the ship of Peter if Peter is not at the helm?[2]

To Luther's adversaries the principle involved could not have been simpler. *Exsurge Domine* had already been promulgated in the Netherlands by order of the emperor. It remained only for Charles to show himself a dutiful son of the Church by taking the same action in Germany. Charles had no desire whatsoever to revive the papal-imperial dispute over temporal authority in Christendom but he was powerless to avoid doing so. It was an unhealed wound that had been festering for centuries and the Wittenberg heresy had ripped away the bandages.

At the end of November the emperor issued an invitation to Frederick to bring Luther to the impending diet in order that he could be heard by learned scholars. Three weeks later the proposed hearing had been aborted – by the action of both parties. Frederick was incensed by the burning of his professor's books. Since this had been implicitly countenanced by the emperor Luther's case had been, in effect, prejudged and Frederick took this as a personal affront. He penned a diplomatic but firm refusal. But by then Charles had, in any case, withdrawn his invitation. The man who caused him to vacillate was Leo's special commissioner, Jerome Aleander.

Aleander was the envoy charged, along with Eck, in gaining co-operation for the condemnation of Luther throughout the lands north of the Alps. While the Dominican grasped the nettle of Germany, Aleander had the supposedly easier task of wooing the emperor and the intellectual leaders of the Netherlands and the Rhineland. If anyone could ensure commitment to the orthodox cause it should have been Aleander. He was a widely respected humanist scholar with a good knowledge of the 'new' studies of Greek and Hebrew and had been rector of the Sorbonne before joining the papal entourage in Rome. Like Eck, he set out with high expectations and, like Eck, he was shocked to discover that the seeds of Wittenberg heresy were readily taking root. Aleander reported back to the curia that, while the new emperor was 'in the bag', several of his advisers were far from 'reliable'. This was partly because of the complex diplomatic relations with the German princes but also because of alarmingly widespread hostility towards Rome. The further one ventured down the social scale, he reported, the more critical the situation became. The books and tracts of the Lutheran camp were everywhere. It was not only immature students who were infected with heresy. Monks and friars were reading the forbidden books. As for the illiterate and semi-literate lower orders, their anti-Roman prejudice was being fed by Lutheran theology which they could not possibly understand. Aleander complained that he was having to endure shouted personal abuse, deliberate obfuscation of the papal case, rabid pamphlet attacks and obstruction by civic and university authorities. Luther's partisans made a mockery of the book burnings by consigning to the flames copies of canon law and works of scholastic theology instead of the heretical books they had been instructed to bring.

However, the pope's man was confident that all would turn out well. What was needed was a show of force. If pope and emperor worked together as the leaders of Christendom nothing could stop them. The imperial edict had gone out through the Low Countries. It remained only to secure the same result in the German-speaking Rhineland, after which political and military force could be relied on to crush the raucous, but ultimately powerless, heretics. Aleander threw himself into the task. His first objective was to have Luther's invitation to Worms cancelled and he achieved this with a scholarly tour de force. He gained permission to argue his case before Charles and his German advisers and he prepared himself thoroughly for the meeting. He spent several days in libraries and archives to assemble and marshal his evidence and he tailored his address to his audience. He would not attempt to overawe the secular ministers with theological argument (such, after all, would be to play the game according to Luther's rules). His reasoning was based entirely on historical precedents designed to prove the universal authority of the pope. Deny that, he warned, and the Christian West would face the threat of political disintegration and anarchy, a horror of which the ruling class lived in permanent dread. Aleander's hearers were impressed. Within hours an imperial letter was on its way to Elector Frederick, withdrawing the invitation to Luther.

Looked at from the standpoint of those responsible for maintaining peace and order, there was quite a lot of sense in what Leo's emissary said. As frost was at work in the autumn ploughed fields, breaking up the clods by expanding myriads of water droplets within the soil, so the new teaching was boosting principles and prejudices at all levels of society to the point at which they would create their own fissures. Western Christendom would, indeed, fall apart. However, this was not how most German people viewed what was happening. In the period leading up to and following the Diet of Worms Luther was at the zenith of his fame. He was a national figurehead, a popular hero, a charismatic focus of various aspirations, most of which were but vaguely understood. Aleander was quite right when he complained that few people had any understanding of the theological issues at stake. But this was the strength of the Wittenberg movement, not its weakness. Every man could assume that Luther was fighting *his* battles for him. Whatever oppression a person might feel himself to be suffering, Luther was his liberator. Historians may discern nationalistic aspirations, anticlericalism, resentment at intellectual oppression or indignation over ecclesiastical taxation as 'causes' of the Reformation, and all these motives certainly existed. But overarching them all was something altogether more powerful, albeit ill-defined. The human spirit always aspires to be free and it was freedom – exciting, intoxicating, invigorating freedom – that Luther appeared to be offering. To gain this those who felt themselves oppressed would cheer, follow and support their champion. They would stand behind him against the forces of Antichrist, now clearly identified by Luther as the fiend of Rome. Adoration showed itself in numerous ways.

In 1520–2 'Lutheranism' became a sect. When he realised what was happening the reformer was appalled; he insisted that people must follow Christ, not Luther. But by then he had become, in the popular imagination, a saint, a miracle-worker, a prophet, the apostle of the last days, almost a reincarnated Christ. He had been allotted a place in the multi-layered mythology of the German people. Writers of popular apocalyptic, like Haug Marschalk, portrayed the Wittenberg monk as one character in the end-time scenario alongside Charlemagne and Frederick III, past heroes who, according to legend, would reappear to revive Christendom, crush Rome and reform the priesthood. In *Von dem weyt erscholle Name Luther: Was er bedeut und wie er wirt missbraucht*, an elaborate allegory, Marschalk depicted Luther, Melancthon and Karlstadt as the three Marys, going to the Easter sepulchre to be greeted by the risen Messiah and receiving from him their commission to proclaim the truth of the Resurrection in defiance of a guard of Roman clergy who were trying to keep Christ entombed. Other writers had no hesitation in overlaying Luther's sufferings on the passion of Christ. As the hagiography became more intense, stories of 'St Martin's' miracles began to circulate, some of which found their way into print. Luther was divinely shielded from pieces of dislodged masonry which Satan hurled at him. When enemies cast his picture into a bonfire it declined to burn. Aleander, himself, reported how a peasant rushed up to touch the hem of Luther's garment. There is a distinct irony about the fact that this reformist scholar who set his face firmly against superstition became encoiled in the tentacles of traditional, semi-religious fable.[3]

This sanctification was most powerfully embodied in pictorial printed images designed for mass circulation. A whole, new Lutheran iconography sprang into being with astonishing rapidity. Humble folk adorned their walls with pictures of Luther, portrayed as a haloed saint. Broadsheets rolled from the presses replete with ribald or cynical images of Catholic oppression. The leading artist, Hans Baldung Grien, represented the Wittenberg monk with his books and the Holy Spirit descending on him in the form of a dove and in a popular pamphlet Luther was shown treading a fire-breathing devil under his feet. By now there was not the slightest reticence in the propaganda supporting Luther about identifying the pope and his minions with the cohorts of hell. An Augsburg tract of 1521 depicted Leo receiving his instructions personally from the prince of darkness.

Such pictures may strike us as excessively 'pointed' but their impact on contemporaries was much more dramatic. Simple people brought up on medieval imagery were painfully familiar with the daunting depictions of Christ the judge, despatching sinners into the gaping, fiery maw of hell. Lurid paintings on church walls and in stained glass windows warned mortals of the wrath awaiting those who died without the sacramental grace dispensed by the priesthood. They were important implements in the educational toolbox of the Catholic hierarchy; aspects of the carrot-and-stick regime which discouraged disobedience and suppressed honest doubt. The new imagery turned the old on its head. Now it was the Catholic hierarchy who were destined for the unquenchable fire which would consume the devil and all his works. Doubt and scepticism about traditional teaching, resentment and indignation at clerical behaviour were liberated. A man might make his own peace with God and all the anathemas of a corrupt papal regime lay stripped of their power to hinder him. The emotional impact of the Luther movement as mediated to Europe's rank and file can scarcely be exaggerated. These images had a far greater impact than the measured theological expositions of the man at the centre of the storm. For most people the Reformation was not an intellectual movement. Historical truth and doctrinal intricacies were minor considerations in the diatribes pouring from every major press north of the Alps. Thus, the account of a celebrated trial of four Berne Dominicans for deceiving people with fake miracles showed Luther among the prosecutors, labelled, significantly, 'PATRON LIBERTATIS', 'upholders of liberty'. In fact, at the time of the event in question Luther had been still a law student at Erfurt.

Within a few years the upsurge of popular support would convulse Germany but, for the moment, it was the backing of the powerful and influential classes that was more important. The gaudy retinues of princes were observed making their way to the obscure little town on the Elbe to meet Luther, dine with him and hear him preach. The radical professor was positively embarrassed by frequent gifts of money from wealthy, well-intentioned patrons. Such offerings caused him genuine twinges of conscience. He who had condemned the acquisitiveness of church leaders feared that he was being subjected to the same temptation to seek worldly wealth. It was a real dilemma. If he had pocketed all the donations being made to him he would have handed valuable ammunition to his detractors. They could have claimed that this 'pious hypocrite' was only in it for the money. He solved this particular problem by giving away most of the cash offerings he received.

Luther was still being feted amongst the humanistic intelligentsia as the standard-bearer of free intellectual inquiry who exposed the stupidity of scholastic methodology and the restrictive practices of the traditionalist academic hierarchy. One of the most forceful images of the reformer was that engraved in Basel in 1523. The Swiss city had become Europe's leading centre of free debate; a haven where religious thinkers of all stamps could work and worship without fear of persecuting authorities. In the printshops and taverns lining the steep streets running down from the cathedral to the Rhine university students rubbed shoulders with such intellectual giants as the radical Ulrich Zwingli, the gentle Lutheran, Johann Oecolampadius, and even the great Erasmus. It was from Basel that the superb publishing houses of Froben, Amerbach and Petri (often referred to as the 'guild of three') sent out their mouth-watering prospectuses of new books which kept the ongoing theological-philosophical debate at white heat. Artists, too, were drawn to this frenziedly busy anthill of intellectual activity. Among them was the younger Hans Holbein. In 1521 or 1522 someone commissioned him to create an image expressing how the German reformer was viewed in humanist circles.

It was a remarkable conception and one which gave rise to consternation on both sides of the Reformation conflict. It was violent. It appealed to the classical idealism of the cognoscenti by depicting Luther as the Greek super-hero and god, Hercules. The scourge of scholasticism was depicted laying about him with a viciously spiked club. Aristotle, Aquinas, Occam, Duns Scotus and Nicholas of Lyra already lay bludgeoned to death at his feet and the German inquisitor, Jakob von Hochstraten was about to receive his fatal stroke. Suspended from a ring in Luther's nose – like some hanged felon – was the figure of the pope. What was clever about this print (and what has made it difficult for later ages to determine its true message) was that it was capable of various interpretations. Followers of Luther could see their champion represented as a truly god-like being of awesome power, the agent of divine vengeance. Classical scholars, delighting in the many subtle allusions (such as the representation of the triple-tiaraed pope as the three-bodied monster, Geryon) could applaud the vivid representation of Luther as the champion of falsehood over medieval error. Yet, papalists could look on the same image and see in it a vindication of Leo's description of the uncouth German as the destructive wild boar in the vineyard and, for this reason, the engraving received a very mixed reception in Wittenberg. Many scholars believed that they could detect Erasmus's inspiration behind the ambiguous imagery. It was well known that he welcomed Luther's stand against the 'mad sophists' identified in the text accompanying the picture, while deploring his unrestrained, 'uncivilised' methods. Yet, whether sympathetic to or critical of the new Hercules, the image was powerful and highly effective.

Everywhere, but especially throughout the German lands, people were interpreting this new Lutheran phenomenon in terms of their own

Luther – the German Hercules, Hans Holbein, 1523

experience and aspirations. Of no 'group' was this more true than of the
nationalists. Luther's revolt both fed and fed off the rise of Germanic
consciousness. Two men who gave particularly virulent expression to this
desire for self-identification and self-determination were Ulrich von Hutten
and Franz von Sickingen. They were members of the *Reichsritterschaft*, the
community of imperial knights, which had a proud military heritage but
a future which seemed to them to be increasingly problematic. Squeezed
by economic and social forces which they but scantly understood, they
saw themselves losing their once-powerful position in the Empire and they
looked around for people to blame. High on their list were the ecclesiastical 'princes' who encroached on their lands and usurped their local
authority in the name of a distant, effete Italian pope. Hutten, no mean
scholar, penned several works of virulent satire against the Roman curia
and their representatives in Germany. Sickingen was a simpler man of
action who put himself at the head of a movement which proposed a military solution to the nation's ills. This turbulent Rhineland warrior had
already added considerably to his patrimony by picking quarrels with his
neighbours and he now believed that the time had come for a major historical conflict. When humanist and radical scholars found themselves
attacked by church authorities they found in Sickingen a ready protector.
By providing refuge for several such critics of the papal regime in his
various castles the knight was throwing down a challenge – to the pope,
the emperor, and to any German prince not prepared to side with reform.
It was inevitable that such men should see Luther as a convert to their
cause and Sickingen offered to extend his protective cloak over the
Wittenberg monk. Such friends Luther did not need, especially when they
tried to force his hand by attacking the Archbishop of Trier's territory in
order to provide a permanent base from which to launch a 'Gospel crusade'
(the so-called 'Knights' War'). Luther can only have been relieved when
the precipitate action of his unwanted allies failed in 1523. Sickingen was
executed when his last stronghold fell to the enemy and Hutten died a
fugitive shortly afterwards.

However, such events lay in the future in the winter of 1521 when the
diplomatic wires were still buzzing over the issue of whether a pronounced
heretic should be permitted to plead his case before the imperial diet.
When the various princely cavalcades trundled into Worms during the
last days of January it soon became clear to Aleander that his earlier triumph
had not settled the matter of Luther's condemnation once and for all. He
was soon complaining about 'self-important' and 'independent-minded'

princelings who refused to be guided by the imperial council. Several members of the estates claimed the right to be consulted on Luther's fate and resented any attempt by pope and emperor to go over their heads. They were all conscious of the delicate political situation in their territories and had to take into account Luther's mounting popularity. If their hero were to be condemned by imperial diktat, then imprisoned or burned, the mood of the people would almost certainly turn ugly. Many members of the diet were more anxious to please Frederick the Wise than Charles V and Charles himself could not afford to alienate the Saxon elector. He had an eye to the long-term situation in Germany and the marriage of his sister to Frederick's nephew (son of George, the heir apparent) was an important part of his strategy. The nuncio scurried from duke to elector to pressure group, becoming increasingly frustrated by their procrastination. Instead of meeting together and making a clear-cut decision they indulged in interminable arguments (some extremely heated) and exchanged written policy statements. On 12 February Aleander harangued the assembled representatives for three hours. He offered various *douceurs*: a hundred crowns for the emperor's secretary, a favourable decision for the imperial chancellor in a case before the papal court, a benefice for the underage son of a favourite member of one of the electoral courts. It did no good. When, a week later, the German leaders finally presented their considered opinion to Charles it was a refusal to allow Luther to be condemned without a hearing. They went further: they asked for a full investigation into the widespread complaints about ecclesiastical abuses. Aleander ranted. Charles squirmed. From his point of view he was faced with a trial of strength, a clash of authorities. If he was to be master in his own house he had to issue an edict against Luther and his works.

Charles, Aleander, Frederick, Sickingen and most of the minor players in the German drama were blinkered activists who could see only their own narrow agendas. They pursued personal or political advantage. They saw the problem – or affected to see it – in simple black and white. They stuck labels on the issues confronting them: 'heresy', 'ecclesiastical corruption', 'national identity', 'obedience', 'loyalty'. They lacked a wider vision. They could not see, as Luther, Erasmus and, perhaps, only a handful of contemplative scholars could see, that issues of eternal truth were at stake. The Wittenberg movement had removed the lid from deep spiritual longings that clamoured to be satisfied. No amount of imperial decrees, papal anathemas or cobbled-together political solutions could silence the tumultuous expressions of hope, indignation and aspiration against which the participants in Worms would gladly have covered their ears. But history is made by little men as well as visionaries and they all had their part to play in this turning point in the story of Europe and the world. Little men resolve their differences by violence or compromise. Charles or his secretariat produced a formula which, rather like a tightrope walker's pole, was designed to enable him to keep his balance without falling on one side or the other. Accepting that there was no alternative to reissuing his invitation to the heretic, he sent his own herald to Wittenberg with a politely worded personal letter and an offer of safe conduct. But, at the same time, he made it clear that he would countenance no debate. The meeting would simply provide an opportunity for Luther to declare whether or not he stood by his condemnation of the Church of Rome. Charles now at last issued the ban for which Rome had been clamouring for months but he found a formula which would soften its impact. Instead of demanding Luther's arrest and handing over to ecclesiastical authority, it simply stated that he had been summoned to give an account of himself. It condemned Luther for disseminating opinions at variance with the faith of the Church Catholic and ordered that anyone possessing writings by the heretic must hand them over to the authorities. The whole 'solution' was riddled with contradictions as Charles knew and as Aleander did not hesitate to point out. A condemned heretic was being addressed in the invitation as 'Dear, honoured and pious Dr Martin Luther'. Instead of being publicly burned, his books were simply ordered to be confiscated (a futile instruction that would be largely ignored). Worse than all this from Rome's point of view, the man responsible for the subversive contagion daily spreading farther and farther throughout Europe was to be provided with a public platform and then allowed to travel home again under the emperor's personal protection.

On 16 April Aleander's worst fears about this unprecedented climbdown were realised when months of argument climaxed in Luther's appearance in Worms. His was a triumphal arrival, compared in contemporary letters by Luther and others to Christ's entry into Jerusalem. When his wagon, preceded by the emperor's liveried herald and a contingent of imperial troops, was still several miles from the city, a large crowd surged out to greet the man of the hour. Thousands more people lined the streets to cheer him from the east gate to his lodging in the convent of the Knights of St John and trumpets blared a welcome from the tower of the cathedral.

Faced with this delirious reception of the most celebrated man in Germany all Aleander could do to minimise its impact was to render

The Imperial Diet

Luther's appearance before the diet as much as possible an anticlimax. The papal nuncio knew well Luther's propensity for self-promotion and was determined to deny him the oxygen of publicity. To this end the investigation needed to be as brief and witnessed by as few people as possible. He arranged with the imperial secretariat for it to be staged in a small audience chamber at the bishop's palace. He schooled the chairman of the tribunal, Johann von Eck (no relation to Luther's erstwhile adversary) in the technique to be employed. The accused was to be confronted with his writings and asked two questions: did he acknowledge them as his own and, if so, did he recant of their contents? In Aleander's vision of the proceedings the heretic would be confined to monosyllabic answers. It must have galled him that he was obliged to absent himself from the event. As the pope's representative he could not attend without appearing to lend it an air of legality.

The room was already so crammed the next afternoon when Luther was led in at about three o'clock that onlookers had to be pushed back to make a space for him to stand before the imperial throne. The atmosphere was scarcely such as to overawe the monk who came face to face with all the leaders of the German people. It is difficult to gauge how Luther felt and comported himself at this crisis moment in his career, because the accounts differ. His enemies reported that he shuffled nervously and was visibly shaken to find himself before such a tribunal. Luther's supporters, on the other hand, claimed that their champion was composed and relaxed, fully in command of the situation. The proceedings, conducted in both Latin and German so that clerics and princes could all understand, began immediately but it soon became evident that they would lack the brevity his enemies were counting on. Eck began the interrogation by indicating a huge pile of books and pamphlets, stacked, as Luther later recalled, on a window sill. Did the accused acknowledge these as his writings, the chairman demanded. If the assembled works of the scholar monk were a comprehensive collection the sight of them must have made a considerable impact. Could one man still under the age of forty really have written all this? Might not the tall columns of books have been bulked out with manifestly seditious material from other hands as a means of tricking the accused into condemning himself? It is small wonder that, before Luther could answer, one of Frederick's men called out, 'Let the titles be read'. This was solemnly done by a clerk and then Luther quietly confirmed that he was their author. So far, so good for his accusers. Next came the big question: 'Do you recant, in whole or part, what you have written?' This was where the meticulously planned prosecution came unstuck. By assembling such a large body of work covering a wide variety of subjects they had opened up a chink in their own armour. Luther could reasonably argue that it was not safe for him to give an immediate 'yea' or 'nay' in response. There were, he pointed out, solemn issues at stake – divine truth, the word of God and the salvation of souls. He asked for time to consider his answer. Charles looked around at his advisers and may even have retired with them to discuss the request. Eck protested, doubtless fearing that delay would give the heretic precisely what he had been ordered to deny him – time to prepare a speech. But when proceedings resumed he had to hear the young emperor declare that, of his clemency, he had decided to order a twenty-four hour adjournment. Eck tried to regain the initiative with a long, censorious speech in which he accused Luther of dividing the Church and distorting Scripture but, according to a report by one of the reformer's friends, the audience paid little attention, preferring to chat among themselves.

News of what had passed was all round the city before nightfall. Everyone knew that the following day's hearing would be crucial and scores of well-wishers visited Luther's lodgings over the next few hours to encourage him and ensure him that, whatever happened, they would not allow him to be burned. The opposition were also gathered together elsewhere to fine hone their tactics for the morrow's crisis confrontation. Aleander and his associates spent hours going over with Eck the best ways of dealing with the 'slippery' Wittenberg heretic.

The assembly was set to reconvene at 4 p.m. on 18 April but by mid-morning people were already queuing in order to secure good vantage points. It rapidly became obvious that the hall designated for the hearing would accommodate only a fraction of the crowd jostling for admission. If large numbers were turned away there was a real risk of riots. The authorities had no alternative but to yield to pressure and make available the largest auditorium in the bishop's palace. Four o'clock came and went. Luther and his antagonists were assembled. The windows steadily darkened. Torches and lamps were lit. The room became stuffy and hot. Sixteenth-century noses were not as sensitive as ours but the stench of human sweat must have been oppressive. Not until six o'clock did Charles and his suite appear. According to one account, soldiers had to elbow a way through the crowd for the emperor to reach his chair (he was the only person in the hall to be seated). He called upon Eck to continue and the chairman treated the assembly to another lengthy diatribe.

When it came to Luther's turn to respond to the challenge to recant he was determined to deliver a carefully prepared address and, of course, most of the audience were agog to hear it. It has been pieced together from Luther's own later account and those of others who were present and, though incomplete, has entered the canon of the world's most important speeches. But we must ask the question, 'Why was he allowed to get away with it?' It was the one thing his adversaries were determined he should not do and either Eck or the emperor could have silenced him as soon as it became obvious that he was launched upon a long oration. Yet, apart from one intervention by Charles (only recorded by Aleander, who was not present), Luther was able to explain himself fully – in both German and Latin – and to repeat his attack on the Roman hierarchy. No answer to this question is obvious from the written records. We have to go behind the documents and place ourselves among the shuffling, expectant crowd packed uncomfortably into that audience chamber, straining their ears to hear everything being said and peering between the heads of those in front for a glimpse of the charismatic radical. They had been patient. They had waited on the emperor's pleasure. They had endured Eck's pompous sermon. It is not difficult to guess what their mood would have been if Luther had now been forced into a muttered, monosyllabic response. Young Charles' position was awkward. He was confronted by a tightly packed mass of his German subjects, most of whom were on the side of their national champion. He might want to assert his authority and his Catholic orthodoxy but nervousness and wisdom both counselled caution.

It was not his presence which dominated the occasion. The man of the hour was Martin Luther. He had the audience in the palm of his hand. The gifted preacher and scholar had a complete grasp of his material and an acute sense of the mood of his hearers. He began with a humble submission to the assembled rulers of the people, presenting himself as a loyal subject and certainly not a ranting, half-crazed heretic bent on tearing holes in the social fabric. On the contrary, the speaker declared that he was motivated by the wellbeing of Germany and its divinely appointed rulers. A serious situation existed in imperial territory, thanks largely to papal oppression (that went down well with the crowd) and it was his duty to do all in his power to bring the light of Scripture to bear upon it. Those who wished to silence him had condemned *all* his works but, as he pointed out, some dealt with issues of Christian faith and morals and even his worst enemies could not take issue with them. For the rest, they came into two categories: denunciation of papal doctrine and practice, and attacks on individuals who had taken issue with him. For the latter, Luther conceded that he might occasionally have exceeded the bounds of propriety but in doing so he had been impelled only by his passion for the truth.

On the substantive issue of his teaching, he cunningly asserted that he was prepared to be corrected by the leaders of the nation (but not the leaders of the Church in Rome):

I ask by the mercy of God, may your most serene majesty, most illustrious lordships, or anyone at all who is able, either high or low, bear witness, expose my errors, overthrowing them by the writings of the prophets and the evangelists. Once I have been taught I shall be quite ready to renounce every error, and I shall be first to cast my books into the fire.[4]

Luther knew that what was disturbing many of his noble hearers was the disruptive impact of his writing and preaching. Many of them were ambiguous about his theological challenge to the official religion but the possibility of social upheaval certainly worried them. The speaker now addressed himself to this problem. His hearers, he said, should not be surprised that the Gospel provoked dissension.

> [Christ] said, 'I have not come to bring peace, but a sword. For I have come to set a man against his father, etc.'[5] Therefore, we ought to think how marvellous and terrible is our God in his counsels, lest by chance what is attempted for settling strife grows rather into an intolerable deluge of evils, if we begin by condemning the Word of God. And concern must be shown lest the reign of this most noble youth, Prince Charles (in whom after God is our great hope), become unhappy and inauspicious.[6]

Luther referred to the terrible fate of Old Testament kings of Egypt and Babylon to point out what happened to rulers who relied on their own wisdom rather than God's. 'And so', he concluded, 'I commit myself to your Majesty and to your lordships. I humbly beg you not to condemn me without reason because of the passions of my enemies.'[7]

It was clever polemic: Luther had focused attention on what he saw as the essential contest between the leaders of the Roman church and the God they purported to serve. He had turned the argument away from his own recantation and, instead, had politely challenged the emperor to decide whose side *he* was on. Eck could not tolerate such equivocation. Angrily he demanded a straight answer – 'without horns or teeth' – to the question whether the accused would renege on his published opinions. And so Luther, his back to the wall, made that statement which has reverberated down the centuries:

> Since, then, your Majesty and your lordships desire a simple reply, I will answer without horns or teeth. Unless I am convicted by Scripture and by plain reason [i.e. plainly understood, without recourse to allegorical or spiritualised interpretations] (I do not believe in the authority of either popes or councils by themselves, for it is plain that they have often erred and contradicted each other) in those writings that I have presented – for my conscience is captive to the

word of God – I cannot and I will not recant anything, for to go against conscience is neither right nor safe. God help me, Amen.[8]

The words, 'Here I stand; I can do no other' were only added in later versions of the speech.

The die was cast. It remained only for Charles formally to pronounce the ban and insist on its enforcement for the Luther affair to be brought to a fatal conclusion. Or so one might think. The reality was very different. The foetid atmosphere in the dimly lit chamber was now close to intolerable. The emperor adjourned the session once more and both contending parties left believing that they had had the better of the day. There was a boyish, unrestrained side to Luther's character which, in the explosion of relief in the aftermath of the ordeal, came to the fore. He strode through the narrow streets in the midst of a gang of noisy supporters, laughing and waving his arms in ebullient victory salutes. As the cavalcade passed there were some who jeered from doorways and windows and shouted, 'To the flames!' but there was not the remotest chance of Luther being arrested in Worms. There were even rumours, supported by a pamphlet distribution, of a rising of armed knights against the papal party. For their part, Eck, Aleander and their associates were not fazed by such jubilant demonstrations. They were politicos, content to work behind the scenes and they were sure of their man, the emperor. The heretic had shot his bolt. Condemned by his own truculence, Luther would surely be apprehended by some loyal member of holy church and, once safely under lock and key, no amount of bluster by loutish Germans could save him.

But others were also adept at political manoeuvring. When Charles, the following morning, declared that he expected all Germany's rulers to co-operate with himself and the pope by ensuring that Luther was arrested, the electors and princes sent a deputation urging compromise. Reluctantly the emperor agreed to an *in camera* debate between Luther and a group of theologians. This duly took place and, of course, settled nothing. Aleander fumed at the continued delay and at Charles' determination to allow the heretical monk to return to Wittenberg under safe conduct. Once back among his own people and protected by his own stubborn prince Luther might be free to continue his arrogant defiance of Rome. Despite all his efforts Aleander could see his quarry escaping.

Luther certainly did escape – but not quite in the way that the papal legate had envisaged.

III

Liberty and Restraint
1521–1526

'I almost believe and think that it is because of me that the devil is making such a mess in the world.'

Letter to John Ruhel, May 1525

9

Junker George

'"Are these your books?" "Yes." "Will you revoke them or not?" "No."
"Then get out!"' In those words to his artist friend, Lucas Cranach, Luther
summarised his Worms experience. He was being ungenerous. Several
people, on both sides of the religious divide, had tried to find a compromise which would enable all parties to walk away from the diet with a
modicum of honour. They were aware of the social and political consequences of allowing the theological conflict to escalate into rebellion – or
something worse. Luther, on the other hand, was not interested in face-
saving deals. He was fighting for principles whose truth and universal application he believed in with every fibre of his being. But the rickety structure of human society is held together by a myriad compromises, and principles are like battering rams whose impact can be devastating. Did Luther
see where his unrelenting assault on medieval religion might lead? No, he
was profoundly shocked when, in 1525, furious radical revolutionaries
claimed him as their patron saint. If he could have foreseen the excesses
his teaching might inspire would he have been less forthright in asserting
his convictions? Probably not. He saw himself as but the agent of an angry
God who was using preached and printed verities to turn the world upside-
down, as he explained to Staupitz a year after the Diet of Worms:

> He is doing this without us, of course, without the help of a human
> hand, solely through the Word. The Lord knows the end of it. The
> matter is beyond our power of comprehension and understanding.
> Therefore there is no reason why I should delay until someone is

able to understand it. Because of the greatness of God, it is most fitting that there should arise proportionately great disturbance of minds, great causes of offence, and great monstrosities . . . You can see in these things God's counsel and his mighty hand.[1]

Luther left Worms on Friday 26 April with a protective guard of twenty horsemen, under the impressive leadership of the imperial herald. The wagons lumbered their ponderous way northwards to Frankfurt before taking valley roads (more or less the route of the modern E40 *Autostrasse*) towards distant Eisenach, familiar to Luther from his childhood. They seemed to be in no hurry. Luther took the opportunity to call upon relatives, to spend time with bands of well-wishers and to preach (something expressly forbidden by the terms of his safe conduct). At Friedberg, on the 28th they overnighted at a local monastery and while there Luther wrote a long letter to the emperor which is fascinating in the light of subsequent events. In earnest prose oozing with expressions of humble loyalty and devotion, he rehearsed all that had passed in Worms, from his own point of view, and repeated his request for an unbiased jury to examine his books and pass judgement on them in the light of Scripture. For Luther the Bible was the philosophers' stone which alone could transform the base metal of worthless medieval religion into the gold of true faith. And he was passionately concerned that Charles should understand that it was only his total commitment to sacred writ which was the crux of his argument with Rome.

I am still absolutely ready to stand, under Your Sacred Majesty's protection, before trustworthy, learned, free, secular, as well as ecclesiastical judges, and to be instructed by Your Sacred Majesty, by the Imperial Estates, by councils, doctors, or anyone else who can and is willing to do it. [I am ready] to submit my little books and my teachings most willingly to all and to endure and accept their examination and judgement, excepting nothing, *provided only that the Word of God remain unobstructed, clear and free* [my emphasis]; certainly [the Word of God] ought to remain above everything and be the judge of all men.

For this reason I now make my humble petition, not on my behalf (since I am of no importance) but on behalf of the whole church . . . With my whole heart I desire, of course, that Your Sacred Majesty, the whole Empire, and the most noble German nation may be served in the best possible way, and all be preserved in God's grace as happy people. Hitherto I have sought nothing but God's glory and the welfare of all men. Even now I have not considered my own advantage, whether my opponents will condemn me or not. For if Christ my Lord prayed for his enemies while on the cross, how much more should I, with joy and trust in Christ, be concerned about and pray and plead for Your Sacred Majesty, for your Empire, for my most beloved superiors, and all native Germany. I expect nothing but the best from them, relying on my afore-mentioned offer.

With this I commend myself to the shelter of Your Sacred Majesty's wings. May the Lord guide and keep you for our well-being and happiness. Amen.[2]

It was a personal apologia. It was a statement of evangelical faith. But was it something else? Was there a sub-text to this letter of humble submission? For the truth was that Luther was *not* prepared to trust to the 'shelter of Your Sacred Majesty's wings'. He had already agreed (albeit reluctantly) to accept protection elsewhere and to be concealed in a secret location. A plan had been formed to 'snatch' him before he reached Wittenberg and to make him disappear in the hope that it might be generally believed that he had been captured by his enemies. The letter, with its allusions to the constant danger Luther faced, might have been part of a smokescreen. Furthermore, the imperial herald was charged with delivering the letter to his master and this may have been a ruse to get the troublesome official out of the way.

Six leisurely days later the party was in Eisenach where, once again, Luther spent time renewing old friendships. It was on the outskirts of this town that the fake kidnapping was put into effect. As the party rode through the forest, almost within sight of the ancient walls, they were startled by the sound of urgent hoof beats and the shouts of armed soldiers, wearing no livery, who suddenly appeared through the trees. Luther's guard was quickly overpowered and he was dragged unceremoniously from his cart. His captors hoisted him roughly onto the back of a saddled horse, before plunging back into the forest and riding off with him at speed. It was all over in a few minutes. When the emperor's men had recovered from their surprise they gave chase. But eventually they were obliged to abandon their search, return to barracks and shamefacedly report that Luther's enemies had made good their threats to seize their charge and, presumably, put a violent end to his heretical career. Rumours immediately began to circulate that Catholic zealots had taken it into their heads to fulfil the emperor's decree without waiting for the expiry of the safe conduct he had issued.

In fact, Luther was neither dead nor a prisoner in some foul-smelling dungeon. He was lodged in the Wartburg, the formidable fortress perched on the hill above the town. When Sickingen and other knights had offered Luther sanctuary he had declined. He always claimed that he would not run away from his accusers; that he was ready to face persecution, if need be. It is not doubting his sincerity to point out another reason for his reluctance: he was not prepared to tie his fate to that of such firebrands as the warlike knights. However, when his own prince, Frederick the Wise, offered the same deal Luther took it more seriously. Towards the end of his time in Worms members of the elector's suite came to urge him to accept refuge in one of their master's strongholds. Frederick, himself, took no part in the plot and did not want to know its details. That way he could, if pressed, truthfully deny all knowledge of his protégé's whereabouts. But there is no doubt that he was the brains behind it. He had done everything in his power to ensure Luther an impartial hearing at the diet and many people would have considered that he had amply fulfilled his obligations as patron. Yet, now this most circumspect of men engaged in an act of covert defiance against his overlord. His assessment of the events at Worms was that the young emperor lacked the power and resources to impose his will on his German subjects. The diet had eventually passed an edict outlawing Luther and condemning all his works but this was only after Frederick and several of his colleagues had already left, so the elector did not feel himself bound by it. The reality, as he understood it, was that he and his fellow princes were free to enforce the ban against Luther or not, as their own inclination led them. Furthermore, Charles' ardour for a marriage alliance with Saxony had cooled. All in all, Frederick had a clear conscience about pursuing his own policies and he was certainly not prepared to throw his celebrated professor to the wolves.

But that does not fully explain why he was so concerned to wrap his mantle round the shoulders of a condemned heretic. The elector never became a Lutheran (unlike his nephew and eventual successor, John Frederick, the Magnanimous) and it would be anachronistic to regard him as a defender of free speech. He was not even overly concerned about the return of the professor to his teaching post at the university. The situation in Wittenberg was very volatile. If there was to be a spontaneous outbreak of pro-Luther demonstrations, neighbouring princes, and especially his rival, Duke George, might conceive it as their duty to march in and restore order. Frederick envisaged Luther remaining indefinitely in hiding and was later annoyed when the reformer cut short his sojourn at the Wartburg. I believe that there are two, interconnected reasons for Frederick's engagement in this cloak-and-dagger exercise. He had a deep and sincere admiration for the reformer. Their long relationship, albeit carried on through intermediaries, had been fruitful. Frederick, who has been called the 'Maecenas of the Northern Renaissance', had an unerring eye for talent. It would have appalled him to think of this independent-minded scholar and profound religious thinker being silenced by Catholic prejudice. Frederick hoped that Luther's disappearance might lead to a cooling-off period. Also, he did not want to lose his most celebrated author-teacher to some other prince. Luther was, at this time, seriously considering a career move and may well have discussed it with Spalatin. Much as he loved Wittenberg, it was off the beaten track and he was anxious to find some more prominent platform from which to preach and teach. Erfurt and Cologne were in his mind as possibilities.[3] Frederick might very reasonably have considered that, after all the support Luther had received from his patron, he owed him more loyalty. Whatever his motives, Frederick had Luther safely and secretly installed at the Wartburg and there he would remain for the foreseeable future.

It was, for the trained monk, a very strange experience. Gone was the monastic habit; the castle's guest was clad in the tunic and breeches of a German knight. Gone (gradually) was the tonsure; after a few months Luther sported a luxuriant head of hair and bushy beard. The man of religion had been transformed into a man of war, Junker George. He must have found the change of daily routine difficult to adjust to. No longer was his life encased in a strict regimen, with times set for worship, study and meals. He had become a layman. He was left to his own devices and had to organise himself. Yet, without doubt, what he found most difficult to come to terms with was not being at the centre of things. For more than three years he had been the most talked-about man in Europe. He had come to regard himself as the lead actor in God's own drama (and, indeed, he was) and, like a stage star, he found it difficult to cope with 'resting'. The play was going on without him and he had little means of knowing how it was faring in the hands of other performers. He longed to be back in front of the footlights.

His life now was more solitary than it had ever been in Augustinian cell and cloister. Luther was lodged in two rooms in a tower above the

quarters occupied by Hans von Berlepsch, warden of the castle. He had a
stove and basic furniture and, by the standards of the day, was quite
comfortable. But he was, in reality, a prisoner. His 'minder' controlled
access to the guest chambers, which could only be reached by a circular
staircase. Apart from Berlepsch, Luther's only visitors were two servants
who attended to his daily needs. Other members of the household were
told that their anonymous guest was a knightly hostage being held by the
elector. Increasingly, Luther craved company. He lived for the letters sent
on by Spalatin, who now became his only regular contact with Wittenberg
and the wider world.

   But if he was deprived of friends and colleagues, he also lacked distractions. No pastoral or teaching obligations encroached on his energies and,
more importantly, he was freed from the exhausting business of religious
controversy (Spalatin was very circumspect about the writings of his enemies
which he passed on). So there was nothing to keep Luther from writing.
He only had a few books with him – notably the Hebrew and Greek texts
of the Bible – and he sorely missed his access to good libraries but there
was so much that he wanted to say stored in his mind and now he could
devote himself completely to exegesis and devotional works. Over the
preceding few years countless people had approached him wanting to know

Luther's lodging in the Wartburg, 1521–2

the practical implications of his new teaching. His insistence on the primacy of Scripture meant that there were numerous issues of church doctrine and practice which stood in need of fresh understanding and he had been inundated with requests to provide guidance to clergy and local authorities who were setting up reformed programmes. Thus, in his lofty eyrie with its breathtaking views over the forest-clad Thuringian hills, Luther once more took up his pen.

If his literary output before had been phenomenal, it now became almost miraculous. The standard Weimar edition of his works runs to sixty-seven volumes, covering his writing over more than a quarter of a century. His output during the ten months he spent in the Wartburg accounts for three of those volumes. He wrote a series of sermons (a postil) expounding the Scripture passages set for the Sundays of the year. These addresses were designed to be read by clergy who lacked the education or talent for regular preaching but there must have been many such who found rather daunting the printed material now provided for them. One of Luther's 'sermons' ran to 173 pages! What the postil really demonstrated was how the Bible could be expounded and related to contemporary issues – local and national politics, relations between ruler and ruled, the shortcomings of monasticism, public order, etc. Treatises followed on the abolition of private masses, reform of the practice of confession and the portmanteau subject of vows – something fundamental to all relationships in sixteenth-century society. Luther's primary interests here were the commitments made by young men or women entering on a life of religion and the attendant issues of celibacy and marriage. However, much more was at stake. When Luther concluded that vows made to or in the name of God were of the nature of 'works' and, therefore, contrary to faith, and that Christian freedom liberated people from such obligations he realised that this would cause 'a change in public affairs'. All promises that could be regarded as not having been voluntarily entered upon by all concerned parties were, by this argument, null and void.

Luther was undertaking the monumental task of creating a whole evangelistic system of theology and ethics. Moreover, he was making the individual conscience the sole arbiter in such matters. No other authority governing human conduct existed than the word of God and no ecclesiastical or civil power could be placed above it. The Christian was bound by the written revelation but at the same time free to study it for himself. This was explosive. As the realisation grew of just what followed from his basic understanding of grace and faith, Luther became more anxious about how others would interpret it. It had the potential to blow society apart if wise councillors were not on hand to channel the force of the new liberty. The news from Wittenberg which reached the lodger in the Wartburg only reinforced his worst fears. He was frustrated not to be there as a guiding and restraining influence. For the moment he could only encourage, inform and admonish through his letters and books.

It was not a role he could patiently accept. 'Lazy and full, I sit here all day long.' So this prodigious writer complained to Spalatin. He demanded to know from Melancthon whether people were saying that he had deserted them. His ineffectiveness prayed on his mind so that long hours spent rushing pen across paper were interspersed with periods of black depression. On another occasion he wrote, 'Sitting here all day, I picture to myself the state of the church. God, what a horrible picture of his wrath is that detestable kingdom of the Roman Antichrist! I abhor the hardness [of my heart] that I am not completely melted to tears.[4] Such introspection in solitude was inevitable – but not conducive to health of mind or body. He spent days racked by constipation and nights tormented by insomnia, sexual frustration and demon-haunted dreams. 'I can tell you in this idle solitude there are a thousand battles with Satan. It is much easier to fight against the incarnate devil – that is, against men – than against spiritual wickedness in the heavenly places,' he bewailed to another correspondent. His host, in his rough and ready way, tried to find diversions for him. Luther later recalled being taking on a hunting excursion. This had involved uncomfortable hours spent jogging about on horseback watching a sport for which he had no taste. He tried, unsuccessfully, to preserve a rabbit from slaughter. Walks in the forest could only be permitted in the company of his two appointed servants who were always on the watchout for locals or travellers who might show an unwelcome curiosity about their charge. Luther referred to the Wartburg as his 'Patmos', the barren Dodecanese island which had served as a Roman penal colony and where it was believed that St John had written his gospel and the Book of Revelation. His friends were at a loss to know how to comfort and encourage him and it may have been in an effort to keep him 'in touch' with the continuing conflict that they sent him some of the diatribes that continued to be published by his enemies.

Luther responded during these months to two Catholic tracts denouncing him and his works. None of his enemies broke new ground and Luther could do little more than reiterate old arguments. He enjoyed the opportunity to sharpen his claws and lash out with sarcasm and devastatingly detailed citations from Scripture. Yet, each time he expounded his basic doctrine of faith and grace Luther moved to a more profound understanding of the mysteries of salvation. His progress was 'like the ascent of a spiral staircase, where the same point is reached but at a new level and with a wider perspective'.[5] The most effective of his polemical works at this time was his *Refutation of Latomus's Argument on Behalf of the Incendiary Sophists of the University of Louvain.* Latomus (Jacques Masson) was a leading theologian at Louvain, the intellectual centre of reactionary theology, whence came a continuous stream of books and pamphlets attacking humanistic and reforming initiatives. (Erasmus, it will be recalled, had left Louvain for the more tolerant atmosphere of Basel.) But Latomus's assault was more important than most because he went to the heart of the matter by challenging the evangelical interpretation of sin, grace and free-will. Since he supported his case with numerous biblical citations Luther felt obliged to reply. In what was for him measured language Luther insisted that while his opponent was bent on using proof texts to underpin current church practice, he sought only to understand and expound what the plain word of God actually said.

From his reading of St Paul and his observation of human nature Luther was in no doubt about the universal, persistent and irrevocable nature of sin. In Romans 7 the apostle had clearly set out the moral man's predicament: 'I know that good does not live in me – that is in my human nature. For even though the desire to do good is in me, I am not able to do it. I don't do the good I want to do; instead I do the evil I don't want to do.' He used as a metaphor the Roman practice of shackling prisoners to the bodies of the dead or dying: 'What an unhappy man I am! Who will rescue me from this body that is taking me to death?' It was a state of utter despair that Luther himself and many others had experienced and he had come to realise the futility of trying to pull himself up by his own moral bootstraps. Even his charitable works, he recognised, were tainted by the sin of mixed motives. Latomus acknowledged the disposition over which Paul agonised but for him the apostle's words were not a gut-wrenching *cri du coeur*. The 'sin-tendency' was not a condition which totally alienated man from God. It was an inclination which man, with divine help, could overcome. Man remained in control of his own destiny. 'Now we come to the chief point of disagreement,' Luther stated in his response. 'Is it only by forgiving mercy, or is it by its very nature, that this sin – or, as you prefer, infirmity – is not opposed to God and his law? Doesn't this summarise our dispute?'[6] What would later be labelled the doctrine of 'total depravity' became

fundamental to the Protestant world view. Escape from the human predicament was only, as Paul had stated, through personal faith in the saving
work of God: 'Thanks be to God who does this through our Lord Jesus
Christ . . . There is no condemnation now for those who live in union
with Christ Jesus.'⁷ The Catholic take on human will was that it *was*
capable of performing acts pleasing to God and that it was to assist this
behaviour that the Church had been entrusted with sacramental means
of grace. Luther asserted with every fibre of his being that the Christian
could not, *dared not* rely on such externals, nor on his own moral efforts.
Evangelical individualism enabled a man to live, like St Paul, at one and
the same time, as accepted by God (justified) and yet still a sinner, being
transformed (gradually and often painfully) by the new experience of being
'in union with Christ Jesus'. Latomus was committed to defending the
status quo whereby man has to strive for perfection by following the path
laid down by tradition and as a member of the corporate Christian body.
There could be and can be no common ground between these two positions. Ecumenically-minded theologians have tried over the centuries to
bridge the gap between them but it remains as wide as it was in 1521.
Human free-will versus sovereign divine grace – that is what was at issue
in Luther's debate with Latomus and what would later be at issue when
Luther and Erasmus, the greatest minds of the age, finally rode into the
tourney field against each other in 1524–5.

There remains one other work of Luther's 'Patmos' months to be considered and it is the most important of them all. If the word of God was to be
the supreme and unassailable authority for the Christian it followed that it
should be readily available. Vernacular Bibles had existed in Germany for
more than half a century and no less than eighteen versions were in existence but none of them was such as to set the reader's heart racing. They
were translations from the Latin Vulgate and they had about them the aura
of medieval 'churchiness'. It was not just that they lacked the advantages
of the latest scholarship (notably the study of Greek); their glosses emphasised current ecclesiastical practice (such as the sacrament of penance) and
their (often vivid) woodcut illustrations reproduced those dramatic and
miraculous aspects of the biblical narrative that appealed to the painters of
church murals – Noah's ark, Jonah and the big fish, etc. Luther realised the
need for a translation which would be not only purer linguistically but would
direct attention to those passages that clearly expounded the Gospel. Towards
the close of 1521 he personally undertook to translate the New Testament,
using Erasmus's Greek text as his source. He produced a first draft within

three months and subsequently completed the work at Wittenberg where he had colleagues and a good library to help him. Luther's New Testament was published in September, 1522.

The German New Testament shows us a new Luther: Luther the poet. By this time the Bible had become part of him. He knew much of it by heart and he was particularly steeped in the thought forms of the epistles. He had also developed a fluency in High German, a language which was distinct from regional dialects and which was being adopted in the princely courts and chancelleries. With the New Testament Luther staked a place at the very forefront of the development of German literature. His style was vigorous, colourful and direct. Anyone reading it could almost hear the author proclaiming the sacred text and that was no fortuitous accident; Luther's written language was akin to the oral delivery of his own impassioned sermons. His translation was couched in compelling prose. But what did it compel – or entreat – people to believe? This was no objective rendering of a Greek original into a sixteenth-century vernacular. Having, as he believed, fathomed the 'true' gospel, Luther was intent on communicating his insights to others. Each book was provided with its own preface and marginal glosses, designed to instruct the reader in the understanding of all the key concepts – 'law', 'grace', 'sin', 'faith', 'righteousness', etc. Anti-Roman polemic also had its place in the new translation. Luther did not hesitate to point out the contemporary application of first-century teaching. For example, the papacy was clearly identified as the beast of Revelation in Luther's glosses and the vivid woodcuts provided by Lucas Cranach. Luther's New Testament was the campaign manual of the Reformation.

> The fervent zeal of those Christian days seemed much superior to these our days and times, as manifestly may appear by their sitting up all night in reading and hearing: also by their expenses and charges in buying of books in English, of whom some gave five marks, some more, some less, for a book; some gave a load of hay for a few chapters of St James or of St Paul in English.[8]

This phenomenon that appeared in England a few years later had its beginning in Germany in the early 1520s. Bible mania is something the modern reader may well find difficult to understand. In an age when the Bible remains the least read best-seller and is widely regarded as out-dated and irrelevant we find it hard to get inside the minds of people who risked arrest, imprisonment and death by owning, reading and selling copies of the sacred text. Luther's New Testament was, of course, banned and, of course, that only boosted sales. For young scholars and other radically minded people the fact that this fruit was forbidden only added piquancy to its taste. Like Tyndale's English version a few years later, the book attracted excited, devoted students. The lengths the authorities went to to lay their hands on smuggled volumes is testimony to its success. The emperor ordered all copies to be handed in and some senior ecclesiastics even offered to pay for the books thus surrendered. Not many were.

Why did this translation, coming when it did, strike such a common chord? It was because books were, for the first time, becoming part of the everyday experience of people's lives. For some they were, doubtless, little more than status symbols – statements of their owners' wealth and sophistication. But for others they opened whole new worlds of knowledge and imagination hitherto available only to the well-educated (primarily senior clergy and the sons of aristocrats). An extensive 'middle class' could now afford to buy what was coming from the presses. And the most intriguing book of all was the Bible. For as long as anyone could remember priests and friars had talked about it, theologians had argued about it, artists had represented scenes from it in paint and stained glass and now the controversy over what it actually meant had 'hit the headlines'. It was *news*. Small wonder, then, that people flocked to acquire copies, to become literate in order to read them or to resort secretly to the homes of neighbours where the forbidden words were expounded. Bible study became a swelling, unstoppable underground movement. Scripture written in language that ordinary literate people could understand emerged as the symbol and guarantor of personal freedom. Men and women no longer had to take their religion from the priest, to accept uncritically 'truths' proclaimed by men for whom they had limited respect. They could read the Gospel for themselves, interpret it at will, and even write their own religious tracts, expounding and applying holy writ. As we shall see, one result of the publication of Lutheran Bibles was the releasing of a flood of books and pamphlets written by laymen (and women!). Merchants, artisans, soldiers and housewives turned into theologians and rushed into print.

But it was not just the serum of a purified biblical text that Luther set coursing through the veins of Germany. Translation implies interpretation and it was his exposition of the New Testament message that made such a dramatic impact. In the introductory notes and the marginal glosses he wrote for the New Testament books Luther identified and laid out the methodology that later ages would call 'Evangelicalism'. This was far and away the most important contribution of Martin Luther to the history of religion. To this great task he brought all his spiritual experience, theological understanding and critical awareness. His was no blind fundamentalism, asserting like his medieval predecessors that every word of Scripture had equal validity. He saw himself as a servant of the Gospel but not as a slave of the word of God written. The rigid rationalism which obliged him to expose the errors of scholasticism and sacerdotalism would not allow him to turn a blind eye to the differences of interpretation and even the contradictions existing within the New Testament corpus. He drew up his own league table of canonical books. At the top stood St John's Gospel and the Epistle to the Romans, the latter categorised by Luther as 'the purest gospel'. Then came the other Pauline letters and 1 Peter. The remaining books followed in due order, with Revelation and the Epistle of James at the bottom of the list. The Apocalypse, which both Catholic preachers and the wilder sort of heretics had used to strike terror into their hearers, was dismissed for its lack of clarity. 'A revelation should reveal,' Luther expostulated. As for James, the translator scorned it as being sub-apostolic in date and theologically faulty. It extolled the importance of good works as opposed to faith in the achievement of salvation and, thus, was a 'straw-like epistle lacking gospel verity'.

Luther faced the basic problem of every translator: that of converting the original into the idioms and thought patterns of his own day. In wrestling with the writers' first-century, market-place Greek he possessed one quality that may be regarded as an advantage or disadvantage, according to one's point of view: he saw all Christian truth through the eyes of St Paul. By now he had totally absorbed the apostle's theology. He lived and breathed the converted Pharisee's interpretation of the message and mission of Jesus and he was passionately committed to propagating it. So convinced was he that he understood the teaching of the great evangelist that he did not hesitate to add to the original text when he felt Paul's meaning was not absolutely clear. Thus, for example, in the key verse, Romans 3.28, 'We reckon a man is justified by faith without works of the law', Luther added the word 'alone' to provide greater emphasis: 'We hold that a man is justified by faith alone apart from works of law.' There is no doubt that the apostle's tightly packed reasoning needs elucidation for any reader, whether in the sixteenth or twenty-first century, and Luther still stands as the foremost of all his commentators. Paul gave the gentile world the evangel. Luther gave it evangelicalism.

I would like to know who fills my pulpit. Is Amsdorf still snoring and lazy? Also, what is Doctor Karlstadt doing? May the Lord guard and strengthen you in what you write concerning the prosperity of the university.[9]

The exile feasted eagerly on every scrap of news that came from Wittenberg and from the elector's court. Like anyone deprived of the comfort of friends and colleagues, Luther took an exaggerated interest in the little details of their lives. He congratulates Amsdorf on gaining a benefice and Karlstadt on his marriage. He urges Melancthon to preach on festival days in order to divert people from excessive drinking and rowdyism. He accuses the humanist scholar, Wolfgang Capito, of hypocrisy and, through Spalatin, advises the elector against a 'peace at any price' policy. Luther's letters from the Wartburg reveal the mutually contradictory emotions of a leader who longs to be in control yet wants to encourage others to stand on their own feet. He chides his young protégé, Philip Melancthon,

I cannot believe what you write, that you are going astray without a shepherd . . . As long as you, Amsdorf and the others are there you are not without a shepherd. Don't talk that way lest God be angered and we be found guilty of ingratitude. Would that all the churches . . . had one fourth of your share of the Word and its ministers!

And he tells the same correspondent (is it with ruefulness or 'fatherly' pride?): 'You are already replacing me; because of the gifts you have from God, you have attained greater authority and popularity than I had.'[10] Yet both men implicitly accepted that Luther was the master. Melancthon wrote letter after letter describing the fast-moving events at Wittenberg and Luther was not slow to respond with lengthy advice.

What was happening in the distant Saxon town was inevitable. It was a direct consequence of Luther's challenge to religious authority. He had set out in all his writings a programme of reform. He had introduced the powerful narcotic of freedom with all the risks that that entailed. Would Wittenberg's spiritual clinicians be equal to the task of administering it responsibly? Might not some incautious students and citizens be tempted to overdose? Melancthon had good cause to be worried about the direction events were taking without the presence of the one man who commanded the respect of all sections of Wittenberg society. He knew, despite the words of reassurance and encouragement that arrived from the Wartburg, that he lacked Luther's charisma and authority. Moreover, there was among his colleagues one man who did not share Melancthon's humility and reticence; and who was more than ready to step into the master's shoes. The unfortunate truth was that this man, Andreas Bodenstein von Karlstadt, lacked both the temperament and the understanding of complex issues to handle the rapidly developing crisis at the very centre of the Reformation.

It is easy to characterise Karlstadt as, at best, unstable and, at worst, a buffoon. He was neither. He was a scholar of moderate intellect who had the misfortune to live in the shadow of genius. Luther was a creative spirit who, even while making his most obstinate assertions, was still seeking deeper truth. Karlstadt received the new radicalism as though it was written on tablets of stone and applied it with vigour and rigour. He enthusiastically endorsed the Lutheran programme. He saw clearly – perhaps too clearly – the logical conclusions of those policies and initiatives Luther was drawing from Scripture but he had no experience of the years of spiritual struggle which had led Brother Martin to formulate those revolutionary new orthodoxies. Karlstadt studied problems, reached

Andreas Bodenstein von Karlstadt

rational solutions and imposed them stringently, often without the humanity which would have softened his uncompromising dogmatism. In his zeal for reform, Karlstadt turned a fresh way of embracing religion into a hard party line. While Luther was absent and, according to common rumour, brutally done to death by the agents of Antichrist, Karlstadt, as head of the theology faculty at Wittenberg, saw it as his responsibility to continue the creation of a purified Christian commonwealth. There were problems that had to be dealt with on a day-by-day basis. Priests were forsaking their vows and getting married. Monks and nuns were abandoning their convents. Anticlerical riots were becoming widespread. If the new movement was to be saved from disintegration and was, on the contrary, to advance boldly, *someone* had to unfurl the religious banner behind which it would march.

Moreover, the reform was under danger from erstwhile friends. Frederick and several leaders in the town and the university were desperately hoping that, in Luther's absence, everything would *settle down* and return to 'normality'. In the early summer of 1521 they had been delighted and relieved when Karlstadt had agreed to go to Denmark to help with the establishment of the Reformation there. Unfortunately, King Christian II was only interested in religious change as a means of extending royal power and Karlstadt was altogether too extreme for his purpose. Within weeks the traveller had returned to Wittenberg. Frederick's advisers tried in vain to induce him to go back and continue the godly work in Copenhagen but they were stuck with him. Luther's attitude in all this was to demonstrate solidarity with colleagues by supporting them in all his contacts with the elector, while offering them encouragement and constructive criticism. It was only gradually that his and Karlstadt's paths diverged and then disagreement was more over the pace of change than the content of the reform programme.

In the summer of 1521 Karlstadt went public with his views on some of the most pressing problems. He published tracts on celibacy, religious vows and communion for the laity in both kinds. Copies soon reached the Wartburg where Luther read them with anxiety. This was not because he fundamentally disagreed with his old colleague but because he found fault with Karlstadt's exegesis. 'I don't want [you at Wittenberg] to be publishing anything based on obscure and ambiguous Scripture passages, since the light which is demanded of us has to be brighter than the sun and all the stars,' he writes. He also disapproved of Karlstadt's tendency to proclaim as truths binding on all Christians some issues which, Luther believed, were matters of individual conscience: 'We are certainly a people on whom no law should be imposed – especially not for the whole of life – but to whom everything should be left free.'[11] In order to rectify matters Luther now wrote his own treatises on vows and private masses; if the Wittenberg movement was to take a stand against these things it should do so upon a properly-thought-out scriptural basis. There was nothing eirenical about the stance he took and on most issues he did not show himself more moderate than Karlstadt. Having scoured the Bible, he reached clear conclusions: there was no divine warrant for monastic vows or for the mass to be regarded as a sacrifice or offering to God. Both smacked of 'works religion' and were, therefore, to be disregarded. These treatises were radical in the extreme but they were nowhere near as inflammatory as *Against the Idol at Halle*, a blistering attack on the Archbishop of Mainz who had embarked on another indulgence sale. In a separate letter to the archbishop Luther had the effrontery to issue an ultimatum: if the pernicious indulgence traffic had not been halted in fourteen days he would denounce it publicly by having *Against the Idol at Halle* published. As was his custom, Luther sent all these documents to Spalatin to arrange publication or onward posting as appropriate. But the electoral minister, under orders from his master, locked them away. They were far too dangerous to be released into what was already a highly volatile situation.

Poor Frederick was in a quandary. He had Luther bottled up in the Wartburg and could exercise a degree of control over him and his contacts with the outside world. He might have hoped that exile would have had a calming effect but, so far from becoming more reasonable, Luther was clearly growing more extreme. At the same time events in Wittenberg were becoming daily more alarming. There was an exodus from religious houses. Radical clergy were refusing to say private masses for the dead (thereby putting at risk valuable endowments on which the churches relied heavily for their maintenance). There were fresh outrages against priests carrying out their sacerdotal duties. The town council even made a formal request to the elector for liturgical reform, which Frederick rejected on the reasonable grounds that one small German city could not unilaterally inaugurate changes which affected the whole of Latin Christendom. If the elector had hoped that moderate voices would make themselves heard as soon as Luther was out of the way he was clearly disappointed. Karlstadt, Melancthon and their like-minded colleagues had grasped the initiative and were doing nothing at all to calm the situation or restrain impatient elements who wanted root-and-branch reform and wanted it NOW. On the contrary, the religious leadership in Wittenberg was, if anything, more difficult to handle than the guru in Eisenach. Yet, for Frederick and the political leaders there was worse to come.

By December Luther's frustration reached breaking point. He made a short, incognito visit to Wittenberg, which was kept secret from the elector. It was then that he discovered that his latest writings had been suppressed. He was furious and, as soon as he had returned to the Wartburg, he vented his feelings in a letter to Spalatin. After reporting on his reunion with his 'sweetest friends', he referred to the mysteriously missing manuscripts:

> There is nothing that would disturb me more at this moment than to know that [they] had reached you and that you were holding them back, since I have dealt in these little books with themes that require the greatest possible haste. Therefore if you have them, for goodness sake curb that moderation and prudence of which I suspect you, for you accomplish nothing by rowing against the stream. What I have written I want published, if not at Wittenberg then certainly somewhere else. If the manuscripts have been lost or if you have kept them, I will be so embittered that I will write more vehemently than ever on these points. Whoever destroys lifeless paper will not also quench the spirit.

Luther added truculently, 'Everything else that I see and hear pleases me very much. May the Lord strengthen the spirit of those who want to do right!'[12]

'Themes that require the greatest possible haste' – Luther, it seems, now sensed that there was a very real urgency about the changes necessary in the life of the Church. He challenged the forces of conservatism which were bent on slowing the impetus of reform. The exciting things that were happening at Wittenberg and elsewhere were, he believed, God's initiatives. Yet he was not blind to the dangers of heedless haste. In the same letter to Spalatin he made passing reference to 'the improper conduct of some of our people' and he promised to address the wilder spirits in an exhortation which could be read in the churches. Within days he had kept his word. In *A True Admonition to All Christians to Guard against Insurrection and Rebellion* he pointed out that in the warfare against Antichrist there was no need to use Antichrist's own weapons of violence and defiance of civil authority. The word of God was already at work undermining the citadels of false religion and could be trusted to complete the task. Rebellion was always wrong.

This is the first indication of the most painful dilemma Luther had to face in the explosive days that lay ahead. He never was a political thinker. His attitude to worldly power was simple, even simplistic. Church leaders, whether acting in their spiritual or temporal capacities, were always to be held accountable to the word of God. Secular authorities were always to be obeyed, even when they were wrong, because power had been entrusted to them from on high and resistance could only lead to the breakdown of all law and order. The difference of attitude is apparent in all his personal dealings with his superiors; there is a stark contrast between the almost fawning respect he showed to the elector and the emperor and the contempt he had for the pope and his adjutants. Luther honestly believed in the doctrine of what came to be called the 'godly magistrate'. Kings, princes and city councils, under the guidance of ministers of the word, alone had the ability to root out papist error, to divert funds from the maintenance of lazy monks to the care of the poor, to close centres of superstitious pilgrimage. In his vision of the Reformation this is exactly what would happen. It was unthinkable that the impatient lower orders would take the law into their own hands in order to expedite the work of the Gospel. That would bring the whole evangelical movement into disrepute. Given the complex state of German politics in which civil and ecclesiastical powers were inextricably intertwined and given also the heady libertarianism inherent in the Gospel message, such convictions were naïve in the extreme. Events in Wittenberg were about to expose their shortcomings.

Luther's friends had been overjoyed to see him and vastly encouraged by his expressions of support. It seemed to them that he had set his seal of approval on all that they had been doing and, when he departed again, he left in his wake an atmosphere of euphoria. It seemed to Melancthon, Karlstadt and members of their party that the Wittenberg reformation was now on course and they pressed ahead zealously. They laid out a spiritual and moral agenda for the godly republic and presented it to the city council. Among its provisions were: communion in both kinds, regular preaching of the Gospel, tighter regulations against drunkenness and prostitution, the abolition of religious lay brotherhoods and the confiscation of their funds. Frederick ordered that such demands were to be resisted but it is clear that the initiative now lay with the extremists. Christmas arrived but the celebration of the coming of the Prince of Peace was marked by a dramatic increase of tension. Karlstadt announced that, in direct defiance of the elector, he would celebrate festal mass with some very visual changes: he would not be wearing vestments; he would not elevate the host; he would conduct part of the service in German; and he would give the chalice to communicants as well as bread. This symbolic break with tradition fuelled an excitement that was already red hot. Ribald groups emphasised their adherence to the new order by bursting into churches where ordinary services were being held and drowning the voices of the celebrants with coarse songs.

All this activity was not taking place in a vacuum. In towns throughout Germany and into Switzerland and France new religious thinking was loosening social and political conventions. The evangelical wing of the Church periodically has a tendency to bifurcate into word-based and Spirit-based elements, between those whose only authority is the Bible and those who seek direct divine 'anointing' in the form of dramatic experiences and signs such as prophecy, miracles and glossolalia. Exponents of the latter, 'charismatic' understanding of the faith inevitably generate excitement, particularly among the illiterate. They offer not merely a flamboyant expression of Christianity but experiential religion which owes little to patient study and appears to be self-authenticating. Several of these exuberant preachers were thrown up by the intellectual and spiritual ferment of the 1520s. One place where tumultuous events were taking place was Zwickau, a prosperous textile-manufacturing and silver-mining centre close to the Bohemian border, some 150 kilometres south of Wittenberg. At Zwickau fanaticism made its frenzied entrance into the Reformation drama. It took the form of Cerberus, and its three heads were millenarianism, iconoclasm and charismania. Despite certain superficial similarities, what burst onto the religious scene from Zwickau was quite distinct from anything being advocated by Luther or even by his over-enthusiastic followers. Luther's challenge to religious tradition was born of spiritual struggle. The Zwickau revolt was generated by social conflict. Where wealthy merchants and mine owners lived cheek-by-jowl with exploited labourers and artisans it was inevitable that there would be conflict between the haves and have-nots. This was the unstable world into which burst prophets preaching the imminent and violent overthrow of the existing order by an angry God.

Thomas Müntzer was five years younger than Luther and an ardent disciple who eagerly embraced the freedom explicit in the reformer's message. Like Luther, he was attracted by the intense inner spirituality of the mystics but he was not drawn to the contemplative life. Müntzer was an activist. He was impatient for the revitalisation of the Church. Like Karlstadt, he was always inclined to cut corners in order to achieve social and religious change. But he was more extreme – and dangerous – than Wittenberg's dean of theology. At some point during his early manhood he discovered – and the realisation was pregnant with future disaster – that he had the gift of oratory. He could sway crowds, play on the strings of their emotions, move them to tears of self-abnegation or roars of indignant rage. Müntzer was obviously going to be an influential figure in the newly emerging Germany. The only question was the message to which his remarkable talent would be harnessed. In 1520 there seemed no reason to doubt that he was marked out as an evangelist of the true Gospel and Luther had no hesitation in supporting his application for the post of pastor of St Mary's church in Zwickau. Unfortunately, in that unhappy town he came under the spell (and the metaphor is particularly apt) of Nicholas Storch.

Storch was an impoverished weaver with a grudge against the world and particularly its wealthy and powerful leaders. His unassailable conviction, his extensive knowledge of the Bible and the revelations which he claimed to receive from the Holy Spirit made him a formidable 'prophet'. Those who came in contact with him either stood in awe of his holy zeal or in fear of his mounting influence. Storch possessed the magnetism often enjoyed by those who claim to be in direct communication with God and the recipient of unique revelations. Few if any of his critics were able to confound him from their own superior understanding of the Gospel. Müntzer immediately attached himself to the body of Storch's disciples. They made a formidable team and Müntzer became the mouthpiece for a violently millenarian message. He went further and further beyond the Wittenberg prospectus. Like all apocalyptics, he bolstered his hatred of the existing world order by proclaiming imminent divine judgement against it. Mankind was on the verge of extinction and only the elect would survive fiery retribution. The elect, of course, were those who subscribed to the Zwickau message. Opposition only strengthened Müntzer's argument: suffering in this world was a mark of the elect. Suffering was not long in coming. After a series of violent riots the city authorities threw the prophets out in April 1521. Müntzer went on tour with his inflammatory manifesto, becoming steadily more manic and extreme. He told any who would listen that he had been chosen to purge the world in preparation for the *dies irae*:

Harvest time is here, so God has hired me for his harvest. I have sharpened my scythe, for my thoughts are strongly fixed on the truth and my lips, hands, skin, hair, soul, body, life curse the unbelievers.

Drive Christ's enemies out from among the elect, for you are the instruments for that purpose. Dearly beloved brethren, don't put up any shallow pretence that God's might will do it without your laying on with the sword . . . Christ is your master, so don't let them live any longer . . . a godless man has no right to live if he hinders the godly.[13]

Unsurprisingly, this preacher of sedition was drummed out of town after town. Storch and some of his close adherents, meanwhile, remained in the vicinity of Zwickau where they continued to make a nuisance of themselves until, in December, Duke John of Saxony ordered an investigation into their activities. This was the moment when these wild men, who had always asserted their willingness to embrace persecution and martyrdom, fled. They pitched up in Wittenberg.

The Zwickau prophets arrived in the middle of a tense and confused situation – and made it worse. Their zeal was infectious; their root-and-branch attitude to reform compelling. Karlstadt found their egalitarianism chimed with his own convictions and broke down still further the distinction between clergy and laity. He now boldly affirmed other teachings of the newcomers, such as rejection of infant baptism and the veneration of images. He told his congregations that pictures and statues of the saints were 'graven images', condemned by the Ten Commandments, and he encouraged his hearers to remove them. Thus it was that the first iconoclastic outbursts of the Reformation occurred at Wittenberg. While academics, clergy and ill-disciplined enthusiasts went their own diverse ways, the city council, itself very divided, was faced with the task of maintaining some semblance of order. Any attempt to clamp down the lid on what was happening would have built up the pressure. The only way to ensure peace was to make concessions. Thus the Ordinance of the City of Wittenberg came into being. It was the first attempt to legislate for an evangelical urban commonwealth and gave formal sanction to the reforms proposed in December.

What was lacking in all these tumultuous events was coherence. Untried policies, novel ideas, liturgical innovations and secular laws tumbled out of the religious cornucopia without order and without any clear strategy. There was only one man who could sort the sheep from the goats in Wittenberg's reformation. Melancthon wrote to him asking for his advice.

Thomas Müntzer preaching

Luther's reply was, as usual, biblical and common sensical. Having dealt with the controversial theological issues, he told his young colleague that on no account were the Zwickau charismatics to be taken at their own valuation. He was inclined to believe that they represented a diabolical attempt to destroy the reform from within and he gave Melancthon a simple litmus test to apply: 'examine them and do not even listen if they speak of the glorified Jesus, unless you have first heard [them speak] of the crucified Jesus'.[14]

Once more, Luther expressed his complete confidence in the younger man's ability to handle the situation in Wittenberg but this was little more than a gesture of encouragement. He had already made an important decision, as he explained in a letter to Spalatin four days later:

I shall definitely return in a short time; if I don't stay in Wittenberg I shall certainly stay somewhere else [nearby] or wander around. *The cause itself demands it* [my emphasis].[15]

10

The Parting of the Ways

For Luther it was inconceivable that any who had followed him along the path out of the dark forest of papist error should want to go rushing on ahead into the swamps and mires of heresy. He and his colleagues had set free the Pauline gospel, long chained-up in the dungeons of scholastic theology and sacerdotal religion. The implications of that act of liberation for the everyday life of the Church were still in the process of being worked out. A good translation of the Bible had to be produced; liturgy had to be made to reflect the new theology; issues of monastic vows had to be faced; the nature of priesthood needed to be redefined and that meant taking a fresh look at celibacy and marriage. These and other practical matters had to be discussed and resolved and that was why the exile was pleased with most of what was going on in Wittenberg. Truth had been established. It was only necessary to apply it. Anyone who came forward with rival truth was a liar. Worse, he was an agent of Satan. Writing to advise Melancthon what to do about the men from Zwickau, he observed:

I hear of nothing said or done by them that Satan could not also do or imitate . . . God has never sent anyone, not even the Son himself, unless he was called through men or attested by signs. In the old days the prophets had their authority from the Law and the prophetic order, as we now receive authority through men. I definitely do not want the 'prophets' to be accepted if they state that they were called by mere revelation . . . I have always expected Satan to touch this sore, but he did not want to do it through the papists. It is among us and among our followers that he is stirring up this grievous schism, but Christ will quickly trample him under our feet.[1]

Luther, who had, through his own spiritual experiences, been propelled into rebellion against the highest authority in the earthly church, saw no irony in the fact that he was repudiating preachers of novelties for the same reason that he had been repudiated by Rome: they were setting themselves up against divinely appointed authority.

What stung him were the taunts of his old enemies. They had pointed out the inevitable disintegration of his movement once the unifying obedience to Rome had been shrugged off. The reformers did not have the propaganda battle all their own way. Rome experienced no lack of witty champions able to wield their pens with devastating effect. In 1522, the Franciscan, Thomas Murner, lampooned the Wittenberg leader in a long verse satire entitled *The Lutheran Fool*. He denounced the arch-heretic as a revolutionary disloyal alike to his spiritual and temporal superiors and set to plunge the empire into chaos. Worse, Luther's rejection of the sacraments was blasphemy against God. There is no doubt that such attacks struck home and made Luther determined to demonstrate his obedience to his prince and his abhorrence of public disorder. Weeks later we find him writing to the elector to justify his decision to return to Wittenberg:

I myself was so overwhelmed by the calamity that had I not been certain that we have the pure gospel, I would have despaired of [our] cause. Whatever I have suffered hitherto for this cause has been nothing compared with this. I should willingly have averted the trouble at the cost of my life if that had been possible. We can answer neither to God nor to the world for what has been done. And yet it is blamed on me and, what is even worse, on the gospel. This pains me deeply.[2]

Luther was faced with the problem that faces all radical reformers, whether religious or secular: the limitations of liberty. He had freed people from the shackles of priestly domination by making available to them the 'pure gospel'. He believed that Scripture and reason would always lead seekers to the spiritual deliverance he had found. What he could not come to terms with was the phenomenon of other teachers using his own exegetical methods and reaching different conclusions.

Something must be said at this point about Luther's personal situation throughout the crisis years 1523–6. No longer did he face ever-present danger as he had in the period leading up to the Diet of Worms. Instead, he had to cope with novel experiences – uncertainty and the deprivation of daily routine. He returned to the cloister and was, once again, an Augustinian friar. Off came Junker George's beard. Back came the tonsure. But, wholly as a result of his own teaching, the numbers in the Wittenberg convent were steadily dwindling as, one-by-one, his brethren abandoned their vows. Luther did not immediately follow suit. It was the autumn of 1524 before he put aside his habit. Monasticism was dying but it offered the only structure for life that Luther knew. Materially he was now less well provided for than he had been in the Wartburg. His work at the university was unpaid and he received nothing for his pastoral responsibilities. He could have looked for a teaching post elsewhere but that would have meant leaving the safety of the Elector Frederick's territory. For someone who believed firmly, as Luther did, in vocation – that every man and woman had a divine calling to fulfil – all this was a disorienting experience. He agonised in prayer to discover what God wanted of him. He had championed the Gospel against the papists but now new combatants were appearing and he could not put up his sword. In addition visitors and letters arrived almost daily seeking his advice on the establishment of the reforms in various towns and regions. Others came knocking on his door seeking refuge – ex-monks, converts disowned by their families, nuns who had fled their convents. Congregations throughout Saxony wanted him to come and preach to them. The demands on his time and energies were unceasing. He worked all the daylight hours and on into the night, at length falling, exhausted, onto an unmade bed.

Overwork, irregular diet, living conditions that were less than ideal – they were the ingredients for poor health, both physical and mental. Luther was prone to digestive disorders, to insomnia, to bouts of nervous exhaustion and to a general debility which left him easy prey to any bugs that were around. If he had not possessed a sturdy, peasant constitution he would probably have succumbed at an early age to some ailment that proved fatal. As it was, his most devastating affliction was what he called *Anfechtung*, a psycho-somatic disorder for which the word 'depression' is an inadequate translation. Mystics called it 'the dark night of the soul', a state of alienation in which God seems to be absent, leaving the believer prey to doubts and black despair. Luther's bouts of inner turmoil had not come to an end with his discovery of salvation by only faith. Sometimes, during his spiritual journey he would fall by the wayside, incapacitated by questions to which he received no easy answers – was he really right and the world wrong?; why, when other evangelicals were facing martyrdom, was he living in ease and safety?; was he counted unworthy to suffer for his Lord?; why was the unleashed word of God not sweeping all before it? In the loneliness of private devotion Luther wrestled with angels and demons – sometimes not sure which was which. On these occasions he was gripped by the fear of losing faith and, therefore, having nothing to look forward to but death, the complete annihilation of body, mind and spirit.

Always he turned for comfort and enlightenment to the Bible, especially the Psalms and the gospels. The Old Testament poet had had the same experience: 'O Lord . . . listen to my cry! If you do not answer me, I will be among those who go down to the world of the dead' (Psalm 28). And had not Jesus experienced the very depths of alienation when he cried from the Cross, 'My God, my God, why have you forsaken me?' Rationally Luther understood that such experiences were necessary for spiritual growth. Only when all other props and stays have gone and the believer is left clinging to faith by his fingernails will God lift him out of the pit and into the sunlight of his presence.

Contemporaries and later analysts based their judgement of Luther on his terrible, uncompromising certainties. They deplored his violent language, his unyielding dogmatism, his arrogance. What they failed to grasp was that public assertion was the obverse of private doubt. It was not that Luther did not question his own teachings and his application of Scripture, nor that he blithely failed to calculate their effect. On the contrary, it was precisely because he *did* wrestle with these things in the bleak seclusion of his own soul that he emerged for the fray encased in impermeable armour. He *had* confronted God's aweful, magisterial, holy truth. He *had* been almost crushed by it. He *had* submitted to it. It only remained for him to proclaim it – for the enlightenment of others and for his own self-assurance. If it drew from readers and hearers howls of protest, these were nothing compared with the impassioned entreaties he had, himself, made to the Almighty.

The immediate situation in Wittenberg was easy enough to rationalise: heretical teaching had been introduced and this had resulted in civil unrest, which manifestly demonstrated its diabolical origin. The Zwickau doctrines were causing concern to the town's religious leaders while Frederick and the civic authorities were profoundly disturbed about the breakdown of public order. Luther dealt with the first problem in letters to Melancthon in which he expounded Bible teaching on ecstatic religion and infant baptism. The second problem was more difficult to combat. The city council urged him to return as the only man who could command sufficient respect to restore concord. The elector, on the other hand, needed Luther to stay in hiding in order to preserve the fiction that he did not know where the condemned heretic was and could not, therefore, execute the imperial ban. In his Wartburg eyrie the exile struggled with his conscience. He longed to return to Wittenberg to defend 'the cause' but he hesitated to defy his prince. How could he urge others to submit to authority if he himself was not doing so? His letters reveal him trying to squirm his way around this moral dilemma by suggesting compromises. He needed to return in order to complete his work on the New Testament. He was anxious to begin, with others, the translation of the Old Testament. Perhaps he could simply move closer to Wittenberg to keep an eye on things without actually coming out of hiding. Not until the third week of February, 1522 did he make up his mind. He had already returned when, on 7 or 8 March, he wrote a tactful letter to Frederick. There were three reasons for his action, he said. The first was the entreaty he had received from the leaders at Wittenberg. The second was that 'Satan has injured some [members of the flock] which I cannot heal with any writing.' The third reason was doubtless designed to overcome the elector's scruples but also indicates that Luther accurately understood the worsening general situation.

> I am rather afraid (and I worry that unfortunately I may be only too right) that there will be a real rebellion in the German territories, by which God will punish the German nation. For we see that this gospel is excellently received by the common people; but they receive it in a fleshly sense; that is, they know that it is true but do not want to use it correctly. Those who should calm such a rebellion only aid it. They attempt to put out the light by force, not realising that they are only embittering the hearts of men by this and stimulating them to revolt.[3]

Luther was alarmed that the wilder spirits were urging their followers to overthrow all authorities which showed themselves hostile to the brand of religious enlightenment they were peddling. He, who had blazed the trail of challenge to the Roman Antichrist, was appalled that others were commanding disobedience to the divinely ordained power of *secular* rulers.

A millennium of interaction between church and state had created a situation in which the two were completely fused. Luther had no desire to separate these Siamese twins; indeed, the very concept would have been incomprehensible to him. Nor did he accept the eschatological manifesto of those who preached the sweeping away of the existing order in preparation for the rule of the saints. He genuinely believed that Christian society could be regulated by godly princes. This was the fundamental flaw in his political application of his gospel. It begged the question of who was to decide when a ruler was or was not 'godly'. Nor did Luther set a faultless example. When it came down to daily practicalities he was prepared to defy secular authority while demanding that others give it unquestioning loyalty. The letter he wrote to Frederick about his proposed return to Wittenberg smacks of almost Jesuitical reasoning:

> Inasmuch as I do not intend to obey Your Electoral Grace, Your Electoral Grace is excused before God if I am captured or put to death. Before men Your Electoral Grace should act as an elector, obedient to the authorities and allowing His Imperial Majesty to rule in your cities and lands over both life and property, as is his right according to the Imperial constitution. Your Electoral Grace should by no means offer any resistance or request such resistance or any obstruction on the part of others if [His Imperial Majesty] wants to capture me or put me to death. For no one should overthrow or resist authority save him who ordained it; otherwise it is rebellion and an action against God.[4]

This confident ('arrogant' would not be too strong a word) attitude towards his patron marks a fresh stage in Luther's psychological development. His evolution as a great figure in world history had begun as a young man in the cloister struggling with new thoughts. He had gone on to become the teacher of a new way. Now he emerged as the leader of a new movement. He had defied the two most powerful men in the western world – the pope and the emperor – and God had protected him from their wrath. He had been withdrawn from the fray and everything that he had achieved had come under threat. It was now clear to him that God intended him to take command of the missionary endeavour which was spreading throughout Germany and beyond. The man who returned from the Wartburg was not the belligerent controversialist who had entered the castle (though he would still, when necessary, employ a sharp tongue or pen). He was a man intent on setting out a programme for practical reform and he went about it with quiet assurance.

His first task was to set everything to rights in Wittenberg and, considering all the turbulence and confusion of the last few months, he accomplished this with remarkable speed. He was doubtless helped by the mood of most sober citizens who were angry and frightened by what was happening in their midst. When the news spread that the local hero had returned and that he proposed to address his congregation, people flocked to hear him. He delivered a series of eight daily sermons between the ninth and the seventeenth of March in which he covered comprehensively all the controversial issues facing the city. The burden of his message was patience, moderation and quietude. Certainly there were abuses to be addressed but little would be gained by hasty change and nothing would be gained by violence. Thus, he agreed with Karlstadt that religious images gave rise to superstition but he opposed their wholesale destruction. As he put it in his homely way, men were often led astray by women and strong drink but that was no reason to abolish them both. Familiar patterns of worship, similarly, needed reform but to sweep away old customs without adequate explanation and preparation could only cause confusion. He restored the services in his church to the *status quo ante*. While this was all reassuring to the majority, it inevitably puzzled the 'keener' Christians of Wittenberg. The erstwhile revolutionary seemed to have gone soft. Luther's response was, as ever, well thought out. To force change on people against their will – for example, by obliging them to receive communion in both kinds – was no better than the priestly domination of the old dispensation. Every individual had to make his own faith response to God and God would then enlighten him. No human intermediary should compel him into religious acts which had no inner meaning for him.

The more precisely Luther defined his stand on specific issues of church teaching and practice the closer he came to defining his own movement over against, not only Catholicism, but also the belief systems of those humanists and evangelicals who could not follow him in every particular. Here we see another inconsistency between the reformer's praxis and lexis. His insistence on not bruising the consciences of his congregation by imposing radical beliefs meant that he was building a broad church. Yet, erecting new doctrinal barriers implied just the opposite: a gathered church of subscribers to Lutheran orthodoxy. To those who had held sway during his absence the returned leader's 'peace at any price' stance seemed like dishonourable compromise. When he abandoned liturgical innovations and sent the Zwickau 'fanatics' packing Karlstadt and his allies had to consider their position.

Karlstadt was a man confused and inconsistent. He had been hauled before the elector and had agreed to stop preaching novelties. He had taken a back seat on Luther's return. Then he wrote a trenchant treatise defending his hard line on images. His behaviour became increasingly eccentric. When lecturing he put aside his doctor's gown and took to addressing the young students as his 'dear colleagues'. Soon he was neglecting his academic duties altogether to spend time on his nearby farm. He took no pleasure in his old friends and companions in the war on the papacy. Instead he found consolation in correspondence with, of all people, Thomas Müntzer. In 1523 he left Wittenberg to take up a post as vicar of Orlamünde, where he could promote his own version of the faith without Luther breathing down his neck.

Karlstadt was not the only old friend whom Luther lost as Latin Christendom sundered into confessional fragments. His mentor, Johann von Staupitz, was also unable to follow his erstwhile protégé. In fact, the Augustinian vicar general became so frustrated with the divisions and political manoeuvring within his order that he left it and joined the Benedictines. Luther heard from mutual friends of Staupitz's news and of opinions he had expressed of events in Wittenberg. It pained him and he wrote in the hope of rebuilding bridges:

> . . . I beg of you, for the sake of Christ's mercies, do not indiscriminately believe the accusations that are made against . . . me. You say that my teachings are praised by those who patronise brothels and that my recent writings gave great offence. I am not surprised or afraid of this. Certainly we have done nothing here other than publicise the pure Word among the people without [creating] a disturbance and this we are [still] doing. Both the good and the bad are making use of the Word and, as you know, it is not in our power to control [what they do] . . . We will do what Christ predicted when he said that his angels would gather out of his kingdom all causes of offence. My Father, I must destroy the kingdom of abomination and perdition which belongs to the pope, together with all his hangers-on . . . The Lord knows the end of it. The matter is beyond our power of comprehension and understanding. Therefore there is no reason why I should delay until someone is able to understand it. Because of the greatness of God it is most fitting that there should arise

proportionately great disturbance of minds, great causes of offence
and great monstrosities. Do not let all these things disturb you, my
Father . . . You can see in these things God's counsel and his mighty
hand . . .[5]

What Luther desperately wanted his old friend to understand was that the
turbulence which was building up around him was proof positive that his
cause was holy and just. He saw himself as a battlefield commander in the
cosmic conflict between good and evil, truth and falsehood, order and
chaos. He would have been worried had there *not* been disturbances,
disagreements and divisions. Others lacked this certainty. They put more
obvious interpretations on surface events. To them it seemed that Luther
had unleashed the hounds of hell rather than the cohorts of the Lord of
Hosts. This was certainly Staupitz's position. His transfer from the
Augustinian order to the more rigid Benedictine system was a declaration
of the validity of monasticism at the very time that Luther was denouncing
it. He made no reply to the reformer's letter and, fifteen months later,
Luther wrote again, in genuine anguish, beseeching the man who had
taught him to cast aside reliance on pious works and embrace the Cross
in simple faith, to come back to the truth.

> . . . But if you have become another man towards us – Christ forbid
> (to be frank with you) – I will waste no more words, but invoke
> God's mercy on you and on us all. You see, therefore, Reverend
> Father, with what great doubts I am writing, because through your
> extended silence you have left us uncertain for such a long time about
> your feelings towards us. On the other hand you can be most certain
> about our thoughts and feelings. I am sure you do not really despise
> us, although we may displease you in everything. I shall certainly not
> cease in wishing and praying that you may be turned away from . . .
> the papacy as I am, and as certainly you once were. May the Lord
> hear me and take you to himself, together with us. Amen.[6]

This time Staupitz did reply. He applauded his old friend's courage in
combating those errors which had crept into the life of the Church but
gently pointed out that things had gone too far. The freedom Luther
preached had led to licence and disorder. Disposing of vows might relieve
Luther's burdened conscience and aid a few other troubled souls but it had
lured the majority into an unholy liberty and given them apparent divine

sanction to follow their own lusts. This, as far as we know, was the last communication between the two men who had once been so close. The breach was never closed and, by the end of 1524, Staupitz was dead. Luther ever afterwards honoured his memory and spoke with gratitude of the spiritual guidance his father in God had given him. He seems to have closed his mind to Staupitz's 'defection'.

Death removed other supporters. Franz von Sickingen and Ulrich von Hutten both died in 1523 (see above, pp. 161 ff.). Luther had always been careful not to tie himself too closely to the German knights but they had eagerly espoused his movement and provided refuge to scores of evangelical and humanist activists.

In his last extremity Hutten turned for aid to an erstwhile humanist friend, Desiderius Erasmus. But he appealed in vain to someone who was desperately trying to avoid any taint of heresy. The age's leading man of letters had fled the dogmatic, unforgiving, unyielding traditionalism of Louvain for the intellectually eclectic atmosphere of Basel but he discovered to his chagrin that there was no haven where a quiet scholar could escape the burning issues of the day. He was beset by entreaties to confront Luther in print. Catholic leaders from the pope down identified him as the obvious champion of orthodoxy and there were many others who, perplexed by the battle of beliefs and ideas, wanted to hear what the great Erasmus had to say. Year after year he warded off such pleas, claiming somewhat disingenuously that he had not read Luther's works and so had no opinion about them. Luther, himself, urged the Dutch scholar to maintain his vow of silence but the poor man found himself in a no-win situation. By refusing to challenge the Wittenberg rebellion he appeared to confirm the suspicions of those who were convinced that he was secretly in league with the heretics.

Thus it was that, in September 1524, Erasmus bowed to the inevitable and delivered to the press a hastily compiled anti-Lutheran tract, *Diatribe seu collatio de libero arbitrio (A discussion or comparison of teachings about free-will)*. In December of the following year Luther responded with *De Servo Arbitrio (The Enslaved Will)*. This exchange went to the heart of the Reformation debate. With hindsight we can identify it as the point at which Reformation and Renaissance parted company. Yet, at the time it proved to be something of an anticlimax, for if intellectual Europe expected a clash of Titans it was disappointed.

This was a contest of style and substance and the two were easily confused. The combatants never really met head-on because they represented very different attitudes and viewpoints. Erasmus was a detached scholar who sought fragments of truth in classical writings and the Christian fathers as well as the Bible. It was Luther's boast that he preached and taught only the word of God. Several years before, he had identified exactly where his response towards the problems facing the Church differed from that of Erasmus. Describing something by the great humanist that he had just read, he explained ruefully, 'It is so agreeably, learnedly and wittily put together, that is, so thoroughly Erasmian in fact, that it compels one to smile and jest on the subject of the faults and misfortunes of the church of Christ, which, however, it is every Christian's duty to deplore before God in deepest grief'.[7] Erasmus, the liberal intellectual, found such earnestness, coupled with religious certainty, repellent. What stuck in his throat when confronted by evangelicalism (and this has always been a problem for rationalists who distrust religious emotion) was the seeming arrogance of those who claimed to *know* that they were among God's elect. He was impatient with all dogmas and dogmatists. His religion, his *philosophia Christi*, was essentially an ethical system: one did one's best to follow the teachings of Christ. Luther's heartfelt response to this was 'Been there, tried that; it doesn't work.' He had found his way to certainty based on Scripture so that he could react to Erasmus's apparent intellectual humility with the claim, 'To take no pleasure in assertions is not the mark of a Christian heart; indeed, one must delight in assertions to be a Christian at all.'[8]

Erasmus saw the conflicting beliefs which were tearing Europe asunder as, in part, the agencies of civilisation and barbarism. He wanted to set dogma aside in order to reconcile divergent views. He believed cracks could be papered over in the interests of peace. He felt almost physical revulsion at the fierce partisanship which tore down 'superstitious' images, consigned 'heretics' to the flames and threatened to plunge Christendom into even more serious internecine strife. For Luther compromise in the name of a spurious concord was anathema:

> You make it clear that this carnal peace and quiet seems to you far more important than faith, conscience, salvation, the Word of God, the glory of Christ, and God himself. Let me tell you, therefore – and I beg you to let this sink deep into your mind – I hold that a vital and solemn truth, of eternal consequence, is at stake in this discussion; one so crucial and fundamental that it ought to be maintained and defended even at the cost of life, though as a result the

whole world should be, not just thrown into turmoil and uproar, but shattered in chaos and reduced to nothingness.[9]

The differences between the two great men went far deeper than issues of mere style. In their controversy over free-will and grace it is Erasmus who appears as the true radical. He places man at the centre of the universe (although, of course, he would have denied that), walking tall and in command of his own destiny. Reason is his guide and he needs only to *understand* the loving divine purpose in salvation to order his life in response to God. For him a Christian is someone 'who has embraced Christ in the innermost feelings of his heart and who emulates him by pious deeds'. Luther is the one who remains firmly in the medieval tradition which saw man as caught up in a cosmic conflict between God and Satan.

> Satan is the prince of this world, and reigns, as Christ and Paul tell us, in the wills and minds of men, who are his prisoners . . . Will this roaring lion, this restless implacable enemy of the grace of God and the salvation of men, suffer man, who is his slave and part of his kingdom to make endeavours towards good at any time, or by any movement whereby he might escape Satan's tyranny? . . . You, who imagine that the human will is something placed in an intermediate position of 'freedom' . . . find it easy to imagine that there is at the same time an endeavouring of the will in either direction; for you imagine that both God and the devil are far away, mere spectators, as it were, of this mutable free-will; you do not believe that they are the prompters and drivers of an *enslaved* will, each waging relentless war against the other . . . Either the kingdom of Satan in man is unreal, in which case Christ will be a liar; or else, if his kingdom is as Christ describes it, 'free-will' will be merely a beast of burden, Satan's prisoner, which cannot be freed unless the devil is first cast out by the finger of God.[10]

The specific issue over which these two astute minds locked horns was as old as Christianity itself. St Paul had tackled it in his letters to the Romans and the Galatians. Augustine and Pelagius had clashed over it. Christian theologians had struggled with it for centuries. Others would continue to do so long after Luther and Erasmus were dead. It is fundamental to Christianity but, in the last analysis, remains an enigma. In that it affects humankind's eternal destiny it very properly exercises the minds of religious thinkers. In that it involves a probing of the character of God it is beyond human comprehension. As early as 1517 Luther had put his finger on his fundamental disagreement with Erasmus: 'the discernment of one who attributes weight to man's will is different from that of him who knows of nothing else but grace'.[11] Luther's determinism was based on his commitment to the belief that God's will is sovereign. Nothing and no one can influence his resolve to accept or reject whomsoever he decides to accept or reject. It follows that every helpless individual's fate is predestined; he is either saved or damned and there is nothing he can do about it. Such a doctrine appalled Erasmus, nor did Luther fail to appreciate why it should do so. How could he fail – he who had experienced the very depths of despair in his efforts to reconcile himself to a just and holy God? He acknowledged:

> . . . it gives the greatest possible offence to common sense or natural reason that God, Who is proclaimed as being full of mercy and goodness, and so on, should of his own mere will abandon, harden and damn men, as though he delighted in the sins and great eternal torments of such poor wretches. It seems an iniquitous, cruel and intolerable thought to think of God.[12]

It *is* an intolerable thought but the alternative, Luther insisted, is worse. If man, by the unaided exercise of free-will, can influence God, then, not only does the sacrifice of Christ on the Cross become superfluous, but God ceases to be omnipotent. And without an omnipotent God the entire created order collapses into chaos. All the subtleties of theologians who, over the centuries, had tried to reconcile free humanity with all-powerful divinity, had, in Luther's opinion, failed totally, just as Erasmus was failing now.

Yet, so intractable was the problem that Luther himself was no stranger to rationalisations that smacked of sophistry. Common sense dictated that man was not a machine whose every move was predetermined. Luther acknowledged that in all the decisions of day-to-day living – what to buy in the market; when to set out on a journey; who to marry – people acted independently. They made free choices. They could even opt for good or evil. Luther tried to get round this problem by distinguishing between the 'lower sphere' of human activity and the 'higher sphere', which concerned relationship with God. It was only in this upper realm that the will was bound, unable to connect with the divine until it was infused by grace. Thus, Luther had driven into a logical cul-de-sac. He had put limits on that very omnipotence he had set out to safeguard.

To the modern reader this looks like the worst kind of obscurantism. Erasmus and Luther both confessed that God is inscrutable. His reasons for saving some of his human creatures and condemning others were locked up in his own unfathomable will. What might appear to man as unfair and cruel was, in the eternal scheme of things, holy and just and good. On this the contenders agreed. Could they not just leave it at that? The negative answer to that question has its roots in the characters and personal history of the two men. Erasmus, the erudite savant, lived in an isolated world of books and ideas where his superior intelligence handled with assurance the wisdom of the ancients. Luther was a *pastor*, who inhabited the world of ordinary men and women. Not only had he endured his own solitary sojourn in the valley of the shadow, but, on a daily basis, he performed his duties as a confessor and guide to others with troubled consciences. It was the *practical* implications of their rival theologies that mattered. Follow Erasmus and you developed a spirituality based on inner contemplation and outward charity, hoping to gain divine approval. Take the Lutheran path and you cast yourself in faith upon a just but loving God, acknowledging your own sinful and helpless nature.

There could be no meeting of minds on this and neither combatant shifted his position. The controversy put an end to any mutual respect that had existed between the two participants. They both tried to observe the conventions of civilised debate but they could not prevent their emotions breaking through. Luther, particularly, found restraint difficult, as he acknowledged: 'If I seem too bitter . . . you must pardon me. I do not act so out of ill will; but I was concerned that by the weight of your name you were greatly jeopardising the cause of Christ.'[13] Such a disclaimer was hardly likely to mollify his opponent. Erasmus smarted under the scorn heaped upon him. Over and again Luther acknowledged his adversary's superior eloquence but managed to convey the impression that linguistic cleverness was a charming mask covering a pock-marked intelligence. His own chosen metaphors were even more pungent: 'my heart went out to you for having defiled your lovely, brilliant flow of language with such vile stuff. I thought it outrageous to convey material of so low a quality in the trappings of such rare eloquence; it is like using gold or silver dishes to carry garden rubbish or dung.'[14] From this point matters went from bad to worse. Erasmus accused Luther of spreading lies about him and, at the same time, delighted to pass on scurrilous rumours concerning Luther. He went into print with a lengthy two-part rejoinder – the *Hyperaspistes*

(*'Defensive shield'*) *Diatribae adversus Servum Arbitrium Martini Lutheri.*
Luther did not bother to reply. In later years he had no hesitation in desig-
nating Desiderius Erasmus as the greatest enemy of the Gospel he had ever
encountered. But by this time the wandering scholar had other foes to
worry about. He discovered Basel to be filling up with heretics even more
extreme than Luther. In 1529 he moved on again. He who had once been
the darling of the European intelligentsia was now a man out of sorts with
the times. Neither protagonist would have been flattered if he could have
known that, in 1559, Erasmus's writings would be placed alongside Luther's
on the Catholic index of banned books.

Luther regarded *The Enslaved Will* as his finest work and it is not difficult to see why. He was quite sincere when he thanked his antagonist for
marking out the ground for their debate. In turning away from peripheral
issues such as indulgences and papal authority and penning his views on
the theological subject of how salvation 'worked' Erasmus had gone to the
heart of the matter and provided Luther with the opportunity to set out
for all to see the essential elements of the evangelical gospel. Luther was,
fundamentally, a medieval theologian who protested, not only at the corruption of traditional practice and teaching, but also at the 'post-modernism'
represented by Erasmus. He was no prophet, able to foresee the mounting
challenges that emerging 'science' would present, over the coming centuries,
to the biblical concept of a proactive, interventionist God but he was well
aware that humanism, by its very nature, severed the cord of dependence
between man and his Creator, restricting the Almighty to the role of audience in a world theatre in which men and women not only occupied the
stage but also wrote the script.

There were some opponents of Luther who poured out the vials of their
wrath in absolutely uncompromising invective:

> You wily fox! By your lies you have made sad the heart of the right-
> eous man, whom God has not saddened, and thereby you have
> strengthened the power of the ungodly scoundrels, so that they shall
> continue in their old ways. Therefore things will go with you as with
> a fox when it is caught.[15]

So Thomas Müntzer ranted in a tract directed against 'the unspiritual soft-
living flesh at Wittenberg'. In 1523 the peripatetic revolutionary had come
to rest at Allstedt, not twenty kilometres from Luther's home town of
Eisleben and within months had enflamed the whole region with his violent

apocalyptic. The peasantry – identified by Müntzer as the true elect – were intoxicated by the preacher's fiery denunciations of their social superiors, the princes and the clergy. These enemies of the Lord were to be cut down and the demagogue called upon God's servants to sharpen their sickles for this gruesome and glorious work. They should on no account listen to Luther, who had sold out to the secular rulers and had been abandoned by God.

The instigators of reform could not wholly escape responsibility for the violence which convulsed Germany in the 1520s. If events got out of control it was, in part, because they had misjudged the impact of their own teaching. Just as Erasmus was alarmed at the aggressive extremism of Luther, so Luther resented those who had moved further to the 'left' than he was prepared to go. Both men had essentially made the same mistake: they had underestimated the mood of the people. When Erasmus mocked the superstitious worship of images he did not reckon with the rampant fury of axe-wielding mobs freed from age-old enslavement to the empty veneration of painted wood, stone and canvas. When Luther proclaimed the priesthood of all believers he did not appreciate the egalitarian vengeance which would be unleashed against clergy who had conned people into according them spurious power and status. The more radical preachers had their ear closer to the ground and were not beyond exploiting popular emotions for their own ends.

All Luther could do was anathematise the satanic troublemakers and distance his movement from their excesses. It was clear to him, as to many others, that if Müntzer's mobs were not stopped from setting fire to Catholic shrines and threatening any authority figures who stood in their way, worse anarchy would swiftly follow. In the following summer, at the same time that he was working on his reply to Erasmus, the reformer wrote *A Letter to the Princes of Saxony*. He contented himself with a brief theological exposition on the word of God and the work of the Holy Spirit, pointing out that these two could not be in conflict. He condemned the devilish spirit which inspired Müntzer and other 'prophets' and declared his willingness to confound them publicly out of Scripture. The princes should not suppress preaching, but allow it to wither in the scorching sunlight of divine truth. In this, as in every controversy in which he was involved, Luther believed that the word of God was powerful enough to win the victory unaided. However, he reminded his princely readers that they had been entrusted with the sword and must not be afraid to wield it: when false prophets 'want to do more than fight with the Word, and begin to destroy and use force, then your Graces must intervene . . . and banish them from the country'.[16]

It was not only against such obvious sectaries as the Zwickau prophets that Luther set his face. Matters between him and Karlstadt came to a head at about the same time. The headstrong, irrepressible professor was very popular in and around Orlamünde and was greatly enjoying his ministry there. But his activities presented two problems to the authorities: his sermons and writings showed that he was still influenced by Müntzer and Co. and he had not resigned his positions in Wittenberg. Thus, while neglecting his teaching and preaching duties in the city, he was drawing a salary as well as a stipend for his pastorate at Orlamünde and using the money to promote dubious doctrines. Karlstadt's teaching was an idiosyncratic mixture of anticlericalism, iconoclasm and anabaptism garbed in mysticism. By implication, if not directly, it denounced half-hearted reformers, like Luther, who failed to go all the way in establishing the 'true church'. Like all fundamentalisms it held a great allure for people unaccustomed to thinking for themselves, many of whom, for whatever reason, felt themselves alienated from society. Luther's verdict on Karlstadt was, 'an untamed desire for glory and fame is consuming this man'[17] but it is possible to feel a certain sympathy for 'Brother Andrew', as he now insisted on being known. He had supported the revolt of his younger colleague and shared with him the papal anathema. He saw himself as joint leader of the Wittenberg movement but Luther was incapable of working in tandem with anyone and Karlstadt increasingly felt the need to escape from his friend's shadow, hence his flirting with the Zwickau prophets and his attempt to set up a rival Wittenberg at Orlamünde.

By the summer of 1524 the electoral authorities had failed to solve the Karlstadt problem. They had deprived the pastor of his post but he declined to move. Duke John Frederick, nephew and heir of the elector who was now much incapacitated by illness, urged Luther to undertake a preaching tour of the area under the renegade's influence in order to re-establish moderate doctrine and obedience to the secular power. The excursion was not a success. Everywhere he went Luther was met by Karlstadt's partisans who heckled his sermons and jostled him in the street. The climax came in a confrontation between the two men in the Black Bear Inn at Jena. In the middle of a crowded room Luther tossed a gold coin to his adversary. It was a conventional gesture symbolising their enmity. Later, at Orlamünde, Luther failed to bring the town authorities to heel and, as he left, they ordered all the church bells to be rung as a sign of their own champion's triumph.

Their exultation was short lived. The authorities had had enough of the troublemaker and ordered his immediate exile from Saxony (even though this meant leaving behind his pregnant wife). Karlstadt made for eclectic Basel, but took in on his way several towns and cities of southern Germany and Switzerland in which he preached and distributed fiery tracts. Luther's cautious reformation and concern for tender consciences he lampooned as faint-hearted compromise: 'Oh, the weak, the weak, the sick, the sick, not so fast, slowly, slowly does it!' Karlstadt would have nothing to do with such shilly-shallying. If one saw a child playing with a sharp knife would one lecture it calmly about the danger of such implements or snatch it away immediately? Just so must the true pastor be decisive in pruning churches of idolatrous images and stopping such practices as infant baptism and communion in one kind. Since this sort of root-and-branch reform could not happen on a regional, let alone a universal basis, it followed that each church should decide what was for itself true doctrine and practice and adopt it immediately, *without tarrying for any*. This slogan became emblazoned on the standard of the radical wing of the Church. For the first time congregationalism was provided with a measure of theological respectability.

Luther could only regard such 'anarchy' with utter dismay. His own preference was for a Catholic Church wholly reformed. He believed that teaching and preaching from the word of God would bring this about. He called upon godly princes to aid in this work and that inevitably meant the emergence of state churches. He called for change that was *cautious* and *controlled*. But the world had moved on. Luther was no longer the unchallenged champion of reform. The evangelical movement was in a state of confusion. Wandering preachers travelled from place to place proclaiming subtly different versions of the faith. Books and pamphlets were cascading from the presses. Luther was never in any doubt about movements that differed from his own. He saw the issues involved in stark black and white. Writing to a friend in May 1524 he insisted,

Satan is setting up a sect among us, at yet another place, and this sect supports neither the papists nor us. [The members of this sect] boast that they are being moved by pure spirits, without the testimony of Holy Scripture. This shows that our word is truly the Word of God, since it is being harried not only by force, but also by new heresies.[18]

Another new feature of intellectual life in Germany was the number of self-taught, lay theologians who now ventured into print with works of devotion and exhortation. It was an exciting time – many believed it to be the endtime. New converts, freed from priestly oppression, were on fire with a message of liberation and religious certainty. To take just one example of how ordinary people were being transformed into bold advocates or pestilential troublemakers (according to one's point of view) let us consider the activities of Argula von Stauffen, a Bavarian lady of modest means but with some aristocratic connections. Although she had no Latin she eagerly read the vernacular works of humanists and reformers and, by her mid-twenties, had become thoroughly steeped in the Bible. In 1523–4 she shot into the 'headlines' with a series of letters to authority figures which she immediately had published. What provoked her literary career was the persecution of a Lutheran student at the university of Ingolstadt. Indignantly demanding from the university senate justice for a young man whom she had never met, she defended her action from Scripture. 'The word of God is constantly before my eyes,' she wrote, 'reminding me of my obligation to confess Christ, an obligation from which neither man nor woman is excluded.' The Bible was replete, she argued, with examples of holy female champions upon whom God had poured out his Spirit. Having established her credentials, she sailed into deeper theological waters. She assailed the Roman Antichrist and accused the university authorities of being in thrall to the papacy. Emboldened by her cause (and perhaps by a publisher who saw profit in encouraging controversy), Argula next wrote an open letter to her prince, Duke William of Bavaria. Widening her range, she denounced corrupt clergy, celibacy and the entire monastic system. She called upon the duke to reform the church in his territories. Social justice as well as divine mandate required a rigorous redistribution of wealth:

> . . . bring [the clergy] into court to see how much they really earn and see that the money is put to some common use, so that the poor man is not quite so overburdened. Stop absentee priests with benefices that they never visit, filling them with foolish vicars who know nothing! The rector in Voburg receives 800 guilders income from his benefices but in a whole year never gave a sermon.

Further published letters followed to the city fathers at Ingolstadt, Elector Frederick of Saxony and the Count Palatine, all urging reform based on Scripture. Reaction was not slow in coming. Argula's husband was ordered to silence her and, when he proved unequal to that task, he lost his job. According to one rumour the poor man had even been instructed to cut off two of his wife's fingers to put an end to her epistolary activities. She was denounced from pulpits. How dare mere women presume to lecture men and even admonish their social and spiritual superiors, one incandescent priest ranted. They were 'pompous children of Eve, bitches and scoundrels' who assumed 'that just as Christ lived in Mary, so he might live in any Christian'. This was the devilish doctrine of Martin Luther and his satanic brood. Argula's response was interesting. 'I am not a Lutheran,' she claimed. 'I confess Christ, not Luther', and she appropriated for herself the label 'evangelical'.[19] But what was 'evangelical'? This was the question troubling many ecclesiastical and civic leaders confronted by the babel voices of rival preachers.

Strasbourg is a city which, in the 1520s, found itself coming under the influences of Lutheranism spreading from the North and a rather different form of evangelical Christianity which was taking root in Switzerland and south-western Germany (see below). The man emerging as one of the leaders of Strasbourg's religious life was Martin Bucer, ex-monk and humanist who had been present at the Diet of Worms and associated himself closely with Luther's reform. He and his colleagues were trying to establish patterns of theological teaching and church order which would be acceptable to the civic authorities, who, like secular rulers everywhere, were concerned about the impact of radical ideas on the lower orders. After Karlstadt had passed through with his anti-Lutheran programme of social levelling Bucer wrote urgently to Luther and to Ulrich Zwingli in Zurich asking for their opinions on certain basic issues – infant baptism, religious images and the nature of Christ's presence at the communion service.

Zwingli's teaching had certain surface similarities to Karlstadt's but a more solid biblical base. He had followed a conventional career, studying theology at university and then taking up an appointment as a parish priest. But he early came under the influence of humanism and was, for a while, a follower of Erasmus. At about the same time that Luther was wrestling with the real meaning of justification Zwingli also and independently came to understand the centrality of personal faith not reliant on priestly intermediation. His powerful preaching, like Luther's, struck a common chord. Thousands followed and the Swiss reformation was established. The implications drawn from a fresh approach to biblical exegesis were similar to those which had held sway in Wittenberg during Luther's exile. Monks fled monasteries, clergy married, churches were cleared of superstitious 'clutter' and the mass was replaced by a vernacular service of the Lord's Supper. This transformation was at its most turbulent in the years 1523–5.

Zwingli had a great regard for Luther but in no way did he consider himself a follower of the German reformer. 'I do not want to be labelled a Lutheran by the papists,' he wrote. 'It is not Luther who taught me the doctrine of Christ, but the word of God. If Luther preaches Christ he does the same thing as I do. Therefore I will not bear any name save that of my chief, Jesus Christ, whose soldier I am.'[20] In fact, there were important differences between the two leaders which inevitably came out in their theology. One was the difference of nationality. Luther was a German with a respect for discipline and those aristocratic leaders in whom authority was invested. Like many of his countrymen, he was deeply prejudiced against the more democratic Swiss. 'Look at the government of the Swiss,' he wrote to a friend. 'There is no discipline or obedience among them and they are nothing but mercenaries.'[21] Zwingli was proud that his forebears had fought for and gained their independence from more powerful neighbours and his upbringing had conditioned him to thinking of power coming from below, from the people. Also Zwingli was the better linguist. He founded all his teaching on an understanding of the Bible culled, wherever possible, from study of the most reliable early documents. He had carefully reached his own conclusions about, for example, the nature of sacraments and he was not prepared to abandon them because they had been challenged by a German of no more than modest intellectual attainments.

Luther took the opportunity of Bucer's invitation to write a long and detailed refutation of the novelties being taught by the radicals – *Against the Heavenly Prophets in the Matter of Images and Sacraments*. The writer was as forthright in his attack primarily on Karlstadt, the 'deserter', as he had ever been on Tetzel, Eck and other papal spokesmen. Indeed, he saw little difference between Catholics and radicals. They were both, in his estimation, propagating works religion: teaching that salvation was to be achieved by human actions rather than by dependence on divine grace. Over and again he pressed home the question, 'How does anyone become a Christian?' If it is by *sola fidei* why are the radicals devoting all their energies to peripherals?

These honour-seeking prophets . . . do nothing but break images, destroy churches, manhandle the sacrament, and seek a new kind of mortification, that is a self-chosen putting to death of the flesh . . . And if they had now altogether succeeded so that there were no more images, no churches remained, no one in the whole world held that the flesh and blood of Christ were in the sacrament and all went about in grey peasant garb, what would be accomplished thereby?

Fame, vain glory and a new monkery would well thereby be achieved, as happens in all works, but the conscience would in no way be helped. Thus such false prophets do not care where faith and love are to be found, just as the pope does not care but presses on if only he can make sure of the works belonging to his obedience and laws.[22]

Luther's forthright denunciation of fellow evangelicals as satanic agents and enemies of the Gospel alarmed even some of his closest supporters. They feared he was widening breaches that needed to be closed and so it proved. As happens not infrequently, the evangelical cause was becoming bedevilled by two kinds of rivalry: divergent interpretations of Scripture and the authority conflict between the Bible and the Holy Spirit. The devout anxiously scrutinised each other to determine who were 'sound' and often the issue resolved itself into a consideration of which leader had the most dynamic personality. Karlstadt, Zwingli, Müntzer and other extremists were striking celebrities who attracted devoted followings. Luther was far and away the most famous figure in the reformed camp but he no longer had the stage to himself and his uncompromising denunciations of other leaders did him more harm than good. In Strasbourg, for example, the reform followed the Zwinglian and not the Lutheran model, as did Basel under the leadership of Luther's old supporter, Oecolampadius. Undoubtedly Luther's harsh reaction to those who differed from him on relatively minor issues was coloured by the eccentric behaviour of Karlstadt. He felt deeply his ex-colleague's defection and, thus moved, tended to tar with the same brush all those whose teachings bore any resemblance to those of Brother Andrew. If he had been free to move about Europe and discuss basic issues with other evangelical scholars he might have developed a greater respect for the likes of Zwingli, Oecolampadius and Bucer. As it was, the 'Protestant Reformation' was divided before it had scarcely begun.

Zwingli, like Luther, was being forced to define his doctrine with greater precision because of pressure from both sides. He also had trouble with extremists demanding that he should go still further. One of his own ex-pupils, Balthasar Hubmaier, had his own version of reformed Christianity. Having stirred up trouble in Alsace he removed to Zurich, where he expected a more sympathetic hearing but his old mentor was appalled by Hubmaier's agenda which included rejection of infant baptism and the swearing of oaths. Since solemn vows were a vital part of the making and sustaining of all relationships – master and apprentice, lord and servant, mercenary general and paymaster, what Hubmaier's followers (soon to be dubbed Anabaptists) proposed was nothing less than a breakdown of society. Indeed, several Anabaptist preachers required believers to withdraw completely into their own communes, where they could live a shared, holy life according to their own pietistic reading of Scripture. Zwingli eventually had Hubmaier arrested and forced a recantation out of him (thereby resorting to old Catholic practice) but, when freed, the heretic escaped to resume preaching elsewhere.

Yet what appears in history as the most significant development of these years, the division of the evangelical movement into Lutheran, Reformed and Anabaptist segments, was not what grabbed the attention and roused the anxieties of contemporaries. Many of them awaited with foreboding what the year 1524 would bring. Astrologers had long prophesied that it would be the year when the world was deluged in misery and woe. For all the planets would be conjoined in Pisces, the constellation of the Fish, which could only presage disaster. And, in the middle of that year, right on cue, there began a series of events which convulsed the German lands with violent rebellion and savage repression. Mobs rampaged, the smoke of looted buildings hung in the air and blood ran in the streets. For most people caught up in these terrifying events esoteric discussion about predestination and the nature of Christ's presence in the Lord's Supper were beyond their ken at a time when nuns were being forcibly turned out of their convents and farmers' sons ridden down by sword-wielding *Kurassiers*.

11

The Brief Reign of Ploughman Jack

If there were thousands more of the peasants, they would still be altogether robbers and murderers, who take the sword simply because of
their own indolence and wickedness, and who want to expel sovereigns and lords and [to destroy] everything, and to establish a new
order in this world. But for this they have neither God's command-
ment, authority, right, or injunction as the lords have it now. In addition, the peasants are faithless and are committing perjury toward
their lords. Above all this, they borrow the authority of the divine
Word and gospel [for covering up] their great sins, and thus disgrace
and slander [God's name] ... if God wants to pour out his wrath
upon us and devastate Germany, then these enemies of God, these
blasphemers, robbers, and murderers, these unfaithful and perjuring
peasants are suitable for this.[1]

Luther wrote thus to a friend in May 1525 when the so-called Peasants'
War was at its height. He divorced himself forcefully from a sequence of
violent events which had already cost hundreds of lives and which would
cost very many more before the sporadic rebellions were crushed. But if
he thought he could disassociate himself from the worst disturbances in
living memory he was mistaken, as a pamphlet published as early as 1521
demonstrates. *The Divine Mill* specifically connected the work of humanists, reformers and social revolutionaries. The thesis is graphically portrayed
in the title-page illustration. Christ is shown pouring 'grain' in the form
of the teaching of prophets, apostles and evangelists into the hopper.

The Divine Mill – illustration from a pamphlet depicting humanists, reformers and the common people involved in the dissemination of the new religion

Erasmus gathers the resulting flour into a sack which Luther then makes into the 'bread' of evangelical doctrine for distribution to the people. Pope and clergy reject this but above them rises the figure of '*Karsthans*', who is laying about him with a flail. *Karsthans* in popular legend was the John Bull of the German peasant class. We might translate the name as 'Ploughman Jack'.

It is not surprising that simple folk failed to see the subtle nuances in Luther's teaching. He had offered them 'liberty' and thousands of them had grasped it with outstretched hands. But each understood the gift and used it in his own way. As Milton was to point out in his 1649 tract *The Tenure of Kings and Magistrates*, 'None can love freedom heartily, but good men; the rest love not freedom, but licence.' Luther had struck off the chains of Roman autocracy and priestly sacerdotalism which shackled humanity's eternal wellbeing to the worldly rules and rituals of a religious caste. But he had said nothing about other kinds of oppression – unjust taxes, encroachment on peasants' land rights, the very institution of serfdom itself. Indeed, Luther had bolstered the authority of temporal rulers by urging them to take over power which senior clergy had usurped. To the underclass of German society the new teaching appeared to give divine sanction to a movement for social reform – violent if need be. When Luther opposed them they were mystified and outraged. They turned their ears instead to radical preachers who energetically wielded the big spoon of liberty to stir up ancient resentments and class hatred. To all this Luther reacted – perhaps overreacted – with alarm, because he saw everything he had fought and suffered for being swept away in a tide of bloody anarchy.

We have already seen how deliberately the enemies of reform charac-terised it as a disruptive movement which threatened social and political chaos. This was a trump card which the ecclesiastical hierarchy readily played in their efforts to mobilise emperor and nobility against heretics. Ever since Luther had been denounced as the wild boar in the vineyard he had been sensitive to accusations that he was a revolutionary influ-ence. He had responded by stressing his obedience to all temporal authority. In his correspondence with the elector, the emperor and other princes he always adopted a tone of what appears to the modern reader as fawning sycophancy, and this cannot be fully explained by reference to the conven-tions of the time. In his writings he strove mightily to distinguish between his opposition to the power wrongly wielded by the papal machine and that exercised under God by secular rulers. However, this was no mere reaction to criticism. Luther was sincere in his deference to traditional authority. His lack of sympathy for the peasants was, in part, the emotional reaction of one who was conscious of having risen from humble origins and attained a superior, more enlightened and civilised attitude to life but there was more than that to his fierce opposition to rebellion. Luther had no political philosophy beyond that which he deduced from the pages of the Bible, and Scripture very clearly enjoined obedience to 'the powers that be'. His teaching, his beliefs and prejudices, the very credibility of his cause were put severely to the test during the traumatic events of 1524–6.

In these crucial months the situation throughout German lands was so *mouvementé* and so multi-faceted as to almost defy description and analysis. The forces of France and the Empire were locked in fierce combat from which Charles V emerged as the master of Italy. This obliged the new pope, Clement VIII, to assess his political options. Thus, not only was Charles too preoccupied to pay close attention to the religious situation in Germany, but the common front of emperor and pope against heresy was seriously weakened. Evangelical activists were not the only ones to take advantage of Charles' preoccupation. The estates in the imperial diet had for several years been working towards greater autonomy and now they were in a strong position to assert it. This was particularly true of the free cities, which had their own house in the diet. It was precisely these cities in which Lutheranism was making its most dramatic progress. Civic authorities were under pressure to make the same kind of changes as Wittenberg in relation to public worship, monasticism, clerical celibacy and the privileges of the clergy. The diet met in Nuremberg in the early weeks of 1524 and received a demand from the imperial chancellery, backed by Rome, for a more energetic enforcement of the Edict of Worms. The cities refused to countenance an anti-Lutheran witch hunt. Their official reasons were pragmatic rather than religious but everyone present was able to read between the lines:

> Because now the Common Man everywhere thirsts after God's Word and the Gospel, which . . . have recently spread much more widely than before . . . If we accept, approve or allow to be enforced even the slightest barrier to the Gospel's spread, the honourable, free and Imperial cities . . . could not only not enforce such a law, but they would doubtless provoke widespread disturbances, rebellion, murder, bloodshed, yes, total ruin and every sort of evil . . .[2]

It was a realistic assessment of the situation. Things had gone too far. The forces of reaction had failed to nip the new movement in the bud and now it was in full flower. A programme of severe repression could only backfire and the fact that several princes and municipal corporations were sympathetic to reform meant that a co-ordinated attack on the evangelical movement would have been impossible. City leaders had cause to be concerned for their own position for they, in turn, were under pressure from democratising elements within their walls who were calling for a greater share in their own government. For example, Nuremberg itself was under the influence of its own charismatic cleric, Andreas Osiander, whose pulpit denunciations were, at Easter 1524, turning from the detestable enormities of Rome to the constitutional imbalance in his own city.

To avoid the charge of simply being negative and obstructive the cities suggested that the appropriate forum for deciding the religious issue was a general council of the Church. This was a difficult pill for the papal party to swallow. It implied acknowledging that the Lutheran breakaway was not simply another heresy which Rome had the right and duty to extirpate but a schism within the Church which could only be resolved by theological disputation between *equal* parties. This was what Luther had always demanded and what his enemies had always refused. The news that the diet had accepted the cities' proposal was rapturously received in Wittenberg. Luther allowed himself to believe that a peaceful resolution of the religious issue might yet be possible. But the proposed general council was never summoned. Within months Germany was preoccupied with more immediate and extremely unpleasant matters.

Trouble broke out in the Black Forest in the middle of 1524. It spread in a haphazard way, like a heath fire at the whim of changeable winds. Some areas were severely scorched, while others remained relatively untouched. Nor was there any cohesion. This was not a 'movement' possessing leadership and common aims. Catholics were caught up in it as well as Lutherans, Zwinglians and members of radical sects. Some activists campaigned for a wholesale reordering of society and others addressed themselves to a programme of clearly defined reforms. In some places the peasants, so far from being socially disruptive, looked to local clergy or landowners for guidance. There was nothing new about peasant unrest. The inequalities of society bore down on the rural working population and at any time a local dispute could spark the firedamp of resentment and frustration with perceived or actual injustices. What marked this uprising out as different – apart from its geographical extent – was the evangelical standard hoisted by several of the peasant groups. Some marched under gaudy banners bearing religious images or slogans such as 'The Word of the Lord Abides Forever'. In February 1525 two citizens of Memmingen, an imperial free city in Bavaria, provided their revolt with a manifesto. One of them was none other than the Zwinglian pastor, Christoff Schappeler and the *Twelve Articles* bear the stamp of his thinking. Among the demands contained in this document was autonomy for every congregation and the right to have only such pastors as should 'preach the holy gospel to us clearly and purely'. The rebels asked for the restoration of ancient rights they claimed had been eroded, such as the use of common land, the restriction of free labour owed to landlords and fair rents. But the author of the *Twelve Articles* justified every one of the demands by reference to Scripture. Thus, he insisted that there should be no restriction on the countryman's hunting and fishing rights because God had given men authority over all animals. And he rejected serfdom on the equally weak grounds that Christ's sacrifice availed for all men. In essence what the rebels were asserting was that they would obey their masters in all ways that were agreeable to the word of God – and *they* would determine what was and was not 'agreeable to the word of God'. This was no more than the freedom of conscience that Luther had claimed at Worms and some of the peasants' leaders cited him as an arbitrator to whom they would readily submit their claims. The difference was, of course, that Luther confined his rebellion entirely to matters spiritual. What the rebels were now claiming was that distinctions between the heavenly and earthly realms were false; that the Gospel had clear political application.

Luther's attitude towards the mounting crisis, doubtless like that of many other commentators, changed as that crisis intensified. In the spring of 1524 his approach to current events may be summarised as follows: He abhorred violence as a thing evil in itself but also because it played into the hands of his enemies and because in his mind it was inextricably linked with the twisted apocalyptic of those false teachers he lumped together as *Schwärmer*, 'fanatics'. On the other hand, he felt considerable sympathy for the underdogs of the social system who did have genuine grievances. Life was fairly quiet in Wittenberg and Luther had several other things on his mind. Elector Frederick was dying and though his brother, Duke John, and his nephew, Duke John Frederick, were more committed supporters of reform, the imminent change of regime inevitably involved a certain amount of adjustment. Luther was deeply engrossed in his translation of the Old Testament as well as overseeing a process of peaceful liturgical and doctrinal change. Then there was his reaction to Erasmus to be carefully thought out. In the midst of all his labours Luther was only able to form an opinion of what was happening elsewhere from the conflicting rumours that reached him. It was not until he set off for Eisleben in April 1525 to visit relatives and arrange for the opening of a new school that he began to meet eye witnesses who told horrifying tales of monasteries burned and looted and outrages committed against their inmates. Rapidly his trip turned into a preaching tour and from pulpit after pulpit he condemned the insurgents for taking the law into their own hands. But everywhere peasant blood was up and the message was badly received. Not now was Luther widely hailed as a popular nationalist hero. For the first time he experienced being shunned or verbally abused by ordinary German people. In one church locals rang all the bells while he was preaching in an attempt to drown out his voice. All this was very hurtful and Luther reacted to such opposition, as he now increasingly did, with white hot anger. Not only were the people rejecting him, he insisted, they were rejecting the word of God.

At Eisleben he began a written reply to the insurgents, *An Admonition to Peace on the Twelve Articles of the Peasantry in Swabia*. In it he tried to be even-handed. He upbraided the rulers. They had brought this peril upon themselves by squeezing their tenants, workers and servants in order that they could live in ostentatious luxury. Their arrogance and exploitation were not only offensive to their social inferiors, they were anathema to God. The chastising hand of the sovereign Lord was to be seen in the current turmoil. Back in Wittenberg, the reflective and pain-racked Elector Frederick acknowledged as much when he confided to Spalatin that if the overthrow of princely rule and the dominion of the peasants were to come about, he would accept it as the will of God. Luther did not share his prince's fatalism. Even if the peasants were being used as divine agents, they were also limbs of Satan and must be resisted to the last drop of Christian blood. What prevented the writer being truly impartial in this controversy was his commitment to the medieval belief that society was divinely ordered. The teaching of the New Testament, he insisted, had nothing whatever to do with bringing about political change and attempting to create a more equitable society. We are strangers and pilgrims here; our citizenship is in heaven. Like Augustine, Luther adhered to the conviction that in the kingdoms of this world two 'cities' were intermingled, those of believers and unbelievers. It was the Christian's role to influence his fellows for good but not to overthrow the state.

So, when he moved on to address the peasants, Luther's language became increasingly severe. Christian freedom, he pointed out, must not be confused with licence. The rebels have no mandate from God to challenge their masters and, as Jesus had shown by his rebuking of Peter who had drawn the sword in the Garden of Gethsemane, violence was never an option for the Christian. Vengeance and the righting of wrongs belonged to God. As for the devout believer, his lot was, 'Suffering, suffering, Cross, Cross!' Luther reserved his choicest invective for the false prophets who had, for their own purpose, taken advantage of the plight of the poor and egged them on to rebellion. Not only were they misleading their followers, but they had the effrontery to cite Scripture in support of their lies. He had no doubt that the real villains were Schappeler and, behind him, Müntzer. These 'prophets of murder' were endangering the immortal souls of those they inveigled into following them. They it was who lured the peasants away from trusting only in Christ for any amelioration of their lot. What, then, should the poor people do; how could they achieve redress? Luther went through their twelve demands. The abolition of serfdom was fanciful nonsense; equality under the Gospel does not translate into the removal of social grading. Without class distinctions society would disintegrate into anarchy. By the same token, the withholding of tithes would be an unwarranted attack on the economic working of the prevailing system. To the desire of congregations to choose their own pastors Luther could not but be sympathetic but even this was only acceptable within the existing legal framework. If the local ruler did not grant such autonomy, the people might not take it. Luther declined to legislate on the specific issues of land rights, taxation and disputes over ancient customs. These were matters for lawyers, not preachers. In conclusion, he urged both sides to seek a solution by peaceful conciliation.

Within days of hurriedly completing this treatise Luther received news from Wittenberg that the failing elector had sent for him and he hurried home. Sadly, he did not arrive in time to say farewell to the one man in the world to whom he owed his widespread influence and, indeed, his life. Frederick the Wise died on 5 May. His passing was a severe loss to Germany. It was among his dying wishes that his brother princes would show mercy to the peasants and his mediation might well have averted the worst of the bloodbath into which the country was to be plunged in a matter of days. For the moment there was hope. Luther had learned with joy that at Easter a treaty had been signed by the leaders of the Swabian League (a confederation of municipal councils, princes and knights whose territory straddled the German-Swiss border) and the local peasant leaders. But cruel disillusionment followed swiftly. Fresh insurrections broke out and now they were much nearer home. Peasant hordes were on the move in the Rhineland, Thuringia and Saxony. Towns and villages which Luther had visited recently were caught up in the violence. The most furiously boiling cauldron of unrest was Mansfeld, where his father had worked in the mines and where several of his relatives still lived. And it was precisely in these new risings that the mobs got out of control. There was little appetite for dialogue with local rulers; no presentation of demands for reform. This new wave of rebellion sought not to reform existing society but to create a new one by fire and sword. Their apocalyptic preachers assured them that in the new, divine order they would be kings.

From his headquarters at nearby Mühlhausen Thomas Müntzer now took up the leadership of the Peasants' War. His battle cry was clear, uncompromising and spattered with biblical allusions:

Go at them, and at them, and at them! It is time. The scoundrels are as dispirited as dogs ... Take no notice of the lamentations of the godless! They will beg you in such a friendly way, and whine and cry like children. Don't be moved to pity . . . At them, at them, while the fire is hot! Don't let your sword get cold! Don't let it go lame! Hammer cling, clang on Nimrod's anvil! Throw their tower to the ground! So long as they are alive you will never shake off the fear of men . . .[3]

Greed, resentment and bloodlust were now freed to do their devastating work washed in the absolving waters of divine purpose. Consciences became numb. The rebels broke into ducal and monastic barns and carried off the stored grain. They slaughtered animals to roast over their camp fires. They smashed their way through churches and laid siege to castles. They left monasteries ablaze in their wake. They cut down any of the 'godless' who stood in their path.

Luther's response to this frightening, escalating crisis was the most vitriolic pamphlet he ever published. *Against the Thievish, Murderous Hordes of Peasants* was dashed off in a few furious hours. There was no time for mature reflection. The situation was urgent. It was an exhortation to the princes to rouse themselves and deal ruthlessly with this threat to the peace of Germany. Hitherto the rulers, like Frederick, had hesitated. They were confused, not because they did not know how to deal with peasant unrest, but because this specific rising had taken on the character almost of a religious crusade and they feared that it might, in very truth, be an act of God. It was to dispel any such misgivings that Luther emulated Müntzer's language in what would be his most notorious tract. He assured the rulers that rebellion, whatever excuses were given for it, was an offence against God and he reminded them that they bore the sword as agents of God. It would be disastrous for them to delay longer. The fire of revolt was spreading and, if not checked, would have widespread, disastrous results.

Title page of Luther's tract *Against the Thievish, Murderous Hordes of Peasants*, 1525

Rebellion brings with it a land filled with murders, the pouring out
of blood, and makes widows and orphans and destroys all, which is
the worst misfortune imaginable. So then, anyone who can should
smash, strangle and stab, secretly or openly, remembering that nothing
can be more poisonous, harmful or demonic than a rebellious man,
just as when one must kill a mad dog, for if you do not strike him,
he will strike you and the whole land with you.[4]

The words are terrible because of their hot violence but also because of
their cold logic. The situation had got out of hand. Reports reaching
Wittenberg told of peasant armies 18,000 and 20,000 strong. Müntzer was
urging his host on to the great Armageddon which would usher in the
overthrow of all existing authorities and the establishment of the rule of
the saints. There *was* a need for immediate and firm action. Luther was
justifiably anxious about the breakdown of all law and order. He was
convinced that distorted religion – whether that of papists or *Schwärmer*
– lay at the root of the current trouble and that gave him the right, as a
theologian, to make public pronouncements on it. He had just learned
that Zwingli had perpetrated what might be almost the ultimate blasphemy
of having the mass made illegal in Zurich and that will not have improved
his temper. In *Against the Thievish, Murderous Hordes of Peasants* Luther
condemned wholesale slaughter by one section of society while advocating
its employment by another. To many commentators over the centuries this
inconsistency and the savageness with which it was urged has seemed
unforgivable and certainly far divorced from the life and teaching of the
Prince of Peace.

Plainly, there are contradictions within Luther's formulation of biblical
truth and the ways he sought to apply it to specific issues. He was not
a systematic theologian; he was a thinker and pastor who was passionately involved in contemporary issues and dealt with them as they arose.
He was also a creature of the prevailing culture. European societies were
authoritarian in both their temporal and spiritual aspects. Like the arches
of a Gothic cathedral, they only held together – and glorified God – if
all structural pressures and tensions were evenly distributed and were
borne downward from the apex, through stout pillars to the foundations.
If those foundations shifted the results could only be devastating. That is
why rulers in church and state were terrified by the prospect of rebellion
and heresy. The sixteenth century was still an age of certainties, in which
philosophers were only just beginning to question the assumptions (mostly

theological) which provided society with its *raison d'être*. Some human-ists, such as the Swiss reformer, Joachim Vadianus, might pen idealistic prose about the 'noble peasant' but they fell noticeably silent after 1525. That being the case, preservation of the status quo was an end which justi-fied whatever means might be employed to secure it. A dozen years after the Peasants' War, Henry VIII of England ordered savage reprisals against conservative rebels who had dared oppose his radical socio-religious poli-cies. In 1572, Pope Gregory XIII would celebrate with a joyful *Te Deum* the extirpation of more than five thousand French evangelicals during the St Bartholomew's Day Massacre. Luther, therefore, was not out of kilter with the spirit of contemporary officialdom. Where, I think, he can be criticised is for not getting to grips with the implications of his own theology of spiritual egalitarianism and freedom under the Gospel. Karlstadt, Müntzer and other firebrands may have wandered from the path of peacefully securing social reform, political development and human rights but they had followed a signpost erected by Luther and it would have been helpful if he had been prepared to engage them in dialogue, just as he had earlier demanded an impartial hearing for his own views. As it was, his movement lost and never regained the mass support of the common man. Lutheranism would develop as a state religion closely allied with the ruling class.

In May 1525 that class probably did not need his exhortation to 'smash, strangle and stab'. After weeks of indecision they had at last got their act together. Duke John had, initially, been as reluctant as his brother to meet the rebels with the limited force at his immediate command but now he sent urgent messages to Philip, Landgrave of Hesse, a twenty-year-old ruler with the determination and clear-headedness of youth, who already had a reputation as a military leader. He brought to his banner contingents from the neighbouring dukedoms and marched swiftly towards Müntzer's camp.

On 15 May the two armies met in hilly terrain at Frankenhausen, just outside Mühlhausen. The rebels had the numerical advantage but they were facing trained infantry and cavalry supported by cannon. It was a case of professionalism confronted by zeal. For days Müntzer had been screwing up the courage of his followers with fervent oratory and prom-ises of a radiant future beyond the immediate ordeal. When a rainbow appeared in the sky he claimed it as a divine omen, an endorsement of his mission, a proof that the hosts of heaven were on his side. Thus supported, he assured his untrained levies, the missiles of the enemy would be unable to harm them. They cheered him to the skies and shouted defiance at the enemy. Proceedings began, as convention demanded, by an exchange of heralds. Philip urged the peasants to give up their leaders and promised leniency if they would lay down their makeshift arms. The rebels, however, remained mesmerised by their charismatic prophet, who laughed off the threats of the princes with the taunt that he would catch their bullets in his sleeve. With that Philip's artillery opened fire. The first round fell short and was greeted by howls of derision from the peasants. Then the gunners found their range. The next cannon balls did not miss their mark. It was all over. Or, rather, the decisive moment had passed. For the defeated rebels, at Frankenhausen and elsewhere, all was far from over. Expert troops rode down the fleeing would-be revolutionaries and massacred five thousand of them, with the loss of half a dozen of their own number. That was just the beginning. Müntzer was dragged from a cellar where he had tried to hide, was tortured and executed, as were all the other ringleaders on whom the victors could lay their hands. Meanwhile, all over Germany, the mopping-up operation got under way as the princes exacted their revenge and reasserted their authority. Men who had taken up arms or simply spoken against their masters or who fell foul of informers were imprisoned or beheaded. Towns which had harboured the wild preachers found themselves burdened with swingeing fines. To any unbiased commentator, then or since, the reaction has seemed to be out of all proportion to the offence.

It certainly blackened Luther's name. News of the savage reprisals circulated at the same time as the publications in which he had demanded draconian measures. Friends and disciples, as well as enemies, challenged his judgement and his lack of compassion. He was forced to defend himself in print. Characteristically, though he upbraided the nobles for their merciless pursuit of the innocent along with the guilty, he would not retract his earlier writings. As at Worms, he insisted that he had Scripture and conscience on his side. It would be unsafe for him to preach and teach any other message.

Terrible as all these events were, Luther had more immediate preoccupations during the summer of 1525. He saw the recent tragedy in the light of that larger, spiritual struggle which, for him, always lay beneath the surface of human affairs. The recent upheaval was the work of Satan and Luther knew he must resist the enemy uncompromisingly and by all the means at his disposal.

Müntzer and the peasants have done much damage to the gospel here, [and] have revived the spirits of the papists so much that it seems we have to begin building all over again. This is the reason that I have now testified to the gospel not only by word but also by a deed[5]

When Luther wrote those words in a letter in August he had just completed *An Open Letter on the Harsh Book Against the Peasants*, the pamphlet in which he tried to make clear to critical friends why he had taken such a firm stand. He was also completing his much more profound and detailed response to Erasmus on the subject of free-will. Such writings constituted the 'word' he was referring to. The 'deed' was something which appeared to those who knew him well to be a much more dramatic and uncharacteristic event. He had married.

For a long time he had encouraged monks and nuns to abandon their vows and, along with priests, to espouse the married state but his answer to friends who asked whether he, too, would take a wife had always been, 'No'. His stated reason was, not that he was immune to sexual desire or feminine charms, but that he did not want to involve a woman in his stress-filled and insecure life. He frequently declared that he expected martyrdom – if not from the fire, then from the assassin's knife. The reasons he gave for his change of heart in 1525 were his father's desire for grandchildren and, more importantly, his determination to silence the wagging tongues of his enemies. Some critics accused him of being all talk; of being afraid to do what he encouraged others to do. He still lived in the Augustinian cloister and had only recently abandoned the cowl. Yet, whatever explanations he gave to others (and, perhaps, also to himself), it is obvious that he was particularly susceptible at this time. He had entered the physiological 'roaring forties' (he was five months short of his forty-second birthday) when a middle-aged man's fancies lightly turn to thoughts of love. Never had he felt more alone and in need of support. In these months, when enemies were more numerous than ever, friends were wavering and his old protector was dead, it seemed to him that he stood alone – Luther *contra mundum*. Moreover, temptation lay close at hand. The deserted Augustinian monastery had recently become the refuge of a group of single women.

It was in April 1523 that Luther came to the aid of these maidens in distress. There were nine of them,* all daughters of not very well-to-do

*Some sources suggest the number was eleven.

noble families. Like so many others of their class, they had been given to the religious life as a means of sustaining them without their relatives having the expense of their maintenance. Now, doubtless for a variety of reasons, they wanted to escape from their incarceration in the Cistercian convent at Nimbschen, some sixty kilometres upriver from Wittenberg. Their relatives refused to let them leave so they were doomed to the frustration of seeing friends restored to the outside world with the possibility of finding husbands while they remained, 'cabined, cribbed, confined', prisoners to a way of life that they had not chosen and for which they had no vocation. Emboldened by Luther's denunciation of enforced vows, the ladies appealed to him for help and he planned a dramatic rescue with the aid of Leonhard Koppe, a local merchant who supplied the nunnery with food. One evening he drove to the tradesmen's entrance with barrels of beer and salt fish. That done, he and his men loaded his wagon with the empties. By now it was dark and no one noticed that the barrels were not as light and easily manoeuvrable as they should have been. By the time the escapees were missed they were well on their way to Wittenberg. Of course, this quixotic, outrageous *Entführung* rapidly became the talk of Germany and, of course, there were repercussions, not only from the women's angry and humiliated fathers and brothers, but from religious authorities and other noble families who found themselves facing a clamour of demand from their womenfolk for similar deliverance.

Luther was not the sort of man to keep his head below the parapet. He readily confessed to his part in the escapade and, far from being apologetic, used the plight of the runaways to launch a fresh attack on the monstrous injustice of coercing young girls into a lifetime of religious devotion to which they had not been called by God. He went into print again on his attitudes towards marriage, virginity and celibacy, notably in a little commentary on I Corinthians chapter 7, on which some of his opponents relied in order to claim that the single state was holier than the wedded one. He patiently pointed out that both were gifts of God and could be channels of great blessing. Moreover, any different principles adduced from St Paul were erroneous. Theory was all very well but what was he to do with a houseful of ex-nuns with active hormones and no experience of the real world? It was a real headache, not least because he did not have the money to support his unpaying tenants. However, over the months, thanks to careful education, help from wellwishers and patient negotiation with the families concerned, most of the ladies were returned to their homes or were found husbands. But all this close, personal and practical involvement in coping with a problem largely of his own creation did make him reconsider his position. While never conceding that his critics might be right, Luther had to ask himself whether he should 'walk the walk' as well as 'talking the talk'.

The last of the Nimbschen refugees on his hands by 1525 was Catherine von Bora, a woman from a noble family near Leipzig, who had spent twenty-one of her twenty-six years in the convent. There was no possibility of her returning to her own homeland where she faced imprisonment for breaking the law. But she was not prepared, having escaped one servitude, to submit to another by meekly doing Luther's bidding. Catherine was comely (perhaps even plain); she was intelligent; and she had a mind of her own. She set her face against being married off to the first man who would have her. Rather than that, she worked for two years as a servant in the house of the artist, Lucas Cranach. At length a suitor was found who did please her. This was Jerome Baumgartner, a wealthy, young burger from Nuremberg. Sadly, Baumgartner's family persuaded him that he could do better for himself and a disconsolate Catherine was left on the shelf. Luther now determined that his charge should marry Caspar Glatz, a fellow theologian and pastor of the parish of Orlamünde, recently vacated by Karlstadt. Catherine would have none of it. She appealed to Nicholas von Amsdorf and he wrote to his friend on her behalf: 'What in the devil are you up to that you try to persuade good Kate and force that old skinflint, Glatz, on her. She doesn't go for him and has neither love nor affection for him.'[6] Luther was irritated by Catherine's stance. Here was someone as stubborn and self-willed as himself, a wretched ingrate who apparently was insensitive to the trouble and expense he was being put to on her behalf. She seemed to be determined to marry no one but her protector. Out of the question! Matters came to a head when he called on his parents during his spring tour in 1525. His father confronted him: how long was Martin going to go on advising other ex-monks to marry while refusing to set an example himself? Old Hans had never happily accepted his son's commitment to celibacy and now he wanted to see him 'settle down' and provide himself and Margaretta with grandchildren before it was too late. Did Luther still experience a degree of guilt about his relationship with his father? After all that had passed between them did he feel that he owed the old man something? In his explanation to friends he certainly cited Hans' wishes as a motivating factor in his decision. Inviting Nicholas von Amsdorf to the wedding banquet on 27 June, he wrote:

The rumour is true that I was suddenly married to Catherine. I did [this] to silence the evil mouths which are so used to complaining about me . . . In addition, I also did not want to reject this unique [opportunity to obey] my father's wish for progeny, which he so often expressed. At the same time I also wanted to confirm what I have taught by practising it; for I find so many people timid in spite of such great light from the gospel. God has willed and brought about this step. For I feel neither passionate love nor burning desire for my spouse.[7]

So it was that, amidst the terrible and tumultuous events of the summer of 1525, Martin and Catherine Luther set up one of the most famous and influential family households known to history. The reformer assumed a new identity, the genial host and *bonhomme*, dispensing homely wisdom from his table and hearth. But this transformation only took place slowly and was not apparent, in 1525, to those in Wittenberg and elsewhere who were shaken by the news of Luther's almost clandestine marriage.

Melancthon, for one, was gobsmacked – and, in this instance, the modern slang is permissible. In a letter to a friend the young theologian expressed both his annoyance that the leader had not taken any of his intimates into his confidence and also his belief that Luther had acted unwisely. Philip could not understand how, 'in these unhappy times, in which good people are suffering so much, this man lacks compassion and rather, as it seems, revels and compromises his good reputation, precisely at a time when Germany stands in particular need of his spirit and authority'. Casting around for some explanation, Melancthon concluded that the fault must lie elsewhere: '. . . the nuns plied all the arts to draw him to their side. Perhaps this manifold association with the nuns has weakened and taken the fire out of his noble nature and greatness of soul. This is apparently how he tumbled into such an untimely change in his way of life.'[8] Friends and supporters found it difficult to accept Luther's assertion that he married to put a stop to criticism – and they were right. There was much more to it than that. Luther was in a dilemma over getting married: he was damned if he did and damned if he did not and he must have known that. After the event enemy tongues were soon wagging with new rumours, the most obvious being that Luther found himself having to formalise his relationship with Catherine, for the obvious reason.

It is as we cast a last look back over these turbulent months in Luther's life that we can see that the impulse wedding was all of a piece with his extreme reactions to peasants and heretics. His decision was the involuntary mental spasm of a man who must respond – decisively, dramatically – to life's pressures. He could never float on the stream of events. He had to influence and control them. When he discovered that he could not control them, this intellectual giant acted irrationally or lapsed into depression – often both. His manic personality would not allow him to leave any task unfinished, any challenge unmet. His literary output alone is incredible testimony to the long hours he spent, pen in hand, hunched over his desk, and when he was not writing there was a full programme of pastoral and teaching responsibilities to be addressed. It is no wonder that most nights he tumbled into sweat-stained sheets which had not been laundered on a mattress whose straw had not been changed. The idea of a helpmeet must have become suddenly attractive.

Luther's violent denunciation and personal abuse of those he considered to be enemies of the Gospel have embarrassed his biographers and made it easier for his critics to belittle his arguments. His unrestrained language can, in some measure, be explained by his method of working. The words poured from him, not only with white-hot passion, but with amazing fluency. He had no time to edit his work, nor did he acknowledge the need to do so. No first drafts were discarded. Never did he pause for that reflection which might have persuaded him to modify his language. For Luther the importance of his message, the crisis of the times and his conviction that death lay in wait for him every day created a sense of urgency that could not be denied. For our part, we must be careful not to judge him solely as the defiant pugilist of the polemical works. The genial, playful and affectionate Luther of the *Table Talk* and the *Letters* presents us with an equally vivid picture. Here was a man who loved children, who enjoyed a good joke, who drank wine and beer heartily, who never tired of making music with friends, who was always available to students, whose purse was so wide open to the needy that poor Catherine was often in despair at his profligacy.

There could be a considerable difference between what Luther wrote about his opponents and how he behaved towards them. We have seen how charitable he was to the dying Tetzel. Even more remarkable was a magnanimous event which occurred in the summer of 1525. The first long-stay guest Martin and Catherine entertained in their new home was none other than Andreas von Karlstadt. The man whom Luther had, only six months before, denounced as the spawn of the beast of Revelation (in

Against the Heavenly Prophets) arrived in Wittenberg seeking refuge. In the aftermath of the peasants' insurrection the countryside was scoured by armed posses sent to round up the usual suspects. Karlstadt went into hiding and sent his wife to intercede with the erstwhile colleague and leader he had deserted. Luther agreed to meet him and, then, not only did he accept Karlstadt's grovelling apology, not only did he conceal him in his house for several weeks, he also interceded for him with the elector. It did no good. Like Mr Toad, Karlstadt was prone to forswearing his foolish ways with hot, penitential tears, on one day, and kicking over the traces on the next. The remaining sixteen years of his life were replete with crises, trials and tribulations. But that was not Luther's fault.

Ultimately, Luther's change of marital status and lifestyle must be attributed to his prime motivation – faith. As such, it inevitably defies rational analysis – and even Luther's own attempts to explain it. His firm conviction was, as he told Amsdorf, that 'God has willed and brought about this step'.[9] To what extent the divine instruction was mediated through the importunity of Catherine and her friends (as Melancthon suspected) we cannot know. Certainly the new Mrs Luther was a determined and strong-willed woman. Some of her husband's friends found her bossy and shrewish but that may tell us more about her critics than it does about her. Here was a woman who had presumed to intrude herself into the very centre of a gentlemen-scholars' club. Catherine, like most women, had very little book learning and less inclination to extend it. 'I've wagered her 50 guilden if she can read the whole Bible by Easter,' Luther reported to a friend. We have no information about who won the bet. When the master of the household was discussing weighty theological issues with friends and students Katie remained in the background. It may be significant that in a woodcut of the Luther family at table with guests the only figure missing is Catherine. But if she could not provide her husband with intellectual stimulus, she had many other gifts which he fully appreciated and which made for a harmonious and successful marriage. Indeed, it is difficult to see how Luther's ministry could have continued throughout his middle and later years without the stability and creature comforts provided by his domestic life.

Up to this point Luther had been in limbo. The dwindling community in the Augustinian cloister had left him, one colleague and a few servants rattling about in a large building like pebbles in a tin. The place had lost not only its routine but also its *raison d'être*. The cloister buildings had reverted to their donor, the elector, and he had granted permission for the residents to go on living there. But there was neither the structure of daily life nor the material necessities to make it moderately comfortable. Looters had taken advantage of lax security to strip it of provisions and there was no income to purchase fresh supplies. Luther received no salary for his university work until Duke John, the new elector, agreed to pay him a far-from-generous allowance of 200 guilden p.a. The buildings became shabby and untidy. Arrangements for cooking, cleaning and laundry deteriorated. It was all awaiting a woman's touch and this Mrs Luther provided.

With no money and with, what was worse, a husband who had no money sense, she set about turning the sparse and dusty convent into a home. She solicited gifts from wealthy friends of the reform movement. She augmented the slender stock of furniture with fresh purchases. She established a vegetable garden and orchard. She obtained fishing rights in a local pond. Her principal income came from taking in lodgers. In a university city there was no shortage of demand for cheap accommodation, and students were delighted to receive bed and board from Catherine because her charges were reasonable and they could enjoy the privilege of sitting at table with the great Dr Luther. For some years the couple had a hand-to-mouth existence but it was a happy one – even more so when children arrived.

Martin did his best to support the domestic economy but his best did not amount to much. He helped in the garden and, with self-deprecating humour, boasted of his skills as a builder of walls and grafter of trees. At one point he took up carpentry but DIY was certainly not his *métier*. He could, and perhaps should, have become quite wealthy from his writings. Between 1520 and 1546 one-third of all published vernacular literature in Germany came from his pen, and printers all over Europe issued and re-issued his Latin works. The middlemen grew fat on the results of Luther's genius. Yet, from them he took never a pfennig. As a high-minded academic and a religious enthusiast Luther was interested only in the dissemination of divine truth. Financial reward had no place in his calculations. As a member of the Augustinian order he had embraced poverty and had had no need to generate income. His simple needs were met in the cloister. That otherworldliness which had so annoyed his father years before had, by middle age, become a fixed principle by which he lived. He simply believed that God would provide for the needs of himself and his family. Jesus promised, 'be concerned above everything else with the Kingdom of God and with what he requires of you, and he will provide you with everything else',[10] and that was the end of the matter. Catherine must frequently have thought that her husband took this principle to extremes. He was a 'soft touch', who would give his last coins to someone in need even when his own debts had not been cleared. Yet, she saw her role as supporting Martin in his great and ongoing work. She provided him with the stability which was the launchpad for his creativity. Regular meals, a daily routine and care for his basic necessities were luxuries he had not experienced since his return from the Wartburg.

No marriage is without its tensions. The best are those in which love either resolves or surmounts them. This was the kind of marriage that Martin and Catherine built. Their affection was deep and enduring. Though Luther poked gentle fun at his wife's lack of intellectual accomplishment, sometimes referring to her as 'Doctoress', he kept her well informed about his work and concerns, as is clear from the few surviving letters that he wrote to her when he was away from home. Within a year their first child was born and was christened 'Hans' in honour of his grandfather. By the end of 1534 Catherine had given birth five more times. Martin took a middle-aged father's delight in his children. In letters to friends he exuberantly described their little milestones as they passed through infancy, from cutting their teeth to reading the Bible. Luther's own childhood had been hard and he probably reacted by spoiling his own offspring. He believed that encouragement was more important than chastisement as the following letter to his four-year-old eldest son indicates.

Grace and peace in Christ! My beloved son: I am pleased to learn that you are doing well in your studies, and that you are praying diligently. Continue to do so, my son [and] when I return home I shall bring you a nice present from the fair.

I know of a pretty, beautiful, [and] cheerful garden where there are many children wearing little golden coats. [They] pick up fine apples, pears, cherries, [and] yellow and blue plums under the trees; they sing, jump, and are merry. They also have nice ponies with golden reins and silver saddles. I asked the owner of the garden whose children they were. He replied: 'These are the children who like to pray, study, and be good.' Then I said: 'Dear sir, I also have a son, whose name is Hänschen Luther. Might he not also [be permitted] to enter the garden, so that he too could eat such fine apples and pears, and ride on these pretty ponies, and play with these children?' Then the man answered: 'If he too likes to pray, study and be good, he too may enter the garden, and also Lippus and Jost. And when they are all together [there], they will also get whistles, drums, lutes, and all kinds of other stringed instruments; and they will also dance, and shoot with little crossbows.' And he showed me there a lovely lawn in the garden, all prepared for dancing, where many gold whistles and drums and fine silver crossbows were hanging. But it was still so early [in the morning] that the children had not yet eaten; therefore I couldn't wait for the dancing. So I said to the man: 'Dear sir, I shall hurry away and write about all this to my dear son Hänschen so that he will certainly study hard, pray diligently, and be good in order that he too may get into this garden. But he has an Aunt Lena, whom he must bring along.' 'By all means,' said the man, 'go and write him accordingly.'

Therefore, dear son Hänschen, do study and pray diligently, and tell Lippus and Jost to study and pray too; then you [boys] will get into the garden together. Herewith I commend you to the dear Lord['s keeping]. Greet Aunt Lena, and give her a kiss for me.

Your loving father, Martin Luther

Wife, children, colleagues and their families, friends, young students, visitors and household servants – the Luther ménage was a busy and lively place and one that did much more than provide the pleasant background for the reformer's remaining years. It established a pattern. With the advantage of hindsight we can see that what came out of the white-hot kiln of 1524–6 was a set of new 'pots', practical concepts of the Christian state with an evangelical glaze. In what would emerge as 'Protestant' lands, the vision for society, promoted via pulpit and press, was essentially a Judaeo-Christian paternalism which drew its inspiration from Scripture. The family unit was invested with a new sanctity, was, indeed, promoted as the very bedrock of society. The disappearance of religious houses hastened the changing balance in population between single and married people. Wealthy burgers, who attributed their success to their devotion to God, commissioned family group portraits, sometimes showing themselves seated with their households around the open Bible. No longer was the married state regarded as a second best to lifelong virginity. The pastors of reformed communities would be, for the most part, married men patterning a different kind of ideal to that of the celibate Catholic priests. They moved into large houses where their large families – theoretically at least – suggested a foretaste of the intimate joys of heaven.

For the state, too, a new pattern was emerging. In town and principality governments emerged which took over several of the functions
hitherto performed by the Church and were charged with overseeing care
of the poor, education and the institution of laws based on the Christian
moral code. Luther became quite tetchy when he was asked to adjudicate
on marriage cases. 'I'll give him something to remember me by for impli-
cating me in such matters!' he responded when a pastor wrote to him with
such a request. 'Such matters belong to the government. These are external
things that are concerned with dowries and inheritances. What do they
have to do with us!'[11]

A radically different lifestyle was emerging in those lands where Luther's
influence was strongest and most long-lasting. Several novelties made an
immediate impact: the extension of civil law over the clergy; the disappearance of excommunication and other threatened ecclesiastical sanctions;
the withering of the pilgrimage trade; the encouragement of individual Bible
study; vernacular services; the rejection of most sacraments. But it was
only slowly that the deeper implications of Luther's teaching on everyday
life in Germany manifested themselves and the reformer, himself, could
not foresee just how major his contribution would be to the moulding of
a new Germany.

IV

Wars and Rumours of Wars
1527–1532

'Christ's cross must always be carried'

Letter to the Elector John,
18 November 1529

12

Alliances and Misalliances

'I advise that Your Electoral Grace, together with the other sovereigns and cities who are united in their faith, give a humble reply to the Emperor, and in all humility sue for peace from His Imperial Majesty.'[1] This was Luther's response to the Elector John who wanted to form a political alliance of German evangelicals to resist imperial religious coercion. To those evangelicals who happened to disagree with him over the precise meaning of Christ's words at the institution of the Lord's Supper – 'This is my body . . . This is my blood' – his reaction was very different. 'The fanatics strangle Christ my Lord and God the Father in his words, and my mother church, too, along with my brethren . . . they would like to cultivate love in their relationship with me . . . but, in spiritual matters, we intend to shun, condemn and censure them.'[2] In political matters he permitted room for manoeuvre, even compromise, but on what would to most people seem to be an issue of doctrinal trivia or one which might be left to individual conscience he was implacable. For him the Reformation was, from first to last, a movement for *religious* freedom. But it was, inevitably, becoming politicised. Luther's refusal to be part of this process made him yesterday's man. He who had been both the figurehead of protest and its driving force was edged by others further and further into the wings. His tragedy was that he was an actor who wanted to remain centre stage, but found himself with fewer and fewer lines to speak that were relevant to the unfolding drama.

It was clear to all the lead players that the survival of the Reformation would depend on the enforcement or non-enforcement of the Edict of Worms. At a deeper level its impact would rest to a very great extent on the unity or disunity of evangelicals. Neither of these considerations featured prominently on Luther's agenda. With the benefit of hindsight we can see that he was wrong. The father of the Reformation bastardised some of his children and exercised an unhelpful authority over others. Great leaders have great egos and find it difficult to tolerate any challenge to their own convictions. This tendency is multiplied if they have had to struggle for recognition. One could cite Oliver Cromwell, Horatio Nelson and Winston Churchill among those whose stubborn conviction of their own rightness led them into monumental disasters as well as brilliant triumphs. Luther's vision was a *biblical* vision. Time after time he had been driven back to the word of God in his quest for truth, for enlightenment, for consolation, for guidance in the varied problems which beset him daily. No one knew the Scriptures better than he. He came to see himself as, if not the only interpreter of the Bible, at least its most honest and fearless exponent. This self-evaluation was reinforced by the steady flow of people who came to consult the oracle of Wittenberg. Students, clergy, burghers and princes sought his advice and even kings sent emissaries. The leading Catholic scholars implicitly acknowledged him as their equal every time they locked horns with him. The *enfant terrible* had become the elder statesman, a leader who expected his authority to be accepted by everyone within the evangelical fold.

The international situation in the aftermath of the Peasants' War favoured the consolidation of evangelical forces in the empire because pope and emperor were still preoccupied with more pressing problems and because the recent unrest had demonstrated to the princes that German problems were most readily solved by German rulers acting in concert. In February 1525 Charles V had won a victory at Pavia which was famous for two reasons. It was the first time that handheld firearms were used in battle and the fate of Italy was settled. The imperial army had a corps of 1,500 Spanish harquebusiers, a shock force which decimated the ranks of the French infantry. The result of the annihilation of Francis I's army was that Charles became master south of the Alps. He took the French king prisoner during the battle and, early in 1526, imposed a humiliating peace treaty upon him. The two sovereigns left Madrid; Francis sullenly harbouring thoughts of revenge and Charles happily travelling to Seville for his marriage to a Portuguese princess. The twenty-six-year-old emperor had every cause to feel satisfied with the progress of his reign and he confidently espoused the vision of himself as the Catholic champion who would unite his extensive dominions into a league for the protection and advancement of the true faith. This would include dealing, once and for all, with the Lutheran menace. He ordered a new, large and magnificent palace to be built in Granada which would be a material expression of his lofty ideals. It did, indeed, become a symbol of his hopes and dreams, for it was never finished.

Within months messengers were bringing him unwelcome news from several quarters. Francis I had abrogated the Treaty of Madrid by forming a new alliance with Pope Clement and Henry VIII of England. This League of Cognac was a direct result of Charles' triumph. He had become *too* powerful and his neighbours were determined to curb his ambition. Worse information was to follow. Suleiman the Magnificent was on the move from Istanbul at the head of a mighty army. Ottoman encroachment by land and sea had been steady ever since the new sultan's accession in 1520 but the current campaign was on a much larger scale. Suleiman actually enjoyed the support of Francis I with whom he had just negotiated a treaty. The objective was obviously to oblige Charles to divert troops to his eastern border while France and her allies reversed the results of the Battle of Pavia. The cynical *realpolitik* which saw a Christian king entering into alliance with the great enemy of the faith was soon matched by the emperor. He mobilised troops from his central European lands to descend on the Papal States. Not only was this an attack by the great Catholic champion on the head of the Catholic church, it was patronage of heretics by the great enemy of heresy, for Charles employed mercenaries and German troops, many of whom were Lutherans. Even the appalling news of an impressive Ottoman victory in Hungary did not cause the emperor to rearrange his strategic priorities. In August 1526 Charles' brother-in-law, Louis II of Hungary, impulsively launched an attack on the superior forces of the Muslim invader at Mohács and paid for this temerity with his life. His army was annihilated and the Turks continued triumphantly to Buda. Habsburg Vienna lay a mere 250 kilometres away up the Danube and was only saved because Suleiman, diverted by problems at home, turned back. He left political chaos behind him. Charles' brother, Ferdinand of Austria, who was regent in the eastern Habsburg lands, claimed the vacant crown but was opposed by János Zápolya, a Hungarian nobleman who had the backing of the Turks. The result was thirty years of intermittent civil war and the ultimate partition of the country. For Charles this meant that his eastern frontier was terribly vulnerable. Yet he considered the situation in Italy to be more pressing, so much so that he initiated a massive military incursion. He ordered Ferdinand to send troops from Germany across the

Alps. He negotiated the aid of Italian states which had their own reasons for hostility towards the Medici pope. And he sent a Spanish contingent by sea. Strategically this was a move which ensured success. Morally it was a disaster. Charles certainly had every justification in defending his Italian possessions but that was not the only reason for the invasion which he unleashed against Rome and its allies. He reacted with the righteous wrath of a man betrayed. Francis had gone back on his word. As for the devious Medici, he had been a party to the Frenchman's duplicity. He had even connived at the involvement of the enemies of the Christian faith. From the emperor's perspective he was defending the Church's values against the head of the Church, who had forsaken them. Probably the irony never occurred to him that this was precisely what Luther had been attempting for the last decade. Thus, in the spring of 1527, the terrible cavalcades converged upon the eternal city. Men with long memories might fancy that they could hear the high-pitched laughter of Savonarola echoing round the courts of heaven.

Most of the soldiers who had made their way through the frozen winter passes of the Alps or were now enduring the heaving decks of a Mediterranean crossing had no exalted motives. Rome was a honeypot and the forces that converged upon it from various directions were driven by the once-in-a-lifetime prospect of fabulous loot. After some futile attempts at negotiation, the long-dreaded assault began on 6 May. 25,000 soldiers, only notionally under the leadership of their commanders, poured through the breaches and coursed along the narrow streets of the city, breaking into houses, churches and convents in their quest for easy wealth. What followed was an orgy of murder, rape and pillage such as Europe had not seen since the sack of Constantinople by 'holy' crusaders in 1204. Armed soldiers fell mercilessly on a civilian population, for there was no military presence to speak of.

Reports of the atrocities shocked all of Europe. The marauders spared nothing and no one. Altars were stripped, tombs broken open, shrines wrecked and the contents of precious reliquaries thrown into the street. As for the residents who had not managed to flee the stricken city, they became the victims of unimaginable horrors at the hands of brutal foreigners forcing them to divulge the whereabouts of their treasures.

> Many were suspended for hours by the arms; many were cruelly bound by the genitals; many were suspended by the feet high above the road or over the river, while their tormentors threatened to cut the cord.

Some were half buried in the cellars; others were nailed up in casks or villainously beaten or wounded; not a few were branded all over their persons with red-hot irons. Some were tortured by extreme thirst, others by insupportable noise and many were cruelly tortured by having their teeth brutally drawn. Others again were forced to eat their own ears or nose or their roasted testicles, and yet more were subjected to strange, unheard-of martyrdoms that move me too much even to think of, much less describe.[3]

So wrote one eye witness, Luigi Guicciardini, brother of the celebrated historian Francesco Guicciardini. As many as twelve thousand people were butchered, their bodies tossed into the Tiber or left cluttering the streets. Soon damage and disease had rendered three quarters of the city uninhabitable and the only respite gained by the survivors came when the soldiers deserted Rome to escape the plague.

It might have been thought that the Germans, and especially the Lutherans, with their xenophobic disdain for effete Italians, would be the most barbaric and ruthless of the invaders but contemporary observers seem to have concurred that the most savage members of the imperial host which rampaged through Rome and its environs for nine months were the Spaniards and Italians. Certainly Lutherans relished the opportunity to make rough and ready religious comment, such as scrawling graffiti, smashing cultic images, spitting on the host, dressing up in rich vestments and holding mock ceremonies, or ensuring that nuns would no longer be able to claim to be virgins. Some Germans held a mock papal election in which Luther was elevated to the throne from which Clement had been ejected. However, Catholic commentators would never be able to make propaganda capital out of the outrages committed in 1527 because their own co-religionists held the papal regime in just as much contempt as did the heretics. With drunken gusto they ripped down altar paintings, made bonfires of sacred books and hacked priests to death. They stabled their horses in St Peter's and turned convents into brothels. Catholic and evangelical observers close to the action were agreed in prophesying the welcome end of the papacy.

Of course, it was no such thing. Charles V was satisfied at having defeated his more immediate enemies but he was genuinely appalled at the devastation he had unwittingly unleashed against the Holy See. In the aftermath of the invasion the emperor's major concerns were the extraction of the maximum political capital from the situation and the silencing of all the outraged critics who condemned the invasion. The abolition of the papacy did not enter his thinking at all but an adjustment of the relationship between emperor and pope was an urgent priority. He kept Clement a virtual prisoner in his fortified refuge, the Castel Sant'Angelo, until December, when the pontiff escaped to Orvieto disguised as a merchant. His independence in the subsequent peace negotiations was largely illusory; he had nothing to bargain with. But Charles' position was far from secure. The French were still in the field and, for several months, threatened to entrench themselves and their allies firmly in Milan, Florence and Naples. Not until the summer of 1529 was a lasting peace concluded between all the parties. Renewed friendship between Charles and Clement was impressively cemented the following December in a coronation ceremony at Bologna, at which Charles V became the last emperor to be crowned by a pope. The continuance of a tradition reaching back seven hundred and twenty-nine years seemed to restore the unity and integrity of Christendom, and Clement comforted himself with the hope that Charles would now divert his attention to protecting Europe from the Turk and to eradicating heresy from his dominions.

There was, however, one fly remaining in the papal ointment: Charles and the imperial princes were still insisting on the immediate summoning of a general council to deal with all those abuses which had precipitated the Reformation. This was the one issue on which Clement was determined to dig in his heels. He was not prepared to have his own record and that of his half-brother, Leo X, exposed to public scrutiny and criticism. As a Venetian diplomat reported to his government, rather than permit that, Clement was prepared to forego the emperor's friendship and risk a second sack of Rome. For his part, Charles urgently needed a council. It would enable him to offer his recalcitrant German princes what they had, all along, been demanding. It would take the religious issue out of their hands and place it in those of the theological experts. Whatever the outcome, the dissident members of the diet would be morally obliged to accept it. Charles and Clement played a game of bluff and counter-bluff. But it was now the pope who had the stronger hand. He knew that the emperor could not risk a second showdown. Thus it was that, when all the other terms of a general peace had been decided, the demand for a general assembly of the Church was shelved. On the religious issue it was sensitive Medici pride and ingrained Vatican secrecy that triumphed over political wisdom and ethical transparency. The rejection of this last opportunity of the Church Catholic to reform itself proved disastrous.

In the 1940s the American scientific and military communities developed the technology that would enable them to manufacture a nuclear bomb. The theoretical possibility of such a weapon made inevitable its practical use in a war situation and led to the horrors of Hiroshima and Nagasaki. It is not fanciful to use this analogy in order to elucidate what happened in Europe between 1527 and 1530. If the evangelical gospel was the equivalent of $e=mc^2$, its political application lay in individual states being able to choose their own confessional allegiance. Theology, like nuclear physics, would be taken over by the men of power and used for their own purposes. Once that happened, the empire and Christendom itself would be blown apart and the fallout would be felt for generations. The ardent Archduke Ferdinand set the process in motion in 1524 when he called upon all loyal princes in South Germany to unite in support of the Edict of Worms. In the following year Catholic princes in the North, including Duke George of Saxony and the Electors of Brandenburg and Mainz met at Dessau to form a league pledged to the defence of the old faith. The Peasants' War was a godsend to these reactionary princes and they grabbed the opportunity to exterminate all the Lutheran preachers they could lay hands on. Such rulers were essentially traditionalists who, whatever their misgivings about the exercise of imperial authority, regarded the unifying power of religion as more important. This was the situation in which one of the more tragic figures of the Reformation forced his way into a position of leadership. The twenty-year-old Philip, Landgrave of Hesse, was an energetic, impulsive, independent-minded young man who had already had to fight long and hard to establish his authority in his own territories. He was Duke George's son-in-law but he resolutely refused to be led by that implacable enemy of Luther. Instead, he proclaimed himself a supporter of the reformers, especially of Melancthon, and he threw in his lot with Elector John.

Having decided where his religious allegiance lay, Philip proclaimed it with a bravura which frequently embarrassed the reform leaders in Wittenberg. He was scarcely the best advocate for the evangelical faith. His sex life was an open scandal; he was not above duplicity and bullying in the pursuit of religious freedom; and he was incapable of keeping a low profile when delicate situations called for it. Thus, his preparation for the Diet of Speyer in 1526 was provocative in the extreme. Knowing that Lutheran priests were forbidden to officiate in the city churches, Philip arrived with an entourage of evangelical preachers whom he set to declaiming in the streets and squares of Speyer. Then, on the first Friday, a meatless fast day, he presided over a public ox-roast. What such uncompromising behaviour did achieve was an emboldening of those rulers committed to or tending towards reform and a demonstration to their opponents that they were prepared to stand by their principles. Charles V, not present at the diet and fully occupied elsewhere, was in no position to insist on religious orthodoxy. As a result the confessional issue was largely avoided and this, in effect, left rulers free to decide autonomously what policy to adopt. More than anything else it was the fact that the emperor's hands were tied that decided the political outcome of the Reformation.

While centralised control grew weaker the religious factions jostled for supremacy. Philip worked like a beaver to build up a strong evangelical alliance. He enlisted the support of several north German states and the cities of Augsburg, Strasbourg, Ulm and Nuremburg and his messengers scurried busily around other courts and council chambers. Philip had grandiose ideas of an evangelical crusade which would eradicate papal error – if necessary at swordpoint – and to this end he sent diplomatic missions to Bohemia and France. There was a certain strategic logic to his thinking. Following the sack of Rome the empire was in a state of confusion. France and her allies had not been crushed; Ferdinand was absorbed in the problems of Hungary; and there could be little doubt that the Turk would soon be on the march again. It must have seemed to the headstrong Philip that this was a God-ordained moment to make a strike for the truth of the Gospel. At the same time the archduke's advisers were screaming for reprisals against the rebellious and heretical German leaders. On both sides pamphleteers whipped up warlike feelings. It was a state of affairs in which rumour and suspicion flourished and this accounts for the success of the Pack letter. Otto von Pack, one of Duke George's agents, showed Philip a copy of a document purporting to reveal plans agreed in a meeting at Breslau for a pre-emptive strike by the Catholic states against their heretical neighbours. On the strength of it Philip urged his supporters to gird themselves for war. But the whole episode was an exercise in mischief-making. Pack was an avaricious double agent and his letter was a forgery. Whether Philip was duped or part of a conspiracy to create a false *casus belli* has never been clear. What is evident is that sabres were being noisily rattled on both sides.

It was when Elector John came under pressure from his ally to mobilise his forces in the summer of 1528 that he turned to Luther for advice. Luther had watched from afar, preserving his non-political stance. When he replied it was in a joint letter with Melancthon. Not for a moment did the two theologians think strategically or weigh the chances for military success or consider the pros and cons of failure. They simply laid down the biblical principles as they saw them. Ferdinand had ordered all the estates of the empire to preserve internal peace and it was this injunction that the writers seized upon.

> . . . this mandate was issued by our regular governmental authority, which has been established by God, and which we are duty bound to obey; and this is especially so since . . . no evil is commanded, only good and peace, and neither our [interests] nor those of the other party are considered, but only the common good of the Empire is being sought . . .

To reject the clear instruction of the emperor's deputy would put the evangelical princes in the wrong just as much as the peasants had been. They would 'have no good conscience before God, no legal ground before the Empire, and no honour before the world. This would be dreadful and terrifying.' Luther and Melancthon denounced the proposal to take up arms as a satanic temptation and there was more than a hint of blackmail in what they went on to say would happen if their advice was rejected:

> . . . we would be compelled to speak out and to testify against Your Electoral Grace, our most beloved lord . . . we would have to leave Your Electoral Grace's territory and emigrate . . . for the sake of the gospel, in order to avoid having all this disgrace appear to fall justifiably on the innocent word of God.[4]

The Wittenberg theologians were determined that the Reformation should not be hijacked by warlords. It was a religious movement and Luther, more vehemently than his colleague, insisted that it should not be tainted by politics. This was naïve. In their conflict with Rome the preachers had looked to the secular power for support and protection and their developing vision was for state churches in which the clergy defined Christian belief and practice and the magistracy framed and enforced the laws which enshrined that belief and practice. Such collaboration was an unrealistic ideal, depending, as it did, on the goodwill and, ultimately, on the holiness of the prince or the civic authority. Princes and councillors would expect, as they always do, quid pro quos in dealing with church leaders. But we should not judge Luther by the cynical realities of a modern secular society. The relationship of church and state had been debated by theorists for centuries and that debate was intensified in the sixteenth century by the fresh insights gleaned from classical authors as well as the Bible. Evangelical thinkers were becoming much exercised by considerations of how to establish a 'godly commonwealth'. Luther took no part in such esoteric discussions except insofar as he deemed it right to advise rulers on how to apply biblical principles. His priority was a simple – even a simplistic – one: 'What says the word of God?' He was out of his depth in any consideration of the subtle circumstances which might cause a subject or a territorial prince to defend his faith against his overlord. In any such debate Luther was driven by two passions – adherence to Scripture and concern for the reputation of the evangelical movement. The Bible was clear that the Christian should not put his trust in chariots. Divine truth would ultimately prevail without the assistance of military might. If, in the course of his battle with the satanic enemy, a prince should suffer, even unto death, well, this was no more nor less than Christ, himself, had called him to. In another letter to the elector Luther urged him to not to be provoked by imperial sanctions:

> . . . such an undertaking of the Emperor is only a threat of the devil, which will be without power and will finally grow into a catastrophe for the opposition, as Psalm 7[.16] says: 'His mischief returns upon his own head, and his violence will descend upon him'. In addition, Christ tries us (as is right and necessary) through this [to see] whether or not we . . . take his word seriously and uphold it as firm truth. For if we wish to be Christians and have life eternal in the world to come then we cannot be better off than our Lord himself and all his saints were and still are. Christ's cross must always be carried . . .[5]

This exhortation begged several questions, not least among which was the moral responsibility a prince had towards his own subjects. Passive disobedience and a willingness to accept martyrdom are all very well for the individual believer but can they be embraced by the Christian prince? Was he, for example, to stand by and see his people slaughtered by an emperor who launched a religious war against them? And was he justified in sending his troops into battle against an external enemy such as the Turk or an internal foe like the Anabaptists? These were urgent, practical issues for Germany's rulers in the late 1520s and it was little help to them to urge them to keep their own hands clean and look to heaven for their reward. Luther did realise this and he did address his mind to the complexities of the real world. Yet he only wrote about them in response to enquiries from those who sought his aid: seldom, if ever, did he venture into print with long, reasoned tirades against erroneous teaching on political matters as he had done when confronting Rome and its minions over such issues as indulgences or papal authority.

Luther has been accused of inconsistency because he gave different advice on the use of force at different times and to different people. Certainly, he lacked the unalterable conviction of the man who advocates the same policies always and everywhere. But there is another kind of consistency – that which holds to basic principles and interprets their application afresh in every situation. Luther was wise enough to know that policy must be decided by both principles and circumstances. The problem was understanding how to advocate action that would be effective, without compromising Christian truth. Convinced as he was that God's word written was the final arbiter in all questions of faith and conduct (and we should remember that it was during these years that he was completing his masterly German translation of the Bible), he wrestled daily with the divine text and the advice he gave reveals this ongoing, creative *Kampf*.

It was a military man, Assa von Kramm, who provided Luther with the opportunity to set out his ideas on the ethics of war. Kramm was a cavalry leader who had served in several campaigns, but it was the massacre at Frankenhausen which troubled his conscience. There, he and his men had cut down helpless peasants, trampling under hoof the religious banners which proclaimed the rebels' Christian convictions. He asked Luther to resolve the problems confronting him and the title of the book which Luther wrote in response indicates the seriousness of Kramm's worries. *Whether Soldiers, Too, Can Be Saved* came off the press at the end of 1526 and covered several political issues as well as the culpability (or otherwise) of the man wielding sword or pike. It is very far from being Luther's best work. It leaves some crucial aspects of the subject unresolved. It is not in the same category as the painstaking, point-by-point treatises in which he explored the great central doctrines of the Church. Rather, it should be thought of as an extended pastoral letter in which the pastor/confessor shines the light of Scripture onto the complexities of governmental authority and responsibility.

Luther's political thinking was locked into the conventional, medieval pyramidal pattern. All authority spread downwards from God; all

responsibility extended upwards to God. At no level did the individual
have any right to challenge his superior. Was this, then, a recipe for
tyranny? No, because every individual in the pyramid had a duty of care
for those below him. As long as everyone fulfilled his function, justice (a
manifestation of the divine law) would prevail. The alternative was chaos,
inspired by the prince of chaos. In all this Luther shared the convictions
of Aquinas and other traditional Catholic authorities. This world was but
the outer courtyard of God's eternal palace. Man's responsibility in it was
to save his soul. Political units had to be organised in ways that would
facilitate this sacred task. But, of course, Luther's pyramid was *not* the same
structure as that designed by his predecessors. It was built without ecclesiastical bricks. Popes, bishops, cardinals and abbots had no place in his
political scheme of things. This stemmed from his reading of Scripture but
we should be clear that the diminution of clerical influence in government was a process that was already underway. Throughout Europe senior
ecclesiastics were being replaced by men trained in common law as opposed
to theology or canon law. The practical secularisation of government was
already happening. Bold contemporaries unflinchingly grasped the implications of this. Machiavelli had written his *Principe* and *Discorsi* while
Luther was still a young monk. His premise was that what works in government is what works in government and that a ruler can properly fulfil his
function only if he is not unduly hampered by exalted religious and ethical
considerations. Far removed from the Italian thinker, though just as unin-
hibited in their application of logic, were some of the sects commonly
called 'Anabaptist'. They held that secular governments were manifestly
evil. Wherever they looked they saw corruption, exploitation, cruelty and
inter-state war. Under most regimes – both Catholic and evangelical –
they suffered persecution. How could they doubt that such states were
under the control of Satan? Their reaction was to separate themselves,
refusing to be bound by man-made laws and, in many cases, leading peripatetic lives until they could find sympathetic landowners who would give
them somewhere to settle.

   Luther did not accept that the subordination of church to state meant
the abandonment of the latter to amoral pragmatism. But if the spirituality were no longer in political partnership with the temporality how were
Christian ethics to be upheld and the Gospel to be propagated? The answer
lay in the appointment of ministers of the word by whom rulers would be
guided. It may be that Luther had been 'spoiled' by his relationship with
the electors of Saxony. Through Spalatin he had enjoyed easy access to

Frederick and John and both had sought his counsel. Their heir, John Frederick (who succeeded in 1532), was an even more committed supporter of the reform. Luther had always been very frank in his dealings with the princes and they had, by and large, accepted his advice. This experience provided the model for the evangelical states of Germany which Luther now envisaged. His solution was idealistic. It was, perhaps, impracticable. It raised as many questions as it solved. How, for example, could individual freedom of belief be squared with the existence of territorial churches? This and many other day-to-day issues had to be left open to negotiation and compromise. Yet, if the evangelical objective was to create new-style Christian states which avoided the extremes of theocracy and secularism, it is difficult to see what better pattern could have been advanced. Certainly, it is unfair to label Luther as the apostle of absolutism. The assertion that 'had there been no Luther there could never have been a Louis XIV'[6] is wide of the mark. Luther was only one voice among many in the sixteenth century which (for a variety of reasons) were calling for secular powers to assert authority over a monolithic church which had become too powerful and corrupt. In his schema, the prince *was* responsible only to God but this did not imply that he was a semi-divine being, as more extreme divine right theories would claim. It was the Christian minister's responsibility to devote himself to prayer and study of the word and to keep his prince in line with the will of God. If the prince chose to reject such guidance, he could not overbear the conscience of the subject, and methods of resistance, short of armed rebellion, were open to the subject.

It was conscience that was at issue in the appeal of the soldier, Assa von Kramm. Luther was at pains to reassure him. The military profession was an honourable one which a man might pursue with diligence and pride. Just as a prince might, under certain circumstances, go to war, so his subjects might fight in his army. But the soldier's prior duty was to God. While it was not his responsibility to probe the motivation of his superiors, if he had good reason to believe that his master's cause was unjust he should obey his conscience and refuse to fight. Ultimately, said Luther, the servant of a tyrant could not take refuge in the excuse that he was just 'obeying orders'. What of the soldier who fought and killed only for pay? This was the age of the professional warrior, the man who belonged to a war band, ready to serve anyone, anywhere if the terms were favourable. Those terms usually included rights of plunder which could lead to appalling acts such as the sack of Rome. Surely, there could be no defence of such arrangements on theological grounds. Yet, Luther refused to dismiss mercenaries out of hand. Unpalatable as was the reality of paid thugs in the service of ambitious princes terrorising help-less villagers and townspeople, the use of professionals did, at least, save some men from being impressed into military service. Better that a man toughened and trained for war should risk his life than that the peasant should be taken from his plough or the weaver from his loom. That said, it followed that the labourer was worthy of his hire. He might even transfer his allegiance from one master to another. But, again, what mattered was his own motivation. He should offer his sword to the prince with the purest cause, not the one with the deepest pocket.

If the Christian taking up this violent trade was expected to weigh care-fully the ethics of every campaign he was called upon to engage in he would need guidance as to how to judge the rights and wrongs of each case. Luther, therefore, had to offer some insights on the ethics of war. Princes were responsible to God for the punishment of evil and the protection of their subjects. Thus, putting down rebellion and engaging in defensive wars were included in their duties. What evangelical princes might not do was combine to offer military resistance to the emperor or aggression to their Catholic counterparts. Let them strive mightily to preserve peace and refuse to wage war for personal gain.

All this idealistic exhortation left aside one area of potential conflict and one which loomed large in the minds of many contemporaries: war against the Ottoman Empire. One tactic Philip of Hesse proposed was to refuse mili-tary assistance to Charles V until the religious issue was dealt with to the satisfaction of the evangelical leaders. Luther finally dealt with this in detail in 1529, when he published *On War Against the Turk*, dedicated to Philip. In accord with what he had already written about war, the author affirmed that the emperor was not only allowed, but also obligated, to defend his people against the incursions of another ruler who was his political equal. Therefore, Philip and his allies were not justified in bargaining with Charles for their support. Their overlord was within his rights in ordering them into battle. But, in this instance, the ethics of conflict were complicated by the historical and religious background of war between 'Christian West' and 'Muslim East'. Luther absolutely rejected crusading idealism. The emperor should not enter the fray as the champion of the faith whose arms were blessed by the pope and whose troops were encouraged by the offering of indulgences and other spurious spiritual incentives. No mere mortal could launch a 'holy' war. The only army that fought for the Church was the angelic host. The success of Suleiman suggested to Luther that God was holding his heavenly legions in reserve. Christendom was being punished for its errors and its neglect of the Gospel.

Luther's enemies made great play with his seeming pacifism. What could be plainer proof that he was in league with the devil than that he preached non-intervention against the Islamic hosts of Satan? *On War Against the Turk* fiercely refutes this charge. Certainly, it states, Islam is an alien faith at war with Christian truth. It must, therefore, be countered, first and foremost, on the spiritual plain. Let every Christian, ruler and subject, pray for deliverance from the infidel – not forgetting to intercede for divine judgement upon papal error and wickedness. Then, let them rally to the imperial standard, as men called upon to fight a just *temporal* war. Having, as he believed, blown away the fog of religious claptrap which obscured the centuries-old clash between Christendom and Islam, Luther gave his advice on the best way to conduct any war with the Turk. It all came down to common sense military strategy. Suleiman had so far been successful because his enemies were divided. While Charles waged war against France and Rome the Ottomans had conquered Hungary. Let all Christian princes now unite to repel the common foe.

Ferdinand of Austria was desperate for such unity in the face of the Turkish menace but his clarion call sounded an altogether more strident note. He used the threat of foreign invasion in an attempt to bring the heretic states back into line. He denounced those princes and cities which had strayed from the Catholic fold and insisted that Christendom must unite or perish. The threat was real. Since the Battle of Mohács Hungary had been an unstable buffer state and a cause for diplomatic confrontation. Ferdinand had demanded the return of confiscated Habsburg territory and, by way of reply, the sultan had promised to march his army to Vienna in order to 'discuss' the disputed territory beneath the walls of the capital. In May 1529 news reached Austria that he was about to make good his promise. Suleiman had set out from Istanbul.

13

Family Squabbles

The imperial diet was meeting at Speyer when messengers on lathered horses arrived with the alarming news. Faced with this crisis, the representatives of evangelical towns and principalities supported Ferdinand by promising contingents to a combined force of 20,000 troops to defend Vienna. But there was a price to be paid. They resisted the demand to suppress reformed preaching and abate the secularisation of church property. 'In matters which concern God's honour and salvation and the eternal life of our souls, everyone must stand and give account before God for himself' – this was the nub of the famous 'Protestation' advanced by Philip of Hesse, John of Saxony, George of Brandenburg, Wolfgang of Anhalt, Ernest and Francis of Brunswick-Lüneburg and the leaders of fourteen imperial cities. They had drawn a line in the sand. They had brought into being a new politico-religious entity whose people would henceforth be called 'Protestants'. If a moment has to be defined when Luther finally lost control of the movement he had started, this is it.

Now, it was Landgrave Philip who took the lead in matters, not only tactical, but also theological. He saw clearly that the strength of the evangelicals depended on their unity. It was time to persuade the religious leaders to sink their differences. Accordingly, he invited them to his castle perched above the town of Marburg-an-der-Lahn, north of Frankfurt, to draw up a common declaration of faith. It would probably be true to say that all the delegates responded with mixed feelings, desiring amity while fearing further rifts, but, in late September and early October, they all came – Luther, Melancthon, Zwingli, Oecolampadius, Bucer and other interested parties. Cautiously they confronted each other in what must go down as one of the sad might-have-beens of history.

Church councils are not known for being gatherings at which disputes are charitably and prayerfully resolved in an eirenic spirit. Where contenders believe that they are the champions of immutable, divine truth there is little room for manoeuvre. Participants tend to depart more firmly entrenched than before in their own convictions, whether or not there has been a polite papering over of cracks. What can be said in favour of the Colloquy of Marburg was that it was conducted in complete honesty and with a degree of politeness which might not have been expected in view of the years of controversy that preceded it. The outcome may have confirmed to the Catholic world that 'Protestantism' was, by nature, fissiparous and that those who had left the ship of faith were vigorously rowing away from it in several directions but, when we remind ourselves that earlier Christian councils had often been marked by the vigorous exchanging of anathemas and that even murder was not unknown, the Colloquy of Marburg emerges as a pretty tame affair. In fact, the delegates reached agreement on fourteen out of fifteen articles. The core beliefs of evangelicals were confirmed. These included justification by faith, the primacy of Scripture, the nature of the person of Christ, the priesthood of all believers, baptism and church-state relations – matters on which there was and had been for centuries considerable disparity of opinion within the traditional church. Bearing in mind that, as Samuel Butler observed, 'definition is the enclosing of a wilderness of idea within a wall of words', these evangelical delegates did rather well. Yet the hoped-for unity was not achieved because the delegates were unable to find a wall of words to confine what happens in the central act of Christian liturgy. What did Christ mean when at the Last Supper he referred to bread and wine as his body and blood?

The background to this debate was six years of mounting antagonism between Luther and other radicals – but mainly Zwingli – on the nature of Christ's presence. When he had said 'This is my body; this is my blood' did he intend the words to be taken literally or figuratively? Luther insisted on the 'real' presence. If, at the Incarnation, God had entered a human body and if, through faith, Christ took up residence in the heart of every believer, there should be no difficulty in accepting that the divine had chosen to enter into bread and wine. The Swiss reformers were determined to distance themselves as far as possible from the crass materialism they believed to be inherent in the medieval concept of a sacrament. Zwingli abhorred the very word 'sacrament'. 'I wish the Germans had never let this word get into their theological vocabulary,' he wrote. He refused to accept that the consecrated elements had some intrinsic power of their own to convey holiness. This undermined the faith and the will of the recipient. The Lord's Supper was a powerful stimulant of faith but nothing more. For him and his supporters the word 'is' in Jesus' inauguration of the fellowship meal could only mean 'signifies'. Luther was closer to the traditional doctrine of the mass than Zwingli and Co., a fact he made no bones about. 'I'd rather drink blood with the pope than wine with Zwingli,' he scornfully stated.

Both reformers had set out on their doctrinal journey from the same station. They rejected sacerdotalism, the belief that power, authority lies in the consecrating priest to perform the miracle of the mass, to effect a change in the elements, to transform bread and wine into flesh and blood. It was this beyond anything else that had underpinned the power of the medieval priesthood as a caste of men set apart from ordinary mortals and alone able to connect them with the eternal realities of heaven. Luther and Zwingli were also on common ground in rejecting Aquinas' explanation of how this metamorphosis takes place, so that the broken body of Christ becomes present in the elements even though no obvious change can be observed by sight or taste. However, from this point the thinking of the two men had diverged. Zwingli had followed a humanist line of reasoning: since transubstantiation was nonsense it followed that Christ's body was not and could not be *located* within the stuff of the physical universe. The Bible taught that the risen and ascended Christ was now seated at the right hand of the Father in heaven. What Jesus had instituted at the Last Supper was a memorial of the new relationship he was about to set up with believers by his sacrifice at Calvary and not a mystic re-enactment of the crucifixion.

To Luther this was arrant blasphemy because it contradicted the plain word of God, understood literally, and so, in effect, made Christ a liar. He had proclaimed 'This is my body; this is my blood', and that was an end of the matter. The Christian's response was simply to accept this by faith, as he accepted everything else written in the word of God. *How* it happened was not his concern. Zwingli, in his efforts to rationalise what was taking place at the altar, was, in Luther's view, as guilty as Aquinas of futile logic-chopping. For the Wittenberger this could not simply be a matter for courteous disagreement. Divine truth was absolute and non-negotiable. That is why, when the delegates sat down round a table at Marburg, he scrawled on its surface, *Hoc est corpus meum*. If his opponents tried to squirm their way out of these plain words, they were not of God. And if they were not of God they were of the devil. In *That these Words of Christ, 'This is my Body', Still Stand Firm Against the Fanatics (1527)*, Luther, in his usual forthright way, accused Zwingli, Oecolampadius and Bucer of being Satan's unwitting agents in tearing down the very theological fabric of the Church. Their master would not stop when he had disposed of the truth about Holy Communion. He would 'carry on and attack more articles of faith, for his eyes are already agleam, saying that baptism, original sin and Christ are nothing'.[1] Neither of the two principal contenders was in a mood to compromise but it was Luther whose mind was not only closed but barred and bolted. Facing Zwingli across a narrow table, he challenged his opponent to prove that Christ was not bodily present in the elements but, when Zwingli attempted to do just that, pointing out other occasions on which Christ had used colourful, symbolic language to refer to himself, Luther simply brushed his arguments aside. 'Now, you're being obnoxious,' he snorted. It can never have occurred to him that he was doing exactly what his Catholic adversaries had done in the years leading up to the Diet of Worms – demanding capitulation and denying his opponent the courtesy of a debate among equals.

Luther identified himself as a spiritual guide and the Swiss delegates merely as leaders of a religious movement. He was calling the whole Church back to the truth of Scripture. They were fomenting nationalist rebellion and giving it a spurious biblical gloss. Inevitably, Zwingli and his colleagues, in justifying themselves, simply turned the tables. It was *they* who were grappling with the truth of the word of God and fearlessly applying it and Luther who had defected to the enemy by, for example, refusing to condemn the veneration of images or distance himself totally from the Catholic mass. Meanwhile, Philip of Hesse, John of Saxony and other princes hovered in the wings, intent on ensuring that the evangelical movement had political muscle and requiring from the theologians the doctrinal unity that would give confessional rigidity to their stand against the emperor and the pope. Later commentators have rather tended to align themselves with the politicians. It is common to see the failure of the Colloquy of Marburg as a 'lost opportunity' to create an evangelical consensus. The reality is more complex.

Zwingli, Oecolampadius and Bucer presented Luther with an uncomfortable new reality. Hitherto he had crossed swords with papists, radical fanatics and humanist scholars. The one thing they all had in common from his point of view was that they were not firmly rooted in the Bible, the only source of Christian truth. Now he was facing evangelical theologians whose devotion to the word of God was as great as his own. The freedom of Christians to interpret that word which he had insisted upon was now rising up before him as a spectre of spiritual anarchy. The reason he found it impossible to argue with other evangelical scholars was that he could not accept that the truth he had reached through such anguish of soul could be contradicted out of Scripture. When he did enter the exegetical lists he suffered reverses. Thus, for example, when Zwingli insisted that, according to the Bible, Christ was seated at the right hand of God and could not therefore be on earth in the form of bread and wine, Luther retorted that the phrase 'right hand of God' could not be taken literally as a location. But, if that was the case, why should the words of institution not also be understood figuratively? The fact was that there were no criteria for deciding in what way any text of Scripture was 'true'. Consensus was one possible key and here Luther had the majority of Christian progressives on his side. Most humanists and evangelical theologians sided with him on the communion issue. The mass miracle was so deeply embedded in the religious consciousness of Europeans that even the most radical Renaissance rationalists were emotionally unable to detach themselves from it. It was something at once sacred and familiar. To jettison it or even to devalue it was unthinkable. Luther could thus feel secure in his conviction that those who opposed him at Marburg were merely a minority group of heretical sectaries.

All parties came to Marburg with a heavy load of psychological and emotional baggage. At root there was a mutual suspicion between Germans and Swiss. Specifically for Luther, there was a fear of being tarred with the sacramentarian brush. He was also concerned not to offer gratuitous offence to the emperor by appearing to side with religious extremists. He aspired to the creation of a national church stripped of allegiance to Rome and based squarely on the biblical revelation but remaining in most outward essentials Catholic. He believed in the power of the word of God to continue the reform and to make 'his' church a model for others. Just as he had opposed the peasants for taking the law into their own hands, so he opposed the destruction of religious images, the rejection of vows and all other manifestation of 'root and branch' reform. He saw no need for the evangelical consensus that Philip of Hesse was trying to manufacture. It was politically suspect and could never be based upon a dishonest theological compromise. As the conference drew to a close Luther reported to his dear Katie, 'the Landgrave is negotiating [to see] if we could be united, or whether, even though we continue to disagree, we could not nevertheless mutually consider ourselves brethren, and members of Christ. The

Landgrave works hard on this matter. But we do not want this brother-and-member business, though we do want peace and good[will].'² And, when the assembly broke up, he could not bring himself to shake Zwingli's hand. It was testimony more to the persistence of Philip and his advisers than to any fraternalism on the part of the delegates that the principals were able to set their hands to a common statement of belief, the Marburg Articles. This itemised fourteen points of agreement and on the crucial matter of the Lord's Supper stated,

> . . . we all believe and hold concerning the Supper of our dear Lord Jesus Christ that both kinds should be used according to the institution of Christ; also that the mass is not a work with which one can secure grace for someone else, whether he is dead or alive; also that the Sacrament of the Altar is a sacrament of the true body and blood of Jesus Christ and that the spiritual partaking of the same body and blood is especially necessary for every Christian. Similarly, that the use of the sacrament, like the word, has been given and ordained by God Almighty in order that weak consciences may thereby be excited to faith by the Holy Spirit. And, although we have not at this time reached an agreement as to whether the true body and blood of Christ are bodily present in the bread and wine, nevertheless each side should show Christian love to the other side insofar as conscience will permit, and both sides should diligently pray to Almighty God that through his Spirit he might confirm us in the right understanding. Amen.
>
>
>
> Martin Luther
> Justus Jonas
> Philip Melancthon
> Andreas Osiander
> Stephen Agricola
> John Brenz
> John Oecolampadius
> Huldrych Zwingli
> Martin Bucer
> Caspar Hedio³
>
>

All things considered, this was a remarkable achievement.

It was an achievement that Philip of Hesse could only regard as having been secured in spite of Luther, rather than with his aid. If the evangelical caucus were to capitalise on this and win the right to follow their own religious path the great German theologian might well be an obstacle in the showdown that was approaching. The struggle would be hard enough without Luther's unyielding acrimony towards all those who opposed him. In the autumn of 1529, the tide which had been running in favour of the Protestant princes turned. First of all, in August, came the signing of the Peace of Cambrai at which Charles V and Francis I settled their differences. A few weeks later, Suleiman the Magnificent, camped before the walls of Vienna, packed up his tents and marched homeward. The city had bravely resisted his assaults and, with his supply lines dangerously extended, the sultan had no option but to raise the siege. By a combination of ruthlessness and laborious diplomacy the city states of North Italy were pacified. The removal of imperial troops from papal territory enabled emperor and pope to patch up their relationship and, in February 1530, their renewed amity was solemnly symbolised when Charles received the imperial crown at the hands of Pope Clement. It remained only for pope and emperor to re-establish themselves as the joint leaders of a united Christendom and this they set themselves to accomplish. This meant that the Lutheran menace now rose to the top of the imperial agenda. For the first time in nine years Charles was able to give his undivided attention to the affairs of Germany. The thirty-year-old ruler, the most powerful man in Europe, had, perforce, learned the arts of government rapidly during the previous turbulent decade and felt confident that he could complete his God-given task of restoring true religion to his dominions. This would mean reversing the Reformation. He had recently gone on record as saying that he wanted future historians to record that a movement which had begun in his reign had also ended in it. He proposed to employ two tactics to this end: he would bring all the German leaders together to agree a common religious policy and he would persuade the pope to summon a general council to thrash out the theological issues which lay at the root of the problem. He failed in both these enterprises.

Charles called a meeting of the imperial diet to convene in the spring of 1530 in Augsburg, a city which was, itself, torn between Catholic and evangelical factions. In mid-March Elector John set off for the meeting with his leading theologians, including Luther, in tow. The party made their slow way, lodging at the elector's residences, along the Magde valley to Grimma and thence to Weimar, before proceeding through the Thuringian forests to Coburg on the edge of Wettin territory. From here they continued southwards – but not with Luther. On the night of 23–24

April he was smuggled into the fortress high above the town. In the following weeks, while his friends were waging intellectual and spiritual battle in Augsburg, Luther lived a frustrated, reclusive life, bearded and wearing the tunic of a simple squire. It was the Wartburg all over again.

There was a good and genuine reason for leaving Luther in the safety of Electoral Saxony. He was still under the imperial ban and could, legally, be arrested, although it is doubtful whether Charles would have sanctioned such a provocative act while sensitive negotiations were underway with the Protestant princes. Of course, not even the emperor could protect him from armed Catholic zealots. However, it is difficult to avoid the impression that the evangelical spokesmen at Augsburg were relieved not to have the embarrassment of Luther's presence. Elector John tried to persuade the councillors of Nuremburg to provide lodging for Luther during the course of the diet but they declined. Philip of Hesse and his supporters were intent on winning concessions from their overlord and knew that their efforts would not be helped by any display of tactless defiance on Luther's part.

The reformer spent a hundred and sixty-five days at Coburg, during which time he suffered loneliness, personal grief, bouts of illness, anxiety about the activities of his colleagues at the diet and, above all, boredom. Whether or not the forty-seven-year-old leader consciously acknowledged to himself that he was being sidelined we cannot know. What is clear is that he did everything he could to influence the deliberations at Augsburg. Before setting out from Wittenberg, he and Melancthon, Justus Jonas and Johann Bugenhagen had carefully prepared their manifesto and were agreed on the case they would present to the diet. This did not stop Luther immediately he arrived at Coburg from sitting at his desk to pen an *Exhortation to all Clergy Assembled at Augsburg*, a point-by-point catalogue of everything that had divided him from Rome ever since the indulgence controversy. He assured his friends that he had reined in his indignation in writing this pamphlet but they must have found that difficult to believe when they read such passages as this addressed to his Catholic opponents:

> . . . you are the devil's church! She is a liar against God's word and a murderess, for she sees that her god, the devil, is also a liar and a murderer . . . You should not, therefore, say to us so much, 'Church, church, church'. you should rather make us certain that you are the church. That is the crux of the matter! The devil can also say, 'I am God, worship me', Matthew 4[.9]. The wolf can also say, 'I am a

shepherd', Matthew 7[.15], John 10[.1] . . . God help you to a reformation on this point . . . We want you to be forced to it by God's
word and have you worn down like blasphemers, persecutors and
murderers, so that you humble yourselves before God, confess your
sins, murder and blasphemy against God's word . . . We are willing
to stake everything on this and fight it out with you on the basis of
God's word, which you persecute . . .[4]

Luther had the pamphlet printed and five hundred copies shipped to
Augsburg, where it caused a sensation and sold out, despite Charles' attempts
to suppress it. While Melancthon and the others were making serious
efforts to reach a compromise solution, their mentor, like some prophet
of old, was despatching from his mountain retreat messages of fiery denunciation and exhortations to his friends to stick to their guns.

Luther really did see himself as a prophet in the Old Testament mode
and increasingly used the word to describe the vocation to which God
had called him. It was his role vis-à-vis temporal and spiritual rulers to
advise, warn, exhort, predict and anathematise. Every reverse he suffered
only served to reinforce his self-identification, for what prophet had there
ever been who had not been denounced, persecuted, rejected by those to
whom he was sent, or put to death? Even this skulking away in Coburg
was reminiscent of Elijah fleeing the wrath of Ahab and Jezebel. In his
fortified retreat, guarded by a garrison of thirty soldiers, Luther went through
rapidly changing moods. Sometimes he wrote with his accustomed energy,
concentrating largely on his Old Testament translation but also beginning
a new version of Aesop's *Fables* (never finished). But then the old depression returned or he was distracted by headaches, constipation, failing
eyesight and tinnitus. All these conditions were aggravated by overwork
but enforced leisure did nothing to ease his situation, for he only fretted
when he was idle. Distanced from his family, his students and the action
at Augsburg, he felt useless.

Then came a hammer blow. On 5 June, he received news that his father
was dead. He had learned early in the year that the old man was gravely
ill. At that time Martin had made the decision not to travel to Mansfeld.
'I did not dare to venture into danger,' he wrote by way of explanation,
'at the risk of tempting God, since you know how lords and peasants hate
me.'[5] All he could do was offer spiritual counsel and enquire whether his
father was strong enough to be moved to Wittenberg so that he could
fulfil his filial duty in looking after his aged parents. In his letter of 15

February Luther had movingly urged old Hans to fix his mind on the things of God and submit himself to the divine will.

> Herewith I commend you to him who loves you more than you love yourself. He has proved his love by taking your sins upon himself and by paying [for them] with his blood, and he has let you know this through the gospel, and has given it to you freely to believe this by his Spirit. Consequently, he has prepared and sealed everything in the most certain way, so that you are not permitted to worry about or be concerned for anything except keeping your heart strong and reliant on his Word and faith. If you do this then let him care for the rest. He will see to it that everything turns out well . . . May he, our dear Lord and Saviour, be with you and at your side, so that (may God grant it to happen either here or there) we may joyfully see each other again. For our faith is certain, and we don't doubt that we shall shortly see each other again in the presence of Christ. For the departure from this life is a smaller thing to God than if I moved from you in Mansfeld to here, or if you moved from me in Wittenberg to Mansfeld. This is certainly true; it is only a matter of an hour's sleep, and all will be different.[6]

There could be no simpler or clearer definition of Luther's gospel. The paraphernalia which, in the old religion, surrounded death – the anointings, the prayers, the priestly incantations, none of which could assure the departing soul of its reception in heaven – had been swept away. At the end of his earthly sojourn the Christian, by faith, could rejoice in the assurance of salvation. Yet, the conviction that his father had gone to be with Christ, there to await a joyful reunion with his son, could not deliver Luther from grief mingled with guilt. Hans had suffered much as a result of his son's notoriety and though the old man had died secure in the faith of Christ, Martin could only reflect on the cares and troubles with which he, himself, had repaid paternal love. He must also have reproached himself that, at the last, he had thought more of his own safety than his father's comfort. It took Luther several days to recover his composure.

Meanwhile, events at Augsburg pursued a serpentine course but one which could only have a single destination. Charles V, stiffened in his resolve by the intransigent papal legate, Cardinal Campeggio, and by Johann Eck, also come to enjoy the humiliation of his old enemies, was determined to curb the Protestant princes and burghers. But they had travelled too far along the road of religious freedom to be turned back. There was, to be sure, a willingness on the part of several participants to seek, if not a compromise, at least a *modus vivendi*. The anxious Melancthon sagged under the burden of responsibility. He was too gentle not to be upset by the sheer hatred of the Lutherans' enemies but he had to cope, not only with the Catholic onslaught (Charles had made his position clear by forbidding evangelical preaching during the diet), but also with efforts by the Swiss to win Philip of Hesse to their cause. Worse still, he had the absent Luther, as it were, breathing down his neck through a constant stream of letters. Melancthon wanted to demonstrate that he and his colleagues were reasonable, prepared to make concessions in the name of peace and unity. The appearance of Luther's *Exhortation* did nothing to support the impression he was trying to create. Not surprisingly, he did not exert much effort in reporting to Coburg the details of the Augsburg negotiations and, not surprisingly, Luther fumed and fretted that he was being kept in the dark. Angrily he told his friends that he would not reply to their letters if they persisted in keeping him short on details.

Not until 25 June was the Lutheran manifesto, which soon came to be known as the Augsburg Confession, read to the emperor and Melancthon sent a copy to Coburg the next day. It is easy to see the reason for his diffidence. Although the statement was in essence what had been agreed back in Wittenberg, Melancthon had watered it down. The first twenty-one of its twenty-eight points re-affirmed basic Christian teaching and were intended to demonstrate the authors' unimpeachable orthodoxy. The remaining seven articles dealt with abuses that had crept into common usage – the doctrine of the mass, communion of the laity in one kind, priestly celibacy, auricular confession, indulgences and similar examples of 'works religion', monastic vocations as a means to merit grace, and excessive episcopal power. No mention was made of papal corruption, purgatory or distortion of the word of God. Moreover, when he felt the arctic chill with which the statement was received, Melancthon was prepared to entertain even further concessions, including declaring respect for the Roman See and returning Lutheran churches to episcopal obedience. Luther's response to this was predictable. He accused his deputy of making dubious ends justify unacceptable means. The objective of the Confession was not the restoration of unity but the setting forth of the truth. He was prepared to accept the document in its altered form but set his face firmly against further compromise.

Had Campeggio and his party possessed any diplomatic subtlety they would have exploited the rifts in the evangelical camp. Not only were there differences between Melancthon and Luther, but other delegates were incensed at Melancthon's havering. The Swiss and the Strasburgers each produced their own confessions. With the archdemon securely shut away in some Saxon safe house, the pope's men might have cajoled and bullied his subordinates into at least an apparent surrender. The Catholic side was not without its eirenic members and Charles, himself, could see the political advantages of reaching some sort of accommodation with the Protestant princes. But the pace was set by Campeggio and Ferdinand of Austria and they would settle for nothing less than a complete reversal of the Reformation. In an open letter to the diet Luther pointed out that this could never be achieved without bathing the whole of Germany in blood. He declared that a religious settlement was impossible and urged the secular leaders to reach a political accord so that the empire could enjoy internal peace. The diet had other business to occupy itself with and it was not until 3 August that the Catholic response was ready. This *Confutation* had been drawn up by the pope's representatives and endorsed by the emperor as the official answer to the dissidents. There was to be no discussion. Once again the evangelicals were presented with a take-it-or-leave-it proposition – with dire warnings of what would happen if they left it. Three days later Landgrave Philip went home in disgust without bothering to obtain the emperor's permission. The agents of goodwill were loath to leave Augsburg with nothing to show for their pains and desultory talks *did* continue for the rest of the month. All the Lutherans gained was an undertaking from Charles that he would persuade the pope to summon a general council to discuss the doctrinal issues. He did honour this pledge by sending a special envoy to Rome. The message that came back was far from encouraging: 'the pope and the cardinals would sooner see this council in hell than on earth'. Faced with recalcitrance on both sides, the Holy Roman Emperor, ruler of more than half of Europe, was powerless. Once again the religious issue was shelved and Charles had to be satisfied with a face-saving formula. When the diet came to an end on 23 September the evangelicals were enjoined to make their submission by the following spring and not to enforce their religion on their Catholic subjects.

The Protestant leaders were not cowed. More than ever they were determined to give their confessional community some political rigidity and military muscle. Three months after the end of the diet Philip of Hesse achieved what he had long been seeking. In a meeting at Schmalkalden, on the Hesse-Saxon border, he and John of Saxony headed a conference of Protestant states and cities which formed themselves into a defensive league. By the following spring the Schmalkaldic League could boast the membership of eight princes and eleven cities. They were united in loyalty to the Augsburg Confession and prepared to support each other in resisting any attacks on their faith or territory. Between them they were prepared to commit 10,000 infantry and 2,000 cavalry to fight for the right to believe and worship as evangelicals without interference from pope or emperor. Luther was very lukewarm about this development. It mattered little. No one had formally consulted him.

14

Defining the Church

... our wiseacres do nothing except to slander us and say, 'Luther
has indeed destroyed the papacy but he can't build a new church',
that is, can't introduce a new form of worship and new ceremonies.
These wretched men think that building up the church consists of
the introduction of some sort of new ceremonies. They don't realise
that building up the church means to lead consciences from doubt
and murmuring to faith, to knowledge, and to certainty.[1]

Those *obiter dicta* of Luther's go to the heart of what he thought of as his
vocation. They warn us off a treatment of his career which has marked the
approach of some biographers. I refer to the tendency to see the reformer's
life after *c.*1530 as a coda. We are presented with a man whose life work –
at least when viewed in historical terms – is complete. What follows can
only be an anticlimax, a winding down. He is yesterday's man and the
Reformation henceforth goes on without him. It is true that the more sensational events of his life – the confrontations, dangers and world-changing
publications – now lay in the past. It is also true that age and illness robbed
him of the extraordinary energy that he had expended in his prime. But
Luther certainly did not think of his latter years as a time when he had
accomplished all that God had put him on earth to accomplish. He did not
even think that his mission had fundamentally altered. His task was still 'to
lead consciences to faith, to knowledge, to certainty'.

Any life of Luther must, perforce, concentrate on the dramatic events
which he precipitated or in which he was caught up. For him, however, they

were punctuation marks in the chronicle of the passing years. His calling was to be an evangelist and a teacher. He taught and preached the Gospel as he understood it from the plain word of Scripture and he dealt individually with the pains, griefs and anxieties of the many people who sought his spiritual counsel. His letters provide abundant evidence of his concern for his students, his congregation and his friends and these are supported by the unofficial notes taken by young men who were guests under his roof. In order to help make ends meet, he and Catherine provided board and lodging to several students. Accommodation was at a premium in Wittenberg's crowded university and there was no shortage of potential lodgers who needed a roof over their heads and who also felt privileged at being able to sit at the great man's table. They listened with awe to Luther's conversation and made notes on the verbal gems which fell from his lips. Some of these collections were later amalgamated and published as Luther's *Table Talk*. The interesting (and perhaps remarkable) fact about these hastily scribbled notes is that they wholly support the character portrait of the reformer that emerges from his own writings. The man whom we glimpse in the informality of his own household is the same earnest, forthright, dogmatic, jokey, passionate, compassionate, sometimes vulgar controversialist of the *Babylonian Captivity* and the meticulous teacher of the commentaries on Romans and The Psalms.

Thus, Luther could advise a depressed and introverted Melancthon to get out and about more:

I, too, often suffer from severe trials and sorrows. At such times I seek the fellowship of men, for the humblest maid has often comforted me . . . a solitary life should be avoided as much as possible.

On human depravity he observed,

The world is like a drunken peasant. If you lift him into the saddle on one side, he will fall off on the other side. One can't help him no matter how one tries. He wants to be the devil's.

Exhorting his students to regular Bible study, he revealed his own habit:

For some years now, I have read through the Bible twice every year. If you picture the Bible to be a mighty tree and every word a little branch, I have shaken every one of these branches because I wanted to know what it was and what it meant.

As a preacher ever on the lookout for good illustrative material, Luther loved the fables of Aesop and delighted to quote them:

> A lion, a wolf, an ass and a dog captured a deer. The lion asked for his share. The wolf, being famished, divided the game into four equal parts. For this he had his throat cut by the lion, who pulled the wolf's hide off over his ears. Seeing this, the ass gave all four parts to the lion. The lion asked, 'Who taught you to divide this way?' The ass replied, 'That doctor over there with the red biretta,' as he pointed to the mangled wolf.

Luther could be quite impatient with the constant stream of people seeking his advice. Once someone came to his bedroom when he had already retired to seek help for a widow who was looking for a new husband. On another occasion a visiting member of the Hussite Brethren, who was, presumably, well acquainted with the Bible, pressed him to say whether fornication was as bad as adultery. He pointed the enquirer to I Corinthians 6.9 and snapped,

> Paul made no distinction . . . I can't make a law for you. I simply point to the Scriptures. There it is written. Read it for yourself. I don't know what more I can do.

The question often arose in the inner circle of friends and students about the use of logic in Christian apologetic and controversy. Luther's opinion on this was drawn from long experience of crossing swords with the finest theological and philosophical minds of his age. In the cosmic scheme of things, he said, it was an illusion to suppose that a man's intellect could be independent.

> Reason that is under the devil's control is harmful and, the more clever and successful it is, the more harm it does. We see this in the case of learned men who on the basis of their reason disagree with the Word. On the other hand, when illuminated by the Holy Spirit, reason helps to interpret the Holy Scriptures . . . reason that's illuminated takes all its thoughts from the Word.

For Luther, theology was something to be lived or it was nothing. From pulpit, lecture platform and from his own chair at the head of the meal table he urged his hearers to shun barren argument. He even discounted some of his own writings as being too intricate. The liberalism of scholars like Erasmus, for whom intellectual debate was as the breath of life, was, to Luther, anathema.

> True theology is practical and its foundation is Christ, whose death is appropriated to us through faith. However, today all those who do not agree with us and do not share our teaching make theology speculative because they cannot free themselves from the notion that those who do good [will be rewarded]. *This is not what is written . . .* speculative theology belongs to the devil in hell.

But alongside such dogmaticism went an open acknowledgement of his own weaknesses, temptations and doubts – his *Anfechtung*.

> . . . I advise you young fellows . . . beware of melancholy, for it is forbidden by God because it's so destructive to the body . . . My temptation is this, that I don't think I have a gracious God . . . It is the greatest grief and, as Paul says, it produces death.[2] God hates it and he comforts us by saying, 'I am your God' . . . I'm not going to devour you. I'm not going to be poison for you . . . We ought to know . . . that above all righteousness and above all sin stands the declaration, 'I am the Lord your God.[3] (But I preach to others what I don't do myself.)[4]

As has already been mentioned, Luther established a new pattern, the Protestant pastor as family man. The old Black Cloister at Wittenberg, though spacious, became a crowded and bustling place when it was transformed into the Luthers' home. First, there were the couple's six children but other visitors and residents came and went in a never-ending procession. Martin and Catherine practised Christian hospitality as an economic necessity and a religious duty but above all because of their love of company. The monastery became a haven for several of the couple's poor relatives as for dispossessed nuns and monks. The buildings were always full of energetic, noisy young students and the doors were ever open to guests. It was a religious phenomenon the like of which western Christendom had never seen before and its social impact can scarcely be exaggerated. It endorsed the family and it brought clergy and laity closer together. No longer were parishioners second-class Christian citizens, unable to aspire to the holiness of their self-denying priest. The abandonment of celibacy also removed one of the major causes of scandal of which generations of lay people had complained.

It was Catherine who bore the main domestic burden – feeding her large household, organising and disciplining the servants, bringing up the children, nursing them and her spouse when they fell ill, and husbanding the family's slender financial resources. Luther had little free time to help with the chores. He had a demanding academic lecture schedule to fulfil. He had to preach, not only on Sundays and festival days, but when required to 'perform' before the elector and when travelling – since wherever he went folk expected a sermon from the great man. He had no official pastoral role in Wittenberg but he always stood in for the local pastor, Johann Bugenhagen, whenever he was absent (as he was for much of 1530–1). And, on top of all this he continued to maintain an extraordinary literary output.

The implications of evangelical doctrine included fundamental rethinking of the conduct of regular worship. If the mass was no longer a sacrifice and if the priest no longer had a sacerdotal function it followed that the congregation were not now mere observers of a cultic act but full participants in the drama of the liturgy. Here Luther, like all religious reformers, faced a major challenge. People may respond readily to vigorous preaching, especially when it highlights clerical abuses, but they tend to cling with stubborn affection to the familiar externals of worship. For Luther's contemporaries this included a Latin liturgy which few of them understood. Luther had been very critical of Karlstadt and others who had swept away images and insisted on administering communion in both kinds whether the congregations wanted it or not. He insisted that such insensitivity would bewilder and alienate people. Far better to proclaim the word of God faithfully so that listeners would come to realise the need for change. Yet the new teaching *was* at odds with the old ritual and Luther could not avoid the responsibility of transforming worship in order to make it an effective vehicle for the Gospel. Moreover, evangelical religion did make greater demands of believers. They were expected to understand their faith. If possible, they should read the Bible for themselves and certainly not just rely on automatic performance of rituals. It was difficult to persuade them to embrace this greater involvement in religious life.

Throughout the later 1520s Luther nagged away at this problem. His first innovation was the provision of vernacular hymns. Hymns were not new; what was new was that they were in German and that they rapidly became a popular part of worship. This had several advantages: it did not remove or alter any elements of the traditional liturgy. Illiterate congregations could learn the words off by heart (Luther organised weekday rehearsal sessions).

In so doing they 'absorbed' doctrine from the lyrics. Hymns involved the congregation in singing the praises of God; they were not confined to listening to a choral 'performance'. More than that, music enabled them to make an emotional as well as an intellectual response to the Gospel. Luther, who had always passionately loved music, later extolled its virtues:

> Music is to be praised as second only to the word of God because by her are all the emotions swayed. Nothing on earth is more mighty to make the sad gay and the gay sad, to hearten the downcast, mellow the overweening, temper the exuberant or mollify the vengeful . . . this precious gift has been bestowed on men alone to remind them that they are created to praise and magnify the Lord.[5]

Luther sought out musicians and poets able to create suitable hymns. He wrote some himself and discovered that he had a gift for religious verse. The result was a series of hymnals, the first of which, a modest volume of eight items, appeared in 1524. When considered alongside all the mighty tomes of biblical exegesis, Christian apologetic and religious polemic that poured

Fraw Musica.

Fur allen freuden auff Erden /
Kan niemand kein feiner werden.
Denn die ich geb mit mein singen /
Vnd mit manchem süssen klingen.
Wie kan nicht sein ein böser mut /
Wo da singen Gesellen gut.
Die bleibt kein zorn / zanck / has noch
Weichen mus alles hertzeleid. (neid
Geitz / sorg / vnd was sonst hart anleit.
Fert hin mit aller trawrigkeit.
Auch ist ein jeder des wol frey /
Das solche Freud kein sünde sey.
Sondern auch Gott viel bas gefelt /
Denn alle Freud der gantzen Welt.
Dem Teuffel sie sein werck zerstört /
Vnd verhindert viel böser Mörd.
Das zeugt Dauid / des Königs that /
Der dem Saul offt geweret hat /
Mit gutem süssen Darffenspiel /
Das er jnn grossen Mord nicht fiel.
                                A iij   Zum

Lady Music: Verse introduction by Luther to John Walther's
Glory and Praise of the Laudable Art of Music, 1538

from Luther's pen, it must be conceded that, with the exception of the German Bible, nothing that he wrote had a greater or more lasting impact on ordinary people than his hymns. Folk who never read a word of his scholarly exposition of justification by only faith grew up familiar with,

> With thee is naught but untold grace
> Evermore forgiving.
> We cannot stand before thy face,
> Not by the best of living.
> No man boasting may draw near.
> All the living stand in fear.
> Thy grace alone can save them.
>
> Therefore in God I place my trust,
> My own claim denying.
> Believe in him alone I must,
> On his sole grace relying.
> He pledged to me his plighted word.
> My comfort is in what I heard.
> There will I hold forever.[6]

Hymns were the paving stones of the road that led away from Catholicism. They familiarised evangelical pilgrims with a truth that differed from what adherents to Rome believed and they enshrined that truth in forms of congregational worship which were quite distinct from the old priest-and-people pattern.

These additions to conventional rituals could only be a first step. Evangelical innovation had its own impetus. Luther, ever reluctant to impose his own ideas, had to follow where the word led. The word was of central importance. That meant that the sermon had to be incorporated into the mass. Hitherto, preaching had been a distinct activity conducted (if at all) in a separate service before the sacramental rite. Now, space had to be found for it in the liturgy. This, of course, meant altering the structure of the mass and this posed problems that were not merely technical; any new arrangement had to balance word and sacrament – and that involved making value judgements. Several churches (not only those of the extremist sects) had already established wholly vernacular worship and were discovering that doing so stirred up a hornets' nest of resentments. Luther, who had yet to work out the most appropriate worship pattern for

Wittenberg, was being approached by other pastors and town councils to sort out their liturgical problems.

With the Peasants' War, the refutation of Erasmus and rolling conflict with the sects Luther had quite enough on his plate but the worship issue could not be put off. He identified two basic difficulties: authority and style. Who had the right to sanction new services? The old Latin mass was universal. It was subject to minor regional variations but was basically the stoutest binding cord of Christendom. A traveller could attend mass in Bristol or Bratislava, Granada or Gdansk and be familiar with what was going on. Vernacular services would put an end to this universality. So be it; the word must be sovereign and expressed in language that regular worshippers could fully understand. But fragmentation must have its limits. Every church should not be encouraged to do its own thing. Luther concluded that this particular circle could only be squared by regionalism and by common consent. New worship patterns should only be introduced if the prince or local council, the pastors and the individual congregations were in accord. In effect this meant that uniform patterns of worship were to be imposed by the secular authorities. By 'style' Luther understood all that was involved in translation and the careful marriage of words and music. It was not sufficient simply to change Latin words into German ones. With his acute ear for the rhythms of poetry, prose and music he knew full well that to 'work' an act of worship had to be an aesthetic whole. 'Text and notes, accent, melody and manner of rendering,' he wrote to one enquirer, 'ought to grow out of the true mother tongue and its inflection, otherwise all of it becomes an imitation the way monkeys do it'. Luther moved cautiously. He celebrated his first German mass at the end of 1525 and published it together with an explanation of everything that was unfamiliar to the congregation. It was not meant to be his last word on the subject, a formula set in stone. For example, he believed that the altar should be moved from its place against the east wall so that the celebrant could face the congregation but he allowed this change to wait until a later time.

What is, perhaps, most intriguing about all Luther's writings on this subject is the vision he expressed of an ideal form of evangelical worship which was quite distinct from the solemn Sunday mass. His immersion in the New Testament had given him a picture of the essential elements of corporate life in the primitive church. He theorised that it should be possible to recreate the intimate gatherings of the apostolic era which would enjoy a form of worship shorn of the accretions of one and a half millennia: 'Those who want to be Christians in earnest and who profess the gospel with hand and mouth should sign their names and meet alone in a house somewhere to pray, to read, to baptise, to receive the sacrament and to do other Christian works.'[7] He envisaged this house church type of assembly as being short on formality and long on love and service. This going back to basics would appeal to many brands of evangelicals over the ensuing centuries and the cell church would be reinvented many times over whenever traditional churches were stirred up by revival. Luther never attempted to turn his vision into reality because, as he said, 'I have not yet the people for it, nor do I see many who press for it.' He had to deal with the church as it was, a mix of the 'hot', the 'cool' and the 'lukewarm'. But there can be little doubt that his dream was of a vibrant, growing, spiritually aware body of believers whose expression of their faith went far beyond the formalities of Sunday worship.

Paintings and prints by Cranach and other propagandists show eager listeners gathered round Luther's pulpit, standing or seated on stools to hear him expound the word of God. We have to be cautious about accepting such images at face value. Any idea we might have of Wittenberg as a 'hotbed' of evangelical religion is rapidly dispelled by a study of Luther's comments on the behaviour of the local congregation. At times he became extremely frustrated with them. He spoke of Gospel preaching as casting pearls before swine. Citizens who had grown up with a concept of the mass as something which they simply turned up to watch found it hard to adapt to a more committed concept of worship. Luther admonished them for wandering in and out during the service. He had to cajole them into playing their part in the reformed rituals. Over and again he pressed them to receive communion regularly. He was appalled at their unashamed ignorance; few of them could recite the Lord's Prayer, the Ten Commandments or the Creed off by heart. Sometimes worshippers behaved without appropriate reverence. On at least one occasion Luther had to thunder his reproof at a baptism party who turned up noisy and inebriated. Then, there were the Wittenbergers who had never accepted the evangelical faith and simply voted with their feet.

As to public and personal morality, there were certainly no dramatic displays of mass repentance, no bonfires of the vanities, such as had marked the response of penitents to the emotionally charged preaching of such reformist friars as John Capistrano and Girolamo Savonarola. Since salvation was no longer preached as dependent on a purged conscience and good works there was less incentive for people to seek the path of holiness. It is impossible to know whether conditions really were worse than before the Reformation or whether offences were simply highlighted by vigorous preaching. Luther certainly complained frequently of sexual immorality, sharp commercial practice, gluttony and lack of charity. He was no puritan but he vigorously denounced 'lewd dancing', fornication and the adulterating of beer. He had no hesitation about excommunicating unrepentant offenders, including Hans von Metzsch, the city governor, whose affairs were notorious. And then there was the lack of charitable giving. Since generosity no longer 'bought' salvation there was a marked reduction in contributions to the common chest out of which alms were paid, as well as the preachers' remuneration.

Any move towards Luther's ideal of reformed church life would rely heavily on education. The concept of the priesthood of all believers placed a far greater responsibility on every baptised member of the flock than had been the case under the old dispensation. Since it was vital for every Christian to know the Bible Luther pressed on with his translation of the Old Testament whenever he had the opportunity (see below). He knew that it was particularly important to 'catch 'em young'. All children should be thoroughly catechised so that they would know the Lord's Prayer, the commandments and the basic tenets of the faith. Luther understood the value of the home as the essential schoolroom of faith and he did not exclude parents from the pedagogic process. In 1529, he published a *German Catechism* and *Small Catechism*. The latter was a brief textbook of fundamental doctrine in the form of passages to be committed to memory with questions to be posed by the teacher to ensure that the pupil understood what he or she was reciting. The other book was a teacher's manual. Its author envisaged the preacher or pastor going into parishioners' homes and taking whole families through a course of instruction. If Wittenberg did not become a shining example of a devout Christian community the fault could not be laid at Luther's door.

Such were Luther's everyday concerns but the world was moving on – rapidly, and in a direction he did not like. The formation of the Schmalkaldic League raised the spectre of rebellion against the emperor and civil war in Germany. The signatories had taken this fateful step because they believed they were facing an imminent crisis. In March 1531 the imperial demand for a return to papal allegiance would be issued. Their religious convictions would not allow them to have Catholicism re-imposed upon their people by force and they had no intention of giving up their freedom to order their own internal affairs. They, therefore, took pre-emptive action. But the evangelical cause in Germany was far from united. Landgrave Philip continued to try to obtain some theological formula which would give at least a semblance of ideological unity to the league. Luther still refused to co-operate in any stratagem which could be no more than a papering over of cracks. In political terms, there was considerable disquiet about offering defiance to the emperor. The Nuremberg council and the Margrave of Brandenburg-Ansbach declined to join the league. Everywhere people wanted to know where Luther stood on the issue of resistance to authority in the name of God. He was no less anxious to make his position clear – the more so since it had changed significantly in the aftermath of the Diet of Augsburg.

In April 1531 he published *Dr Martin Luther's Warning to his Dear German People*. He explained that he had come to the view that, in extreme and specific circumstances, Christians might take up arms to resist their rulers. He had reached this conclusion reluctantly and only after agonising prayer and study. His was the eternal pacifist's dilemma: at what point might a man legitimately abandon his abhorrence of war in order to defend himself, his loved ones and his fundamental beliefs? For Luther the answer was that rebellion was always rebellion *except* when it was in defence of the Gospel. The imperial government (and Luther was careful not to blame Charles in person) had no right to demand that subjects abandon their faith. Therefore, if they did so they were no longer exercising power as God's deputies. Rather they were abusing that power and might be resisted – if all other options to settle differences had been tried.

Luther went to great lengths in this little treatise to prove that he and his friends had, in fact, worked hard to preserve peace. Augsburg had been their Last Chance Saloon. They had presented their statement of belief and asked that it be considered but the Romanists had balked them at every turn. They had demanded unconditional surrender. Their *Confutation* had not been a point-by-point refutation of the evangelical position. They had not allowed discussion of their *Confutation*. They had threatened the use of force to back up their *Confutation*. They had duped the emperor into endorsing their errors and blasphemies. Therefore, it was they who were the enemies of peace. Luther directed his message to those who might be summoned by emperor or prince to take up arms against their Christian neighbours. Their answer should be humble but firm:

... dear Emperor, dear prince, if you keep your oath and pledge made in baptism, you will be my dear lord and I will obey you and go to war at your command. But if you will not keep your baptismal pledge and Christian covenant made with Christ, but rather deny them, then may a rascal obey you in my place. I refuse to blaspheme my God and deny his word for your sake; nor will I impudently rush to spring into the abyss of hell with you.

As always, Luther looked beyond terrestrial conflict to the spiritual battle-field:

... he who fights and contends against the gospel necessarily fights simultaneously against God, against Jesus Christ, against the Holy Spirit, against the precious blood of Christ, against his death, against God's word, against all the articles of faith, against all the sacraments, against all the doctrines which are given, confirmed and preserved by the gospel, for example the doctrine regarding government, regarding worldly peace, worldly estates, in brief, against all angels and saints, against heaven and earth and all creatures. For he who fights against God must fight against all that is of God or that has to do with God ... What is worse, such fighting would be done consciously; for these people know and admit that this teaching is the gospel ... Therefore, no Turk can be as vile as you and you must be damned to hell ten times more deeply than all Turks, Tarters, heathens and Jews.[8]

Luther poured out the vials of his wrath against perfidious Rome. He drew upon his visit there years before to expose the corruption, hypocrisy, immorality, cynicism and downright atheism of the Vatican. He seasoned his diatribe with spicy anecdote: the curia once proclaimed that cardinals should restrict the number of boys they kept for their pleasure but Pope Leo vetoed this, 'otherwise it would have been spread throughout the whole world how openly and shamelessly the pope and the cardinals in Rome practise sodomy'.[9] Was this the kind of regime Germans were prepared to fight Germans to defend?

It was but a short step from morality to theology. If Germany placed itself once more under the papal yoke it would be obliged to suffer again all the old doctrinal atrocities:

It was not enough that they venerated the saints and praised God in them, but they actually made them into gods. They put that noble child, the mother Mary, right into the place of Christ. They fashioned Christ into a judge and thus devised a tyrant for anguished consciences, so that all comfort and confidence was transferred from Christ to Mary, and then everyone turned from Christ to his particular saint.[10]

If people wanted to know where Luther stood on the burning issue of the day, he gave them a clear answer. He closed the treatise with a personal statement:

> . . . I do not wish to incite or spur anyone to war or rebellion or even self-defence, but solely to peace. But if the papists – our devil – refuse to keep the peace and, impenitently raging against the Holy Spirit with their persistent abominations, insist on war and thereby get their heads bloodied or even perish, I want to witness publicly here that this was not my doing, nor did I give any cause for it. It is they who want to have it that way. May their blood be on their heads! I am exonerated; I have done my duty faithfully.[11]

The firm political and religious stand taken by evangelical Germany made a bloody showdown impossible. There was no chance of an internal crusade such as the hawks of Rome were calling for. The Ottoman threat had not gone away. Charles' Netherlands subjects were restive. His southern coasts were threatened by the Moors of Algeria. His diplomats reported a new rapprochement between Clement VII and Francis I. The truth was that the Holy Roman Empire was vastly overextended. With an effort Charles could defend its territorial integrity *or* he could restore its religious unity. He could not do both. There would have to be further negotiation.

In reality negotiations had never really stopped. Several diplomats and theologians were trying to patch up some accord between the emperor and the Schmalkaldic leaders. It was clear that Charles would have to back down from his demand that the Edict of Worms should be enforced in every region of the empire but pride demanded that the Protestants give up something in return. Luther was not directly involved in any of the talks but his position remained clear: nothing of doctrinal substance could be yielded but bargains might – and, indeed, should – be struck on lesser matters in the interests of peace. His immediate goal was maximum freedom of worship and expression for evangelicals. If part of the price to be paid was permitting communion in one kind or allowing the Latin mass to be celebrated where the people wanted it, so be it. He was not in the business of coercing men's consciences. Agreement was near by March 1532, when the diet was convened to meet at Regensburg. Its importance was reinforced a few weeks later by reports that the sultan was once more on the march with a quarter of a million troops at his back. It was in July at Nuremberg that a final agreement was reached. The entire religious issue was put on hold indefinitely – pending that elusive church council. The evangelicals had won their fight for toleration. In response they were ready to contribute to the army of more than 115,000 men which Charles led personally to face the great enemy. He wrote to his wife. 'With God's help, as I act in his cause, I will be helped and favoured, so that he may be served and our holy faith be exalted and strengthened.' But the Christendom as whose champion he went forth no longer existed. It had now, by mutual agreement, been divided.

V

Vanity of Vanities
1533–1546

'The work and the problems with which I am loaded down every hour'

Letter to Martin Bucer, 14 October 1539

15

The Problems of Peace

'We heard the English themselves, while they were here, complaining about their King and admiring our freedom.'[1] These words, written to the Strasbourg leader, Martin Bucer, with whom Luther was now on better terms, are indicative of much that was happening in Europe during the 1530s. In North Germany the evangelical cause had become ineradicably established. As a state religion in several principalities and cities it could not be dismissed as just another heresy. Unlike many earlier manifestations of Christian radicalism, it had been the product, not of wild-eyed, manic zealots or of semi-educated spokesmen for a repressed underclass. German Protestantism was promoted and led by scholars and by temporal rulers who were, for the most part, sincere about their convictions. In the lands of the Schmalkaldic League, as in the regions which espoused what came to be called the Reformed tradition, the Reformation was a political as well as a religious reality. Thus, as the new ideas spread along the commercial and intellectual grapevines, through word of mouth, through preaching and through the dissemination of Bibles and banned books, governments had to reckon with them and the movement fuelled by them. It was not just a case of internal discipline – the suppression of troublesome minorities. Taking the movement seriously could have significant political or diplomatic implications. Thus, for example, Henry VIII, who had actually written (or collaborated in the writing of) a book refuting Luther's 'heresies' and, thereby, won the title 'Defender of the Faith' from a grateful pope, came to realise that the spread of evangelicalism could be an effective whip to wield against that pope's successor. The decline of monasticism in North Germany and the reversion of monastic lands to temporal rulers provided him with a valuable model when he decided to grab for himself the wealth of the English abbeys. And flirting with the Schmalkaldic League could be a useful diplomatic ploy when negotiating with France or the Empire. Across Europe, kings, bishops, scholars, itinerant preachers, merchants, lawyers, students, diplomats and courtiers were all, for their own reasons, interesting themselves in evangelical doctrine. The Reformation had gone international. Reformation celebrities became household names. Their books were avidly translated and read. Men travelled long distances to consult them. The biggest celebrity was, of course, Martin Luther. Visitors and messengers arrived in Wittenberg in an ever-growing stream.

Luther remained committed primarily to his own 'dear German people' and, though he rejoiced in the spread of the Gospel, he did find burdensome the problems attendant on success. He only had a small team around him in Wittenberg and when, for whatever reason, Melancthon, Justus Jonas or other close colleagues were absent he missed them greatly. 'I need you people here,' he wrote when several of them had fled a minor outbreak of plague. 'I am forced to carry these burdens alone and answer by myself because of that plague (that is, the devil), which rejoices that it is able to keep us apart for such a long time through one or two funerals.'[2]

Death, inevitably, intervened to change ongoing situations. In 1531 it removed two of Luther's theological opponents. Zwingli, ever the militant soldier of Christ, was slain in battle. Civil war had broken out between the Catholic and evangelical cantons of Switzerland and a decisive battle was fought at Kappel, on the border of Zurich and Zug. Zwingli was present as a chaplain and was seriously wounded in the ensuing defeat. Afterwards he was despatched by an enemy captain. His body was burned and his ashes scattered. When Luther heard the news, he commented sourly that those who took the sword perished by the sword. It was only weeks later that that very different Swiss evangelical, Oecolampadius, died. The removal of the two leading spokesmen for the Reformed cause eased relations with the Lutherans and this certainly improved negotiations with Philip of Hesse, who had been strongly inclined towards Zwinglian teaching on the Lord's Supper. In 1534 Clement VII went to an unmourned grave but his replacement by the crudely nepotistic Paul III suggested to Luther that no one should look to Rome for repentance and reform. Luther also outlived another opponent. Erasmus died in Basel in 1536, troubled till the end by religious discord. ''Though I am living here with the most sincere friends,' he wrote, 'I should yet, on account of the differences of doctrine, prefer to end my life elsewhere.'

A death closer to home was that of John the Steadfast (August 1532). He had certainly lived up to his nickname in his refusal to be cowed by Habsburg power and his determination to form a strong alliance of evangelical princes and cities. Luther had respectfully demurred from the elector's forthright politics but he had been much closer to him than to his brother and was personally distressed when John succumbed to a massive stroke at his hunting lodge at Schweinitz. The new elector, John Frederick (known to posterity as the Magnanimous), was more committed to the evangelical cause than his uncle, and even his father, had been. It would scarcely be an exaggeration to say that the young prince was a disciple of Luther. There is a woodcut by Lucas Cranach which emphasises both John Frederick's piety and his adherence to Luther's teaching. The picture is a typical piece of Lutheran propaganda, depicting true and false religion. On the right the 'papal crew' go about their business of selling salvation in order to finance their own craving for wealth and power and offering their prayers to an angry God through the mediation of St Francis. This is contrasted with the left-hand side of the print, where Luther preaches to a devout congregation. He points to the Lamb of God, who, as texts indicate, is the only mediator between man and God. In the forefront of the picture stands John Frederick, who turns his head at a rather uncomfortable angle so that he can be recognised by the viewer. Over his left shoulder he carries a large wooden cross. The imagery is appropriate, for the prince would, indeed, carry his cross and pay dearly for his allegiance to the evangelical faith.

One implacable enemy the new elector and his preacher both had to face was Duke George, head of the rival branch of the Saxon ruling family. His opposition was dynastic as well as religious and, with the passing of the years, his hostility became increasingly frenetic. In the diet he led the Catholic princes in their onslaught against evangelicals. He fiercely persecuted any of his own subjects who displayed 'heretical' tendencies. And he occasionally ventured into print against Luther. The angry pot boiled over in 1533. In the spring of that year an unrepentant evangelical of Leipzig, Dr Augustine Specht, died. The body was denied Christian burial in consecrated ground. That did not stop almost the whole city turning out for his funeral. Furious at this demonstration of defiance, Duke George set his thought police on the offending citizens. Hundreds were interrogated and more than eighty were exiled from the territory. Luther was indignant but

Lucas Cranach the Elder's *True and False Religion*. Elector John Frederick is
shown beneath Luther's pulpit, bearing a cross

he restricted himself to sending letters of support to the victims. This was
sufficient to stir the duke's fury.

He complained to his cousin that Luther was inciting his subjects to rebellion. This was not the kind of affront that Luther took lying down. His
response was a very public one: he published *A Vindication against Duke
George's Charge of Rebellion*, in which he pointed out that the preacher/writer
who had condemned the peasants in 1525 could not be branded as an incendiary by anyone with an ounce of common sense. But, being Luther, he
went further: if anyone deserved the label 'rebel' it was George, who was
acting in defiance of God by ruling tyrannically over the people entrusted
to his care. This sparked off a pamphlet war (carried out on George's side
by clerical ghostwriters) in which neither side held back from hurling insults.
Duke George had good reason to be sensitive over the religious issue. He
was no blind defender of the papacy but he did cling to the old ways and
they were seriously under threat in his territories. His subjects were divided
between supporters of the rival faiths. Worse than that, there were disputes
within his own family. His two sons were safely Catholic but one was
mentally ill and, therefore, unlikely to succeed to the duchy. Should anything
happen to John, the other son, the title would pass to George's brother,
Henry, and Henry was a patron of Lutheran preachers. So great was enmity

between the two brothers that, in 1536, Henry joined the Schmalkaldic League. Early the following year Duke John died. What life remained to his father was filled with the bitterness of knowing that he had lost the religious battle. Luther, of course, interpreted these events as examples of divine judgement on an enemy of the Gospel.

It was not only noble enemies that caused Luther distress; friends and supporters in high places could also trouble him. Philip of Hesse, in particular, was a source of great embarrassment. The personal life of this zealous and forthright evangelical champion was an open scandal. At nineteen he had made a dynastic marriage to Christina, daughter of Duke George of Saxony. Despite the fact that the couple had seven children they were not happy together. Philip was promiscuous (and eventually developed syphilis as a result). His wife became addicted to drink. Their situation cannot have been helped by the religious conflict between Philip and his father-in-law. There was nothing unusual about members of the aristocracy being unfaithful to their spouses and had Philip remained a Catholic he would, doubtless, have quieted his conscience through frequent confession. It is to his credit that he felt guilty and that for long periods of time he would not receive communion but he was dominated by his sexual passion and could not abandon his habit. Like many Christians experiencing the tension between worldly desire and heavenly duty, Philip struggled with Scripture in an effort to discover, if not justification, at least some way out of his difficulty. He could neither find nor engineer any cause for divorcing his wife but might he not take another? After all, the Old Testament patriarchs had practised polygamy and there was no evidence that God had pronounced against it. As early as 1526 he had written asking for Luther's response to the suggestion that he undertake a second marriage. Luther firmly but gently pointed out that such a course was not open to any Christian man unless his wife suffered from some extreme condition – such as leprosy or insanity – that prevented them living together.

This, of course, did not solve Philip's problem and he did not cease trying to reason with Luther, Melancthon, Bucer and other evangelical teachers. If they condemned him to go on living in sin, he argued, they were undermining his authority and his leadership of the cause. He could not punish any of his wayward subjects for immorality. He could not receive the sacrament. He was being robbed of that peace of soul which he needed to fight for the Gospel in the political arena. After several years Philip's problem came to a head when he contracted a liaison with a woman who demanded marriage. Now he put real pressure on his spiritual advisers. If they refused to sanction, publicly or privately, a bigamous marriage he was contemplating, he would seek permission from the emperor. That would doubtless involve reference to the pope for a dispensation and once that became public it would be impossible for him to continue as a leader of the evangelical movement.

At this point the theologians buckled. The prospect of the landgrave's defection from the evangelical camp was too awful to contemplate. Bucer travelled to Wittenberg for emergency meetings with Luther and Melancthon. They eventually devised a solution that was every bit as Jesuitical as anything of which they accused the old Catholic scholars. They told Philip that they fully sympathised with his predicament but they were obliged to point out that bigamy was against church law. His second union, therefore, could not be sanctioned *legally*. However, it might be permitted *pastorally*. The landgrave could be advised, under the seal of the confessional, to ease his conscience by undertaking a second marriage whose details would be kept secret. As far as the rest of the world would know, the 'other woman' would be Philip's concubine, a role quite familiar in European court circles. This sophistry was uncharacteristic of Luther and, inevitably, it backfired on him. Philip did not keep his side of the bargain. Not only did he make the second wedding public, he also insisted, contrary to an earlier pledge, that any children by his new wife would have full inheritance rights. This could only provoke dynastic discord. As for Luther he felt the full brunt of public indignation. His reaction seems to have been to resort to bluff and bluster. When the issue was raised at his own table, he acknowledged that the landgrave's action was certainly scandalous but that it should be judged alongside his many brave and heroic actions on behalf of the evangelical cause. As for the matter of the second wife, well, he added, nonchalantly, 'Stay calm! It will blow over. Perhaps she will soon die.'³ But this lapse of judgement could not be shrugged off. Philip's behaviour and the apparent complicity of the theologians seriously undermined their cause. The Schmalkaldic League suffered a setback from which it never recovered (see below, p. 331).

Catholic commentators gleefully pointed out that Luther's behaviour in the landgrave's case contrasted markedly with his response to another, more celebrated scandal which was sweeping Europe at the same time. It was in 1527 that King Henry VIII of England began to contemplate seriously a rearrangement of his matrimonial affairs. His queen of eighteen years' standing, Catherine of Aragon, had failed to provide him with a male heir and he wanted to wriggle out of the marriage in order to establish a lawful union with his latest lover, Anne Boleyn. Henry believed, not without reason, that all he had to do was appeal to Clement VII for an annulment of his marriage and make the appropriate payment to the papal coffers. He could not possibly have chosen a worse moment to send emissaries to the pope's court. Following the sack of Rome, Clement was completely under the thumb of Charles V and the emperor was not prepared to submit to the humiliation of seeing his Aunt Catherine cast aside by her libidinous husband. There is no need to unravel here all the tangled threads of King Henry's 'great matter', which accelerated England's drift away from Rome and towards evangelical religion, but Luther's role in the protracted affair, though minor, was not insignificant.

The Boleyn faction at Henry's court, in partnership with the king's first minister, Thomas Cromwell, and his pliant Archbishop of Canterbury, Thomas Cranmer, had their own reasons – personal, political and religious – for seeking close relations with the Protestant princes of Germany and with evangelical theologians on the continent. They persuaded the king to seek the opinions of leading academics on the annulment issue. They approached the Wittenberg theologians and sought also the mediation of Landgrave Philip. One emissary involved in these dealings was Robert Barnes, an ex-Augustinian friar-turned-evangelical preacher, who had fled persecution in England and eventually fetched up in Wittenberg. He presented the king's case to Luther and, in September 1531, Luther gave his considered verdict in a long, detailed letter designed to be delivered to the English court. It was a masterpiece of careful biblical exegesis and it was not what Henry wanted to hear from the man many regarded as the leader of evangelical opinion.

It is likely that, from the very beginning, Luther reposed little trust in the English king. It was only nine years since he had responded to Henry's *Assertio Septem Sacramentorum* with a diatribe in which he had surpassed himself for the violence of his language. He had headed his *Against Henry, King of the English* with the words, 'Martin Luther, minister at Wittenberg by the grace of God to Henry, King of England by the disgrace of God'. 'Fool', 'liar' and 'damnable, rotten worm' were just some of the titles bestowed by Luther on an adversary who was accustomed to receiving fawning flattery from everyone with whom he came in contact. A few years later, when he heard an erroneous rumour that Henry was inclined to the Gospel, Luther sent him a fulsome apology. The king grasped the opportunity for his revenge by repudiating the reformer in an open letter which he intended should have the widest possible circulation. Duke George willingly co-operated by having the letter translated into German and sending it to his printer. It was now this king (or his representatives) who was looking to Wittenberg for support. Would Luther relish giving Henry another literary thrashing in full public view? The temptation must have been great. On the other hand, the Gospel was now making progress in England, as Barnes will have been at pains to point out. The ex-monk was about to return home, fully trusting in the change of religious atmosphere. So, would Luther put his shoulder to the wheel of the English Reformation by supporting the annulment proceedings? The answer is that Luther did what, perhaps, he should have done in the first place; he restricted himself to turning the searchlight of Scripture on the arguments adduced by Henry's propagandists.

Their case was based on Leviticus 18.16, which condemned sexual relations between a man and his brother's wife. This text had been regarded as an impediment years before, when Henry had decided to marry the wife of his dead brother, Prince Arthur, and the wedding was only able to go ahead after a papal dispensation had been received. Supporters of the annulment now claimed that the pope had no authority to overrule Scripture. Thus the marriage had been and had, for more than two decades, remained invalid. Luther registered his dismay at the legal setting aside of Catherine which would make her and her daughter, Mary, 'incestuous women'. Then he set about dismantling the biblical argument. The appeal to Leviticus he dismissed as special pleading. He pointed out that the text obviously referred to adultery by a man with his sister-in-law if her husband was still living. The Mosaic law did not condemn marriage with a dead brother's widow. On the contrary, Deuteronomy 25.5 specifically urged that in the event of a man dying without heir it was his brother's responsibility to marry the widow in order to provide a son who could inherit the property. Luther emphasised that the divine law regarding matrimony was that it was for life and that man could not put asunder what God had joined. Any man-made church law which contradicted Scripture was invalid because the word of God must remain supreme. To put the matter beyond doubt, Luther worked his way through the Bible, demonstrating those aspects of the Mosaic law which had been endorsed by Jesus and those which had been superseded under the new dispensation. His conclusion was unequivocal: 'At the risk of losing his salvation and under the threat of eternal damnation . . . the King is to be held responsible for retaining the Queen to whom he is married.'[4]

Does the immovable stance Luther took with Henry when contrasted

with his willingness to accommodate Philip suggest cynical double standards and political expediency? In the landgrave's case Luther certainly
yielded, albeit reluctantly, to emotional and psychological pressure. It really
did seem as though the entire Reformation in Germany was under threat
with the possible defection of one of its political leaders. Henry VIII was
not seen as a central figure in the religious life of Europe and Luther had
already had his fingers burned when he tried to be nice to the irascible
sovereign. However, the Reformation needed all the friends it could get
and, if Luther thought primarily in political terms, it would have been easy
for him to support Henry's matrimonial designs. During the 1530s, as we
shall see, he maintained close contact with the evangelical leaders in England
and did everything he could to encourage them. But Luther did not think
primarily in political terms. He believed it was his duty to give advice,
always based on the Bible, and he agonised over what he should say and
how it might be received. He once complained, 'I give advice but no one
follows me, and they say, "I will rule"; if I give no advice, then it troubles
my conscience. I have no idea what to do.'[5] It remained his rooted conviction that Christians should not put their trust in princes. If they remained
true to the word of God under all circumstances then God would fight for
them and, though in the short term his people might have to endure hardship and suffering, he would, ultimately, prevail. In Henry's case the scriptural record was quite clear and Luther had no hesitation in proclaiming
it. So, did he abandon his principles when it came to counselling Philip?
It has to be said that the biblical case for monogamy is not as clear as that
for the sanctity of marriage. Several Old Testament heroes *did* have more
than one wife, as Philip never tired of pointing out, and no New Testament
writers had criticised them for it. Luther was clear that, under certain
circumstances, God had permitted bigamy as a concession to human weakness. However, throughout the Christian centuries monogamy had become
the norm. To openly flout that convention now could lead to all manner
of complications. Thus the suggestion that Philip might have his own way
but should keep quiet about it. Luther and his colleagues had located a tiny
loophole that *did* exist in the divine law and they had squirmed through
it. Their course of action which could, just about, be defended ethically
turned out to be disastrous politically. That was a great irony.

Their friends in England were obliged to play a subtle political game.
Henry VIII was essentially conservative in religious matters but could be
manoeuvred in an evangelical direction if he could be persuaded that it was
to his advantage to be so. Thus he flirted with the Protestant princes when

he wanted to divorce his wife and sever England from Catholic Christendom. He put an end to monasticism in order to grab the wealth of the abbeys for himself. He gave permission for an English Bible to win the support of those influential sections of society who favoured radical change. He opened negotiations with the Schmalkaldic League because he needed allies when his foreign policy was going through an anti-imperial phase. The new politico-religious entity in North Germany was a force to be reckoned with. It lacked the wealth and military might of the Habsburg and Valois lands but it was commercially significant and was useful as a political irritant to its neighbours. Throughout the 1530s Thomas Cromwell, the man who masterminded religious change in England, worked for a closer relationship with the Schmalkaldic League. He sent Barnes back to Wittenberg in 1535 and the ex-monk was soon joined by members of Henry's Council. They held lengthy discussions with Luther and his colleagues in an attempt to reach a theological accord but the sticking point continued to be the annulment, which the Germans steadfastly refused to endorse. Luther had very quickly become bored with the proceedings and did not believe that they would lead anywhere. He was right. By the spring the international situation had changed and Henry no longer needed a German alliance. The English delegates returned home with nothing to show for their labours.

However, within two years the diplomatic wheel had made another revolution. Talks were on again, and there was a new topic on the agenda. The King of England was once more on the marriage market, his third wife, Jane Seymour, having died after producing Henry's long-awaited heir. There was the real possibility that he might choose a bride from among the German princely families. This time the English were asking for Melancthon to come over at the head of a delegation for theological talks in England. John Frederick refused to allow Melancthon leave of absence but a Lutheran deputation did travel to London. By this time Luther was thoroughly confused about the twists and turns of events in Henry's kingdom, as he explained in a letter to one of the English representatives:

> We speak of you people often and at great length, especially since, in view of the changing conditions in your kingdom, either you are unable to write letters to us . . . or those letters which you did despatch have been intercepted. So, we are hanging in the air and, indeed, are afraid that this persistent silence might, perhaps, be a sign of some harsh blow against the progress of the gospel. In addition there

are some who think that your King, finally ensnared by the Roman intrigues, would like to get back into the pope's good grace. In this affair we pray and, [torn] between hope and fear, wish that Satan may be crushed under your feet.[6]

For another eighteen months mutually contradictory messages continued to arrive in Wittenberg about the progress or otherwise of the London talks. King Henry *did* conclude a marriage alliance with one of the German princely houses but this did not commit him to support for the Schmalkaldic League. His new bride was Anne, sister of Duke William of Julich-Cleves-Berg and sister-in-law of Elector John Frederick. William was in a sensitive position as far as religion was concerned. He was sympathetic to reform but did not carry his leading advisers with him. They had, for example, made it clear that any inheritance in their territory which fell to John Frederick in right of his wife would be conditional on his not introducing religious innovations. In choosing this particular alliance Henry was trying to keep a foot in each camp. The marriage to Anne of Cleves was, as is well known, a disaster and was partly instrumental in bringing down Thomas Cromwell, who went to the block in the summer of 1540. The Reformation in England seemed to have come to a sudden halt. Henry wriggled out of his marriage, to the humiliation of his brother-in-law and the persecution of English evangelicals was resumed. Many observers in Wittenberg were disillusioned as well as distressed. Not so Luther. He had, for a long time, been suspicious of Henry VIII and frustrated by his vacillation. In October 1539 he had clearly expressed his misgivings to the elector:

The King is a dilettante and has no serious intentions. This we have certainly found out from the English who have been here, although at the time out of Christian love we had to believe that he was serious. But finally, when we had debated *ad nauseam* – at great expense to Your Electoral Grace – everything was sealed with a sausage (i.e. worthless) and left to the King's pleasure. The English themselves said, 'Our King vacillates.' And Doctor [Barnes] said several times, 'Our King in no way respects religion and the gospel.'

Luther insisted that the evangelical cause was well rid of the man who had made himself 'defender of the faith' and 'head of the English church' – a virtual pope.

Away, away with this head and defender! Gold and money make him
so cocky as to think that he should be worshipped and that God
could not get along without him. Let the King himself carry his sins,
for which he is not ready to repent; we have enough of our own to
carry.[7]

It is a verdict from which it would be hard to dissent.

It was not only in England that the fate of the Reformation was in
the balance. Much of Luther's correspondence was taken up with the
problems of the faithful who were working for the Gospel in other
German territories and cities. In some cases he advised boldness; in
others patience under suffering; but in one attitude he was absolutely
consistent: ends do not justify means. It was important, nay vital, that
as many people as possible should hear the message of divine grace and
be free to worship God as he desired to be worshipped but such a situation could not be brought about by rebellion or law-breaking or religious compromise; truth and spirituality must never bow the knee to
political expediency.

The success of the Reformation created numerous organisational problems, as Luther commented when responding to one request for guidance
from an evangelical city:

> . . . events occur everywhere so rapidly in our days that church ordi-
> nances cannot be drawn up and instituted everywhere as quickly as
> necessary. Nevertheless, in order to maintain pure teaching and also
> external Christian discipline and behaviour and to prevent much
> wrong from occurring one must daily improve on the situation until
> the Almighty grants more peace and unity both in ecclesiastical and
> secular governments.[8]

The variety of questions which arrived on Luther's desk give us some idea
of the immense upheaval the new worship and teaching brought to people's
lives. Should private confession be allowed to continue alongside the
general confession now included in services? When there was a disagreement over the appointment of a preacher, who should have the deciding
voice, the town council or the church congregation? What should a preacher
do if the authorities tried to drive him out by refusing to pay his stipend?
Did the local council have the right to enforce evangelical worship in a
cathedral, which was, officially, under the bishop's authority? Would Luther

give his endorsement to a member of the Schmalkaldic League bent on wresting a certain territory from Habsburg control? Was it in order for the members of a religious order who had adopted the evangelical faith to continue to live under their rule? Then there were numerous issues of church discipline. If members were to be encouraged to holiness of living what sanctions might be employed against persistent breakers of the moral law or peddlers of heterodoxy? And, in an age when itinerant preachers wandered from town to town claiming a divine call and giving impressive demonstrations of holy zeal or miracle-working power, who was competent to divide the sheep from the goats? Religious revival always throws up such problems. Wise pastors never want to curb enthusiasm but they are charged with maintaining peace and concord wherever possible. Nor were the lives of Lutheran congregations conducting their affairs in a vacuum. Catholic critics were ever ready to point out shortcomings in the common life of evangelicals and the extremist sects were always ready to snap up those who found their reformed church too restricting.

For Luther the answer to every question that was posed or which ever could be posed lay in discerning the principles located in the Holy Scriptures. Translating the Bible became the biggest love affair of his life. He had published his New Testament in 1522 but he was forever revising it and bringing out fresh editions. The Old Testament occupied him, on and off, for another twelve years. It was a tumultuous relationship. At times the translator found himself swept along by the power of the narrative. At others he wrestled for days to unlock the true sense of a single phrase. He was by turns elated and depressed by the results of his labours. In the late 1520s and early 1530s he was frequently called away from the work by public events and he found it difficult not to resent the pull of ecclesiastical and secular concerns.

Luther explained to his students how he went about his work. There were two rules, he said. One was that he did not work alone. He was constantly discussing the text with colleagues. Whenever he came across a word that was difficult to understand or interpret he sought help. There is evidence of this in his letters. On one occasion he was having problems naming beasts referred to by some of the prophets. Many of them would be unfamiliar to readers and when he checked the Latin of the Vulgate that was no use at all. He turned to Spalatin for inspiration.

I am all right on the birds of the night – owl, raven, horned owl, screech owl – and on the birds of prey – vulture, kite, hawk and sparrow hawk.

Title page of Luther's Bible, 1534

I can handle the stag, roebuck and chamois but what in the devil am
I to do with the taragelaphus, pygargus, oryx and camelopard?[9]

It was not just a question of finding a German word to match the Hebrew
original; transferring descriptions, and even concepts, from one cultural
context to another involved making informed judgements if the text was
to be as comprehensible as possible to German readers.

His other, and more fundamental rule was that the Old Testament had
to be interpreted in the light of the New Testament. More specifically, it
had to be understood in terms of the Gospel as clearly set forth in the
writings of St Paul.

> . . . if some passage is obscure I consider whether it treats of grace or
> law, whether wrath or the forgiveness of sin . . . God divides his
> teaching into law and gospel . . . In theology there are law and gospel
> and it must be one or the other . . . So every prophet either threatens
> and teaches, terrifies and judges things or makes a promise. Everything
> ends with this and it means that God is your gracious Lord.[10]

Since the Bible was the story of God's gracious dealings with his fallen
creation it, self-evidently, had a coherent message. Thus, for example,
psalms and prophets prefigured Christ, even where they were not specifically foretelling his coming. Luther made the connections clear in his
glosses to the text and his prefaces to individual books. He was no funda-
mentalist, if by that word we mean someone who considers every syllable
of Scripture to be equally inspired. For example, he would happily have
excised the book of Esther from the canon altogether because it contained
Judaising elements and 'pagan crudeness'.

Wherever he was and whenever he was not distracted by other duties
Luther worked at his translation. His Hebrew text and grammar and other
reference books accompanied him whenever he was on a preaching tour
or attending a theological conference or summoned to the electoral court.
Slowly and painstakingly the work came together. Not only did he have
to work on the words, he also oversaw the production of pictures. The
complete German Bible contained 117 woodcuts and Luther had to satisfy
himself that every one was fully in accord with the passage it illustrated.
At last, in the summer of 1534, the work, including the Apocrypha, was
finished. Pages went to the press in September.

It was rapturously received by the German evangelical community. But did the novelty quickly wear off? Did familiarity breed contempt? Luther seemed to think so. Six years later he mournfully told his dinner table companions,

> This German Bible (this is not praise for myself but the work praises itself) is so good and precious that it's better than all other versions, Greek and Latin, and one can find more in it than in all commentaries, for we are removing impediments and difficulties so that other people may read it without hindrance. I'm only concerned that there won't be much reading in the Bible, for people are very tired of it and nobody clamours for it any more.[11]

16

A Death Too Late?

'One could wish that Luther had died before ever this tract was written'.[1] So wrote Roland Bainton about the reformer's diatribe, *On the Jews and Their Lies* (1543), and it is certain that nothing has done Luther's reputation more harm than this single pamphlet. We will return later to a consideration of his opinions about the Jewish race. For now the wider question remains, 'Did Luther live too long?' If the answer is 'Yes', then his was a fate he shared with very many other great men and women. 'Whom the gods love die young' and it is given to few to ride out on the cresting wave of celebrity and success, leaving behind a mourning world stunned by their departure. In 1540 Luther was fifty-seven, no great age, even by sixteenth-century standards, but his bull-like, peasant frame had long been sabotaged by illness and overwork and he, himself, had no desire to live through another decade. The times they were a-changing and certainly not altogether in ways that he welcomed. Yet, as long as he was 'present in the flesh', he would not and could not relax into a passive old age. The general could not put up his sword; not as long as there were enemies, new and old, to be confronted. If, on the other hand, the answer to our question is 'No' then we are obliged to identify the contribution his continued existence made to the contemporary world.

The issue which topped the religious agenda in these years was the calling of a general council. The Lutherans had long clamoured for it. Charles V was desperate for a congress which would close the breaches within the empire. The Kings of France and England, for their own reasons, were demanding it. Most right-thinking men recognised that such a body was the only means that could be employed to deal with the theological chaos and ethical mire into which Christendom had fallen. As for Luther, he had become disillusioned by Rome's constant blocking of any initiative which would weaken papal authority. In 1535, he still hoped that a council would be called but, as he explained to his prince, he was not sanguine.

> I hope and pray that God will let the papists at least once come to their senses so that they will be forced to undertake in all serious-ness a council which would have to be called free and Christian. But in this matter I am like unbelieving Thomas; I have to put my hands and fingers into the side and scars, otherwise I do not believe it. Yet God, in whose hands are the hearts of all men, is able to accomplish even more than that.[2]

After seventeen years of hopes being raised and dashed this was not an unreasonable attitude but, in fact, preparations for a church council *were* under way. Any attempt to assess the character of the new pope, Paul III (Alessandro Farnese), has to confront some bewildering contradictions. Scarcely less corrupt than his recent predecessors, he appointed a commis-sion to report on the failings of the Roman system. He despatched envoys to treat with leading evangelical theologians in the hope of achieving a rapprochement but, at the same time, he urged Charles V and Francis I to exterminate heresy from their lands. He devoted considerable energy over several years to bringing about a council which would examine freely the need for reform, while refounding the Roman Inquisition, pledged to rooting out free expression and independent thought. What all this suggests is that Paul was a skilful politician and such was the case. He had no intention of going down in history as the pope who sold the papacy down the river but he understood clearly that the clamour for reform could not be ignored. He consulted with several of the leading campaigners in Italy who were critical of the regime and he published widely his intention to call a council. When a papal representative came to Wittenberg, in 1535, Luther declared himself willing to attend, 'even if I knew that you would burn me'. However, the princes of the Schmalkaldic League were cool about the proposed conference and Francis I, for political reasons, categorically vetoed it. Paul tried again, this time summoning representatives to meet at Mantua in 1537. Again, the French refused to consent and the Germans declined to be involved, even though their theologians advised attendance. In 1539 the council was postponed indefinitely. It was not only Luther who thought, 'We've been here before'. He told the elector,

> I have no doubt that the pope or his followers are afraid and would rather see this council thwarted. Yet they would like this to come about in such a way that they could boast – and do so with seeming justice – that [this failure] was in no way their fault, since they had summoned the council, sent out messengers and called the Estates . . .[3]

The reality was more complex. As long as the conciliar idea was being kept alive by supplicants and opposed by the pope there was no need to think about it in detail. When the tables were turned and the initiative came from Rome the potential attendees had to consider carefully what they might be letting themselves in for. The Protestant leaders wanted to be sure that they were not being sucked into a papal trap. They guessed, probably correctly, that at a council held south of the Alps their concerns would not receive a serious hearing but that, nevertheless, they would be obliged to abide by its decisions. The theologians were no more optimistic but they believed that they should attend the pope's council in order to make a well-publicised stand for evangelical truth.

The prospect, however remote it might be in Luther's mind, drove him to a fresh statement of his basic doctrinal position. If there were to be talks with the papists he was determined to set out what was not negotiable in such a way as to remove any possibility of misunderstanding. His sense of urgency about this was coloured by the fact that Melancthon, who was now emerging as the lead negotiator, was more disposed to be conciliatory in his discussions with Catholic theologians. It was a classic case of the old chief being reluctant to hand over the reins to the next generation whom he could not fully trust to act responsibly. Melancthon looked optimistically to the future; Luther pessimistically (he would have said, realistically) to the past. Who was right?

These were crucial years. Many church leaders on both sides were tired and ashamed of the bitter divisions between them. They strove to heal breaches and to reach a degree of concord in advance of the hoped-for council. Others were only interested in using a church synod to reinforce their own positions. Amidst the frenzied activity of the early 1540s there were two big questions participants were asking themselves and each other,

'Will the council ever meet?' and 'If it does, will the hawks or doves prevail?'
Melancthon was at the centre of the eirenical lobby and was striving to
reach understanding with Catholic and Reformed moderates. He advised
the Elector of Brandenburg, who was sitting on the religious fence, about
the cautious introduction of reform measures which would not necessarily
involve a separation from Rome. His friendship with Bucer kept open the
dialogue with the Swiss and Strasbourg reformers and he actually disagreed
with Luther's hard line over the Lord's Supper. He corresponded with
Cardinal Albrecht of Mainz, Primate of Germany, asking him to use his
position to act as mediator between Rome and Schmalkalden. He also
engaged in discussions over several years with the Archbishop of Cologne.
This nobleman/ecclesiastic was one of a number of territorial princes (like
the Elector of Brandenburg) who was following a middle way. He sought
Melancthon's help in drawing up a regimen for his clergy which imposed
moral stringency and demanded proper religious education for the laity.

It is easy to put 'Catholic' and 'Protestant' labels on the leading figures
of the Reformation but there was a great deal of barrier crossing. Many
humanist scholars and dedicated pastors were appalled by the scandal of
disunity and by the moral failings and doctrinal intransigence which had
provoked it. There were sincere, thinking men who, in their own spiritual pilgrimages, changed sides, some of them more than once. Religion
was 'news' and at every level of society people reacted to the challenge of
novel ideas – some positively, some negatively. The Venetian cardinal,
Gasparo Contarini, was one of the Italian reformers who had the ear of
Pope Paul, and who was appointed to a commission charged with identifying abuses in the church and recommending disciplinary action. The
resulting report, De emendanda ecclesia, was brutally frank. It referred to
Rome as the most decadent city in Europe and proposed widespread moral
and administrative reforms. Unsurprisingly, it provoked a gleeful 'told you
so' response in evangelical lands. In 1541, Contarini was sent to Regensburg
as member of a delegation to a colloquy summoned by the emperor as the
latest in a series of meetings between Catholic and evangelical theologians. With Melancthon, Bucer and others he strove manfully to find
compromises which might point a way forward. He was overjoyed when,
among other items of agreement, a formula about justification by faith was
approved. His optimism was short lived. A message arrived from Rome to
the effect that the formula was unacceptable. A similar response came
from Luther in Wittenberg. The hard men were still in command. The
one who emerged as Luther's counterpart at the papal court was Giampetro

Carafa and his career demonstrates how genuine zeal for reform could go hand-in-hand with persecution mania. Carafa was a founder member of the Theatine order, a brotherhood (compared by the historian, Macaulay, to the Wesley brothers' Holy Club) dedicated to charitable works among the poor and to encouraging pious living among the laity. He originally had much in common with Contarini but he had no interest in reaching agreement with Lutherans. Quite the contrary; he wanted to see that vile breed of heretics totally extirpated. After the failure of the Regensburg talks he persuaded the pope that the evangelicals were incorrigible and that a vital step in that reform of the Church Catholic that his holiness so earnestly desired was the setting up of a new disciplinary body which should ruthlessly purge it of error. 'If my own father were found guilty of heresy,' he remarked, 'I would pile the faggots around him.' Thus a new Roman Inquisition, modelled on the body already existing in Spain, was set up in 1542 and immediately Carafa began that persecution which, apart from causing appalling suffering, drove many moderate men out of Italy, some into the arms of the evangelicals. Carafa's uncompromising career, particularly after he succeeded Paul III in the chair of St Peter, slammed the door on rapprochement as firmly as Luther's intransigence.

That intransigence was demonstrated in a spate of writings between 1537 and 1539. They were all directed against the papacy and were intended to constitute a final statement about the Antichrist. There was more to this than the pride of an old dog determined to demonstrate that he still had teeth. Two factors lay behind this concentrated burst of literary activity: Luther was concerned that, in the move towards reconciliation, vital information about the papacy would be deliberately glossed over or otherwise lost to sight. He also feared that he would not be around to counteract Roman propaganda. In 1536 he had suffered minor heart failure. Then, in February 1537 he collapsed and came close to death. This happened at Schmalkalden, where he had gone to take part in a conference designed to prepare the League for the proposed council. After a few days he fell ill with kidney stones and was unable to urinate. As if that were not painful enough, he suffered agonies at the hands of doctors who prescribed a massive intake of fluid and the application of various nostrums, including a potion containing garlic and animal dung. Unsurprisingly, the patient deteriorated rapidly. He prepared himself mentally and spiritually for the end and asked to be transported home to die. He took a solemn farewell of John Frederick, who came to his bedside and promised to take care of Katy and the children. Then, against the advice of the physicians, he was laid in a wagon for the jolting, sixteen-day journey back to Wittenberg. It may be that the lurching motion actually achieved more than the medical practitioners for the urinary blockage was dislodged and from that moment Luther slowly recovered.

Within weeks he had embarked on his literary onslaught. This time Luther abandoned his usual technique of biblical exposition to explore church history. He wrote an attack on the *Donation of Constantine*, the notorious eighth- to ninth-century forgery which had been used as a basis for the papacy's claim to spiritual and temporal dominion throughout Latin Christendom. This document had long been recognised for what it was, a fraudulent attempt to give the pope a superior status to every other western ruler, including the emperor. However, Luther was not offering an unnecessary revelation. The point he was making was that since the pope had no legitimate claim to rule in either the political or the ecclesiastical sphere it was necessary to decide exactly what position he *did* hold. Luther suggested that this would be an appropriate subject for the council's agenda.

The major work of these years was *On the Councils and the Churches*, a lengthy dissertation on the subject of where ultimate authority was to be found. If reformation was necessary, as everyone now knew that it was, who was going to lead it? He surveyed the work of the first four ecumenical councils – Nicaea (325), Constantinople (381), Ephesus (431) and Chalcedon (451) – in order to discover what they had tried to do and how effective they had been. His conclusion was that they had been regulatory. They had adjudicated on contemporary issues of doctrine and practice. As such their authority did not extend far beyond their own time. The same would be true of any new council. It could discern and deal with current untruths (in his definition this, of course, meant beliefs or behaviour not in accord with the Bible) but not establish new truths that would be binding on future generations. Furthermore, it would not be infallible; the fact that some councils had reversed decisions made at earlier assemblies made that quite clear. *Ergo*, councils, like all pastors, teachers and preachers, had but one responsibility: to ensure that the Church remained faithful to Scripture. It was neither pope nor council which had the last and defining word.

It cannot be overemphasised how revolutionary this evangelical contribution to a centuries-old debate was. Hitherto papalists and conciliarists had engaged in a sterile controversy over the question of whether pope or council possessed ultimate, unassailable authority. Both sides shared the conviction that such an authority *must* exist because Jesus had promised that the Holy Spirit would lead the Church into 'all truth' and that, therefore, there must be a conduit for his activity. But there was little evidence that contending parties had ever honestly sought the divine will. Ecclesiastical politics did not work like that. What usually happened was that councils were summoned or demanded by groups in revolt against Rome and that Rome responded either by denying such requests or by setting up more amenable anticouncils. At a stroke Luther cut this Gordian knot with the sword of holy writ. He utterly rejected the concept of progressive revelation:

> The correct definition of a council is this: A council is a consistory or tribunal of the church in which many bishops assemble to defend the pure doctrine of the faith and to purge the church of new heresies . . . They can introduce ceremonies in councils but only insofar as the ceremonies remain free . . . The papists have taught the twelve articles of the faith in the Creed but in the meantime they have invented a multitude of others about purgatory, the sacrifice of the mass, the invocation of saints. Thus one error grows out of another. We must therefore restore everything to its right shape – that is, to conformity with the Word of God.[4]

Now, if councils, like popes, are fallible and if their role is no different from that of all teachers and preachers, namely setting forth the truth as revealed in Scripture, it follows that authority is dispersed, generalised. How, then, is one to define the Church? This was the issue Luther turned to in the final section of the book. He disliked the rendering of the Greek *ecclesia* as *Kirche*, because in most people's minds this suggested a building or an ecclesiastical hierarchy, whereas its original meaning was a 'gathering' (*Gemeinde*). 'Church', therefore, should be thought of as the gathered people of God, either in the local congregation or that 'multitude which no man can number', stretched out through time and eternity. Its membership is essentially invisible, discerned only by the eye of faith. Insofar as it could be recognised in this world, it was a communion of people among whom the word of God was proclaimed, the dominical sacraments celebrated, the Cross exalted, a ministry called out to exercise that priesthood which belonged properly to all the faithful and persecution accepted as the lot of those who followed the crucified Christ. Any assemblies where these marks were to be discerned (and, presumably, Luther believed that this included all the evangelical congregations) stood in no need of any council.

If a general council was eventually convened it would have to (a) be genuinely free – i.e. not under papal control, (b) be able to rectify all the errors that had accreted to the Church over the centuries, and (c) defend the doctrine of justification by faith. Luther had little hope of such an assembly ever being called into being.

But a council *was* convened and on the pope's terms. A window of opportunity opened for the forces of reaction and they made the most of it. The fiasco of Philip of Hesse's bigamy had weakened the morale and the credibility of the Schmalkaldic League. The failure of the Regensburg talks had convinced Charles V that a peaceful settlement of the religious problem was impossible. The various evangelical groupings were unable to find complete unity and, for the first time in twenty years, the initiative passed from them to the opposition. In 1543 the emperor made his first successful military foray into Germany. In the latest round of the Habsburg-Valois conflict the Duke of Cleves had sided with the French. He very soon paid the price. Charles marched into Cleves territory, reduced the supposedly strong fortified town of Düren and imposed peace terms on the duke. Meanwhile, in Rome the likes of Carafa had obtained the upper hand. Once again Paul III sent out instructions for his bishops and cardinals to gather, this time at Trent. The location was cleverly chosen. Trent was in imperial territory but it was also south of the Alps. It was impossible that the evangelical case would have a proper hearing. As at Worms and as at every confrontation Luther and his colleagues had had with the Catholic hierarchy there would be only one agenda – recantation and submission to the Holy See.

Early in 1545, Charles and his brother, Ferdinand, met to fine hone their plans. They secretly sent a message to the pope informing him of their intention to wage war against the Schmalkaldic League and requesting material and spiritual support. Their plans very nearly came unstuck when Paul, unable to keep the good news to himself, let slip what was afoot. The rumour of an impending showdown swiftly spread. The alarmed German princes requested a meeting with the emperor and asked what his intentions were. Charles managed to bluff his way out of the situation but the suspicion and anxiety which had been mounting in northern Germany over recent months reached its highest point. The atmosphere was tense. People sensed that the long-threatened storm was about to burst.

The atmosphere of foreboding – whose cause Luther, as ever, attributed to the devil – goes some way towards explaining the angry tone of his later writings. His letters in these last years varied in mood from depression to stubborn optimism – things were so bad that the return of Christ must be imminent. His dominant attitude was one of weary disillusionment. He told an old friend in December 1544,

> I am sluggish, tired, cold – that is, I am an old and useless man. I have finished my race; it remains only that the Lord call me to my fathers, and that my body be handed over to decomposition and the worms. I have lived enough, if one may call it living . . . I care nothing for the Emperor and the whole Empire except that I commend them to God in my prayers. It looks to me as if the world, too, has come to the hour of its passing . . . There is nothing of heroic virtue left in the sovereigns [he seems to be including some members of the Schmalkaldic League in this condemnation], but only hatred and discord, avarice and selfish lusts which cannot be healed . . . Nothing good can be expected, therefore, except that the day of glory of the great God of our salvation may be revealed.[5]

Luther's health continued to be indifferent. The punishing regime he was determined to maintain allowed his immune system little respite and he suffered a variety of complaints. Headaches, boils, digestive disorders, circulatory problems, recurring tinnitus and the perpetual pain of kidney stones increasingly made life something to be endured rather than enjoyed. But there were worse trials than the running down of a prematurely aged body. At the beginning of 1540, Catherine fell ill and her life was despaired of. Then, in September 1542, their thirteen-year-old daughter, Magdalene, died. The Luthers had, by the standards of the day, been fortunate with the health of their children. Of the three boys and three girls only one had failed to survive infancy. Perhaps for that reason it was hard for the parents to bear Magdalene's rapid deterioration. Luther's elder daughter passed away in his arms and he was distraught. He confided to a friend,

> My most beloved daughter Magdalene has departed from me and gone to the heavenly Father. She passed away having total faith in Christ. I have overcome the emotional shock typical of a father but only with a certain threatening murmur against death. By means of this disdain I have tamed my tears. I loved her so very much.[6]

A little more than a year later it seemed that the remaining girl, Margaret, might also be taken from her parents. There was an outbreak of measles in Wittenberg and the Luthers' daughter succumbed. But as her friends and playmates recovered Margaret lapsed into a severe fever which continued for ten weeks. This time Luther steeled himself to be philo-sophical: 'I shall not be angry with the Lord if he takes her out of this satanic age and world, from which I, too, desire quickly to be taken, together with all my loved ones. For I long for that day and for the end of the raging of Satan and his followers.' It is not surprising that when Luther did take up his pen to write new theological works the acid of wrath and resentment flowed onto the page. If he rationalised these fresh attacks on old enemies it would be to assure himself that those following him would need to be fortified with texts that were totally uncompromising against the subtle wiles of their foes.

It was in the weeks immediately following Magdalene's death that Luther wrote *On the Jews and Their Lies*. It would be unrealistic to relate these two events as cause and effect. He had been developing his ideas on unregenerate Israel for some time. However, the wrath he poured out in his new pamphlet must have given some relief to his deep grief. The imme-diate occasion for this diatribe seems to have been the news that pro-selytising Jews had succeeded in converting some Christian men, who had denied Christ and submitted to circumcision. He recorded that three rabbis had called on him, apparently with the same objective. This was the exact opposite of what, he had long believed, should be happening. Early in his career he had adopted a liberal attitude towards the Jews in the celebrated Reuchlin case (see above, p. 60) when he had supported the eminent Hebraist (Melancthon's great uncle) who was charged by the Inquisition with Judaising and consorting with the enemies of the Church. In 1523, in *That Jesus Christ Was Born a Jew*, he had urged humane treatment of the despised race because Jews and Christians were all descendants of Abraham. He had a certain amount of sympathy for those who were of the same blood as Jesus and could well understand why they were not attracted by the corrupt pseudo-Christianity of Rome. Subsequently, he had hoped that, now that the Gospel was set forth, they would be able to respond to its truth and the gracious behaviour of its adherents. But it simply had not happened. This was to him a genuine surprise and grief. He had pinned his hope on the power of the word of God to change lives and societies. The stiff-necked attitude of the Jews no less than the obsti-nacy of the papists was preventing this transformation.

The two communities were in some ways linked in his mind. Both were willing slaves of legalism. Catholics were wedded to their traditions and the dictates of the pope and thought to earn salvation thereby. Jews were no less addicted to the 'works religion' based on obedience to the law of Moses. In their wilful blindness they were all rejecting the free grace of God obtained by faith. Jews and Catholics were no better than the Turks, who thought to gain paradise by strict adherence to the rules laid down by Mohammed. Luther's work on the Old Testament had involved careful study of rabbinic commentaries. What he discovered was, not only that these Jewish scholars failed to grasp the purposes of God which received their fulfilment in Jesus, but that, generation after generation, they continued to rely on the writings of earlier exegetes rather than going back to the text and seeking fresh insight. In this they were no better than the scholastic theologians who had taken their doctrine from Peter Lombard, Aquinas, Occam and the rest of the medieval rationalists.

Luther devoted the greater part of *On the Jews and Their Lies* to a careful analysis of the Old Testament writings to show how they prepared the way for the Messiah. In this he followed what St Paul and the author of the *Letter to the Hebrews* had attempted fifteen hundred years before. All this has received scant attention from historians who have tended to fix their sights on the final section of the book. In this the author addressed himself to the question of how Christian rulers should treat their Jewish subjects. Attitudes to his harsh and uncompromising advice have inevitably been coloured by the appalling events of later centuries and predominantly by the Holocaust. Luther did a complete *volte face* on his earlier book. In 1523 he had been an assimilationist; now he had become an exclusionist. No longer were the Jews to be won over by kindness. Their rights of domicile should be rescinded. Their synagogues and houses should be destroyed. In 1519 he had opposed a purge launched by the zealous converted Jew, Johann Pfefferkorn, who was bent on burning Jewish books. Now he urged that all their sacred writings should be confiscated and their rabbis forbidden to preach. Their 'ill-gotten gains' should be taken from them and the money used for the support of converted Jews and the elderly and infirm members of their own community. Jews should not be suffered to live alongside Christians and banishment was the preferred treatment for any who refused to embrace Christianity. All this was intolerant and, to modern sensibilities, intolerable. Four hundred years later it was valuable fuel for the author of *Mein Kampf* and those who preached a new world order based on supposed racial purity. But what Luther advocated was very far from being a final solution.

Unusually, he actually found himself in the majority on 'the Jewish question'. Eck and Bucer were among the Christian scholars who had only recently written on the subject and their conclusions (if not their language) were broadly similar to Luther's. Nothing that he advocated was not already church and state policy in several parts of Europe. And much worse was done in the name of God. In Spain the Inquisition had been doing its work for seventy years, forcing Jews by torture and the threat of burning to convert. Hundreds had perished. Thousands had abjured their ancestral faith. Thousands more had gone into exile. The displaced found it difficult to resettle because many territories were closed to them. They had been expelled from England and France and this had obliged many of them to move to Germany. Here, too, they found no welcome in several states. They had, for example, been banned from Electoral Saxony for a hundred years. Italy was their safest refuge. Here, the pope officially deplored persecution largely because, like the rulers of all the neighbouring lands, he needed the Jews' banking and money-lending skills. Wherever they lived the Jews formed 'foreign' enclaves, preserved their own beliefs and customs – and prospered. For this, of course, they were widely resented and became the not infrequent victims of mob violence. For their part the Jews, from behind their cultural barricades, surveyed their neighbours as coarse, uncivilised people. This particularly irritated Luther. He complained that Jews treated Christians as 'worms', 'filth', 'benighted heathen'. They boasted that they were 'the only noble people on earth, in comparison with whom we Gentiles are not human ... not of their high and noble blood, lineage, birth and descent'.[7] Here, again, was another parallel with the papists, for Rome, too, adopted a patronising air in dealing with Germans.

It was to counteract such 'lies' and worse that Luther wrote his 1542 book, as the title states: *On the Jews and Their Lies*. He quoted obscene and blasphemous insults reputedly thrown at everything Christians held sacred. Jews denied the divinity of Christ and scorned him as a charlatan who gained a following by performing cheap tricks. According to their polemic, his mother was a mere whore who had given birth to a freak. They were awaiting the arrival of a messiah who would visit vengeance on Christendom just as the Lord Jehovah had once before harried Egypt and cut down the proud Pharaoh and his cohorts. It was to Luther obvious that such slanders had to be answered. Nor did he intend to allow Jewish controversialists to hold a monopoly of extreme language. He pointed out that the Jews stood condemned out of their own Scriptures:

> What harm has the poor Jesus done to the most holy children of Israel that they cannot stop cursing him after his death, with which he paid his debt? Is it perhaps that he aspires to be the Messiah, which they cannot tolerate? Oh no, for he is dead. They themselves crucified him and a dead person cannot be the Messiah. Perhaps he is an obstacle to them returning into their homeland? No, that is not the reason either; for how can a dead man prevent that? What, then, is the reason? I will tell you. As I said before, it is the lightning and thunder of Moses: 'The Lord will smite you with blindness and confusion of mind.' It is the eternal fire of which the prophets speak: 'My wrath will go forth like fire and burn with none to quench it' . . .
>
> Further, they presume to instruct God and prescribe the manner in which he is to redeem them. For the Jews, these very learned saints, look upon God as a poor cobbler equipped with only a left last for making shoes. That is to say his is to kill and exterminate all of us Goyim through their Messiah, so that they can lay their hands on the land, the goods, and the government of the whole world. They wish that sword and war, distress and every misfortune may overtake us accursed Goyim. They vent their curses on us openly every Saturday in their synagogues and daily in their homes. They teach, urge and train their children from infancy to remain the bitter, virulent and wrathful enemies of the Christians.[8]

We have no way of knowing how exaggerated these claims were but the prejudices Luther described are precisely those harboured by many persecuted religious minorities who curse their oppressors and look towards some great apocalyptic turning of the tables.

The way to deal permanently with them was, as it had been with the peasants in 1525, by state power. It should be made impossible for the Jews to continue propagating their lies and, indeed, to continue their own traditional teaching and worship. They should be pressured to convert and those who would not should be exiled to their own land where they could do no more mischief. Luther did not advocate extermination. And he was not a racist. His objection was entirely to the Jews' religious beliefs and the behaviour that stemmed from those beliefs. He did not support inquisitorial methods to obtain conversions – use of informers, third-degree interrogation, torture and the threat of the stake (though it might be argued that making life difficult for the Jews by the methods he *did* recommend did not fall a long way short of police-state tactics). To individual Jews (of whom he met very few) he was his usual open, generous self. For several years, he supported from his own slender resources the family of Jacob Gipher, a rabbi who converted, taking the name Bernard. When Bernard was forced to leave Wittenberg in search of work it was Luther and Melancthon who, between them, looked after his children. Anti-Semitism was a nineteenth-century invention and it did not come from Luther's workbench. He did not believe the world would be a better place without Jews but he believed passionately that Christendom would be better without Judaism, just as it would be better without papalism and without Anabaptism. He believed that these aberrations could be controlled by secular government and that, in any case, the world was hastening towards its end when a superior Judge would announce his verdict on every single one of its inhabitants. If he was wrong in believing that princes and magistrates had the right and duty to legislate over men's consciences this was a misapprehension he shared with most other political commentators of the age. Four major, exclusivist faiths met in sixteenth-century Europe. Two of them, Islam and Catholicism, had no compunction about using violence. In his last days, Luther also reached the conclusion that limited force might legitimately be used against the Jews.

Luther's anti-Jewish invective was a sideline and resulted in very little action on the part of his followers. No pogroms broke out in German lands as a direct result of *On the Jews and Their Lies*. His main enemy was, and remained, the Roman Antichrist. To the very end of his days he was writing and preaching against the false claims and the perfidy of the papalists. To all the crimes he had earlier identified as emanating from Rome was now added the activity of Paul III regarding the Council of Trent. Luther remained convinced that it was all a smokescreen covering the pope's real intention to join with the emperor in exterminating evangelicalism by force. He was wrong about the council but right about the covert pact between Paul and Charles to wage war against the Protestant princes. His last major book was *Against the Roman Papacy, an Institution of the Devil*, which he sent to the press in March 1545. It was written in the white heat of anger and indignation and it surpassed in violent and vulgar language anything he had written before. When some friends took him to task for this he admitted that his language was extreme but he was unrepentant. What the pope and his agents were doing was so dishonest, so aggressive and so contrary to the

Gospel that people had to be warned in the most sensational manner that he could devise. Luther was still worried about his colleagues being duped by papal and imperial wiles. The Wittenberg scholars had been asked to prepare proposals for the council but Luther knew that they were simply being played like trout by skilful and unscrupulous anglers and that the destination planned for them was the pot. Like another celebrated enemy of appeasement his opposition seemed to be unnecessarily fierce.

The fact that Luther could not even think about the pope without colourful and abusive adjectives tumbling over themselves onto the page was counterproductive. It embarrassed his friends who realised that their leader was becoming increasingly an eccentric, angry old man at odds with the world. It gave unsympathetic historians the opportunity to concentrate on style rather than substance. And it actually obscured the finer points of his argument. He carefully traced the false claims of the papacy from the beginning: the mistaken biblical exegesis which asserted that Peter had been appointed as first pope; the fraudulent assumption of Church headship, a title belonging only to Christ; the evolution of canon law, a web of legalism designed to entrap the Christian conscience; the forgeries with which the papacy had bolstered its pretended authority. Luther urged the rulers of Europe to cast off the papal shackles once and for all and to establish regimes in which evangelicals would be free to preach, teach and worship. His usual painstaking argument was accompanied and partially obscured by crude jibes and biting satire. At the same time, he made an appeal to the illiterate and semi-literate masses by designing a series of caricatures to be engraved by Cranach. They presented, graphically and startlingly, just how popes had abused emperors and secular rulers and how they despised the mass of people over whom they exercised sway. The prints set before people such edifying spectacles as the pope feeding dung to a sow (Paul III trying to impose a council on Germany) and peasants pissing into an upturned papal tiara (the only appropriate worship to be offered to the man who had made himself a god on earth). The most striking image of all, and the one that was used on the title page of *Against the Roman Papacy* was that of an enthroned pope exercising his dominion from the very mouth of hell.

Once again we have to turn our eyes away from such sensational, headline-grabbing events if we are to gain as complete a picture as possible of old man Luther. After Magdalene's death in 1542 the Luthers were left with four children between the ages of eight and sixteen. Domestic life cannot have been altogether easy for this elderly parent of a young family. He was always busy and when he was not busy it was usually because he was unwell. The children will have been warned not to disturb him. A man who was easily moved to indignant rage must have sometimes found it difficult to restrain himself when annoyed by childish behaviour. Martin and Catherine exercised a strict regime especially with the boys. Like most parents of their generation, they believed that sons should not be pampered. Yet, perhaps because the age gap was so wide, Luther could also be sentimentally indulgent.

Title page by Lucas Cranach for Luther's *Against the Roman Papacy,
an Institution of the Devil*, 1545

Because he remembered harsh beatings he had suffered as a child, he had a tendency to spare the rod. There were occasions when he watched the infants at play and commented on their innocence; how trusting they were in their uncomplicated faith; how he envied them. Of his dead daughters he once said, 'I have sent two saints to heaven.' Catherine might well have reflected that if her husband spent more time with the children he might have realised that they were not entirely the angelic beings he fondly imagined them to be. The boys were kept at home for their education, being first tutored by the Luthers' student lodgers and then enrolled in the university. Hans, the eldest, was not sent away until he was sixteen. Luther felt that he should be 'toughened up' and so the boy was despatched to a school of good repute at Torgau, some sixty kilometres up the Elbe. Hans was very soon homesick, which indicates a happy childhood, but Luther ignored the boy's entreaties and urged him to persevere in his studies. After his father's death Hans went on to the university of Weimar, where he studied for a law degree. Luther had once commented that he would sooner see his son hanged than become a lawyer. Did Hans replicate his father's rebellion in reverse? Martin and Paul, the younger boys, were still at home. The elder would eventually, in accordance with his father's wishes, become a theologian. His brother qualified as a doctor. As is so often the case with children of famous fathers, none of the boys had outstanding careers. One feels that they must have been overawed by their forceful and celebrated father. Little Margaret was eight years old when her sister died and nine when she almost followed her to the grave. She would live to become the wife of one of Wittenberg's aristocratic students. We have only fleeting glimpses of life in the Luther household – Martin Junior reading the Gospel at the meal table; a father's deep grief at Magdalene's death – but the overall impression is that the children were happy in this unusual extended family. If their father was habitually tied to his desk or busy with important guests, there were always plenty of young 'uncles' around, as well as their own cousins. And often, when papa's serious friends came a-visiting they brought gifts for the children.

Thanks almost entirely to Catherine's careful husbandry, the Luthers' material prospects improved over the years. In fact, they became moderately well-to-do. Catherine bought from her brother the small family estate at Zulsdorf and the couple also acquired plots of land and houses in and around Wittenberg. They were engaged in an almost perpetual renovation programme at the Augustinian cloister, which required considerable alteration to make it into a workable home for the Luthers' extended family. On their smallholding they tended several domestic animals and a tax return of 1542 listed 'five cows, nine calves, one goat with two kids, eight swine, two sows and three piglets'.[9] Doubtless there were also chickens and other fowl which were untaxable. Catherine was in charge of all this multi-faceted domestic activity and it would be no exaggeration to say that she turned it into a business venture. She bought, sold, disciplined the servants and drove hard bargains. Her very success indicates that she was forthright and combative, the sort of woman whom tradesmen learned to be wary of and about whom neighbours delighted to gossip. Luther sometimes addressed her jokingly as 'My Lady of Zulsdorf'. Doubtless there were others who found Catherine's 'pushiness' less amusing. Martin remained uninterested in material wealth. The object of his investments was to ensure the security of Catherine, who could be expected to outlive her husband by many years. In the will which Luther made in 1542 he instructed that Catherine was to be able to live independently of the children.

One of the crosses that Catherine had to bear was defending her husband against his own good nature. He was generous to the point of impracticability. Generous and gullible, as the following sad incident shows. In 1541 a certain Rosina von Truchsess turned up on the Luthers' doorstep with a tale of woe. She was a lady of noble birth who had lived most of her life in a nunnery and now found herself homeless because her convent had been closed. Martin took her in and Rosina became the principal maid in the household. It was not long before her catalogue of lies was exposed. Rosina was, in reality, the daughter of a rebel who had been executed in the aftermath of the Peasants' War. She confessed and begged forgiveness. Martin (against Catherine's advice?) agreed to keep her on, a kindness she repaid by stealing, cheating and bringing the house into disrepute by promiscuous behaviour. Eventually she became pregnant. It was probably not so much that as her request that another member of the household help her with an abortion that finally tried Martin's patience and goodwill to the limit. He turned her out and she resumed her vagabond life. By way of revenge she delighted in spreading lies about her former employer.

Life for the Luthers was certainly not 'all work and no play'. The constant comings and goings of students and guests ensured that it would never be dull. But each year was punctuated by happy events, some routine and some spontaneous. In Electoral Saxony the plethora of medieval saints' days had been drastically reduced but Martin, his family and close circle of friends celebrated the major festivals eagerly. Christmas and New Year were greeted with joyful hymns, the playing of games and the giving of gifts (New Year). Luther actually revived the ancient celebration of Shrove Tuesday, which involved the choosing of a 'king' to preside over the festivities as a sort of lord of misrule. Every year, of course, included several birthdays and none passed without a feast.

Music played an inevitable part in such celebrations for this was the art form that Luther loved above all others. He continued writing hymns and psalm versions but his appreciation of music extended beyond sacred settings designed, in part, for the edification of Wittenberg's semi-educated congregation. He enjoyed joining with others in the singing of part songs and motets. He was modest about his own vocal ability but not about his enthusiasm and it is easy to envisage the man who could write the following encomium lending a lusty bass to performances by amateur ensembles:

> This precious gift has been bestowed on men alone to remind them that they are created to praise and magnify the Lord. But when natural music is sharpened and polished by art, then one begins to see with amazement the great and perfect wisdom of God in his wonderful work of music, where one voice takes a simple part and around it sing three, four, or five other voices, leaping, springing round about, marvellously gracing the simple part, like a square dance in heaven with friendly bows, embracings, and hearty swinging of the partners. He who does not find this an inexpressible miracle of the Lord is truly a clod and is not worthy to be considered a man.[10]

Luther, then, seems to have been supported in his heavy workload by a happy if hectic home life. It is then surprising to find him writing to Catherine in July 1545 while he was away on a pastoral tour:

> I would like to arrange matters in such a way that I do not have to return to Wittenberg. My heart has become cold, so that I do not like to be there any longer. I wish you would sell the garden and field, house and all. Also I would like to return the big house [the Augustinian cloister] to my Most Gracious Lord. It would be best for you to move to Zulsdorf as long as I am still living and able to help you to improve the little property with my salary . . . After my death the four elements [earth, air, fire and water – i.e. 'everyone'] at Wittenberg certainly will not tolerate you [there]. Therefore it would be better to do while I am alive what certainly would have to be done then . . . While in the country I have heard more than I find

out while in Wittenberg. Consequently I am tired of this city and do not wish to return. May God help me with this.

The day after tomorrow I shall drive to Merseburg . . . Thus I shall be on the move, and will rather eat the bread of a beggar than torture and upset my poor old [age] and final days with the filth at Wittenberg which destroys my hard and faithful work. You might inform Doctor [Bugenhagen] and Master Philip of this (if you wish), and [you might ask] if Doctor Bugenhagen would wish to say farewell to Wittenberg in my behalf. For I am unable any longer to endure my anger [about] and dislike [of this city].[11]

This was not just the sudden outburst of a dyspetic old man who had been upset by some bad news. His friends and colleagues certainly took the threat seriously and it was only personal intervention by the elector that persuaded Luther to change his mind. In his letter he mentioned as reasons for his annoyance Catherine's unpopularity and the performance of a new, 'lewd' dance that had become all the rage but there was much more than that to his decision.

The root cause lies in the words, 'Wittenberg . . . destroys my hard and faithful work.' It was exactly fifty years since Savonarola had held sway in Florence. By simply preaching he had brought about a religious moral revival. More than that he had seen the end of a corrupt government, the introduction of new laws and the outlawing of usury and commercial exploitation. But the reform had been short lived. The fickle mob, egged on by the Borgia court, had turned against the Dominican and his brothers and consigned them to the flames in the piazza where the friars had formerly presided over bonfires of the vanities. Luther's fate was nothing like as dramatic but the underlying mass psychology was identical. Spiritual and moral revivals are always short lived. They may not come to an abrupt end. They may dwindle into a general respectability, as happened in nineteenth-century Britain. But the initial momentum is never sustained. Holiness is too difficult to be kept going when the initial excitement has passed. Luther perceived this happening in Wittenberg and came to the conclusion, not that he had failed, but that evil was too deep-rooted in the hearts of his fellow citizens.

Our usurers, gluttons, drunkards, whoremongers, blasphemers, and scoffers . . . excommunicate themselves. They despise the Word of God, enter no church, hear no sermons, receive no sacrament. If they don't want to be Christians, let them be heathen, and forever! Who cares about this anyhow? If they take the goods of ministers and appropriate everything for themselves, the minister shouldn't absolve them or administer the sacrament to them. They shouldn't be allowed to attend any baptism, any honourable wedding, or any funeral. They should behave among us as heathen, which they'll be glad to do! When they are dying, no minister or chaplain should visit them, and when they have died the hangman should drag them outside the town to the carrion pit, and no student or chaplain should escort them. If they want to be heathen we'll treat them as heathen.[12]

Such outbursts at Luther's table were not uncommon.

As a preacher Luther was a practical man who addressed himself to contemporary issues that really mattered to his hearers. He condemned drunkenness, a vice he thought his fellow Germans were particularly prone to. He attacked sexual immorality. He urged feuding individuals and families to make peace with each other. These may, perhaps, be regarded as the evangelical preacher's stock-in-trade but Luther waxed more passionate about the sins intrinsic to a hierarchical society. In a class structure based on wide differences of wealth and power in which those at the bottom end had no representation in government, exploitation, greed and corruption were the norms. It is not surprising, therefore, to hear Luther inveighing against usury, price-fixing, excessive displays of wealth and the perversion of justice. There were also sins of omission to be counteracted. Luther castigated clergy who fled to the countryside at the first sign of plague, rather than staying to tend their stricken flocks. Regular churchgoers also received the sharp edge of his tongue. Now that they were not 'paying' for their salvation many otherwise devout Christians were failing to contribute to church funds. As a result the number of pastors and preachers was diminishing and buildings were falling into disrepair.

What this largely comes down to is that, in Luther's mind, his work had produced little result. He had expected that when people's eyes were opened to the Gospel they would respond, as he had done. It did not happen – at least, not on the scale he had hoped for. Basically, this was because evangelical faith was demanding. Luther had moved the spiritual spotlight from the corporate to the individual and many found the glare uncomfortable. For generations parishioners had been more or less content to let their priest do their religion for them. Now, it was up to every man and woman to make his/her personal response to God. They were also expected to read the Bible or, at least, to have it read to them. This presumed an intellectual apparatus that most simply did not possess. It was easier for them to respond to the wonder-stories of saints, repeated in popular legend and graphically portrayed in painted fresco and stained glass.

Yet there were other reasons for the coldness of heart Luther detected in the Wittenbergers. The magic moment had passed. Those exciting, liberating days when their city had led the way in challenging Italian religious domination and ruthlessly exposing the hypocrisy and greed of the clergy were now almost a generation away. In the tavern and the marketplace neighbours discussed whether any very profound changes had come over their lives and concluded (rightly or wrongly) that they had not. In their evaluation of Luther one ink-black cloud brooded over him – the Peasants' War. The hero of the 95 Theses and the Diet of Worms, the regenerator of national pride, the man who had preached the equality of all men in the sight of God, had failed them in the moment of crisis. Luther, in the popular imagination, had become the tool of the princes. Nothing was ever the same again. Luther still had supporters and admirers a-plenty but he also had those who were hostile or indifferent to his message. In Wittenberg by 1545 the magic had long gone out of the movement.

The irony was that, in the wider world, Luther's reputation was still in the ascendant. The success of the Schmalkaldic League and the failure of Rome to set up a council which might initiate reform and restore unity encouraged other German lands to commit to Lutheranism. In the other Saxony when the new ruler, Duke Henry, came to power he had immediately set about establishing the Reformation. He invited Luther and a team of preachers to visit churches and convents and propagate the new faith. Henry was determined to stamp his authority on his lands and one way to do this was to reverse his brother's reactionary regime. Pro-Reformation policies continued when his son, Duke Maurice, succeeded him in 1541. In that year, Luther's old friend and colleague, Justus Jonas, was summoned to Halle to oversee the evangelisation of the Archbishopric of Magdeburg. Melancthon travelled to Cologne to assist in the re-organisation of the church in that electorate. After a few confessional see-saw years the Upper Palatinate joined the Lutheran fold in 1544. Every German city and principality followed its own religious path. 'Lutheranism' was a highly patterned carpet. While accepting Luther's basic dogma states varied in the extent to which they abolished old rituals, Germanised the liturgy or abolished vestments and images. By 1545 the Lutheran Reformation was fairly solid from Würtemberg in the South to Mecklenburg on the Baltic. Most of the new evangelical regimes turned to

Wittenberg at one time or another for advice, direction or help in manning their pulpits. While Luther welcomed the spread of the Gospel, this placed a large additional burden on him. It was particularly difficult to meet the growing demand for qualified and trained preachers and pastors.

Beyond Germany evangelicalism had experienced complete success in Scandinavia and the Baltic lands. Christian III (1503–59), aided by some remarkable Lutheran bishops, established a state church on reformed lines in Denmark and Norway. In Sweden, Gustavus I Vasa (1496?–1560), for largely political reasons, harnessed the forces of reform and had established an evangelical state church by 1544. At the same time Lutheranism spread around the northern coastlands to make the Baltic a Lutheran lake. In other parts of Europe evangelisation was complicated by the divisions within the reform camp. To the East, Lutheran churches took their place alongside Hussite assemblies in Bohemia and Moravia. Beyond these lands missionaries carried the faith through Poland and Hungary right up to the frontier of Orthodox Russia.

To the West the Reformation pursued a more contorted and tragic course. Francis I, though by conviction intolerant of evangelicals, was obliged by the dictates of foreign policy to pay court to the princes of the Schmalkaldic League. This allowed the message of Luther and radical French humanists such as Lefèvre d'Étaples to spread with little effective hindrance. Thousands upon thousands of the reformers' books were eagerly snapped up by students, intellectuals, lawyers, merchants, noblemen and women and even members of the royal court. The ecclesiastical authorities, for all their vigilant attempts to intercept forbidden books and to make examples of those caught handling them, were unable to stop the movement. As elsewhere, it was principally in the major towns and cities – Lyons, Montpelier, Troyes, Tours and Paris, itself – that groups of evangelicals met for Bible reading, worship, mutual encouragement and to plan ongoing mission. But the political situation was very precarious and could change at any moment. Unfortunately, some of the bolder spirits failed to realise that they were walking on eggshells. On the night of 17–18 October 1534 *placards* (posters) appeared in several towns throughout northern France. They protested against the papal doctrine of the mass and denounced it as a travesty of the Last Supper. *C'était magnifique mais ce n'était pas la guerre.* An enraged King Francis ordered repercussions. Two hundred suspected 'heretics' were arrested and twenty-four were burned. New laws were formulated and co-ordinated persecution was instigated under secular authority. All this did was drive the movement underground and set up rigid divisions in society which would lead, a generation later, to France's appalling wars of religion.

The situation in England had several similarities. Henry VIII's attitude veered to and fro according to his foreign and domestic policy needs. Right up to the end of his reign (1547) evangelicals were subject to sporadic purges but the nation had an evangelical archbishop, backed by an influential faction at court and they were poised to take control as soon as Henry's underage son inherited the crown.

If we want some kind of statistical evidence for the astonishing success of the Reformation we should realise that, by 1545, probably some thirty per cent of Europe's population were adherents of one form or another of evangelical faith. Luther was not single-handedly responsible for this. Reformers like Zwingli, Oecolampadius and Bucer had reached their theological positions independently of Wittenberg. Without Luther some kind of religious change would have swept the continent. However, without Luther the spread of new ideas would have been much more diffuse. He provided tenacity of purpose, clarity of vision and a prodigious body of written work, covering biblical exegesis, theology, ecclesiology and practical religion. More importantly, he bridged the intellectual gulf between the scholarly elite and the man in the street. Even his worst enemies could not deny the academic rigour of his Latin works but what set their teeth more on edge was that this university professor could express his damnable heresies in vigorous prose (frequently accompanied by lurid woodcuts) that had a ready appeal to the non-specialist multitude.

It has often been lamented that the Reformation fragmented as soon as it appeared. This was certainly something that distressed Luther, which was why he opposed the radicals as vigorously as he castigated Rome. But it was Luther, himself, who had discovered and dug up the treasure of liberty that enabled theologians to develop their own theories. Once people had been permitted the freedom to read and react to the Bible for themselves, an element of divergence was inevitable. What Luther established was the basic galvanising enfranchisement of the individual soul faced with the enormities of eternity and infinity. Enfranchisement and dignity. No longer was a man's salvation dependent upon the prayers and sacerdotal acts of a priestly caste. But if he now stood alone 'coram Deo' (in the presence of God) he found Luther's God stooping to offer him, through the Cross, salvation as a free, unmerited gift. This realisation was exhilarating, intoxicating. It transformed the lives of countless thousands of Luther's contemporaries, as it had done for millions before and would do for millions more in after years. The testimony of Bunyan's Pilgrim, seeing the burden fall from his back into the empty tomb or the description of John Wesley feeling his heart 'strangely warmed' come readily to mind.

The aged Luther was denied this overview, this gift of seeing his life work in broader perspective. He thought of himself as a prophet without honour in his own country. He might well have echoed the words of Elijah, fleeing the wrath of Jezebel and Ahab: 'I have always served you, but the people have broken their covenant . . . It is too much to bear, Lord. Take away my life.'[13] The depression to which he was always prone reached lower depths. Much of the problem was caused by the punishing schedule of pastoral and administration work which never let up. Luther had no official position among the growing number of German evangelical churches but numerous clergy and civic authorities looked to him for advice and help. Often it was a matter of finding suitable pastors for congregations or suitable congregations for pastors. The problem was that there were not enough 'sound' men to go round. Luther sent an applicant to Torgau but with the warning that he had, in the past, had a drink problem. The pastor of Hof sought a move because he did not get on well with his prince. The congregation at Creuzburg asked Luther to do something about their preacher's excessively 'crude' sermons (in reality, what worried them was that his fiery condemnations were too pointed). Frequently there were financial problems to be dealt with. A man's stipend was inadequate or the support he received from his congregation was niggardly, or the house provided was too small for his family. Such were the practical problems Luther had to deal with on an almost daily basis. Most regions had their own church supervisors to take care of such issues but this did not stop petitioners turning to Luther. Often he had to leave home in order to tour parishes which had called for his help or which needed the firm discipline they would only accept from him. Luther had become, in effect, an *episcopus vagans*, a wandering bishop.[14]

Nothing illustrates this better than the mission on which he was despatched in the spring of 1545. When Luther wrote, in the letter quoted above, to tell his wife that he was en route for Merseburg, he was travelling to the town some hundred kilometres from Wittenberg in order to preside at an episcopal ordination. George III, Fürst (Prince) of Anhalt, was appointed as the new bishop. He asked the evangelical Bishop of Brandenburg to perform the consecration but, before any arrangements could be made, the bishop died. There being no other senior ecclesiastic available to take his place, George turned without hesitation to Luther. Luther, also apparently without hesitation, agreed and, on 2 August,

Luther in the last years of his life

he presided over the solemn ceremony in the cathedral at Merseburg.

Among the many people who believed they had a call upon his time were the inhabitants of his own native region of Mansfeld. There was a long-running dispute there between Count Albrecht, whom Luther counted as a friend, other members of Albrecht's family and the copper miners with whom he had close family ties. Luther had made journeys there in the past in vain attempts at arbitration but when, at the end of 1545, his help was requested again, he agreed to come. The aged reformer set out from Wittenberg on 23 January, accompanied by his three sons, and his secretary Johann Aurifaber. Justus Jonas joined them en route. The weather was foul. The travellers' wagons were delayed by flooded rivers glutted with floating ice. It was a tiring journey and one that tapped his failing strength. Nevertheless, he found the energy to preach in towns along the way. In his letters to Catherine he was cheerful and made light of his difficulties but he was more honest when writing to Melancthon:

> During the trip both a loss of consciousness and that illness which you usually call *humor ventriculi* [apparently a circulatory problem]

caught me. For I went on foot, but this was beyond my strength, so that I perspired. Afterwards in the carriage when my shirt also had got cold from the sweat, the cold grabbed a muscle in my left arm. From this came that tightness of the heart and something like shortness of breath. It is my own stupid fault. But now I am quite well again, how long – well that, of course, I do not know, since one cannot trust old age . . .[15]

After five days of such discomfort Martin Luther arrived at Eisleben. It must have been almost exactly sixty-three years since he had been conceived in this very town. Despite his jaunty letters Catherine was concerned about him and he had to gently reprove her:

You prefer to worry about me instead of letting God worry, as if he were not almighty and could not create ten Doctor Martins, should the old one drown in the Saale or burn in the oven or perish in Wolfgang's bird trap [a jocular reference to their servant, Wolfgang Sebergery who tried to catch birds in the garden at Wittenberg]. Free me from your worries. I have a caretaker who is better than you and all the angels; he lies in the cradle and rests on a virgin's bosom, and yet, nevertheless, he sits at the right hand of God, the almighty Father. Therefore be at peace. Amen.[16]

At Eisleben the wearying negotiations between the contending parties dragged on day after day. At one point Luther contemplated a subterfuge to speed things up. Catherine should obtain from Elector John Frederick a letter demanding his urgent recall. Perhaps the prospect of losing their intermediary might concentrate the minds of the warring factions. The emotional strain of getting Albrecht and his cousins to talk to each other, let alone discuss a compromise solution to their problems, further drained Luther's strength, but he gave himself unstintingly to the task. At last, on 14 February (appropriately, St Valentine's Day) an agreement was reached.

By this time Luther was being attended by doctors and his bedclothes were being warmed to counteract the chill that was creeping over his body. His friends urged him to rest but, though he spent much of the ensuing days in his room, he insisted on coming downstairs for meals. On the evening of 17 February he held court at table, as he had done on countless days at Wittenberg. As usual, friends and family were there to record his words of wisdom. About ten o'clock he retired and slept for three hours. Then he awoke in such pain that his alarmed companions sent for the doctors and for his friends. Rapidly the little room filled. Martin's two younger sons were there, as was Justus Jonas, his host and hostess, Count Albrecht and his wife. Later they were joined by other members of the ruling family who had been roused form their beds by the alarming news. Dr Martin was near death. The end came quietly at around 3 a.m. on 18 February 1546.

His body was brought back to Wittenberg and all along the route church bells rang and people turned out to gaze in mute respect on the cortège. It was an impressive procession that made its way from the city gate to the castle church on Monday 22 February.

Ahead of the body, on horseback, were representatives of our Benevolent Elector of Saxony, the two young Gentlewomen and Lords of Mansfeld, accompanied by their fourteen horsemen. Following the hearse on which the body had been placed, came his wife, Katharine Luther, as well as several matrons. Next followed his three sons, John, Martin, and Paul Luther; his brother, Jacob Luther, a citizen of Mansfeld; his sister's sons, George and Ciliax [Cyriakus] Kauffman; citizens of Mansfeld, and other friends. These were followed by the rector of the worthy university, several young princes, gentlewomen and barons who were studying at the University of Wittenberg. After this, the body was followed by Dr Gregory Brück [aide to the Elector of Saxony], Dr Philip Melanchthon, Dr Justus Jonas, John Bugenhagen, Dr Caspar Creutziger [Cruziger], Dr Hieronymus [Schurff], and other senior doctors of Wittenberg University. Next came all the doctors, masters, and the honourable council, together with counsellors; further, a multitude of people, a great number of students and the citizenry; many female citizens, matrons, women, young women, many earnest children, young and old, all with much mourning and sobbing. In all the streets, as well as in the market place, there were such big crowds that many remarked with amazement that they had never seen the like of it in Wittenberg.[17]

In the church funeral orations were delivered by the pastor, Johann Bugenhagen, and Philip Melancthon. The service was read. Then the coffin was lowered into the grave which had been dug close to the pulpit. It was a fitting resting place for the hero of the word.

VI
And Afterwards?

17

God's Word and God's World

Just over a year later, the Emperor Charles V stood on that very spot, gazing down at the grave of the man who had caused him so much trouble over so many years. It was a dramatic moment. A historic moment. The two men had come face to face only once, when Luther had been in his prime and Charles scarcely more than a boy. Now the reformer was dead and the emperor was at the summit of his powers. He had just emerged victorious from a prolonged campaign against the Schmalkaldic League. It was a war the German princes should have won. Their forces outnumbered those of the emperor and they were fighting on their own territory. Yet Charles' brilliant generalship and his utter determination to restore Catholicism by force of arms gave him the victory. He impelled his troops onward through the autumn and winter, though his men were weary and his advisers urged him to wait for spring. At Mühlberg, he won the final battle, took John Frederick prisoner and stripped him of the electoral dignity. It was everything that Luther had feared throughout all those years when he had urged the evangelical princes to put their trust, not in naked steel, but in 'the sword of the Spirit, which is the word of God'. Was this the end of the German Reformation? Luther had embraced death willingly as the laying down of a thankless burden, believing that his spiritual crusade had failed. Now the political aspect of the religious revolt had, similarly, come to nothing. For some weeks or months Charles allowed himself to believe that the war for the soul of his German empire had been won. At Wittenberg he displayed that combination of magnanimity and contempt that can only go with victory. As he stood in the castle church surrounded by his jeering and triumphalist Spanish officers he refused their request to dig up the corpse and burn it, as befitted so great a heretic. Such a symbolic annihilation, for which there was plenty of historical precedent, would have rubbed the evangelicals' noses in their own defeat. But the emperor's dismissive answer was, 'I do not make war on dead men.'

It would be difficult to discover a comment that history has loaded more heavily with irony. Eight years later Charles V abdicated, knowing that he had failed in his mission to unite European Christendom under the combined leadership of pope and emperor. Whatever the Holy Roman Empire had ever meant, it would never mean again and for that Martin Luther was in large measure responsible. Charles had brought under his nominal suzerainty an entity which was territorially and ideologically greater than anything seen since the days of Charlemagne. This monolithic Latin Christendom was sundered by a monk who inserted a wedge into one of its many cracks and struck it with repeated, massive hammer blows until it fell apart. For seven hundred and thirty years emperors had been crowned by popes. There would be no more such coronations and that fact, in itself, is massively symbolic of the end of an era.

The transformation which came over European society in the dynamic sixteenth century was extremely complex and it follows that the reasons for it cannot be reduced to the beliefs and actions of a few individuals, however visionary and creative they might have been. Nevertheless, the point has arrived at which I must attempt an analysis of Luther's contribution to the evolution of modern Europe and, indeed, of the modern world. To do that it is necessary to commit an anachronism. Post-Enlightenment Europe progressively separated religion and politics and today we have reached the ultimate position in which Christianity is a minority hobby in those lands over which the Reformation conflict once engaged the minds and hearts of the majority. But in Luther's time and for two hundred years afterwards it was impossible to disentangle religion and politics. That, however, is what I must try to do – because the historian of the Reformation has, or so it seems to me, an inescapable responsibility to explain what the present owes to the prime movers of that great revolution. Since we live in a secular present the story must be told, partially at least, in secular terms. So, I shall deal with my subject under a false categorisation by dividing it into 'political', 'religious' and 'social/cultural' sub-heads. Having said that, I hope readers will understand when issues of Christian belief elbow themselves to the front of the narrative.

The Political Aftermath

The short-term results of evangelicalism's confrontation with traditional, ritualised religion can be quickly summarised. The attempt to eradicate it from Germany failed, in large measure because it was intertwined with the struggle of local rulers for greater independence from the emperor. Mühlberg was not the last and deciding confrontation between Charles and the German princes. In May 1551 the victor of that battle was fleeing through the Alpine snow with only a handful of attendants from an army of rebel princes led by Elector Maurice of Saxony, the loyal Albertine supporter on whom the emperor had, only four years previously, conferred the dignity stripped from his Ernestine rival. Political, dynastic and nationalistic interests had combined to produce a coalition of forces (even including Charles' brother, Ferdinand) opposed to overweening Spanish Habsburg power. Military activity ended with the Treaty of Passau (1552), at which it was agreed that the religious status quo would remain in place until the next meeting of the imperial diet. This occurred three years later in Augsburg. It permanently settled the religious issue in Germany by subordinating dogma to political expediency. The princes had two concerns above all others: internal stability and the limiting of imperial power. They confirmed the Augsburg Confession as equally valid with Catholic teaching and demanded that allegiance to one confession or the other would be established on a territory-by-territory basis. Within months, Charles had abdicated, yielding Spain and the Netherlands to his son, Philip, and the imperial title to his brother, Ferdinand. The political integrity of Latin Christendom was shattered.

The Austrian Habsburgs remained a power in Germany until 1806, exercising at times a useful unifying influence. But their power was, from the time of Charles V, ineluctably on the wane. As long as the Empire could, with some rationale, be called 'Holy' and 'Roman' it possessed a philosophical identity. Relations between emperor and pope had frequently been troubled but politically they needed each other. Theirs was a symbiotic relationship. When Rome was exiled from several German states the myth of united western Christendom was exposed once and for all. What the Lutheran princes achieved in terms of controlling the externals of church life was copied in England, Scotland, the reformed Swiss cantons and, over subsequent centuries, in all lands where church and state were separated. The principle of *cuius regio, eius religio* brought personal conscience and political power into conflict on a massive scale. The principle, 'one law, one faith, one king' was deeply ingrained not only among the political elite. Shared beliefs and values were essential to the security of the state. Few questioned the conviction that religious freedom and anarchy were soul mates. Not until the eighteenth century would the spread of toleration make it possible for confessional communities to co-exist within state borders and the frequent attempts to impose conformity made the years 1550–1700 the bloodiest in European history before the carnage of World War I.

Luther had been a man of his time when he upheld the right of civil rulers to control church affairs. He had taught that, in most cases, the only choices open to evangelicals when faced by persecution from unsympathetic governments were patient suffering or emigration. In the years following his death the continent was 'alive' with the movements of minorities seeking safe haven. German families sought leave to cross into neighbouring territories. French Huguenots fled to England. The Dutch Republic became a magnet for Protestant asylum-seekers. English evangelicals travelled to Geneva, Zurich and Strasbourg during the reign of Catholic Mary. Dutch and English Puritans took ship for the New World. For many of those who stayed behind severe repression became a reality. Protestants were hounded by the agents of 'Bloody' Mary and Catholic recusants were hunted down by her sister, Elizabeth. Philip II of Spain tried to purge his Netherlands possessions of heresy. Archduke Ferdinand of Styria gave his subjects the option of departing with such belongings as they could carry, converting or going to prison. Catholicism was forcibly restored in Charlemagne's old capital of Aachen, symbolic of western Christendom. In 1589, when, at the Diet of Regensburg, the Catholic majority demanded the return of all church property in Protestant lands, the evangelical representatives walked out and did not return to the imperial Reichstag for forty years. Though the appalling events initiated in Paris on St Bartholomew's Eve, 1572, which resulted in the massacre of 20,000 Huguenots, takes the palm for religious-inspired brutality, the repeated attempts to extirpate Catholicism from Ireland were no less appalling.

At the level of national and international politics religious discord dominated relationships for a century and a half. Just as conscience vied with obedience to the secular power in the life of the individual, so, on the wider stage, the power of ideals struggled with the idealisation of power. Switzerland was enmeshed in decades of strife between Catholic and Reformed cantons. Civil war dominated France throughout the second half of the sixteenth century and, though this conflict cannot with complete accuracy be labelled 'the wars of religion', confessional rivalry was a major contributory factor. The same is true of the revolt of the Netherlands (1566–1648) and the British civil wars (1639–49). But it was the German heartland which suffered the worst and most prolonged devastation. In 1608, the evangelical Rhineland princes formed the Protestant Union and the following year the Catholic League came into being as a counter-threat. Within a decade the empire went to war within itself when the Habsburgs tried to return Bohemia to the Catholic fold. Hussite and Lutheran leaders had united behind a shared confession as long ago as 1575. They were now prepared to swear allegiance to a Calvinist prince, Frederick, Elector Palatine, to avoid being embraced by the coils of Rome. The Thirty Years' War had begun. Most European states were dragged into it at one time or another. Armies rampaged to and fro, destroying villages, sacking towns and trampling good farmland. By the time the exhausted combatants signed the Peace of Westphalia in 1648, some four or five million subjects of the Holy Roman Emperor had perished as a result of battle, disease and famine. If we can identify any sense in which this appalling conflict marked a turning point in the affairs of Europe it is, in the words of C. V. Wedgwood, that the leaders of the nations 'rejected religion as an object to fight for and found others'.[1]

Pope Innocent X denounced the Peace of Westphalia as 'null, void, invalid, iniquitous, unjust, damnable, reprobate, inane, empty of meaning and effect for all time'. He was angry because he had not been consulted about it and because his Catholic champions had not been prepared to fight on till the last drop of blood had been spilled in order to bring the entire continent back under papal allegiance. The treaty makers had, in effect, endorsed Luther's condemnation of coercion in religious matters. In his advice to the Elector John Frederick, to Philip of Hesse, to Asa von Kramm and in his diatribes against the pope and the sectaries he had rejected the use of worldly means to achieve otherworldly ends. The Christian was most certainly involved in warfare but it was a spiritual warfare and could only be fought with the spiritual weapons God had provided.

Yet, can we acquit Luther of all responsibility for the long decades of religion-inspired belligerence which permanently divided Europe into rival faith camps and gave rise to such untold human disaster? Would any of it have happened if the Wittenberg monk had not challenged the scandal of indulgences? The spread of individualism, nationalism, autocracy and libertinism have all been fathered on Luther from time to time. But he did not invent any of these things nor the self-assertiveness which under- lies them all. There had been peasant uprisings before 1525 – and terri- torial rivalries, and kings and emperors who had challenged the power of the Church, and outbreaks of heresy which had called forth Catholic reprisals, and freedom fighters who had based their appeal on rabid nation- alism. If such confrontations intensified from the mid-sixteenth century, other factors are at least partially responsible. Cheap print – both word and image – imparted a new meaning to the word 'propaganda' and encour- aged the spread of prejudice. The availability of affordable books opened to men and women a world of ideas that had previously been restricted to scholars and churchmen. It did not need the arrival of Luther for old authorities to be challenged and old certainties to be questioned. Books also played a major part in the emergence of modern languages. 'France', 'England' and 'Germany' were terms with limited meaning as long as the peoples who lived there only understood regional dialects. The emergence of standardised languages encouraged people to think of themselves as belonging to nations and as clearly different from (and superior to) those of other nations. Latin Christendom, insofar as it had ever been a unity, must have fragmented during the century and a half after 1517 and that fragmentation would certainly have involved a measure of violence.

Luther's contribution to the process was to give – or appear to give – religious sanction to fissiparous political initiatives. There was a potential contradiction at the heart of his message. It was there because he rigidly followed the teaching of Jesus and St Paul. The apostle had laid down that it was no part of the Christian's mandate to subvert the political status quo. Caesar had been appointed by God and, as Jesus said, it was every subject's duty to render to Caesar the things that were Caesar's. Social change *per se* was not on the Christian's agenda because his citizenship was in heaven. Thus, for example, Paul accepted the institution of slavery. However, he also asserted that, in the household of faith, there were no distinctions of race, class or gender; male and female, Jew and Greek, slave and Roman citizen – all were equal before God. It has never been easy to hold these two principles in equilibrium so it is scarcely surprising that both radicals and reactionaries, in their quest for respectable antecedents, should have laid claim to Martin Luther. The centenary of the posting of the 95 Theses in 1617 was proclaimed as a three-day holiday in all the German Protestant states and Luther was tacitly lauded as the initiator of anti-papist secular polity in sermons and broadsheets and by the striking of special medals. At that time several evangelical nations were still fighting sporadically for their political existence and propaganda was important. A century later much of the heat had gone out of confessional confrontation and the celebrations took on a less nationalistic identity. As inevitably happens in religious institutions, factions had by now emerged within the Lutheran fold. Some scholars looked critically at their founder and were anxious to disassociate themselves from his more uncompromising teaching and violent language. Frederick William I of Prussia ordered that no celebratory preaching or literature was to include attacks on Catholicism. This upset traditionalists who tetchily pointed out that critics 'should have the decency to consider that the very freedom of which they speak and write they owe to Luther's Reformation'.

Individual freedom was the great cause to which Luther's name was linked in the later years of the eighteenth century. Johann Gottlieb Fichte, Professor of Philosophy at Jena, was one of many intellectuals of the Enlightenment who were, initially, thrilled by the outbreak of the French Revolution. He saw a ready parallel with the sixteenth-century monk who had 'broken humanity's chain' and was now rejoicing in heaven as he witnessed 'the crops that sprang from the seeds you sowed'. The genie of liberal/radical aspiration who escaped from his bottle in the revolutionary years ranged to and fro over Europe throughout the ensuing century and many of those touched by his turbulent magic claimed the Wittenberg monk as their patron saint. Now, it was no longer Lutherans alone who proclaimed, 'wherever Luther's victorious call echoed, there awoke the free life of the spirit in the service of Truth and Justice'.

By 1871 a new phenomenon had appeared on the political map of Europe – a united German empire. William I of Prussia (now emperor) and his chancellor, Otto von Bismarck, attempted to run the new state on Prussian lines – disciplined, militaristic and ideologically united. The Protestant state church (in Prussia the Lutheran and Reformed traditions had merged in 1817) was seen as an essential prop and Catholicism as an insidious enemy. The Catholics had formed a political party and the First Vatican Council had pronounced the doctrine of papal infallibility. Bismarck launched his *Kulturkampf*, a judicial war against the claims of the religious minority for social and educational rights. But if he had hoped for the solid support of the Lutherans he was disappointed. Protestant politicians were divided over government policy; some regarding Bismarckian autocracy as a greater threat than the continued influence of Rome in German affairs. Government-sponsored initiatives helped to generate a revival of interest in the Reformation. Luther was celebrated in statues, cheap prints, books and plays as a father of the nation. But there were those who could not associate the reformer with the warrior culture of the German Empire. In a Germany looking for its own identity and a place at the top table of major powers there were several versions of Luther. Many pastors held him up before their flocks as the quintessential, home-and-family-loving German. Frederick Engels regarded him as the representative of liberal, bourgeois culture. A contemporary theologian, Walter Kohler, unhesitatingly harnessed his church's founder to the unstoppable military machine that trundled into war in 1914: 'Luther stands before us, a fighter, a hero, a victor, a German, and calls all of us: remain German in faith, in struggle and victory.' Pickelhaubed soldiers marched to the front lustily singing *Ein feste Burg*. Yet to others it seemed strange that the Protestant nation was embarking on a devastating conflict, not against international Catholicism or even just the old enemy, France, but against a sister state, also spawned of the Reformation. However, even those who understood Luther's unremitting opposition to wars of aggression against other Christian nations were caught up in the patriotism of the hour.

If Germany was a schizophrenic nation before the First World War, afterwards it was in a state of humiliation, disillusion, shock and bewilderment. A proud people had become the pariahs of Europe, to be squeezed by the victors, in the words of Britain's First Lord of the Admiralty, 'until the pips squeak'. Worse was to come. By 1924, the economy was totally wrecked and the deutschmark was worthless. Two sinister monsters now rose out of the Stygian depths of the nation's mire: the quest for scapegoats and the longing for firm, authoritarian leadership. There were those who looked to Luther on both counts. Were not the communist and social democrat rabble the modern counterpart of the anarchic peasants of 1525 whom the reformer had urged Germany's rulers to eradicate with the utmost severity and had not Luther denounced the Jews as a race committed to the overthrow of Christian civilisation? To many patriotic Germans Hitler's National Socialists seemed to offer a logical programme of national recovery based on the religious principles Luther had enunciated. 'Ours is an affirmative, truly national faith in Christ, in the Germanic spirit of Luther', so declared the manifesto of the German Christians, one of the nationalist parties thrown up by the ideological turmoil of the times. Hitler's propagandists, of course, eagerly encouraged such secularisation of Luther's theology.

The racist-nationalist-militarist-expansionist programme devised by the architects of the Third Reich drew no legitimate inspiration from the monk of Wittenberg. The tortuous roots of Nazism received their nourishment from pagan myth and nineteenth-century pseudo-science. For a century a theory of 'Germanness' had been built up, layer by layer. Ernst Arndt (1769–1860), professor of history and radical politician, identified his race as the torchbearers of civilisation, the *Lichtvolk*: 'The Germans and the Latins, impregnated and fertilised by them, are the only ones to have made the divine germ flower, thanks to philosophy and theology, and as rulers to animate and guide the surrounding peoples, belonging to foreign species.'[2] Kant, Richard Wagner, and the Brothers Grimm were among a medley of poets, musicians, historians and philosophers who added their voices to the swelling chorus that became loud enough to drown the pleas of reason and balanced argument. In the early days of 1927 Houston Stewart Chamberlain, a naturalised German of British origin, lay dying in Bayreuth. An ardent disciple and ambitious politician came to kneel by his bedside to express his devotion for the inspiration he had received from the old man. The visitor's name was Adolph Hitler. It was Chamberlain, son-in-law of Wagner, who had developed the theory of the Aryan super race, constantly at war with the subversive and corrupting influence of international Jewry.

When the Führer's subservient scholars added their coping stones and decorative flourishes to the impressive-looking but structurally flawed political edifice of German racial purity they cherry-picked ideas and statements from any impressive source that might add credence to their bestial creed. Hitler himself quoted Luther out of context in *Mein Kampf*. It was no accident that the infamous *Kristallnacht* anti-Jewish pogrom of 1938 took place on Luther's birthday. But this was sheer opportunism backed by no tradition of perverted scholarship. There had been no consistent identification of the reformer with persecution of the Jews in the racist rhetoric of the previous hundred years. Nor was there a linking of arms between Nazism and Lutheranism. On the contrary, ministers of the Hitler state labelled the churches as enemies of the National Socialist philosophy precisely because they welcomed people of all ethnic backgrounds and refused to subscribe to notions of racial purity. Moreover Luther had set up the Bible as the standard of belief and conduct and the Bible had been written by Jews! As anyone who took the trouble to read Luther's writings knew, he did not advocate extermination of the church's enemies. His argument had been, not with the Jews as a race, but with proselytising Judaism. There is no well-beaten path that can be discovered from Wittenberg to Auschwitz.

Nor can a convincing case be made for the idea of Luther the anti-democrat. His relationships with the princes of the Schmalkaldic League suggest that he would have been no uncritical supporter of authoritarian government from Bismarck to Hitler. He took his aristocratic supporters to task for creating the genuine grievances which provoked the Peasants' War and he opposed any attempt by temporal rulers to interfere in the teaching of the church. His opposition to the rebels of 1525 rested on the Pauline prescription to obey legally (and, therefore, divinely) appointed rulers. Since he offered no programme of political change it follows that, in the 1920s, he would have supported the democratically elected government of the Weimar Republic. Theologically he would have been at odds with Dietrich Bonhoeffer, the Lutheran pastor who attacked contemporary Protestant preachers for peddling 'cheap grace' (i.e. free, unmerited forgiveness divorced from moral endeavour) but we may imagine him standing alongside the martyr who refused to flee Hitlerite Germany, spoke fearlessly against the outrages perpetrated by the regime and was hanged in April 1945.

That might not have been of much comfort to Bonhoeffer. Like many twentieth-century theologians (both Protestant and Catholic), he rejected Luther's separation of the temporal and spiritual spheres. The premise of liberation theology is that the Gospel is concerned to redeem society as well as its individual members. This entails political involvement. No one can fairly accuse Luther of lacking a social conscience and if he failed to use it as a platform for political protest it was largely because he believed, as did many of his contemporaries, that the end of this world was nigh and that Christian energy was best directed towards the conversion and spiritual edification of men and women. It is as society has become secularised and as churches have become less obsessed with the eschaton that Luther's emphasis on the individual seems, to many Christians, less than adequate. Would Brother Martin, we ask ourselves, have any words of wisdom to offer on climate change or Third World debt?[3]

Social and Cultural Aftermath

Luther enunciated no political programme but has been claimed as a supporter by advocates of various political programmes. The opposite is true of his influence on western culture: he has been responsible for profound changes in the way we think and behave but has seldom been claimed as a progenitor by architects of human 'progress'. Secularist heirs of the Enlightenment prefer to praise the heroes of rationalism for advances in education, housing conditions, law reform and all those improvements which have added comfort, dignity and scope for personal development to the way we live in the twenty-first century. The baby of God's compassionate involvement in history, so fundamental to Luther's thinking, has been thrown out with the bath water of Christian dogma. We prefer to think we did it 'our way'. The truth is that it would be difficult to exaggerate the transforming power of the ideas unleashed by the sixteenth-century evangelicals, of whom Luther was the chief.

Jacques Barzun opens his magnificent *From Dawn to Decadence* with this bald uncompromising statement:

> The Modern Era begins, characteristically, with a revolution. It is commonly called the Protestant Reformation, but the train of events starting early in the 16thC and ending – if indeed it has ended – more than a century later has all the features of a revolution. I take these to be: the violent transfer of power and property in the name of an idea.

Barzun goes on to list the principle points of Reformation impact:

> It posed the issue of diversity of opinion as well as of faith. It fostered new feelings of nationhood. It raised the status of the vernacular languages. It changed attitudes towards work, art and human failings. It deprived the West of its ancestral sense of unity and common descent. Lastly but less immediately, by emigration to the new world overseas, it brought an extraordinary enlargement of the meaning of West and the power of its civilization.[4]

The list, though impressive, is by no means complete but it will serve as a starting point. These were the signs that a whole civilisation had been pointed in a new direction.

Of course, the people of Luther's world had to be ready for such an upheaval. Individuals can lead revolutions; they cannot conjure them out of the empty air. The word 'revolution' does not imply a leap forward to create a brave new world; quite the reverse. The Latin root, *revolvere*, means 'to turn round', 'to come full circle', 'to return to the point of origin'. People *en masse* can never be persuaded to step into the unknown but the idea of going back to some supposed earlier state of well-ordered felicity is one that can engage the common imagination. This is what the reformers offered. For at least three hundred years groups of heretics had appeared whose message was not markedly different from that of the sixteenth-century evangelicals: the Church had taken a wrong turning, was corrupted by power and vice; had forsaken the Gospel of the Galilean Carpenter. There was need for a return to ancient truth. None of these movements had achieved a Europe-wide following. Most had been easily suppressed. But in the 1520s the situation had changed. When Luther challenged the truths people believed or thought they believed or knew they were supposed to believe, large numbers (particularly in the towns and among the educated classes) discovered that the old dogmas did not, in fact, have a firm hold upon their minds. By convincing them that he was promoting, not a novel faith system, but a powerful ancient wisdom, Luther persuaded thousands to follow him.

His teaching and example offered that most powerful of all intoxicants, liberty. Ironically, this was something he did not intend and whose consequences alarmed him. When news of his stand at Worms – his declaration that a man must, above all things, follow his own conscience even if that means resisting his temporal and spiritual overlords – spread throughout Europe it signalled to the majority of people who were, or fancied themselves to be, in some way or other oppressed that they could take on the system and win. When the reformer's teaching on the unencumbered offer of divine grace and free access to the Bible reached them (and many must have heard his theological teaching in a garbled form) they believed they had religious sanction for doing their own thing – even to the point of rebellion. This was not at all what Luther intended. As we have seen, any challenge to temporal authority touched him on a very raw nerve. What was even worse was the prospect of rival evangelicals founding churches based on scriptural revelations that he did not share. Luther's revolution was a very limited one: he intended to return the Church to its New Testament doctrines. What he actually did, without realising it, was to provide oxygen to human individualism. Luther did not invent individualism and it would be a mistake to nominate him as the originator of every advance in the fields of religion, politics, philosophy, science and the arts. But a highly authoritarian society did begin to collapse when assailed by the blasts of his written and spoken rhetoric and in the centuries to come brave individuals who challenged entrenched establishments did owe (even if they seldom acknowledged it) some debt to Martin Luther.

At Worms Luther refused to recant, 'unless I am convicted by Scripture *and plain reason*'. What is sometimes overlooked by commentators on Luther's *sola scriptura* teaching is that qualifying phrase. He was well aware that the Bible can be made to serve any doctrine or, as he would have said, 'even the devil can quote Scripture' but he did not use this as an argument for restricting the availability of the word of God to those indoc-trinated into his own belief system. To be sure, he was convinced that anyone studying the plain word of Scripture with the aid of divine grace would reach the same conclusions that he had reached. To be sure, also, he attached his own glosses to his translations of the two testaments. But he was sure that the student should apply his God-given intellect to solving the problems of faith. It was the refusal of Catholic opponents to dispute with him and their reacting against argument with immovable assertion that angered him in the 1520s. He could not, therefore, demand that others should simply accept evangelical truth solely on his authority. Luther's championing of the spirit of free enquiry led Steven Ozment to claim, 'it is not too much to call the early Protestant movement the first Western enlightenment'.[5] Certainly Luther shared more with a contem-porary like Copernicus than he did with Erasmus. The great astronomer was prepared to pursue the line of reasoning even when it led to jetti-soning fourteen hundred years of received wisdom about the divine ordering of the universe, unlike the wandering humanist who declined to follow his rejection of much Catholic dogma to its logical conclusion.

When Luther gave men the open Bible he gave them permission – by the application of reason to the plain text – to challenge centuries of official Church teaching. Well, if the pope and his minions were wrong, who was to say that other ancient authorities might not also be doubted? Without intending to do so Luther encouraged men to use their God-given intellect to question *everything*. Thus, autocratic power was challenged in sixteenth-century Holland, seventeenth-century Britain, eighteenth-century France and America, nineteenth-century Italy and Germany. In the twentieth century it was the turn of Europe's overseas colonies to apply the same logic to their situations that their rulers had employed in setting up their own republics and constitutional monarchies. The same spirit of open-minded enquiry prevailed in other fields of human endeavour. Empirical science was freed from its theological strait-jacket when scholars were able to make deductions based on their own observations without having to consider cautiously what they *ought* to believe. In the fullness of time the Bible itself went under the critical microscope. By the late nineteenth century linguists, archaeologists, biologists and historians were calling into question the accuracy of the sacred text. In doing so, they found themselves challenged by Luther's evangelical heirs and the battle rages still. Luther knew what we have painfully discovered, that unilluminated reason is no sure guide to human happiness and fulfilment. It is a very mixed blessing. It would be foolish to ascribe to Luther sole responsibility for the empowering and unleashing of the human intellect. In the age of the Renaissance there were many artists and philosophers pushing at the boundaries of human knowledge. Yet, it remains true that no other thinker of the age put into the hands of ordinary (or, at least, literate) people a tool they could use to batter down the locked doors of dogma and prejudice. It is also true that no contemporary so firmly grasped the popular imagination by his personal confrontation with obscurantism backed by naked power.

Since it was desirable for as many as possible to read the Bible, education featured strongly in Luther's thinking about a renewed society and in other reformers' vision of a godly commonwealth. He established no programme for a world that was stumbling towards its imminent end but he laid down basic principles that others would build upon. The home, the church and the state were, he taught, all responsible for the proper upbringing of children and basic education was a vital part of that process. Reading and writing were no longer skills to be associated primarily with the clergy. However, Luther was very concerned about the instruction of potential future ministers. If the people were to be reared on a spiritual diet of good biblical preaching the need for a steady supply of reformed pastors was essential. The lack of such a supply did, indeed, prove to be one of the major problems in establishing the Reformation. The number of ordinations in Germany (as in England) fell drastically as a direct result of the new ecclesiology. When clerical standards were raised and privileges lowered there was considerably less incentive for men to enter the ministry.

This was not Luther's only reason for encouraging the founding of schools. Education was, for him, a good thing of itself. Parents, he insisted, should send their children to school and if they could not spare them for a full day they should, at least, ensure that they spent part of the day at their books. Recalling his own treatment at the hands of dedicated pedagogues, he insisted that teaching should be regarded as a respected profession. Luther's ideal teacher of children was a man who was so committed to the exhausting care of the young that he ought not to spend more than ten years in the job. He urged all municipal authorities to set up schools and local benefactors to finance private ventures. This was one of those 'good works' that was pleasing to God, if undertaken, not as a means of earning salvation, but of gratefully fulfilling one's obligation to care for God's people. The number of schools founded in Germany from the 1530s onward increased, although such growth was not a major factor in changing the basic character of society until Frederick the Great, very much in the spirit of Luther, made elementary education compulsory in Prussia in the 1780s. This put his country at the very forefront of social reform. It would be a century before the rest of Europe caught up with Prussified Germany.

Once again, we must not characterise Luther as the sole originator of a more enlightened attitude towards the rearing of children. It was a given among humanists that sons and even daughters should be encouraged to a genuine love of learning. Thomas More's household is often rightly pointed out as an example of the practical application of the principles advocated by the Spaniard, Ludovicus Vives. Yet, unlike Catholic reformers, Luther did not shrink from the social and religious implications of universal learning. He knew that widespread literacy would shake the existing rigid class structures. Specifically, he accepted that access to the vernacular Bible would turn semi-educated enthusiasts into amateur theologians. Yet, he was not unduly worried when cobblers and even housewives ventured into print on matters of doctrine and church order. More, on the other hand was appalled at the prospect of what might happen,

> When an hatter will go smatter
> In philosophy,
> Or a pedlar wax a meddler
> In theology.[6]

The Englishman probably saw more clearly than his Saxon contemporary that education was a tool of revolution; that it produced new ideas, challenged old conventions and stirred unruly ambitions. He was not alone among Catholic reactionaries who wanted to place social limits on learning and, particularly, to suppress the vernacular Scriptures. But even had Luther foreseen just how potent education would be in shaping western culture he would not have changed his message. He was not built for recanting.

But it was not just the *content* of the German Bible (and the other vernacular writings it inspired) that was formative of a national culture. Luther has been called, with some justification, 'the German Shakespeare'. He introduced, almost single-handedly, a language that was vigorous, colourful and expressive of subtle nuances. It was the forerunner of what would become High German. 'The first transregional unification of the German people was linguistic and cultural, centred round Luther's vernacular sermons, Bible, hymns and catechisms.'[7] Throughout sixteenth-century Europe people were regionally minded, identifying themselves with their village, town or shire, rather than with any wider socio-political reality. They spoke dialects which were so individually developed that, for example, a London tailor would find it almost impossible to understand a Yorkshire herdsman. In 1549 the men of South-west England rebelled against Thomas Cranmer's vernacular Prayer Book because its language was as obscure to them as the Latin of the old mass, which, for all its mystique, did, at least, have the advantage of familiarity. Luther's vernacular, based on the elegant language of the Saxon court, provided a medium which would serve preachers, poets, philosophers, journalists and men of science throughout the centuries to come. He launched it with an astonishing three million copies of his own works (excluding the Bible), which were in circulation before his death. A third of all German-language publications between 1520 and 1546 came from his pen. Nothing was more powerful in creating a sense of national identity and in providing a currency for the exchange of ideas. Moreover, the emergence of a means of intercourse which was not regarded as 'second class', in comparison with Latin, further distanced German people from Rome's domination of the world of scholarship. Of course, the development of printing would have, of itself, led to the emergence of standardised national languages but it was the insistence of Luther, taken up by other reformers, that the Christian faith should be 'understanded of the people' which gave the initial boost to the whole process.

Understanding was the key that unlocked the treasury of divine grace revealed in Scripture. Therefore, words were, for Luther and his spiritual descendants, of primary importance. One way of enabling people, especially the illiterate and semi-literate, to learn and retain the written fundamentals of faith was by song. Thus the close association of poetry, liturgy and music based on vernacular Scripture became probably the most obvious distinguishing mark of Protestant religious life and has remained so. Whatever we think of Salvation Army bands, gospel choirs, the performers of cathedral choral evensong or the purveyors of charismatic 'pop', the underlying element is music as the servant of word. Music for Luther was 'second only to the word of God' and, although hymnody was not unknown in the western medieval church, the tradition of congregational singing was never as developed as in the Orthodox East, and the history of hymns really begins with Luther's first collection, published in 1524. He used simple melodies, often setting verses to well-known folk tunes, but he did not turn his back on the more 'professional' liturgical chant of the old church. On the contrary, he encouraged the training of children to sing in choirs and he sponsored the founding of choral societies. His only stipulation was that the meaning of the words should not be obscured by over-elaborate melodic lines. Much Catholic worship had become extremely intricate in its use of complex counterpoint and for this Luther had no time. Hymn-singing became extremely popular in the Lutheran church but caught on only slowly in other evangelical communions. There would always be an element within evangelicalism which mistrusted 'ceremonial' and even the German Lutherans split over it in the eighteenth century. Calvinists were dismissive of Christian poetry because it departed from the pure word of God. The only concession they were prepared to make was the issuing of books of metrical psalms, settings of the Psalter. Yet, here, too, the hymn eventually forced its way into Sunday worship by virtue of its very popularity. Luther was the fountainhead of that rich stream of congregational singing to which writers such as Martin Rinkart, George Herbert, Isaac Watts, Charles Wesley and hundreds of writers contributed and whose works are *de rigueur* wherever Christians meet for worship.

But Luther's musical influence extended far beyond the provision of sacred song for untrained voices. Chorales and anthems were more demanding but adhered to the simple rule of music as a servant of text and thus came into being the Protestant choral traditions of northern Europe and the United States of America. The biblical oratorio was a natural development. Beginning in 1623 with Heinrich Schütz's *Easter Oratorio*, the tradition of dramatising the biblical narrative developed in the works of J. S. Bach, Handel, Haydn and Mendelssohn. It is not only in church music that the influence of Luther can be traced. In the princely courts of Germany where composers had to provide for the secular as well as religious requirements of their patrons the same principles of chaste, restrained, disciplined writing held sway in the salon as well as the chapel. Italian and French styles might lead fashion in the arts but baroque ebullience and overstatement would never dominate the music (or, indeed, the plastic arts) in Protestant countries. There has always existed an element of cultural restraint in Germany, the Netherlands, Britain and Scandinavia which distinguishes art in those countries from that which has developed in most Catholic lands.

Unlike other evangelical leaders, Luther was not anti religious art. Quite the contrary. He took a very close interest in the production of woodcuts to illustrate his writings, especially the Bible. He understood well the power of the printed or painted image. He was appalled by the iconoclastic outrages perpetrated by followers of Karlstadt, Zwingli and the radical 'prophets'. Writing against the Zwickau extremists, Luther demanded, 'If it is not a sin but good to have the image of Christ in my heart, why should it be a sin to have it in my eyes?' The radicals wanted to sweep away everything that was not explicitly approved in Scripture. Luther's attitude was fundamentally different: he would leave everything *in situ* unless it was explicitly *condemned* in Scripture. First install the Bible at the centre of church life, he insisted, and anything that did not accord with the divine word would gradually disappear without the need for violent campaigns of image-breaking. In nothing was the difference between the old faith and the new more obvious to ordinary people than in the appearance of church interiors. The purified buildings of Calvinists were little more than unadorned meeting halls. The Counter-Reformation deliberately went to the other extreme, stuffing places of worship with gilded reliquaries, overdecked altars, garish paintings and monumental sculptures whose writhing forms were intended to work mightily on the emotions.

This has encouraged over the centuries the simplistic equations, Catholic = aesthete and Protestant = philistine. The truth, of course, is much more complex. We tend to start from a position of admiration bordering on reverence for 'art', an attitude quite alien to our sixteenth-century forbears. Their approach was utilitarian. A painter or sculptor was employed to fill a space in church or chapel and the patrons felt under no obligation to preserve the resultant artefact 'for posterity'. A work might be removed or even destroyed when tastes changed, without the owners feeling any sense of sacrilege. For example, the brothers of Santa Maria delle Grazie in Milan knocked a doorway through the wall on which Leonardo's *Last Supper* was displayed, thus forever removing Christ's feet, and in a later age the whole painting was whitewashed over. There was a strong element of competition involved in the commissioning of works of art. Wealthy patrons wanted to employ the latest in-vogue artists and to be seen to be encouraging new techniques and styles. They did not hesitate to throw out old masterpieces to make room for new ones that would 'score' over their rivals. Religious devotion often took a back seat in such negotiations. Devotion was very much to the fore among the protestors who, for quite other reasons, swept away paintings and statues in iconoclastic frenzy. People touched by new truth were outraged at having been hitherto conned by old falsehood – by supposedly miracle-working statues or images of holy events which distorted Scripture or pictures depicting the fictitious legends of fictitious saints. Art lovers may deplore the loss of many medieval works but their disappearance is not entirely due to the reformers and certainly cannot be lain at Luther's door.

Biblical justification for attacks on images centred on the Decalogue proscription of 'graven images'. Discussion of precisely what this meant and whether adornment of churches constituted image-worship continued well into the next century. By the time theologians had stopped preoccupying themselves with such matters art had moved on. Throughout much of northern Europe it had become secularised (or freed from ecclesiastical restraint, according to your point of view) and masters devoted their talents to representing landscape, classical mythology, ladies and gentlemen of high fashion and even their horses.

The privileged class portrayed by Rubens, Van Dyck or Gainsborough was one Luther would have recognised, even approved of. Its members were part of an ordered, seemingly stable society and one which he saw no reason to challenge. His reading of the Bible and his experience of life combined to endorse the concept of an authoritarian, top-down world in which every individual had a vocation. This applied in the home as much as in the state and the workplace. Men were designed to be husbands and fathers; women to be wives and mothers. Celibacy was unnatural and led to scandal. Marriage was the ordained lot of most people. Sex was only permissible within marriage. Adultery, fornication and prostitution were sins. Apart from the banishing of virginity as a Christian virtue, there was little that was new in his fundamental teaching on relationships. But there was a warmth and humanity about his attitude which had been lacking in the sexual assumptions of the old church. The impression given and often stated in medieval pastoral direction was that sex between husband and wife was OK as long as they did not *enjoy* it too much. For Luther, passion properly directed within monogamous marriage was wholesome and good. Writing to congratulate a friend on his wedding, the reformer remarked, 'On the evening of the day when . . . you receive this letter, I shall also make love to my wife and so feel close to you.'

On the other hand, he was tough on illicit sexual activity. The old penitential system had recognised human weakness and made provision for it by means of the confessional and, for those who could afford it, the granting of papal or episcopal dispensation. Luther rejected what he considered as playing fast and loose with divine law and he also removed matrimonial legislation from church courts. He urged secular rulers to use their powers to create and enforce Christian moral standards. The prince's responsibility was to defend religion and virtue and punish vice. Luther called for harsh penalties against offences which threatened the sanctity of marriage and, by extension, the stability of society. In Calvin's Geneva matters were taken much further. In his determination to set up a godly commonwealth Calvin urged the magistrates to be utterly ruthless in rooting out evil: 'The law of God commands adulterers to be stoned . . . How much more vile and how much less excusable is our negligence nowadays, which cherishes adulteries by allowing them to go unpunished.'[8] It has to be said in favour of the Genevan authorities that they never acceded to Calvin's demand for the death penalty for adulterers but life in the 'godly republic' did approach police-state conditions. Citizens found themselves in trouble for dancing, singing lewd songs, using charms, telling fortunes, laughing during sermons and for daring to criticise Calvin and his ministerial colleagues. A seventy-year-old widow was even prosecuted for contracting marriage with a man forty-five years her junior (no room for toy boys in Geneva!). When spiritual earnestness was transferred from the life of the individual believer and made the basis of public morality Catholic legalism had simply been replaced by Protestant legalism. Puritanism was alien to Luther's spirit but his insistence on biblical standards in public life and on the comprehensive authority of the secular power were always open to this kind of distortion.

More positive was his emphasis on home and family life. His teaching provided the theological basis which underpinned Protestant bourgeois values for centuries. The evangelical minister's household became the model for all members of his flock. Just as he gathered wife, children and servants around him at mealtimes for prayer and exhortation from the word of God, so every leader of a household should act as 'bishop' in his own little 'diocese', bearing rule with firmness and compassion and ensuring that all in his care were brought up in 'the nurture and admonition of the Lord'.[9] The survival of many thousands of family Bibles from the sixteenth to nineteenth centuries throughout Europe, North America and ex-colonial territories testifies to the power of this vision of family life which became the bedrock of society during the years of western expansion.

Religious Aftermath

Whatever else it was, the Reformation was the world's biggest ever evangelical revival. That is, it called all members of the Christian world and, through the work of missionaries, the whole of humanity to sign up to the three fundamentals of evangelical faith: the primacy of Scripture, the centrality of the Cross and the necessity for personal conversion. Luther died a disappointed man because he believed that his message had failed to conquer the hearts and minds of many people. He was right – but only because he set himself high standards. With the benefit of hindsight we can see that religious revival is always limited in its impact and in its duration. German Pietism, the Methodist Revival in Britain, America's Great Awakening, the later movements associated with the names of Dwight Moody, William Booth, Billy Graham and others – they all eventually reached and passed their sell-by dates. Inevitably, zeal wanes, vision fades and vibrant churches become institutions. The old adage always holds good: 'a mission becomes a movement, a movement becomes a machine, a machine becomes a monument and a monument becomes a museum' – until woken up by the next revival.

If the Reformation did not achieve all that Luther hoped for it was for several reasons. The task was enormous and the resources minute. Europe's patterns of religious thought had to be fundamentally changed and there were very few trained ministers available to head up the work. Divisions within evangelical ranks did not help the spread of new religious ideas. Though the impact of the 'lost opportunity' at Marburg has been overemphasised, Catholic opponents certainly made a great deal of capital out of the reformers' internecine strife. However, the most potent enemies the Reformation faced were the determined opposition of organised Catholicism and the strength of subterranean folk religion, composed of superstition, pagan survival, ritualism and libertinism.

After Luther's death, the Council of Trent continued its halting course. Abandoned in 1547, it was reconvened in spring 1551 by a new pope, Julius III, and he was not interested in accommodations and compromises. Politics might be the art of the humanly possible. Religion remained the assertion of divine imperatives. Melancthon, still passionately committed to teasing out doctrinal formulas which might be acceptable to both sides, actually set out for Trent in May but got no farther than Nuremberg. By this point it had become clear to him and his colleagues that the Vatican had moved not one centimetre in the direction of solving fundamental issues of belief. The Lutherans would be permitted to present their confession at Trent but there would be no discussion of it. The Trent fathers were actually in full accord with Luther on the powers of councils: they could affirm the ancient faith and dispose of current deviations but could not create new doctrines. On this basis the insights of the reformers were finally and forever excluded from the creative process of defining belief. It was the victory of elector Maurice that had caused another adjournment in 1552 and the third and final session was not convened for a further decade. Under Pius IV the council was brought to a final conclusion in 1563.

One result of the ecumenical temper of the late twentieth century was the tendency among church historians to replace the term 'Counter-Reformation' with the friendlier 'Catholic Reformation'. Certainly Trent responded to evangelical and humanist criticism, while trying not to appear to be doing so. Religious and ethical initiatives were taken, aimed at putting the Catholic house in order. But for Rome *reform* always involved, as a priority, the assertion and defence of traditional doctrine, and contemporaries on both sides of the ecclesiastical fence saw very clearly that the council was, in reality, all about authority and power. The main Lutheran tenets were firmly dismissed and Pius IV ordered strict obedience to the decisions of the council on pain of excommunication. The Inquisition was given sharper teeth and an index of prohibited books was drawn up. Rome emerged from four decades of crisis with a new self-confidence. Successive popes had worn down the emperor, humanist protestors and spiritually minded reformists. They had won the battle against the conciliarists and emerged from the final session of Trent strengthened for the war against the evangelicals. The leaders of the Catholic church were now committed to waging that war with whatever weapons came to hand. The closing words of this marathon council were, 'Anathema to all heretics, anathema, anathema!'

Looking back on the years since 1520, we can see that the curia was faced with two lessons. One of them it learned well. The other it chose to ignore. The truth that Catholic leaders could scarcely fail to take on board was the urgent need for a spiritual revolution, particularly among the clergy. What they still could not grasp was that heresy could not be expunged by naked violence which was, in itself, a contradiction of the Gospel. The new pope, Pius V (1566–71), was an embodiment of the spirit of the Counter-Reformation. An ascetic of awesome personal devotion, he set his face firmly against corruption at all levels of church life. He was no respecter of persons and the procession of high-ranking ecclesiastics through the church courts sent a clear signal that complaints about nepotism, simony, non-residence and moral laxity were at last being taken seriously. He ordered the closure of Roman brothels, outlawed bullfighting (a proscription totally ignored in Spain) and, like Calvin, wanted to make adultery a capital offence. Laws were issued against profanity and the desecration of Sunday. Puritanism, as Pius demonstrated clearly, was not confined to the Protestant world. And Puritanism is positive as well as negative. It holds Christians to the high standards of their profession. The spirit of the Counter-Reformation disciplined parish priests and the members of religious communities. It reformed the penitential system, finally removing the hawking of indulgences, the issue which had provoked Luther's initial challenge. The post-Tridentine Roman church grasped the importance of educating the laity. New catechisms were issued and devotional aids were encouraged to fill the faith void which might otherwise suck in the growing quantity of evangelical propaganda.

But commendation of the devout was accompanied by harsher than ever condemnation of those identified as enemies of the faith. Pius 'cleansed' the Papal States of Jews (while permitting, for financial reasons, a colony to remain in Rome under humiliating, ghetto conditions). The pope emphasised the enhanced power of the Inquisition by instituting frequent *autos-da-fé* in Rome. Citizens were enjoined to watch these highly theatrical ceremonies which included among the offenders members of noble families, clergy and humanist scholars as well as ordinary people. Always these public trials ended with some of the condemned being beheaded and their bodies being consigned to the flames on the Campo di Fiori or in front of the Castel Sant'Angelo. Some were certainly burned alive. Needless to say many marked men and women, including several printers, did not wait for the knock on the door in the middle of the night. The reign of terror eased after the death of Pius in 1572 but the principle of expunging heresy by force remained firmly locked into the official thinking of the Catholic church. Its leaders firmly believed they were fighting for the soul of Christendom and that, therefore, any means to restoring 'truth' were not only justified but sanctified. Pius nerved Catholic rulers to carry out energetic purges and threatened anathema to any not prepared to shoulder this holy burden. This Catholic ayatollah issued fatwas licensing terrorism. He sanctioned assassination of Protestant leaders and, most famously, 'deposed' Elizabeth of England, discharging all her subjects from their political allegiance. In France, where the growth of the Huguenot minority caused the

royal government serious alarm, the regent, Catherine de Medici, authorised the murder of Protestant leaders in the capital on 24 August 1572. It
was a brutally cynical piece of realpolitik but what followed was much
more shocking. Given the lead by their political masters and their
consciences blunted by the bigotry of their priests, hundreds of French
Catholic communities resorted to mob rule and lynch law. Days of blood-
letting cost the lives of thousands of men, women and children. The significance, as Diarmaid MacCulloch points out, was that, whereas hitherto
wholesale slaughter had resulted from the power politics of princes, now,
'ordinary people were beginning to own the religious labels that the officially agreed confessions and the decisions of Councils were creating: they
found that they were Protestant, Catholic, Lutheran, Reformed'.[10]

Determined persecution, carried out with Machiavellian disregard for
ethical, religious or humanitarian considerations, usually succeeds – up to
a point. As a result of state pressure Protestantism declined in France, the
Empire and the southern Netherlands. Evangelical enclaves in Italy and
Spain were persecuted almost out of existence. But the new faith could
not be wholly eradicated. It was toughened by persecution. Huguenot families who remained in France obliged Henry IV to promulgate the Edict of
Nantes which gave them a significant measure of freedom. It remained in
force for almost a century until another determined Catholic monarch,
Louis XIV, inaugurated a further round of persecution. The migration and
permanent settlement of Protestant fugitives actually brought valued skills
and vitality to the communities which welcomed them.

Just when it seemed that Catholicism had, geographically, recovered
most of its lost ground in Europe, it found its position challenged in the
wider world. It was largely Protestant adventurers who conquered New
England and went on to expand westward as the United States of America
took shape. Catholics were a small minority in the new nation (in 1785
there were only 24 priests serving a denomination of some 24,000 people)
and the separation of church and state provided no opportunity for
Catholics to take their traditional route to power. It would be 1960 before
the USA had its first Catholic president. Elsewhere, Protestant churches
belatedly entered the mission field from the mid-eighteenth century. For
more than two centuries Catholic pioneers had had Asia and the Americas
virtually to themselves. Now Protestant preachers and teachers followed
merchants, explorers and empire-builders into 'heathen lands afar',
frequently setting up rival mission stations in opposition to those run by
Catholic priests.

Confrontation with animism, ancestor worship, shamanism and other alien belief systems should have helped Christian propagandists to get their own differences into perspective. Notoriously it did not. The uncompromising positions taken up by Luther and his equally truculent Romanist opponents dominated church life in Europe and were carried abroad in the essential baggage of the missionaries. What Reformation controversialists could not see and what historians, taken up with minutiae of the confessional conflict, have often been slow to grasp is that European Catholics and Protestants alike were facing the same basic problems – problems not dissimilar to those confronting overseas missionaries: ignorance, the pervasive influence of ancient folk religion and apathy. Luther was very far from being the only pastor to be frustrated by the darkness of prevailing culture and its resistance to the light of the Gospel. A Jesuit working in the Bordeaux area in the 1550s complained that the inhabitants lived 'like beasts of the field. One can find people over fifty years old and more who have never heard of mass, nor heard a single word of faith.' The grumble of an English Puritan about his flock a century later sounds remarkably similar: 'Ask them the meaning of the articles of faith, of the petitions in the Lord's Prayer, or of other common points in catechism, and mark their answers: you shall see them so shuffle and fumble, speak half words and half sentences, so hack and hew that you would think verily they were born stark naturals and idiots.'[11] These were not lone voices. They described a widespread phenomenon; there were vast numbers of unevangelised men and women who never attended mass or listened to sermons and whose moral standards were lamentably uninformed by the Christian revelation. The real battle was not between true faith and false faith, but between faith and unfaith. Yet, even that is an oversimplification. There was a wide overlap between Christianity and magic. People resorted to witches, to wisemen who prescribed herbal remedies to be applied when the heavenly bodies were propitiously aligned and with the repetition of Aves and other religious mantras. The confusion of beliefs defies classification. And, of course, people were not helped towards either Catholic or Protestant conventional doctrines when their advocates were preoccupied with castigating each other, when 'official' religion was whatever happened to appeal to the reigning monarch or when the parish church was served by a bumbling incompetent or not served by an absentee incumbent.

If we have to conclude with some 'grand' statement about Luther and his place in history – and I believe we do – then that statement has to do with the rise and fall of the Bible.

In the West the dominant literary source has been the Bible and the Christian idiom derived from it. Historians and philosophers have tended to underplay this fact and for that reason have underappreciated the power of the Christian metanarrative in Western intellectual life. The abandonment of that metanarrative, which has occurred recently, rapidly and violently, represents an incapacity of history to produce a product meaningful to the Western public at large . . . the present moment presents a crisis or a limit of Western historical consciousness.[12]

Luther himself would have insisted that whatever changes had come over western civilisation in his lifetime were not his doing but had been achieved by the word of God. In this he was right. Making the Bible available to all in vernacular languages was Luther's most enduring legacy, a legacy that was both rich and powerful. The open Bible was a revolutionary document. It was not even necessary for its message to be *proclaimed*. Preaching was, of course, a characteristic element of the Reformation but, for the first time in history, people could sign up to a movement – evangelical Christianity – simply by retreating into their own chambers and reading the New Testament for themselves. We might almost say that the human catalyst of the Reformation was not Martin of Wittenberg, but Paul of Tarsus. Thousands of uneducated men and women set about learning to read for the specific purpose of getting to grips with the Scriptures. In point of fact, literacy was not an essential. Labourers and artisans congregated in small groups in order to listen to 'gospellers' reciting the sacred text. John Foxe recorded of the Marian martyr, John Maundrel, that, though unable to read himself, he yet possessed a pocket testament which he produced when in the company of learned, devout men, so that they might instruct him from its pages, 'having a very good memory, so that he could recite by heart most places of the New Testament'.[13] Maundrel was very far from being unique. Another English convert, Henry Hart, testified that it was the written word which had transformed his life:

> . . . it hath pleased the eternal God which separated me from my mother's womb to lighten the inward eyes of my mind with his grace, and through the knowledge of his word and working of his holy spirit, to work a perfect repentance in me and amendment of my former life . . .[14]

Thousands of people all over Europe were undergoing the same experience – and millions more would undergo it in the following centuries. It is this individual and communal and gradually extending phenomenon of spiritual enlightenment that *is* the Reformation. It was new. It was exciting. It was liberating. It transformed the way many people (including significant numbers of intellectual and political leaders) thought and behaved. It became a major thread in the fabric of western culture. Of course, the collection of texts we call the 'Bible' had existed, more or less in its present form, ever since Jerome had made his Latin translation a thousand years before Luther launched his challenge. Its message had changed innumerable medieval lives. Parts of it had formed the basis of pastoral instruction and devotional life. Over the centuries would-be reformers had used it as the basis for their critiques of the establishment. From time to time vernacular versions had appeared. In Germany, France, Italy, Spain and the Netherlands Bibles and Bible fragments had existed in translation for three hundred years and more before the Reformation. Some had been produced by heretical scholars but others had the blessing of local ecclesiastical authorities. They had given rise to deep devotion to conventional religion and to ecstatic extremism. By and large, when Bible study resulted in dubious doctrines or excessive displays of holy zeal the Church was able to deal with the problem through its pastoral and its repressive offices. But, when all this has been admitted, the fact remains that for a millennium the Bible was the Church's best kept secret. When that secret was revealed its impact was explosive; its results incalculably multifarious.

Scholarly interpretation and re-interpretation over the last half-century has reached the point at which this impact is generally downplayed. One reason for this is the exaggerated, cause-and-effect claims that some historians have made for the Reformation.

> Once it has been reclassified as a transition rather than a revolution, the revolutionary changes commonly said to have flowed from it – deism, secularism and atheism; individualism and rationalism; the rise of capitalism and the decline of magic; the scientific revolution and the American dream; the origins of civil liberties and shifts in the global balance of power – all appear less convincing as time goes by.[15]

Certainly, human history is far too complex for us to draw simple lines linking, for example, the commercial and colonial expansion of Protestant

England and Holland in the eighteenth century and the devotion of their ruling and entrepreneurial classes to Calvinist doctrine. Yet, in revising revisionism, the words 'baby' and 'bathwater' spring readily to mind. There *are* certain developments which can be directly related to responses to biblical principles. Geneva became the leading producers of fine time-pieces and scientific instruments because goldsmiths and jewellers deflected their talents away from the production of 'vanities' which pandered to human pride. Northern painters developed landscape art and portraiture because patronage for religious icons was, it was widely believed, contrary to Scripture. The so-called 'Protestant work ethic' was a reality. For, if we are to accept the prudery and self-righteousness often levelled against Bible-toting Puritans, we must also accept the obverse of that coin: the seriousness, industry and abhorrence of frivolity which marked their approach to all aspects of life, including business. This is not to claim that Catholic merchants and agnostic industrialists were not also hard working. I simply make the point that the prevailing ethos in Protestant lands derived from, or was deeply influenced by, the ethics of the Bible.

'Progress' is a word of which we have rightly become suspicious but if we reflect briefly on what most people would accept as improvements to the human condition – the abolition of slavery, penal reform, universal education, factory legislation and the like – we must acknowledge the debt modern society owes to principles adduced from the Christian scriptures and the courageous men and women who have championed those princi-ples – often at great personal cost. To take one, little known example, consider the career of William Hone (1780–1842). He was so strictly brought up that the only book he was allowed to read as a child was the Bible. His thinking was, therefore, saturated by it. It may have been literary deprivation that caused him to choose the career of bookseller. It was not a wise choice, for he was a poor businessman. This was because he devoted an increasing amount of time to championing numerous social causes. Hone was moved to indignation by the case of Elizabeth Fenning, a servant girl convicted on what many believed to be tainted evidence of the attempted murder of her employers and subsequently hanged. He devoted his energies to researching other possible miscarriages of justice and to berating the judiciary:

> If the people are not moved into some indignation at the neglect of their *soi-disant* guardians the healthful spirit of society is defunct, and the community is degenerating into a base rabble . . . On the other

hand . . . if the people at large should be convinced [of the extent of corruption in high places], it is barely possible that polite people may find the hanging of an innocent person now and then as something more than a bagatelle.[16]

This vociferous campaigner made himself such a nuisance that he was prosecuted before Lord Chief Justice Ellenborough. The jury acquitted and Ellenborough was so incensed by their 'disgraceful' behaviour that he tendered his resignation – an action which only served to underscore Hone's opinion of the bench. This champion of the little man went on to publish numerous tracts attacking establishment corruption, demanding greater press freedom and supporting radical reform of such institutions as lunatic asylums. Hone was little more than a voice in the wilderness. He scarcely merits a footnote in the history books. That is precisely the point. What is relevant is not how significant he was in the process of social reform or even that he was an out and out evangelical. Hone was one of an army of men and women whose sense of justice and injustice, right and wrong were rooted in the Bible. There have been countless other philanthropists who claimed no spiritual motivation for their activities. Yet they, too, had absorbed into their psyches an ethical and religious code conveyed through words listened to, recited and learned at home, in school, at church and in public ceremonies. That code existed *in book form*. It needed no priestly caste to mediate it. It was not dependent on the correct performance of rituals for its efficacy. It was freely available in the language of everyday speech and, until relatively recently, most homes possessed a copy. The language and ideas of the Bible have permeated the common culture of Protestant lands in a way that is not true of Catholic or non-Christian societies.

Post-Tridentine Catholicism found it difficult to deal with the notion of vernacular Scripture because it set up a rival authority to the hierarchy. One party at the council identified modern translations as the 'mothers of heresy'. Yet Rome had no alternative to trying to beat the evangelicals at their own game. Their embarrassment is clear from the preface to the Rheims-Douai English version of the Bible, begun in 1582 and not completed until 1610:

We do not publish upon erroneous opinion of necessity, that the holy Scriptures should always be in our mother tongue, or that they ought or were ordained by God to be read indifferently of all . . . but upon special consideration of the present time, state and condition of our country, unto which divers things are either necessary, or profitable and medicinable now, that otherwise in the peace of the church were neither much requisite, nor perchance wholly tolerable.

Trent's answer to the clamour of humanist scholars as well as concerned pastors for an authoritative text that could be used to refute the errors of the heretics was the sanctioning of a revised version of the Vulgate. The committee set up for the purpose took a quarter of a century and did the job well. Too well. Pope Sixtus V was horrified with the revisers' work. They had corrected such a host of inaccuracies that the reliability of the venerable Jerome's masterpiece seemed to be seriously called in question. Sixtus himself set about a scissors and paste job. This compromise was never issued because the pope died within months of its completion. His successor, Gregory XIV, ordered a revision of the revision of the revision and it was this text, though still far from perfect, which was issued in 1592 by Clement VIII and became the church's official Bible for three centuries.

By the middle of the seventeenth century vernacular Scriptures sanctioned by Rome had become available throughout Europe. But the authorities still tried to restrict their use and availability. The lower orders of society were discouraged from reading or were forbidden to read them without direction from their priests. Teaching orders such as the Jesuits instructed students in the 'proper' understanding of Bible passages and new translations, like the earlier Protestant Bibles, all carried official glosses. When the Jansenists, a group of French radical Catholics based in Paris, suggested that all lay people should be encouraged to study the Bible for themselves and that to deny the holy book to them was a form of excommunication the very idea was denounced by the pope as:

> False, captious, ill-sounding, offensive to pious ears, scandalous, pernicious, rash, injurious to the church and its practices, not only outrageous against the church but even against the secular powers, seditious, impious, blasphemous, suspected of heresy and savouring of heresy . . .

Throughout the Protestant world new translations proliferated in the sixteenth and seventeenth centuries. From Calvinist Geneva came Bibles in French and Italian for home consumption and also for export to regions where vernacular editions could not be printed. There also appeared Latin translations for use by scholars concerned to confront the Vulgate on its own ground. Geneva was also the home of what became for fifty years the most popular English Bible. Produced by refugee scholars during the reign of Mary Tudor, the Geneva Bible, replete with evangelical glosses and marginalia, was the main formative influence in the emergence of the Elizabethan church. But it was not welcomed by all and James I, determined to achieve peace and unity in his new kingdom, commanded a new translation to be made which would take into account the work of earlier translators, incorporate the very latest critical thinking and which would be devoid of all contentious apparatus criticus. Thus, the 'Authorised' or 'King James' version came into being, a book which was to have an impact on the English language second only to that of Shakespeare. A book that would be carried over the oceans to newly settled or conquered lands in North America, India, Australia, New Zealand and Africa which were 'opened up' to British culture. By 1650 the Scandinavian countries and the Dutch Republic all had 'official' translations approved by government authority, used in all churches and popular with the people.

Within a few decades of Luther's death, therefore, all Europe was awash with Bibles in contemporary languages. They came in all shapes and sizes, perhaps the most significant being the pocket testaments that the devout could carry with them at all times so as never to be parted from the 'lively oracles of God'. As the Christian mission extended outwards from its European base a priority for its leaders was always the provision of the sacred text in words that could be understood by new converts. By 2003 the Bible had been translated, in whole or part, into 2,303 languages. This was the richest part of Martin Luther's legacy. He bequeathed to the peoples of the world a collection of religious writings and invested them with supreme authority (or, as he would have said, recognised the supreme authority they manifestly possessed). The descendants of his hottest critics were eventually obliged to concede that ordinary believers and seekers had the ability and the right to search the Scriptures for themselves in their quest for meaning in life. The foreword to the Roman Catholic Jerusalem Bible, Popular Edition (1974) noted:

... the Bible is not only for students undergoing a formal course of study, and there has been an immediate demand for an edition ... which would bring the modern clarity of the text before the ordinary reader, and open to him the results of modern researches without either justifying them at length in literary or historical notes or linking them with doctrinal studies.

It was less than a ringing endorsement of the primacy of Scripture but it was one that would have been welcomed by the man who declared at Worms that he would regard nothing as essential for salvation that was not revealed in the Bible.

Today's western societies have dethroned the Bible and in so doing they have curtained off one of our windows on the past. Deprived of this vital frame of reference it is difficult now for students to understand, not just the religious conflicts of four hundred years ago, but also such cultural landmarks as *The Eisenheim Altarpiece*, *Paradise Lost*, *The St Matthew Passion*, Rembrandt's *Return of the Prodigal Son* or Bunyan's *Pilgrim's Progress*. This puts historians at a disadvantage. We must try to help our readers see that what might to modern eyes seem like futile disputes over obscure points of theology actually *mattered* to those engaged in them; were issues of life, death and eternal destiny. The historiography of the Reformation was, for long years, bedevilled by sectarian commitment. Catholic and Protestant writers took their stand on one side or the other, fighting again the battles of long ago. We are now spared such diatribes. Yet can we really claim to be better off in the hands of agnostic historians who attempt to hover impartially above the field of conflict? Anyone who thinks he can write dispassionately about the Reformation from the superior vantage point of sophisticated unbelief runs the risk of belittling the subject and trying magisterially to cut its prime movers down to size. We cannot do that with Martin Luther. We must feel the force of his passion because, if we do not, we have not got close to the real man. Let us, in conclusion, allow that passion to speak to us one more time as Luther addresses us from the heart of the storm he whipped up about what it was that held together all his thinking, and teaching and arguing and praying and loving and hating and being:

> God's word cannot be without God's people, and God's people cannot be without God's word ... For it is the word of God which builds the Church ... where that is heard, where baptism, the sacrament of the altar, and the forgiveness of sins are administered there hold fast and conclude most certainly that there is the house of God and that there is the gate of heaven.[17]

Notes

Introduction

[1] H. A. Oberman, *Luther: Man Between God and the Devil*, New Haven, 1989, Preface.

Chapter 1

[1] *Luther's Works,** Vol. 54, *Table Talk* (trs. T. G. Tappert), 1967, p. 178
[2] K. Thomas, *Religion and the Decline of Magic*, 1971, p. 35
[3] Thomas à Kempis, *The Imitation of Christ*, Book 3, Chapter 48, pp. 2–3
[4] P. Smith, *The Life and Letters of Martin Luther*, 1911, p. 4
[5] See D. K. Siggins, 'Luther and the Catholic Preachers of his Youth', in G. Yule, ed., *Luther: Theologian for Catholics and Protestants*, Edinburgh, 1985, for an excellent summary of the content of contemporary preaching around 1500
[6] *The Trial of Jeanne d'Arc*, trs. W. P. Barrett, New York, 1932, pp. 320–1
[7] LW, Vol. 54, pp. 473, 150–1
[8] Ibid., p. 69

Chapter 2

[1] See J. Huizinga, *The Waning of the Middle Ages*, 1924, p. 24 (My translation)
[2] F. Braudel, *The Mediterranean and the Mediterranean World in the Age of Philip II* (trs. S. Reynolds, ed. R. Ollard, 1992, p. 80
[3] P. Villari, *Life and Times of Savonarola* (trs. L. Villari), 1888, p. 126
[4] Ibid., p. 298
[5] Ibid., p. 330
[6] Ibid., pp. 518–19
[7] L. W. Forster, *Selections from Conrad Celtis*, Cambridge, 1948, pp. 46–7
[8] See P. A. Russell, *Lay Theology in the Reformation*, Cambridge, 1986, p. 51
[9] F. M. Dostoevsky, *The Brothers Karamazov* (trs. S. S. Kosteliansky), 1930, pp. 11–12

* Hereafter LW.

[10] L. Febvre, *The Problem of Unbelief in the Sixteenth Century*, Cambridge, Massachusetts, 1982, p. 351

[11] For a full description of pre-Reformation Strasbourg, see L. J. Abray, *The People's Reformation*, Oxford, 1985, pp. 21ff

[12] F. Vandenbroucke, in J. Leclercq, F. Vandenbroucke and L. Bouyer, eds, *A History of Christian Spirituality*, Vol. II, 1970, pp. 497–8

[13] S. Ozment, *The Age of Reform, 1250–1550*, New Haven, 1980, p. 199

[14] Kunstmuseum, Öffentliche Sammlung, Basel

[15] See R. W. Chambers, *Thomas More*, 1935, p. 90

[16] Acts 17.21

Chapter 3

[1] Matthew 10.37–39

[2] See R. H. Fife, *The Revolt of Martin Luther*, New York, 1957, p. 92

[3] *LW*, Vol. 54, p. 156

[4] *LW*, Vol. 48, *Letters*, ed. G. G. Krodel, Philadelphia, 1963, pp. 331–2

[5] *LW*, Vol. 44, *The Christian in Society*, ed. J. Atkinson, Philadelphia, 1966, p. 328

[6] *LW*, Vol. 54, *Table Talk*, ed. T. G. Tappert, 1967, pp. 353–4

[7] See G. Rupp, *The Righteousness of God*, 1953, p. 93

[8] Ibid., p. 103

[9] *LW*, Vol. 54, p. 85

[10] See G. Rupp, op. cit., p. 104. It is now almost sixty years since Gordon Rupp delivered the Birkbeck Lectures on which *The Righteousness of God* is based but I do not believe that his careful exposition of Luther's spiritual crisis has been surpassed and I have followed Rupp closely in this account.

[11] *LW*, Vol. 48, *Letters*, ed. G. G. Krodel, 1963, p. 9

[12] G. Rupp, op. cit., p. 118

[13] D. C. Steinmetz, *Luther and Staupitz*, Durham, North Carolina, 1980, p. 33

[14] G. Rupp, op. cit., p. 119

[15] *LW*, Vol. 48, *Letters*, p. 7

Chapter 4

[1] See M. Brecht, *Martin Luther: His Road to Reformation*, Philadelphia, 1985, p. 128 and R. Marius, *Martin Luther: The Christian Between God and Death*, Cambridge, Massachusetts, 1999, p. 86

[2] *LW*, Vol. 48, pp. 21–2

[3] Ibid., p. 28

[4] G. Rupp, op.cit., p. 122

[5] *LW*, Vol. 48, *Letters*, pp. 12–13

[6] *LW*, Vol. 48, *Letters*, p. 14

[7] Ibid.

[8] G. Rupp, op. cit., p. 122

[9] II Corinthians 5.21

[10] G. Shepherd, 'English Versions of the Scripture before Wycliffe', in G. W. H. Lampe, ed. *Cambridge History of the Bible*, II, Cambridge, 1969, p. 363

[11] W. A. Pantin, *The English Church in the Fourteenth Century*, 1962, pp. 132–3

[12] *LW*, Vol. 54, *Table Talk*, pp. 46–7

[13] *LW*, Vol. 48, *Letters*, pp. 24–6

[14] *LW*, Vol. 54, p. 48

[15] Philippians 3.4–9

[16] *LW*, Vol. 48, *Letters*, p. 42

Chapter 5

[1] See R. Bainton, *Here I Stand*, Nashville, 1950, p. 78; M. Brecht, op. cit., pp. 182–3
[2] LW, Vol. 48, *Letters*, p. 108
[3] E. Vandiver, R. Keen and T. D. Frazel, eds, *Luther's Lives*, Manchester, 2002, p. 19
[4] See P. A. Russell, *Lay Theology in the Reformation*, Cambridge, 1986, p. 126
[5] D. Erasmus, *The Praise of Folly*, trs. C. H. Miller, New Haven, 1979, p. 95
[6] LW, Vol. 48, *Letters*, p. 40
[7] See H. Boehmer, *Martin Luther: Road to Reformation*, 1957, p. 213
[8] Ibid., p. 270

Chapter 6

[1] LW, Vol. 48, *Letters*, p. 98
[2] Ibid., p. 100
[3] Ibid.
[4] H. Boehmer, op. cit., p. 225
[5] Ibid., pp. 216–17
[6] See H. Boehmer, op. cit., p. 246
[7] LW, Vol. 48, *Letters*, pp. 101–2
[8] Ibid., p. 107
[9] H. Boehmer, op. cit., p. 272
[10] LW, Vol. 48, *Letters*, p. 113

Chapter 7

[1] See H. Boehmer, op. cit., pp. 282–3
[2] LW, Vol. 48, p. 120
[3] Ibid., p. 110
[4] Acts 17.21
[5] R. Bainton, *Here I Stand*, New York, 1950, p. 116
[6] Ibid., p. 117
[7] R. Marius, *Martin Luther, The Christian Between God and Death*, Harvard, 1999, pp. 184–5
[8] LW, 48, *Letters*, p. 142
[9] LW, Vol. 48, p. 304
[10] I Corinthians 15.5
[11] R. H. Fife, *The Revolt of Martin Luther*, New York, 1957, p. 446
[12] A. G. Dickens, *The German Nation and Martin Luther*, 1974, p. 121
[13] All quotations from this work are from LW, Vol. 44, *The Christian in Society I*, pp. 123 ff.
[14] Ibid., p. 209
[15] I Peter 2.9; Revelation 5.9–10
[16] LW, Vol. 44, p. 129
[17] Ibid., p. 130
[18] Ibid., p. 132
[19] Ibid., p. 134
[20] Ibid., p. 141
[21] Ibid., p. 158
[22] Ibid., p. 175
[23] See A. G. Dickens and W. R. D. Jones, *Erasmus the Reformer*, 1994, pp. 119–20
[24] G. Rupp, op. cit., p. 313
[25] H. Boehmer, op. cit., p. 335

Chapter 8

[1] See A. Wheatcroft, *The Habsburgs: Embodying Empire*, 1995, pp. 117–18
[2] See R. Bainton, op. cit., p. 172
[3] Cf., R. W. Scribner, *For the Sake of Simple Folk: Popular Propaganda for the German Reformation*, Oxford, 1994, pp. 20 ff.
[4] LW, Vol. 32, *Career of the Reformer*, p. 111
[5] Matthew 10.34–5
[6] Ibid., pp. 111–2
[7] See R. Marius, op. cit., p. 292
[8] Ibid., p. 294

Chapter 9

[1] LW, Vol. 49, *Letters*, p. 12
[2] LW, Vol. 48, *Letters*, pp. 208–9
[3] H. Bornkamm, *Luther in Mid-career, 1521–1530*, 1983, pp. 2, 12
[4] Ibid., p. 4.
[5] G. Rupp, *The Righteousness of God*, 1953, p. 247
[6] LW, Vol. 32, *The Career of the Reformer*, pp. 220–1
[7] Romans 7.25–8.1
[8] John Foxe, *Acts and Monuments*, 1837–41 ed., IV, p. 218
[9] LW, Vol. 48, *Letters*, p. 232
[10] Ibid., pp. 234, 257
[11] Ibid., pp. 284, 287–8
[12] Ibid., p. 351
[13] Cf. N. Cohn, *The Pursuit of the Millennium*, 1970, pp. 237, 239
[14] LW, Vol. 48, p. 367
[15] Ibid., pp. 380–1

Chapter 10

[1] LW, Vol. 48, pp. 366–72
[2] Ibid., pp. 389–90
[3] Ibid., p. 396
[4] Ibid., p. 392
[5] LW, Vol. 49, pp. 11–12
[6] Ibid., pp. 50–1
[7] See J. I. Packer and O. R. Johnston, eds, *The Bondage of the Will*, 1957, p. 26
[8] Ibid., p. 66
[9] Ibid., p. 90
[10] Ibid., p. 262
[11] LW, Vol. 48, p. 40
[12] Ibid., p. 217
[13] Ibid., p. 271
[14] Ibid., p. 63
[15] See N. Cohn, op. cit., p. 244
[16] LW, Vol. 40, *Church and Ministry*, p. 57
[17] LW, Vol. 49, p. 73
[18] LW, Vol. 49, p. 82
[19] See P. A. Russell, *Lay Theology in the Reformation*, Cambridge, 1986, pp. 190ff.
[20] See J. Courvoisier, *Zwingli, A Reformed Theologian*, 1964, p. 17
[21] LW, Vol. 49, p. 110
[22] LW, Vol. 4, *Church and Ministry II*, p. 81

Chapter 11

[1] LW, Vol. 49, pp. 109–10
[2] Cf.,T. A. Brady, 'The Reformation of the Common Man', in C. Scott Dixon (ed.), *The German Reformation: The Essential Readings*, 1999, p. 110
[3] N. Cohn, op. cit., pp. 247–8
[4] See R. Marius, op. cit., p. 431
[5] LW, Vol. 49, p. 123
[6] See H. Bornkamm, *Luther in Mid-career*, 1983, p. 404
[7] LW, Vol. 49, p. 117
[8] See H. Bornkamm, op. cit., p. 409
[9] LW, Vol. 49, p. 117
[10] Matthew 6.33
[11] LW, Vol. 54, *Table Talk*, p. 194

Chapter 12

[1] LW, Vol. 49, p. 256
[2] See M. Brecht, *Martin Luther – Shaping and Defining the Reformation, 1521–1532*, 1990, p. 311
[3] See C. Hibbert, *Rome: The Biography of a City*, 1985, pp. 158–9
[4] LW, Vol. 49, pp. 193–4
[5] Ibid., pp. 248–9
[6] J. N. Figgis, *Churches in the Modern State*, 1931, p. 63

Chapter 13

[1] See H. Bornkamm, op. cit., p. 531
[2] LW, Vol. 49, p. 236
[3] LW, Vol. 38, *Word and Sacrament*, pp. 88–9
[4] LW, Vol. 34, *Career of the Reformer IV*, pp. 39–40
[5] LW, Vol. 49, p. 268
[6] Ibid., pp. 270–1

Chapter 14

[1] LW, Vol. 54, *Table Talk*, p. 196
[2] II Corinthians 7.10
[3] Exodus 20.2
[4] LW, Vol. 54, pp. 268, 111, 165, 212, 160, 71, 22, 75
[5] See R. Bainton, op. cit., p. 343
[6] Ibid., pp. 346–7
[7] See H. Bornkamm, op. cit., p. 478
[8] LW, Vol. 47, *The Christian in Society*, p. 35
[9] Ibid., p. 38
[10] Ibid., p. 45
[11] Ibid., p. 55

Chapter 15

[1] LW, Vol. 50, *Letters III*, p. 190
[2] Ibid., p. 111
[3] LW, Vol. 54, p. 382

[4] LW, Vol. 50, p. 39
[5] M. Brecht, *Martin Luther: Shaping and Defining the Reformation*, p. 425
[6] LW, Vol. 50, pp. 179–80
[7] Ibid., pp. 205–6
[8] Ibid., p. 83
[9] See R. Bainton, op. cit., pp. 327–8
[10] LW, Vol. 54, pp. 42–3
[11] Ibid., p. 408

Chapter 16

[1] R. Bainton, op. cit., p. 379
[2] LW, Vol. 50, pp. 84–5
[3] Ibid., pp. 158–9
[4] LW, Vol. 54, p. 333
[5] LW, Vol. 50, p. 245
[6] Ibid., p. 246
[7] LW, Vol. 47, p. 259
[8] Ibid., pp. 263–4
[9] M. Brecht, *Martin Luther – The Preservation of the Church, 1532–1546*, 1993, p. 243
[10] See R. Bainton, op. cit., p. 343
[11] LW, Vol. 50, pp. 238–9
[12] LW, Vol. 54, pp. 422–3
[13] I Kings 19.10,4
[14] See M. Brecht, op. cit., pp. 272 ff.
[15] LW, Vol. 50, p. 294
[16] Ibid., p. 302
[17] *The Last Days of Luther by Justus Jonas, Michael Coelius and Others* (trs. M. Ebon), New York, 1970, pp. 96–7

Chapter 17

[1] C. V. Wedgwood, *The Thirty Years War*, 1938, p. 526
[2] See E. Weymar, 'Ernst Moritz Arndt', in *Das Parlament*, May 1960, p. 322
[3] For concise studies of Luther's impact on European politics, see T. A. Brady, 'The Political Masks of Martin Luther', *History Today*, November 1983, pp. 27 ff., and R. Kastner, 'The Reformer and Reformation Anniversaries', *History Today*, November 1963, pp. 22 ff.
[4] J. Barzun, *From Dawn to Decadence: 500 Years of Western Cultural Life*, 2001, pp. 3–4
[5] S. Ozment, *The Reformation in the Cities*, 1975, p. 116
[6] Thomas More, *A merry jest how a Sergeant would play the Friar*, see R. W. Chambers, *Thomas More*, 1976 ed., p. 90
[7] S. Ozment, *A Mighty Fortress*, 2005, p. 88
[8] J. Calvin, *Commentary on Genesis*, in *Works*, Brunswick, 1863–1900, Vol. 23, p. 499
[9] Ephesians 6.4
[10] D. MacCulloch, *Reformation*, 2003, p. 338
[11] See G. Parker, *Empire, War and Faith in Early Modern Europe*, 2002, pp. 237–8; F. Fernández-Armesto, in F. Fernández-Armesto and D. Wilson, *Reformation*, 1996, pp. 171–2
[12] K. E. Hendrickson, 'The Big Problem with History: Christianity and the Crisis of Meaning', *Historically Speaking*, March/April 2006, p. 25
[13] J. Foxe, *Actes and Monuments*, S. R. Cattley, ed., 1839, pp. 102–3
[14] Cf., J. W. Martin, *Religious Radicals in Tudor England*, 1989, p. 75
[15] F. Fernández-Armesto, op. cit., p. 277
[16] See V. A. C. Gatrell, *The Hanging Tree*, Oxford, 1994, p. 367
[17] See G. Rupp, op. cit., p. 321

The Ninety-five Theses

or

Disputation on the Power and Efficacy of Indulgences

(LW. Vol.31, pp. 25–33)

Out of love and zeal for truth and the desire to bring it to light, the following theses will be publicly discussed at Wittenberg under the chairmanship of the reverend father Martin Luther, Master of Arts and Sacred Theology and regularly appointed Lecturer on these subjects at that place. He requests that those who cannot be present to debate orally with us will do so by letter.

In the Name of Our Lord Jesus Christ. Amen.

1. When our Lord and Master Jesus Christ said, 'Repent' [Matt. 4.17], He willed the entire life of believers to be one of repentance.
2. This word cannot be understood as referring to the sacrament of penance, that is, confession and satisfaction, as administered by the clergy.
3. Yet it does not mean solely inner repentance; such inner repentance is worthless unless it produces various outward mortifications of the flesh.
4. The penalty of sin remains as long as the hatred of self, that is, true inner repentance, until our entrance into the kingdom of heaven.
5. The pope neither desires nor is able to remit any penalties except those imposed by his own authority or that of the canons.
6. The pope cannot remit any guilt, except by declaring and showing that it has been remitted by God; or, to be sure, by remitting guilt in cases reserved to his judgment. If his right to grant remission in

these cases were disregarded, the guilt would certainly remain unforgiven.

7. God remits guilt to no one unless at the same time He humbles him in all things and makes him submissive to His vicar, the priest.

8. The penitential canons are imposed only on the living, and, according to the canons themselves, nothing should be imposed on the dying.

9. Therefore the Holy Spirit through the pope is kind to us insofar as the pope in his decrees always makes exception of the article of death and of necessity.

10. Those priests act ignorantly and wickedly who, in the case of the dying, reserve canonical penalties for purgatory.

11. Those tares of changing the canonical penalty to the penalty of purgatory were evidently sown while the bishops slept [Matt. 13.25].

12. In former times canonical penalties were imposed, not after, but before absolution, as tests of true contrition.

13. The dying are freed by death from all penalties, are already dead as far as the canon laws are concerned, and have a right to be released from them.

14. Imperfect piety or love on the part of the dying person necessarily brings with it great fear; and the smaller the love, the greater the fear.

15. This fear or horror is sufficient in itself, to say nothing of other things, to constitute the penalty of purgatory, since it is very near the horror of despair.

16. Hell, purgatory, and heaven seem to differ the same as despair, fear, and assurance of salvation.

17. It seems as though for the souls in purgatory fear should necessarily decrease and love increase.

18. Furthermore, it does not seem proved, either by reason or Scripture, that souls in purgatory are outside the state of merit, that is, unable to grow in love.

19. Nor does it seem proved that souls in purgatory, at least not all of them, are certain and assured of their own salvation, even if we ourselves may be entirely certain of it.

20. Therefore the pope, when he uses the words 'plenary remission of all penalties', does not actually mean 'all penalties', but only those imposed by himself.

21. Thus those indulgence preachers are in error who say that a man is absolved from every penalty and saved by papal indulgences.

22. As a matter of fact, the pope remits to souls in purgatory no penalty which, according to canon law, they should have paid in this life.

23. If remission of all penalties whatsoever could be granted to anyone at all, certainly it would be granted only to the most perfect, that is, to very few.

24. For this reason most people are necessarily deceived by that indiscriminate and high-sounding promise of release from penalty.

25. That power which the pope has in general over purgatory corresponds to the power which any bishop or curate has in a particular way in his own diocese or parish.

26. The pope does very well when he grants remission to souls in purgatory, not by the power of the keys, which he does not have, but by way of intercession for them.

27. They preach only human doctrines who say that as soon as the money clinks into the money chest, the soul flies out of purgatory.

28. It is certain that when money clinks in the money chest, greed and avarice can be increased; but when the Church intercedes, the result is in the hands of God alone.

29. Who knows whether all souls in purgatory wish to be redeemed, since we have exceptions in St Severinus and St Paschal, as related in a legend.

30. No one is sure of the integrity of his own contrition, much less of having received plenary remission.

31. The man who actually buys indulgences is as rare as he who is really penitent; indeed, he is exceedingly rare.

32. Those who believe that they can be certain of their salvation because they have indulgence letters will be eternally damned, together with their teachers.

33. Men must especially be on their guard against those who say that the pope's pardons are that inestimable gift of God by which man is reconciled to Him.

34. For the graces of indulgences are concerned only with the penalties of sacramental satisfaction established by man.

35. They who teach that contrition is not necessary on the part of those who intend to buy souls out of purgatory or to buy confessional privileges preach unchristian doctrine.

36. Any truly repentant Christian has a right to full remission of penalty and guilt, even without indulgence letters.

37. Any true Christian, whether living or dead, participates in all the

blessings of Christ and the Church; and this is granted him by God, even without indulgence letters.

38. Nevertheless, papal remission and blessing are by no means to be disregarded, for they are, as I have said [Thesis 6], the proclamation of the divine remission.

39. It is very difficult, even for the most learned theologians, at one and the same time to commend to the people the bounty of indulgences and the need of true contrition.

40. A Christian who is truly contrite seeks and loves to pay penalties for his sins; the bounty of indulgences, however, relaxes penalties and causes men to hate them – at least it furnishes occasion for hating them.

41. Papal indulgences must be preached with caution, lest people erroneously think that they are preferable to other good works of love.

42. Christians are to be taught that the pope does not intend that the buying of indulgences should in any way be compared with works of mercy.

43. Christians are to be taught that he who gives to the poor or lends to the needy does a better deed than he who buys indulgences.

44. Because love grows by works of love, man thereby becomes better. Man does not, however, become better by means of indulgences but is merely freed from penalties.

45. Christians are to be taught that he who sees a needy man and passes him by, yet gives his money for indulgences, does not buy papal indulgences but God's wrath.

46. Christians are to be taught that, unless they have more than they need, they must reserve enough for their family needs and by no means squander it on indulgences.

47. Christians are to be taught that the buying of indulgences is a matter of free choice, not commanded.

48. Christians are to be taught that the pope, in granting indulgences, needs and thus desires their devout prayer more than their money.

49. Christians are to be taught that papal indulgences are useful only if they do not put their trust in them, but very harmful if they lose their fear of God because of them.

50. Christians are to be taught that if the pope knew the exactions of the indulgence preachers, he would rather that the basilica of St Peter were burned to ashes than built up with the skin, flesh, and bones of his sheep.

51. Christians are to be taught that the pope would and should wish to give of his own money, even though he had to sell the basilica of St Peter, to many of those from whom certain hawkers of indulgences cajole money.

52. It is vain to trust in salvation by indulgence letters, even though the indulgence commissary, or even the pope, were to offer his soul as security.

53. They are enemies of Christ and the pope who forbid altogether the preaching of the Word of God in some Churches in order that indulgences may be preached in others.

54. Injury is done the Word of God when, in the same sermon, an equal or larger amount of time is devoted to indulgences than to the Word.

55. It is certainly the pope's sentiment that if indulgences, which are a very insignificant thing, are celebrated with one bell, one procession, and one ceremony, then the Gospel, which is the very greatest thing, should be preached with a hundred bells, a hundred processions, a hundred ceremonies.

56. The 'treasures of the Church', out of which the pope distributes indulgences, are not sufficiently discussed or known among the people of Christ.

57. That indulgences are not temporal treasures is certainly clear, for many indulgence sellers do not distribute them freely but only gather them.

58. Nor are they the merits of Christ and the Saints, for, even without the pope, the latter always work grace for the inner man, and the cross, death, and hell for the outer man.

59. St Laurence said that the poor of the Church were the treasures of the Church, but he spoke according to the usage of the word in his own time.

60. Without want of consideration we say that the keys of the Church, given by the merits of Christ, are that treasure;

61. For it is clear that the pope's power is of itself sufficient for the remission of penalties and cases reserved by himself.

62. The true treasure of the Church is the Most Holy Gospel of the glory and grace of God.

63. But this treasure is naturally most odious, for it makes the first to be last [Matt. 20.16].

64. On the other hand, the treasure of indulgences is naturally most acceptable, for it makes the last to be first.

65. Therefore the treasures of the Gospel are nets with which one formerly fished for men of wealth.

66. The treasures of indulgences are nets with which one now fishes for the wealth of men.

67. The indulgences which the demagogues acclaim as the 'greatest graces' are actually understood to be such only insofar as they promote gain.

68. They are nevertheless in truth the most insignificant graces when compared with the grace of God and the piety of the Cross.

69. Bishops and curates are bound to admit the commissaries of papal indulgences with all reverence.

70. But they are much more bound to strain their eyes and ears lest these men preach their own dreams instead of what the pope has commissioned.

71. Let him who speaks against the truth concerning papal indulgences be anathema and accursed;

72. But let him who guards against the lust and license of the indulgence preachers be blessed;

73. Just as the pope justly thunders against those who by any means whatsoever contrive harm to the sale of indulgences.

74. But much more does he intend to thunder against those who use indulgences as a pretext to contrive harm to holy love and truth.

75. To consider papal indulgences so great that they could absolve a man even if he had done the impossible and had violated the Mother of God is madness.

76. We say on the contrary that papal indulgences cannot remove the very least of venial sins as far as guilt is concerned.

77. To say that even St Peter, if he were now pope, could not grant greater graces is blasphemy against St Peter and the pope.

78. We say on the contrary that even the present pope, or any pope whatsoever, has greater graces at his disposal, that is, the Gospel, spiritual powers, gifts of healing, etc., as it is written in I Cor. 12 [.28].

79. To say that the cross emblazoned with the papal coat of arms, and set up by the indulgence preachers, is equal in worth to the Cross of Christ is blasphemy.

80. The bishops, curates, and theologians who permit such talk to be spread among the people will have to answer for this.

81. This unbridled preaching of indulgences makes it difficult even for

learned men to rescue the reverence which is due the pope from slander or from the shrewd questions of the laity,

82. Such as: 'Why does not the pope empty purgatory for the sake of holy love and the dire needs of the souls that are there if he redeems an infinite number of souls for the sake of miserable money with which to build a Church? The former reasons would be most just; the latter is most trivial.'

83. Again, 'Why are funeral and anniversary masses for the dead continued and why does he not return or permit the withdrawal of the endowments founded for them, since it is wrong to pray for the redeemed?'

84. Again, 'What is this new piety of God and the pope that for a consideration of money they permit a man who is impious and their enemy to buy out of purgatory the pious soul of a friend of God and do not rather, because of the need of that pious and beloved soul, free it for pure love's sake?'

85. Again, 'Why are the penitential canons, long since abrogated and dead in actual fact and through disuse, now satisfied by the granting of indulgences as though they were still alive and in force?'

86. Again, 'Why does not the pope, whose wealth is today greater than the wealth of the richest Crassus, build this one basilica of St Peter with his own money rather than with the money of poor believers?'

87. Again, 'What does the pope remit or grant to those who by perfect contrition already have a right to full remission and blessings?'

88. Again, 'What greater blessing could come to the Church than if the pope were to bestow these remissions and blessings on every believer a hundred times a day, as he now does but once?'

89. 'Since the pope seeks the salvation of souls rather than money by his indulgences, why does he suspend the indulgences and pardons previously granted when they have equal efficacy?'

90. To repress these very sharp arguments of the laity by force alone, and not to resolve them by giving reasons, is to expose the Church and the pope to the ridicule of their enemies and to make Christians unhappy.

91. If, therefore, indulgences were preached according to the spirit and intention of the pope, all these doubts would be readily resolved. Indeed, they would not exist.

92. Away then with all those prophets who say to the people of Christ, 'Peace, peace,' and there is no peace! [Jer. 6.14].

93. Blessed be all those prophets who say to the people of Christ, 'Cross, cross,' and there is no cross!

94. Christians should be exhorted to be diligent in following Christ, their Head, through penalties, death, and hell;

95. And thus be confident of entering into heaven through many tribulations rather than through the false security of peace [Acts 14.22].

Bibliography

Suggestions for Further Reading

The literature on Luther is vast. Much of it is only available in German, though most of the major studies have appeared in translation. Since the present book is simply an introduction to the subject for English readers I have listed below only those volumes most easily available to them. Several secondary works contain extensive bibliographies of studies in various languages. I hope this catalogue will provide a starting point for those who wish to take their studies further.

Primary Sources

Dillenberger, J., ed., *Martin Luther: Selections from his Writings*, 1961

Erasmus, D., *The Praise of Folly*, trs. C.H. Miller, New Haven, 1979

Luther, M., *The Bondage of the Will*, eds. J.I. Packer and O.R. Johnston, 1957

Luther's Works, eds. H.T. Lehmann and J. Pelikan, St. Louis, Missouri, and Philadelphia, Pennsylvania, 1955–1986

Naphy, W.G., ed., *Documents of the Continental Reformation*, 1996

Secondary Works

Abray, L.J., *The People's Reformation*, Oxford, 1985

Bainton, R., *Here I Stand*, Nashville, 1950

Boehmer, H., *Martin Luther: Road to Reformation*, 1957

Bornkamm, H., *Luther in Mid-career, 1521–1530*, 1983

Bornkamm, H., *Luther's World of Thought*, trs. M.H. Bertram, Concordia, 1965

Brady, T.A., 'The Political Masks of Martin Luther', in *History Today*, November 1983

Brady, T.A., 'The Reformation of the Common Man', in C. Scott Dixon, ed., *The German Reformation: The Essential Readings*, 1999

Braudel, F., *The Mediterranean and the Mediterranean World in the Age of Philip II*, trs. S. Reynolds, 1992

Brecht, M., *Martin Luther: His Road to Reformation*, Philadelphia, 1985

Brecht, M., *Martin Luther: Shaping and Defining the Reformation, 1521–1532*, trs. J.L. Schaff, 1994

Brecht, M., *Martin Luther: The Preservation of the Church, 1532–1546*, trs. J.L. Schaff, 1993

Brooks, P.N., ed., *Seven-Headed Luther: Essays in Commemoration of a Quincentenary, 1483–1983*, Oxford, 1983

Christensen, C.C., *Princes and Propaganda: Electoral Saxon Art of the Reformation*, 1996

Cohn, N., *The Pursuit of the Millennium*, 1970

Courvoisier, J., *Zwingli: A Reformed Theologian*, 1964

Dickens, A.G., and Jones, W.R.D., *Erasmus The Reformer*, 1994

Dickens, A.G., *Martin Luther and the Reformation*, 1967

Dickens, A.G., *The German Nation and Martin Luther*, 1974

Drummond, A.L., *German Protestantism Since Luther*, 1951

Eire, C.M.N., *War Against the Idols: The Reformation of Worship from Erasmus to Calvin*, Cambridge, 1986

Erikson, E., *Young Man Luther*, 1958

Febvre, L., *The Problem of Unbelief in the Sixteenth Century*, Cambridge, Mass., 1982

Fife, R.H., *The Revolt of Martin Luther*, New York, 1957

Figgis, J.N., *Churches in the Modern State*, 1931

Forster, L. W., *Selections from Conrad Celtis*, Cambridge, 1948

Hendrickson, K.E., 'The Big Problem with History: Christianity and the Crisis of Meaning', in *Historically Speaking*, March–April 2006

Hendrix, S., *Luther and the Papacy*, Philadelphia, 1981

Hoffmann, M., ed., *Martin Luther and the Modern Mind – Freedom, Conscience, Toleration, Rights*, Toronto, 1995

Huizinga, J., *The Waning of the Middle Ages*, 1924

Kastmer, R., 'The Reformer and Reformation Anniversaries', in *History Today*, November 1964

MacCulloch, D., *Reformation: Europe's House Divided 1490–1700*, 2003

Marius, R., *Martin Luther: The Christian Between God and Death*, Cambridge, Mass., 1999

Martines, L., *Scourge and Fire: Savonarola and Renaissance Italy*, 2006

McGrath, A.E., *Luther's Theology of the Cross*, Oxford, 1985

McGrath, A.E., *Reformation Thought: An Introduction*, Oxford, 1999

Oberman, H.A., *Luther: Man Between God and the Devil*, New Haven, 1989

Ozment, S., *A Mighty Fortress: A New History of the German People 100 BC to the 21st Century*, 2004

Ozment, S., *The Age of Reform 1250–1550*, New Haven, 1980

Ozment, S., *The Reformation in Medieval Perspective*, Chicago, 1971

Ozment, S., *The Reformation in the Cities*, 1975

Parker, G., *Empire, War and Faith in Early Modern Europe*, 2002

Pettegree, A., ed., *The Early Reformation in Europe*, Cambridge, 1992

Pettegree, A., ed., *The Reformation World*, 2000

Ritter, G., *Luther, His Life and Work*, trs. J.W. Doberstein and T.G. Tappert, 1975

Rupp, E.G., *Let God be God*, 1949

Rupp, E.G., *Martin Luther and the Jews*, 1972

Rupp, G., *The Righteousness of God*, 1953

Russell, P.A., *Lay Theology in the Reformation*, Cambridge, 1986

Scribner, R.W., *For the Sake of Simple Folk: Popular Propaganda for the German Reformation*, Oxford, 1994

Shepherd, G., 'English Versions of the Scripture before Wycliffe' in G.W.H. Lampe, ed., *Cambridge History of the Bible*, II, Cambridge, 1969

Smith, P., *The Life and Letters of Martin Luther*, 1911

Steinmetz, D.C., *Luther and Staupitz*, Durham, North Carolina, 1980

The Last Days of Luther by Justus Jonas, Michael Coelius and Others., trs. M. Ebon, New York, 1970

Thomas, K., *Religion and the Decline of Magic*, 1971

Vandenbroucke, F. and Bouyer, L., eds., *A History of Western Spirituality*, Vol II, 1970

Vandiver, E., Keen, R. and Frazel, T.D., eds., *Luther's Lives*, Manchester, 2002

Villari, P., *Life and Times of Savonarola*, trs. L. Villari, 1888

Wilson, D. and Fernández-Armesto, F., *Reformation*, 1996

Yule, G., ed., *Luther – Theologian for Catholics and Protestants*, Edinburgh, 1985

Index

Picture Credits

Detail from *Law and Grace*, Lucas Cranach the Elder, c. 1530; The *Schutzmantelbild*. From Ulrich Tengler's *Mirror for Laypeople*, 1509; Albrecht Dürer, *The Four Horsemen of the Apocalypse*, 1498; Savanarola preaching in the Duomo. From *Compendio di Revalazione*, Florence, 1496; Jews being tortured, 1475; The Drummer of Niklashausen by Hans Beheim. From Hartmann Schedel, *Weltchronik*, 1493; The martyrdom of Jan Hus, 1524; Luther sanctified, Hans Baldung Green. From *Acta et res gestae D Martini Lutheri*, Strasbourg, 1521; Johann von Staupitz, engraving after a painting in St. Peter's Abbey, Salzburg; Archduke Frederick of Saxony, 'The Wise', Albrecht Dürer, c.1524; Wittenberg, engraved by Matthäus Merian; Albrecht Dürer, *The Adoration of the Magi*, 1504; The Sale of Indulgences, date unknown; Leo X, engraving by Marcantonio Raimondi; Luther and the devil – different perspectives; The papal bull, *Exsurge Domine*; *Luther – the German Hercules*, Hans Holbein, 1523; The Imperial Diet from a 17th-century map by Hermann Moll; Luther's lodging in the Wartburg, 1521–2. Photograph courtesy of Jürgens Ost + Europa Photo; Andreas Bodenstein von Karlstadt, date unknown; Thomas Müntzer preaching. Woodcut from *The Prophecies of Johann Lichtenberg*, 1527; *The Divine Mill*. From M. Ramminger *Dyss hand zwen shwytzer puren gemacht* Augsburg, 1521; Title page of Luther's tract *Against the Murderous and Thieving Hordes of Peasants*, 1525; *Lady Music*: Verse introduction by Luther to John Walther's *Glory and Praise of the Laudable Art of Music*, 1538, British Library; Title page of Luther's Bible, 1534, British Library; Lucas Cranach the Elder. *True and False Religion*, c. 1545; Title page by Lucas Cranach for Luther's *Against the Papacy in Rome, Established by the Devil*, 1545; Luther in the last years of his life, Lucas Cranach, 1546